TECHNICOLORED

A Camera Obscura book

Technicolored

REFLECTIONS ON RACE IN THE TIME OF TV

Ann duCille

Duke University Press   Durham and London   2018

Library of Congress Cataloging-
in-Publication Data
Names: DuCille, Ann, author.
Title: Technicolored : reflections on race in the time
of TV / Ann duCille.
Description: Durham : Duke University Press, 2018.
| Series: A Camera Obscura book | Includes
bibliographical references and index.
Identifiers: LCCN 2018008223 (print)
LCCN 2018009529 (ebook)
ISBN 9781478002215 (ebook)
ISBN 9781478000396 (hardcover : alk. paper)
ISBN 9781478000488 (pbk. : alk. paper)
Subjects: LCSH: African Americans on television. |
Race on television. | Racism on television. |
Television programs—United States.
Classification: LCC PN1992.8.A34 (ebook) |
LCC PN1992.8.A34 D83 2018 (print) | DDC
791.4508996073—dc23
LC record available at https://lccn.loc.gov
/2018008223

Cover art: Photo: The author and her brothers;
TV: Niels Poulsen DK / Alamy Stock Photo.

CONTENTS

ix   ACKNOWLEDGMENTS

1   INTRODUCTION
Black and White and Technicolored:
Channeling the TV Life

22   CHAPTER 1
What's in a Game? Quiz Shows and
the "Prism of Race"

52   CHAPTER 2
"Those Thrilling Days of Yesteryear":
Stigmatic Blackness and the Rise
of Technicolored TV

83   CHAPTER 3
The Shirley Temple of My Familiar:
Take Two

112   CHAPTER 4
Interracial *Loving*: Sexlessness in
the Suburbs of the 1960s

134   CHAPTER 5
"A Credit to My Race": Acting Black
and Black Acting from *Julia* to *Scandal*

159   CHAPTER 6
A Clear and Present Absence: *Perry Mason*
and the Case of the Missing "Minorities"

183 CHAPTER 7
"Soaploitation": Getting Away
with Murder in Prime Time

209 CHAPTER 8
The Punch and *Judge Judy* Shows:
Really Real TV and the Dangers of
a Day in Court

232 CHAPTER 9
The Autumn of His Discontent:
Bill Cosby, Fatherhood, and the
Politics of Palatability

261 CHAPTER 10
The "Thug Default": Why Racial
Representation Still Matters

285 EPILOGUE
Final Spin: "That's Not My Food"

289 NOTES

311 BIBLIOGRAPHY

325 INDEX

ACKNOWLEDGMENTS

As the following pages reveal, TV viewing began for me in the early 1950s as a shared activity. In some ways, it remains so, even though I am often physically alone when I sit down in front of the television set these days. I have the great gift of counting among my current televisual companions and critical interlocutors a virtual army of family, friends, colleagues, neighbors, and associates, from Nancy and Rhonda, the hairstylists at Sebastian's, to the strangers I have met on trains and planes, in doctors' waiting rooms, and even in the produce aisle at the grocery store. (I won't out the physician who kept other patients waiting while he and I dished about Shonda Rhimes and *Scandal*.) To recognize all my confederates—to thank each deserving partner in crime for the many conversations and critiques, dialogues and debates that have helped call these reflections into being—would mean a list of acknowledgments nearly as long as the book. I offer, therefore, my general but no less sincere gratitude to the many with whom I have talked TV.

Since the early days of watching soaps in the Graduate Center dorms with Gayl Jones and Audrey DuPuy, laughing ourselves silly when Walter Curtain (who had let his pregnant wife stand trial for a murder he committed) drove his car off a cliff in the middle of downtown Bay City, I have enjoyed the good company and intellectual camaraderie of colleagues, friends, and students at institutions ranging from Brown to Wesleyan to the University of California at San Diego and back again. Here, too, it is impossible to name names in a way that would do justice to the many, so I will settle for singling out a few who have been particular champions of this project, including Laura Wexler, who was the first to say I should write about TV, and Indira Karamcheti, who long ago encouraged me to write a memoir.

Elizabeth Weed, Lynne Joyrich, Gina Ulysse, Bill Stowe, Stephanie and Mark Weiner, Marie Rock, and Demetrius Eudell have been the book's loudest cheerleaders. Demetrius, Ellen Rooney, Oneka LaBennett, Elana Bauer, Leah Wright Rigueur, Cecil Thompson, and Richard Slotkin read various parts of the manuscript and offered insightful comments and encouragement. I am particularly indebted to Richie Slotkin for the model of his work as well as for his friendship and support and to Iris Slotkin for the good humor that kept me laughing even in the dark days of the 2016 election. Suzanne Stewart-Steinberg may never forgive me for sending her off into ShondaLand; I am grateful to her and to the Pembroke Center at Brown University for the support that facilitated the book's finishing touches, especially the truly invaluable research assistance, technical know-how, and kind, careful attention of the amazing Arlen Austin. Others whose comments and encouragement helped bring this book along include Pat Sloss, Tricia Rose, Matthew Delmont, David Liao, and especially Jean Tye, who directed me to Norman Lear's new autobiography and kept me well supplied with homemade soups.

My good friend Rebecca Flewelling in Vermont threw me under the bus and gave me up to her son as the reason she was watching so much lame TV. I thank her just the same for all the good times, long talks, and *Say Yes to the Dress* critiques. The same is true for other old friends who have stayed tuned in with me for everything from the imagined communities of *Star Trek*'s several generations to the breaking news of MSNBC and the broken hearts of *Married at First Sight*: Janice Allen, Josephine Bernard, Alfrieta Parks Monagan, Krystal and Az Ndukwu, and John Simmons, with special thanks to the Honorable Julie Bernard for her advice and counsel and to Nathan and Erness Brody for their enduring faith in my work.

Whether we are arguing about *How to Get Away with Murder* or commiserating about politics, Ellen Rooney always inspires me to climb higher and dig deeper. I am grateful to her and to Khachig Tölölyan for the warm and loving friendship that has stretched across decades and continents. I am likewise thankful for and indebted to new friends who feed body, mind, and soul and make my world turn, especially my neighbors at Number 77 who make our building the best place to live in Providence.

This book could not and would not be without the support and encouragement of my editors at Duke University Press, Ken Wissoker and Elizabeth Ault, who believed in the project even when I did not, and Liz Smith, who carried the book through to completion. I am grateful to them and to the production, design, and marketing teams, especially Christine Dahlin, Heather

Hensley, and Chad Royal, with special thanks to Paula Durbin-Westby. My grateful thanks are also extended to the press's anonymous readers, whose careful attention and pointed feedback helped make *Technicolored* a better book. I am indebted as well to Lynne Joyrich for recommending the book to her fellow editors at *Camera Obscura* and to the CO Collective for including *Technicolored* in their series.

My final thanks go to my family who live in these pages with me, especially my younger brother, Danny, my oldest friend and favorite person, and his partner, Linda Pumphrey; my nephew Adrian III, who with his siblings has made "Auntie Ann" my favorite title; and my cousins Oliver duCille and Cecil and Beth Thompson, who remind me of my Jamaican roots, and Neal and Clarence "Sonny" Hogan, who remind me of my childhood and crazy good times with kin.

Black and White and Technicolored

CHANNELING THE TV LIFE

Certainly it comes as news to no one that television has been a mainstay of modern home life since its arrival in the living rooms of American families in the 1950s. The media theorist Lynn Spigel, one of the foremost authorities on mass culture at midcentury, points out that while only 9 percent of American homes had a television set in 1950, postwar consumers purchased the new technology at such record rates that by the end of the decade the number of households with at least one receiver had risen tenfold to nearly 90 percent.[1] Writing with considerable prescience about the new medium in 1956, the sociologist and cultural critic Leo Bogart predicted not only that every household was destined to have a TV but also that as the technology improved and the sets themselves became lighter and less cumbersome, televisions would be spread out through individual homes, with a set installed in nearly every room.[2]

Like most Americans of the baby boom generation, I had lived comfortably with the technological marvel of television ever in the background of my everyday life. It wasn't until I retired in 2011 after more than forty years teaching in and around the university and sixty years with television as a more or less constant home companion that I began to assess the impact of the instrument and the industry on my life growing up as a black viewer in the white suburbs of Boston during the second half of the twentieth century. As a newly unminted English professor, I had expected to do with my newfound leisure what other retired academics have done before me—attend to and indulge in all those pleasures for which there had never been time or space. I would travel to far-off, out-of-the-way places. I would return to the piano and recoup the benefit of years of lessons my parents couldn't afford but somehow paid for nonetheless. I would knit scarves and sweaters and afghans, though I wasn't certain how well I would fare without my late mother the master knitter on hand to fix my mistakes. And more than anything, I would read madly, but nothing in my own field for at least a year—nothing in African American literature or history or culture. But definitely the hot, hip, happening books everyone was talking about—the books that were winning prizes.

My first few attempts at reading on the cutting edge of bestseller glory fell flat. All that glistens is not necessarily my kind of good reading. Soon an assortment of false starts and deflated finishes topped a pile of best-laid plans that went, if not completely awry, not as I had imagined or hoped. Thus it was that through a long and winding road of half-read books, arthritic fingers that insulted the piano, and travel plans that somehow never went beyond the brochures, I wound up spending out the first year of retirement in front of the ubiquitous TV sets (which as predicted presented themselves in nearly every room), endlessly watching fifty-year-old reruns of *Perry Mason*, *Bachelor Father*, *Make Room for Daddy*, and numerous other series and sitcoms from my misspent youth, while also catching up on some of the hot twenty-first-century shows pitched as products of the new postracialism.

As much as a tidal wave of intellectual exhaustion enticed me to think of the *Bachelor Father* daily double or a *Perry Mason* weekend marathon as a mindless escape into the fictions of the 1950s, I know the work of Susan Smulyan and other media theorists too well to take any TV programming for granted or any act of TV viewing as innocent. The opening sentence of Smulyan's essential study *Popular Ideologies: Mass Culture at Mid-century* (2007) was all too apropos and instructive, even as I wanted to wallow in useless abandon: "Complex ideas of race, class, gender, nationhood, and consumption were created, expressed, and worked out in popular culture forms in the middle of the twentieth century."[3] Nowhere were these complex ideas more dramatically on display than in the very shows of yesteryear that I was revisiting daily. All the old familiar stereotypes are as they always were in these classic shows of my youth, but the longer I tracked TV programming across the half century, the harder I was hit by that old adage, "the more things change, the more they stay the same." The old racism I knew so well had been replaced, it seemed to me, by a new racism perhaps even more insidious for its many masquerades as "civility," "reality," "authenticity," and, almost everywhere I turned the metaphorical dial, as eruptions of cultural funk and outcroppings of a buffoonish black performativity, on the one hand, or a depraved indifference to ethics, on the other—what I define in chapter 2 as "stigmatic blackness"—celebrated as the new normal and the new human.

Making a similar point about old racism versus new, Paula Groves Price, a cultural theorist from Washington State University, argues that 1950s televisual images of African Americans as "mammies, Sambos, hoodlums, and Jezebels," among other similarly demeaning representations, "have been instrumental in (re)inscribing ideologies of inequality and white supremacy." But "while many of the same images can readily be seen on television today," she adds, "they often appear under the guise of reality television, black popular culture, or postracial ensemble shows." Television and other forms of mass media appropriate aspects of the black community's responses to a long history of racism, discrimination, and oppression and repackage these cultural modalities as a decontextualized black experience, devoid of any attention to what Price rightly points to as "the sociopolitical conditions that instigate [such] responses."[4] As I address in chapter 10, drawing on the work of the cultural theorist Tricia Rose, gangsta rap, for example, which was born in the inner city as the response of urban youth to the harsh, often hopeless conditions of ghetto life, not only becomes decontextualized by mass culture and commercialized as a celebration of thugs, pimps, and hoes but also becomes what black culture is in the popular imagination. In other words, the history and being of the whole are reduced to the behavior of the few— often presented as the most outrageous or the most countercultural—made to stand in for all black experience. Thus it is that television, as a form of mass communication, Price concludes, works to "reinscribe racist ideologies of blackness by framing it as black culture to the world."[5] Any black is every black, as I describe this regnant racial metonymy in chapter 1, drawing on my mother's wisdom.

But it isn't only what the old folks call "book learning"—the critiques of media theorists like Price and Smulyan—that makes me question how mass media have used "entertainment and consumption to construct and reinforce hierarchies of gender, class, and race."[6] I am a colored child of the 1950s, reared on resisting the racist images that television habitually inscribes as the ways of black folk. Long before I picked up a book on the subject, home training made me a suspicious, even resistant viewer, who early on learned to perceive every detail of television programming through the lens of race. I'm not sure whether to thank or blame my mother for this tinted, if not tainted, view of mass culture, but I do largely credit her as the source of my suspicion.

She was born in 1921, long before the advent of television as a form of home entertainment, but, next to books, cinema was the favorite cheap amusement of her youth. Perhaps because, as a young moviegoer in the 1930s and '40s, she was both shaped and shaken by the demeaning portrayals of blacks she witnessed in Shirley Temple films and elsewhere on-screen, my mother recognized early on the tremendous representational power of the new medium that brought moving images into the homes of everyday Americans. Even when it was very, very white, television was still somehow all about black, with the ability to make or break us as a race. It was in watching TV through my mother's resistant eyes that I first became captivated by and suspicious of a ubiquitous black presence that haunts American television and film, even in seeming absentia, in much the same way that American literature is shadowed by what the Nobel laureate Toni Morrison identifies in *Playing in the Dark: Whiteness and the Literary Imagination* (1992) as a "dark and abiding presence"—a "mediating force" at once both visible and invisible. "Even, and especially, when American texts are not 'about' Africanist presences or characters or narratives or idioms," Morrison writes, "the shadow hovers in implication, in sign, in line of demarcation."[7]

Technicolored: Reflections on Race in the Time of TV was born of a year of living dangerously in front of the television set, but it also looks back over more than half a century of TV viewing through the prism of race. Neither a conventional memoir nor a traditional media study, *Technicolored* uses my own family history and postwar experiences—from the polio epidemic that drove us from the city and ultimately brought us our first TV set, to the propriety concerns that governed what and how we watched—as the framework for a personal narrative of growing up black with the new medium of television, which shaped my childhood. It examines the changing face of racial representation from the early 1950s, when people of color were at once nowhere and everywhere on TV, to the present, when we are everywhere but, perhaps, still nowhere, with many of the same stereotypes of blacks as villains, vixens, victims, and first-to-die disposable minorities still in play, even as new, equally limited and limiting images of blacks and blackness crowd the airwaves. Reflecting on and critiquing the role of race in televisual genres from black sitcoms like *The Beulah Show, Amos 'n' Andy, Julia,* and *The Cosby Show*; to the Shirley Temple films and Charlie Chan movies I watched on TV as a child; to a spate of TV game shows now hosted by black comedians and prime-time dramas headlined by black actors in shows such as *Scandal* and *How to Get Away with Murder, Technicolored* poses critical questions about the roads television has traveled and continues to traverse in its depictions of African Americans, in particular, and what part those depictions play in fixing notions of the racially "othered" in the American imagination.

This last issue—the role that representation plays in stigmatizing black men, women, and children as dangerous and expendable—is a guiding concern of the book and one of the most critical questions of our time. In accepting the Humanitarian Award at the 2016 Black Entertainment Television (BET) award ceremony, the African American actor and activist Jesse Williams delivered a blistering Black Lives Matter manifesto in which he pointed out that data show that "police somehow managed to deescalate, disarm, and not kill white people every day."[8] How is it, then, that black men, women, and children—including most infamously twelve-year-old Tamir Rice fatally shot by police in a Cleveland park while playing with a replica of an air gun—are so often instantaneously killed by law enforcement officers who claim they feared for their lives? Is it because Caucasians are not quintessentially cast on TV and elsewhere in popular culture and political discourse as a dark and deadly menace to society? In perhaps its most important move, *Technicolored* examines the relationship between popular portrayals of African Americans as criminals and thugs and the deaths of scores of unarmed black men, women, and children, among whom the names of Amadou Diallo, Trayvon Martin, Michael Brown, Eric Garner, Walter Scott, Freddie Gray, and Sandra Bland are merely some of the best known in an increasingly long list. At the same time, the less well-remembered names of Eulia May Love from 1979 and Margaret LaVerne Mitchell from 1999—both shot and killed by Los Angeles police (LAPD) officers, infamously in Love's case over a $22 gas bill and over a shopping cart in the case of Margaret Mitchell, who was mentally ill and homeless—should remind us that such shootings are not a new phenomenon.[9] Ultimately *Technicolored* looks to television as an accessory before and after the fact whose color-coded news coverage, stigmatizing storytelling, and clichéd typecasting make TV a potentially deadly form of racial profiling.

These reflections are propelled and made personal by the fact that TV and I have traveled along parallel tracks since our respective births at midcentury. I came into the world in Brooklyn in 1949, just as Jackie Robinson was breaking the color line in Major League Baseball and the new medium of television was beginning to appear in American homes, although it had not yet made its way into my family's second-floor flat in Bedford-Stuyvesant. Radio still ruled the roost. The voice of Edward R. Murrow kept us informed about world events. Heard-but-not-seen characters like Beulah, Amos and Andy, Jack Benny and Rochester, and the Lone Ranger and Tonto kept us entertained. The radio was such a constant companion that I'm told I was nicknamed "Buzzy" because as a baby I made a buzzing sound to the theme music of *The FBI in Peace and War* (CBS Radio, 1944–1958) whenever the show aired. Since the "FBI March" was from Prokofiev's opera *The Love for Three Oranges*, my buzzing along to classical music from the cradle was the first of several false notes that led my mother and father to believe I was musically gifted.

Like most Brooklynites—even transplanted ones—my parents were devoted Dodgers fans; listening to baseball games on the radio was a favorite pastime, second only to watching the Dodgers play in person at Ebbets Field, as my family did regularly. I take some pride in being able to say that from my father's lap, I have watched Jackie Robinson steal home. I don't actually remember any of this, unfortunately, because we left New York for Boston when I was two years old. The fond memories I have of the Dodgers and of the Clifton Place neighborhood that was my first home are from family lore and from the trips we made back to Brooklyn throughout the 1950s to visit my mother's sister, Auntie Bert, and her family and to see close friends and former neighbors we called Aunt Lena and Uncle Troy, who lived in the twin apartment to ours on the other side of the same brownstone row house in Bed-Stuy where we had lived as a young family of four. My mother was originally from Cambridge, Massachusetts, so Boston was close to home for her, but we—that is, my parents, Pearl Louise (Hogan) and Adrian Everard duCille; my older brother, Adrian Jr., and I—didn't linger long in the City on the Hill due to the call of the wild, the white picket-fence dream (more my mother's than my father's, I think) of raising a family in the wide open spaces and fresh air of the suburbs.

Thinking about it now, I suspect there was a motive to my mother's mad rush to leave the city that was larger, more personal, and more profound than midcentury America's generic middle-class fantasy of suburban living. My older brother—her firstborn—had had polio when he was four. He was one of the luckier victims of the polio epidemics that kept the country on edge during the first half of the twentieth century, before the advent of the Salk vaccine in 1954. My brother, Little Adrian, as he was sometimes called, was spared the respiratory problems and paralysis often associated with the

FIGS. I.1 AND I.2
I thought we were going
up over the roof to visit
Aunt Lena in the adjoin-
ing brownstone and
wasn't happy at being
waylaid for picture tak-
ing, but then Aunt Lena
appeared on her way
to our flat, and I was all
smiles, circa 1950.

disease. By some miracle, he made an almost complete recovery and was left with only slightly diminished muscle strength and slower reflexes on one side of his body.

I was a baby at the time and have no firsthand memory of what my brother and my parents went through, but my mother often spoke of the trauma of seeing her little boy suffer, of hearing him wail and cry out for her at the hospital when the doctors were trying to tap fluid from the base of his spine for serological testing in order to confirm the polio diagnosis. She talked of the added anguish of not being allowed to go to her child and comfort and reassure him, because well-meaning medical minds knew better than mere parents. "They whisked him away without letting us explain why he had to go with them," my mother would say. "He would have been all right if they had just let us talk to him, but he probably thought we had abandoned him and his little heart was broken." I would weep whenever my mother told this part of the story. It was a sad, heartrending early chapter in our family history, and even though I knew the story had a happy ending, I felt a kind of grief that lingers still.

But the story did have a happy ending (or so it seemed) and not just because my brother grew to be a straight, strapping 6′3″ and to father four children, but because at some point in the midst of the misery that awful night in the summer of 1950, Little Adrian gave up on wailing for Mummy and Daddy and started yelling at the doctor: "Shut up, Doctor! Shut up! Shut up, I say, Doctor! Shut up!" The funny thing was that, as my mother would tell the tale, the doctor wasn't saying a word and no doubt wondered why this little colored boy he was trying to help was telling him to shut up. Here, my mother would pause for effect and then take great maternal pleasure in informing whoever was listening that *she* had understood instantly why Adrian kept telling the doctor to shut up. It was his way of cussing out the doctor, of telling him off—a four-year-old's "f-you," as it were. He didn't know any real swear words—nobody ever dared curse around my mother or her children—and "shut up" was the worst thing he knew to say.

For all that my mother talked about my brother's bout with polio, for all that she praised the doctors and the nurses who treated him and the March of Dimes who she said comforted and supported the family through the crisis, what she didn't say—but what I in later years surmised or maybe just wanted to believe, since I thought my mother was Wonder Woman—is that she may have saved my brother from permanent paralysis, deformity, perhaps even death. She decided that something was wrong with her son, based on re-markably little evidence: a sudden lethargy one morning, his not acting quite

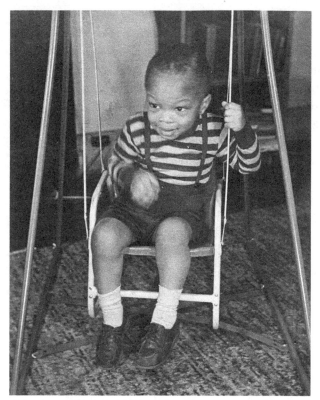

FIG. I.3 Little Adrian in Brooklyn at two years and three months, early 1948.

like himself, especially his not wanting to play with me, the baby sister he had first wished for, then demanded, at one point telling my mother's doctor that if he would "stop squeezing those ladies' arms" (taking blood pressures), he could hurry up and get his baby sister ready. No older brother ever wanted a baby sister more than mine wanted me, or so my mother often told me. For such a little boy, he took being a big brother very seriously and thought it was his personal responsibility to make sure I was properly bathed, fed, swaddled, and cuddled. It was the first, and perhaps only, time I have been unconditionally adored. So when Little Adrian suddenly didn't have the energy to tend to his beloved baby sister's every whimper, my mother knew something was very wrong and insisted on taking him to the hospital. There was no cure for polio then or now and paralytic poliomyelitis has more than one type. My brother's, I believe, was spinal. I'm not sure of the medical facts, but I like to think that early intervention made a difference.

In any case, this must be what it was that drove the move to the country at any cost, the thing that possessed near lifelong city dwellers to light out for territories unknown: polio panic. Rightly or wrongly, polio was seen as the scourge of the long, hot summers in the city, and I suspect that, with one son already stricken, my mother believed her children would be safer as far from the madding crowd as she could get them. So sometime in the fall of 1952—shortly before my baby brother, Danny, was born—we moved to a virgin piece of free land in East Bridgewater, a small town about twenty-five miles southeast of Boston, and began the arduous and unending task of building a house in the country. We began, rather unglamorously, by living in the basement with an outhouse and then, over the course of the next forty years, built up the house around us, block by block.

I don't recall that my father ever talked about the polio event or how close he came to losing his firstborn, namesake son to the disease that paralyzed a president and crippled and killed so many children before the saving grace of Jonas Salk's elixir. I so wish now that I had asked my father about it, about his take on the near tragedy of those Brooklyn days. I think now, though, that this thing that happened on the other side of my memory must be why he—a Jamaican immigrant from the capital of Kingston, yet so much at home among family and friends in New York City and so much more the urbanite—gave in to my mother's family plan for country life.

If the specter of polio—of disease, of hospitals, of a small child necessarily surrendered to the care of strangers—is what drove our family from the city, it also is the thing that brought television into our country sanctuary. At some point in what must have been 1953, when I was four, Little Adrian and I had our tonsils taken out together, I suppose so we would be company for each other. In those days, tonsillectomies weren't the same-day outpatient procedures they are now. They required a hospital stay of two or three days, with at least two nights away from home. I think it must have been hard on our parents, because when they came to pick us up from the hospital, baby brother in tow, they regaled us with tales of how much we had been missed and told us they had a surprise for us, a welcome-home present. I thought it might be a puppy, but it wasn't. It was a new, floor-model console TV set, which I remember as a Motorola.

I loved listening to the radio, but I knew nothing about television. I had seen moving pictures on the big screen at the drive-in to which we went regularly throughout the 1950s, but now the big people of the distant screen were very small and living inside the mahogany box in our den. I loved it, but it also confused me. I thought the people were real and could see me the same way I could see them. I felt connected to them, a part of their lives, and I would lie awake in bed at night, playing out the next chapter of their narratives in my head. It's a sense of television—a mistake almost literally about ghosts in the machine—I have never quite gotten over, which is a dangerous thing for a critic, this difficulty with fact and fiction.

So it is, then, that television and I have grown up together, from our shared infancy in black and white at midcentury, when I thought the people on-screen lived inside the magic box that TV was for me, to a high-technicolored maturity in a new millennium, when I still think the characters on-screen are somehow of and about me as a racialized, gendered subject. *Technicolored* traces our joint coming of age, from those early days in the 1950s to the present, attending in particular to issues of representation and spectatorship that are both historically specific and transgenerational, personal and profoundly racial. It tells the tale of what we watched and how we watched TV against the backdrop not only of my own changing family dynamic but also of the changing times that carried the country through the civil rights and women's movements, the Vietnam War, the Reagan years, the culture clashes of the 1990s, the first black presidency, and the current Black Lives Matter campaign for social justice.

For all its temporal breadth, however, *Technicolored* makes no attempt to be comprehensive in the pioneering footsteps of more traditional studies of race and television such as J. Fred MacDonald's *Blacks and White TV: African Americans in Television since 1948* (1992), Herman Gray's *Watching Race: Television and the Struggle for "Blackness"* (1995), Sasha Torres's edited volume *Living Color: Race and Television in the United States* (1998), and Donald Bogle's *Primetime Blues: African Americans on Network Television* (2001), or a wealth of newer work on the topic.[10] Rather, the scope of the project is limited to and by my own restricted vision, controlled quite literally by my own viewing habits. There is, for example, no discussion of BET as there almost certainly would be in a more traditional examination of race and television in the latter twentieth century. I, however, have been only a casual, sometimey viewer of BET, tuning in selectively for jazz or news reports. But BET was a lifeline for my students for whom it was a link to hip hop and rap music videos and the contemporary cultural scene, and the network's inspired first drama *Being Mary Jane* deserves more careful analysis than my spotty viewing allows for. Nor beyond discussions of series like *Julia, Good Times,* and *The Cosby Show* is due attention paid here to the black situation comedies that have been a primary site and prescribed Hollywood home of black TV programming since the 1950s. It's a genre for which I seem always to have been either too cynical or too critical to appreciate the lowbrow lunacy.

Although presented in the first person, *Technicolored* is not a traditional memoir full of intimate details and family secrets but, rather, a series of personal reflections that correspond to and, I hope, complement an extended critique of television as I have experienced it over the course of the past sixty years. My methodology is perhaps best described as both peripatetic and highly particular, driven more by personal taste and remembrance of things past than by chronology or theme. At the same time, the book does follow the path of my own passage through six decades of what is not only my particular slice of black suburban family life but also a lens through which to glimpse a nation coming of age and confronting some of its demons of difference. Reflections on events both personal and historical provide links to and context for discussions of how television both changed with the times and in some cases helped shape the changing times. Television was out ahead of the general public on the issue of gay rights and same-sex marriage, for example, and helped bring along the president, the populace, and the Supreme Court.

In addition, individual chapters generally do adhere around a specific genre (game shows, for example), subject matter (the danger of TV "syndicourts" like *Judge Judy*), or program (*How to Get Away with Murder*, for instance), held together by overarching questions and concerns about what it means to watch television through a particular set of black eyes—to be at once colored and to watch TV as "technicolored" even when it is in black and white. I use the term "technicolored" broadly in reference to "black shows" or programs with colored characters or racial content. I use the word "colored" in its historical sense to refer to African Americans and to "people of color"—a turn of phrase or term of art with which I have never been completely satisfied.

I come to the well-established field of television studies not as a media theorist but as a literary scholar, which may suggest a certain set of disruptions. As much as I acknowledge and appreciate the conventions of the field, I admittedly tend to read televisual narratives in somewhat the same way that I read literary texts. John Fiske, one of the founding fathers of media studies, warned against treating television as literature in his early study of the medium, appropriately titled *Reading Television*. The "tools of traditional literary criticism do not quite fit the television discourse," he wrote in 1978. The "codes and structure of the 'language' of television are much more like those of speech than writing," he added, also noting that TV's "'logic' is oral and visual."[11] But television has changed dramatically from the "ephemeral, episodic" medium Fiske knew in the 1970s. Increasingly dominated by a new mode of what the media studies scholar Jason Mittell calls "narrative complexity," television programming is coming into its own as a kind of literature.[12] In fact, some artists and cultural critics, including the celebrated writer Sir Salman Rushdie, are now calling modern small-screen dramas "the new literature." Rushdie, who has some TV writing credits of his own, has praised in particular the kind and quality of writing behind U.S. series such as *The Wire*, *The Sopranos*, *The West Wing*, and *Mad Men*. What TV scriptwriters are now able to do with character and story, Rushdie suggests, is not unlike what an author can do in a novel.[13]

Others in media studies seem to agree and have weighed in on the "lure of long-form, episodic television," whose dramatic properties invite comparisons to the big books of Charles Dickens and Henry James. Writing in the *Chronicle of Higher Education*, the cultural historian and film theorist Thomas Doherty, chair of the American Studies Department at Brandeis University, has coined the term "Arc TV" for highly developed serials with long story lines of "interconnected action unfolding over the life span of the series." He argues that while indebted to multi-episode serials from the 1970s and 1980s like *Masterpiece Theater*, *Hill Street Blues*, *L.A. Law*, and especially the deep-cover crime drama *Wiseguy*—the series credited with birthing the term "story arc"—Arc TV's "real kinship is literary, not televisual." Like the great tomes of British and American literature, he writes, Arc TV series are "thick on character and dense in plot line, spanning generations and tribal networks and crisscrossing the currents of personal life and professional duty." Unlike TV series of old with enigmatic heroes such as Marshal Matt Dillon of *Gunsmoke* (1955–1975) whose personal history and inner life were not part of the long-running drama, "Arc TV is all about back story and evolution," where again as in the novel "the aesthetic payoff comes from prolonged, deep involvement in the fictional universe." But Doherty also acknowledges the importance of "stagecraft" in television programming, which inevitably makes TV like theater and film. "For the show to cast its magic," he says, "the viewer must leap full body into the video stream."[14]

Television lives in the visual, then, as the novel lives in language and, of course, demands an interpretive strategy attentive to that difference. I hope *Technicolored* indulges such a strategy, but I am particularly concerned in the book with an element that storied television and the novel definitely do share: narrative. I am concerned with narrative on two levels. First, I'm interested in the various stories different programs and different kinds of programming tell their audiences. While issues of narratology are more immediately obvious in long-form serials that are character and plot driven like the ABC dramas *Scandal* and *How to Get Away with Murder*, other more conventionally episodic programs—from sitcoms and police procedurals, to unscripted tabloid talkfests and even game shows—are not without their storied aspects. Even the impatient star of the eponymous small-claims arbitration series *Judge Judy*, who notoriously cuts everybody off and barely gives complainants a chance to speak, ultimately is still after two sides of a story. Her counterparts from the rival shows *Judge Mathis* and *Judge Faith* make a point of asking litigants to provide a little background. Attention to the smaller stories of such shows leads to the book's second, greater concern with the overarching narrative of race and gender in which all of these programs participate. *Technicolored* explores how this master narrative—from representations of mindless maids, mammies, butlers, and buffoons in the 1950s to depictions of cunning, endlessly calculating, and manipulative moguls and criminal masterminds of today—has both changed and stayed the same.

This book consists of ten essayistic chapters, all but one written since 2012, although a pair—chapter 8 on Judge Judy and chapter 9 on Bill Cosby—take up icons and issues with which I have been concerned for some time, and chapter 3, "The Shirley Temple of My Familiar: Take Two," revisits, revises, and extends an earlier journal article on the cultural power of the pint-size performer and the colored cohorts who did her bidding. Chapter 1, "What's in a Game? Quiz Shows and the 'Prism of Race,'" introduces my family of five as we were in 1952, recently moved from the city to the suburbs of southeastern Massachusetts, and establishes the book's guiding paradigm of reading television through what the game-show host Pat Sajak has blogged about as "the prism of race."[15] It was Sajak's admonition against looking at the world through a racial lens that led me to consider the degree to which that is exactly how I view everything, including his own game show, *Wheel of Fortune*. To do otherwise is a great luxury African Americans can seldom afford. Begun as a simple essay about my mother's love of game shows—especially *Wheel*—the chapter has grown into a critique of the blackening and gendering of a once predominantly white male genre that has become the purview of black comedians like the ubiquitous Steve Harvey, host of *Family Feud*, and a symbol of the hot commodity or black gold that race has become for the television industry in the age of Oprah and Obama and what it means that this black goldmine so often has a sexed-up, dumbed-down, and dirty burnished edge. Drawing on the work of Frantz Fanon and contemporary media theorists such as Lynne Joyrich, chapter 1 raises questions about the power of racial representation and the simultaneous and contradictory sexing and neutering of the black body—issues that resonate as concerns throughout the book.

Building on the notion of television as an instrument of uplift raised in the first chapter, the second, "'Those Thrilling Days of Yesteryear': Stigmatic Blackness and the Rise of Technicolored TV," examines the role of race in early variety programs like *The Ed Sullivan Show* and *American Bandstand*, where black performers provided a cheap but alluring labor that helped build the fledgling television industry even as racism both defined and limited the roles African American actors and entertainers were allowed to perform elsewhere in the medium. These limitations applied as well to other nonwhite entertainers who could be houseboys, sidekicks, savages, and desperados but little else. But while shows like *Beulah* and *Amos 'n' Andy* were criticized for the "stigmatic blackness" they depicted and driven off the air, chapter 2 also considers the extent to which orientalism, noble savage mythology, and other stereotypes of Asians, Mexicans, Latinos, and Native Americans remain alive in regularly aired reruns, from *Bachelor Father* to *Bonanza*, as well as in contemporary programming. In addition to addressing the issue of enduring racial stereotypes, the chapter also explores the impact of the new technology on our family dynamic in the 1950s.

As previously noted, chapter 3, "The Shirley Temple of My Familiar: Take Two," expands an essay that originally appeared in *Transition* 73 in 1998. This revised version contains a new meditation on the orientalism of Charlie Chan movies, regularly shown on TV in the 1950s and beyond, much like Shirley Temple films. Because I encountered these narratives strictly through the venue of the small screen, they played for me and for millions of other child viewers as TV programs rather than as motion pictures, and they are included here as such. In a second added move, this chapter version calls out the small-town educational system of my youth for its relative silence on the subjects of slavery, race, and racism, as well as other cataclysmic historical events such as Native genocide, Japanese internment, and the Jewish Holocaust. It also explores more deeply than the original essay the issue of racial representation from the perspective of the receiver—a black girl living in a white enclave in a body and an identity made all the more strange and undesirable by its telegraphed difference from the white, "perfect-10" cuteness of

Shirley Temple. In a sense, the chapter answers the question Zora Neale Hurston addressed almost a century ago in her essay "How It Feels to Be Colored Me."[16] But through readings of additional visual texts like "#FindKayla-Weber," a disturbing episode of the TNT police procedural *Major Crimes*, the chapter raises a far more pressing question about what it means that in both fiction and fact society continues to devalue the lives of black girls.

Chapter 4, "Interracial *Loving*: Sexlessness in the Suburbs of the 1960s," uses the occasion of the fiftieth anniversary of *Loving v. Virginia*—the Supreme Court case that struck down the Commonwealth's "Racial Integrity Act" prohibiting intermarriage and all extant antimiscegenation laws—to reflect on television's tentative treatment of interracial romance, from the famous *Star Trek* kiss that wasn't to *Another World*'s celibate, mixed-race fiancés who "didn't" and *The Jeffersons'* "Oreo-cookie" neighbors who "did," giving fodder to George Jefferson's endless jokes about their mixed marriage and "zebra" offspring. In as much as 2017 also marks the fiftieth anniversary of my graduation from an overwhelmingly white high school, the chapter likewise ruminates on my own experiences with dating and teenage social life in the suburbs.

Drawing its title from a haunting phrase in Hattie McDaniel's Oscar acceptance speech in 1940, chapter 5, "'A Credit to My Race': Acting Black and Black Acting from *Julia* to *Scandal*," explores the burden of racial representation that fell on the shoulders of early black actors like McDaniel, who briefly played Beulah on the 1950s TV series as well as Mammy in *Gone with the Wind*. McDaniel, who considered herself a race woman, was virtually excommunicated from the race by the NAACP and was panned in much of the black press for furthering demeaning stereotypes. Pioneering black actors of the 1960s and 1970s like Diahann Carroll, who played the title role in the sitcom *Julia*, and Esther Rolle and John Amos, who costarred as husband and wife in *Good Times*, faced similar challenges as national symbols and representative bodies. Attending in different degrees to these and other groundbreaking sitcoms and dramas, the chapter uses biography, autobiography, and interviews to examine the complex dynamics of race, class, gender, and social politics that played out as much behind the camera as in front. The racial anxiety of influence that once haunted black performers is considered in comparison to Kerry Washington's unabashedly wicked, hypersexually explicit role in the ABC drama *Scandal*, where for good or ill positively representing the race is no longer a concern for the series' award-winning star and its black female creator and producer, Shonda Rhimes—at least not in the way it once was.

The lives of black people are disappeared rather than overtly demeaned in the legal detective drama probed in chapter 6, "A Clear and Present Absence: *Perry Mason* and the Case of the Missing 'Minorities,'" even as the series' white star, the magnificent character actor Raymond Burr, seems to have deluded himself that his show particularly benefited "the minorities," who he says learned by watching *Perry Mason* that "the system of justice was for them."[17] Exposing Burr's contention as historical revisionism, chapter 6 offers an admitted fan's cross-examination of the racial risk aversion that countenanced only a handful of African Americans on a show about justice whose nine-year run from 1957 to 1966 directly coincided with the civil rights movement. Far from part of its subject matter, African American "minorities" are at most a present absence in the *Perry Mason* series, called up—with two notable exceptions—in only a few bit parts as local color, including a nonspeaking role in which an absently present black judge seems to mistake moot court for mute court. Against the backdrop of the movement *Perry Mason* ignored, the chapter takes note of the multiracial cast of Hollywood stars who actively championed the cause of equal rights, as well as the racial dimensions and heartbreaking lessons of my family's first trip through the segregated South into the belly of the beast of Jim Crow during the summer of 1960.

Chapter 7, "'Soaploitation': Getting Away with Murder in Prime Time," takes its precolonial title from a mashup of two genres—TV soap operas and blaxploitation films—deployed to denote a new category of shows featuring black actors in leading roles and/or predominantly multiracial casts acting up in over-the-top, twisted plots and endless sexcapades, which seems to me a fitting descriptive for a program like *How to Get Away with Murder.* The chapter posits the series' lead character, a criminal defense attorney named Annalise Keating (Viola Davis), as the would-be successor to Perry Mason, although Keating is more err apparent than heir, more criminal than defense attorney. Considering *Murder* in a reflexive relationship with the white British melodrama *Downton Abbey,* the chapter offers a close reading of *Murder*'s narrative complexity and problematic style of emplotment, as I interrogate my own pleasure in one series and at best ambivalence about the other. Can long-form Arc TV as the so-called new literature and the new novel stand up to the rigors of close reading that are the hallmark of critical analysis? While implicitly addressing this question, the chapter also checks in on my own unraveling family drama, momentarily held together by collaborative work with the local front of Lyndon Johnson's War on Poverty and our volunteer efforts as Democrats in the 1966 senatorial campaign of the black Republican Ed Brooke.

From the outrageous fortunes of soaploitation fictions, chapter 8, "The Punch and *Judge Judy* Shows: Really Real TV and the Dangers of a Day in Court," moves on and into the even more racially exploitative domain of reality TV courtrooms. While the ethical affronts to jurisprudence and the rule of law portrayed in *How to Get Away with Murder* operate within the realm of the imaginary, *Judge Judy* and other arbitration series actively promote themselves as "real": "real litigants, real cases." This chapter argues that therein lies the danger of such shows: their real litigants are disproportionately the poor, colored, uneducated, unemployed, wretched of the earth—not just real people with real problems but real people who are the real problem—the teeming masses of welfare frauds ruining the country, immigrant and colored interlopers specifically cast as "Obama welfare cheats" in the oft-repeated right-wing rhetoric of conservative talk radio and TV and elsewhere in the digital sphere. I argue here that in their unrelenting representations of stigmatic blackness and racialized deviance, these courtroom melodramas and other forms of reality and tabloid TV fan the flames of anti-immigrant and antiminority hate-mongering that heat up national campaigns to do away with political correctness and return America to the truly disadvantaged, silenced majority.

Considering Bill Cosby's spectacular fall from grace in the context of earlier evidence of a flagrant disregard for marriage, wife, woman, and perhaps especially "daughter," chapter 9, "The Autumn of His Discontent: Bill Cosby, Fatherhood, and the Politics of Palatability," argues that the principle of black respectability may be the lever that elevated an alleged sexual predator above suspicion and silenced the cries of rape that so often have led to black men being lynched. The chapter cross-examines Cosby in terms of the palatable, safe, acceptable blackness of his old career as comedian and actor—from the grand good luck of landing *I Spy* in 1965 to his legendary role in *The Cosby Show* in the 1980s—and his new career as the self-appointed moral compass of the black community. It also critiques the ways in which the narrative of Cosby's faultless fatherhood was doubly disrupted in September 1997 by the near simultaneous death of a son and public revelation of a putative daughter, Autumn Jackson, with a woman not his wife. Additionally, as a counterpoint to Cosby's blighted family narrative, this penultimate chapter closes out my own familial history as we have moved from a gang of five to two, on the one hand, and a domestic diaspora of a different sort, on the other, spreading now unto its fifth generation.

In the relatively short time that I have been working on this project as a book proper, more unarmed black men, women, and children than I can count have been killed by police officers and others who, like George Zimmerman, have taken the law into their own hands.[18] These terrible facts and figures would make writing about TV fictions a trivial pursuit were it not for the insidious connection between these fictions and those awful facts. More than a meditation on game shows, sitcoms, syndi-courts, and soaploitation melodramas, *Technicolored* is a book about racial representation, and that, I argue most explicitly in this final chapter, can be a killing force. Chapter 10, then, "The 'Thug Default': Why Racial Representation Still Matters," traces the meaning, use, and blackening of the term "thug" and attempts to demonstrate how televisual image-making, which compulsively stigmatizes the colored Other, functions as a potentially deadly form of racial profiling.

To contend that image is ideology—that what we see on the TV screen colors how we see black boys on the street—is not simply to indulge an old, worn-out argument about positive and negative representation. Nor is it to suggest that audiences are mindless automatons who swallow whole everything they see on the screen—large or small (where "small" these days is often sixty or seventy inches). Rather, it is to consider critically the practical consequences of what media theorists have contended for decades in claiming television as a major conveyance through which prevailing notions of racial, class, and gender difference are both constituted and carried out into the main and minor streams. Race matters at least in part because TV matters, because images matter. I keep thinking about the Frank Capra romantic comedy *It Happened One Night* and all those perhaps apocryphal tales about what a glimpse of Clark Gable's bare chest did to the undershirt in 1934. Reports abound of a precipitous drop in undershirt sales ranging from 40 to 75 percent after Gable removed his dress shirt, revealing nothing underneath during a scene with Claudette Colbert. Of course, there is no empirical evidence that proves Gable's disrobing caused T-shirt sales to plummet, but the fact that so many have for so long believed the claim suggests the power vested in imagery. If a glimpse of white skin could do so much damage to the undershirt, perhaps we really do have to think more critically about how black skin wears on-screen.

And now, a word from our sponsors—that is, a quick note on sources. This project was greatly aided by the Internet. I do not blog, tweet, post, Snapchat, Skype, Instagram, or Facebook; I am much closer to a Luddite than to any sort of technogeek. So the ability to sit at my desk at home and watch on YouTube a sitcom I saw on television sixty years ago or, with a few clicks of the mouse, to retrieve a barely remembered *New Yorker* review from six years ago is an oddly wonderful, yet close to anti-intellectual turn of technology for those of us so much more used to spending hours hunting down sources in the library stacks and days reading microfiche in the archives. I would be a fool not to be grateful for this modern ease of access. But there is something else the virtual world offers that is, as my Jamaican father would say, "beautiful-ugly"—beautiful for the ease of access, ugly for what one may discover when one looks. Whatever the *New York Times* and the *Washington Post* or the pundits and talking heads of MSNBC, CNN, and Fox News may have to say about the state of the union and the ways of our world pales in comparison to what one can learn about her fellow man and woman from the blogs and posts of everyday Americans.

The rapid rise of the real estate baron turned reality TV star Donald Trump, slouching toward the presidency with the aid of birtherism and broadcast bigotry, was utterly unfathomable to me before I began reading online the un-American things my fellow Americans have to say about their fellow Americans. I certainly knew affirmative action and immigration were unpopular, but until I started reading the online outrage over the othered, I had no idea that such a large swath of the American populace thinks ideas like inclusion, diversity, and attention to difference are not only a tyranny of political correctness but also a serious threat to their lives, their limbs, their livelihoods, to homeland security itself. Before I discovered his propensity for blogging and tweeting, I had no idea, for example, that the game show host Pat Sajak, who says he attended a predominantly black high school in Chicago in the early 1960s where "race was a more comfortable subject" than it is today, would be among those who believe it is talking about race that generates racism—that far from a national conversation on race, what America needs is "*less* dialogue on the subject," not more.[19] Nor until I read his words online did I imagine that Clarence Thomas, a Supreme Court Justice who adjudicates cases of race, gender, and other forms of discrimination, would express similar disdain for the attention paid to difference today and the same kind of nostalgia for the 1960s when he, too, claims that the issue of race rarely came up. "My sadness is that we are probably today more race- and difference-conscious than I was in the 1960s when I went to school," he reportedly told a group of college students in 2014.[20] Thomas's nostalgia for the Jim Crow racial stasis of the 1960s and disdain for resistant social consciousness are especially surprising, given his position as a sitting Justice and the historical fact that a black man like him who married outside his race could not have cohabitated with his white spouse in the Commonwealth of Virginia where Thomas and his wife now reside before the Warren Court's "race-conscious" decision in *Loving v. Virginia* in 1967, which struck down long-standing statutes prohibiting intermarriage.

I used to live by the borrowed creed that I would defend to the death the free speech rights of those with whom I disagree. But laissez-faire notions of to each his own cannot stand unchallenged where those in power promulgate dangerous ideas such as the banning and "extreme vetting" of those othered in the name of homeland security, which in the past has given the world concentration camps and crematoria, exclusion acts and internment camps, apartheid and McCarthyism. What is it they say about those who do not learn from the past? Forget history. If you want to know what evil lurks in the hearts of men, turn to the Internet. But in the words of Bette Davis in *All about Eve*, "Fasten your seatbelts; it's going to be a bumpy night."

Chapter 1

What's in a Game?

QUIZ SHOWS AND THE
"PRISM OF RACE"

Does racism still exist? Of course it does, and it always will
among some people, just as ignorance and evil will always exist
in some. But it seems to me we've reached the point at which
racism is considered, at the very least, unacceptable. We will
never be able to eradicate every last vestige of it, just as we can't
completely rid ourselves of any evil.

At some point, however, we have to stop looking at everything
through the prism of race.

—PAT SAJAK, host of the TV game show *Wheel of Fortune*,
blogging at Ricochet.com, August 6, 2010

My mother was a great fan of TV game shows or "quiz shows," as they were
called in the 1950s. She was also remarkably good at many of them. Some of
my earliest childhood memories are of watching her outplay contestants on
picture and word puzzle game shows like *Concentration* in the 1950s and the
original daytime version of *Wheel of Fortune* in the 1970s, which eventually
became the syndicated evening series it is today, cohosted by Pat Sajak and
Vanna White. Mom was a whiz at every game—from *Twenty-One* and *The
$64,000 Question* to *Password* and *Jeopardy*. *Wheel of Fortune* was her all-
time favorite, however, and her greatest claim to fame. She was so phenomenally good at *Wheel* that in the latter decades of her relatively long life, family,

friends, and neighbors would gather in her den weeknights between 7:30 and 8:00 to watch Gramma Pearl, as she became known in the neighborhood, solve puzzles from the comfort of her recliner faster than Vanna White could turn the letters on the puzzle board.

Ironically, though, it was this very puzzle-solving prowess that ultimately caused my mother to quit *Wheel of Fortune* cold turkey in the late 1990s and never watch another episode of her once-beloved show. She was so good at the game that it just became too frustrating when the actual contestants failed to solve what for her were easy puzzles, especially and most particularly when those contestants were black. She had endured decades of white folks' fumbles, shaking her head in disapproval, yet watching and playing on while simultaneously knitting or working a crossword puzzle in ink, usually cheering on the best competitor or the underdog or the good sport or the player who happened to hail from our neck of the woods. But as more black contestants appeared on the show, rooting for the home team took on new meaning and became a kind of racial imperative. If a brother or sister flubbed the obvious, misreading a fully completed puzzle as "WORLD'S LARGEST DESSERT" instead of "DESERT," for example, or "I HAVE NOT YET BEGIN TO FIGHT," instead of "BEGUN," it was more than just a shame, like those darn Yankees beating our beloved Red Sox; it was shame—shame on all our shoulders.

Having grown up in foster care and been forced by circumstances beyond her control to leave high school in her junior year and get a job, my mother knew well the structural inequities and educational disparities that turned *desert* to *dessert* and *begun* to *begin*. Her seemingly unsympathetic response to the verbal faults and epic fails of black contestants was the by-product of an even deeper understanding of the metonymic nature of American racism by which any black is every black—not an individual but a stereotype. The patience and humility she otherwise modeled for her offspring were overridden by the reigning ideology of racial uplift and what Evelyn Brooks Higginbotham, who coined the phrase, identifies as "the politics of respectability," although it would be unfair of me to apply the concept to my parents without addressing the contradictions of their particular prescriptions and proscriptions for being black in the white world.[1] On the face of it, my mother, like many African Americans of her generation, believed that every black man, woman, and child should put his or her best foot forward at all times in order to present colored people to the world as capable and accomplished. Inconsequential as a game-show appearance might seem, the white world was watching one and judging all. It was essential, therefore, that the colored contestant show well—win, lose, or draw—that is, speak well, dress well, play well (even if not winning), and otherwise represent the race in the finest fashion and to the highest standard possible. In this sense, my mother required of black game-show contestants no less than she expected of her own children, even as she rarely judged others, oddly enough, so long as they were not acting up or "playing the fool" in public or on television.

Part of the African American Dream at midcentury, racial uplift is most often associated with the bourgeois aspirations of an educated black elite who believe the best and brightest among them must reach back and pull up the colored masses in the cause of advancing the race. Perhaps the best-known articulation of uplift ideology is the notion of the "Talented Tenth," popularized by W. E. B. Du Bois in an essay of the same name. "The Negro race, like all races, is going to be saved by its exceptional men," Du Bois wrote in 1903, arguing for the higher, classical education of the few who would be leaders among men as opposed to the industrial training of the black majority as advocated by Booker T. Washington.[2] Du Bois goes on to assert that the "worst" of the race will most quickly be elevated by the effort and example of the "best," whom he calls an "aristocracy of talent and character," a few good men, approximately one-tenth of the Negro population, who, by virtue of a virtuous life, liberal education, hard work, and professional achievement, will serve as the "yeast" that will give rise to the entire race.

Not all incarnations of uplift ideology are quite so markedly high-handed and elitist in their "best"/"worst," "us"/"them," top/down divide; and even Du Bois eventually backed away from the notion that only a college-educated chosen few could lead the Negro race to the promised land of equal opportunity and full citizenship.[3] My parents—and my Jamaican father was as full of racial pride as my American mother—were neither middle class nor college educated (although my mother eventually received her high school diploma through night classes and my father earned a bachelor's degree much later in life). Nor was their own commitment to uplift sheathed in either the religiosity or the concern with decorum of the black Baptist church whose women, in particular, Higginbotham maintains, "adhered to a politics of respectability that equated public behavior with individual self-respect and with the advancement of African Americans as a group."[4]

As an ideology associated with the activism of black churchwomen of the late nineteenth and early twentieth centuries, respectability politics has its own internal contradictions, reflecting a "bourgeois vision" that challenged the racist and sexist proscriptions of the day, Higginbotham explains, even as it disparaged the lifestyles and behavior of blacks who acted outside the dictates of what were considered white middle-class norms. Churchwomen displayed their liberal bent in their demands for equality and social justice, but "revealed their conservatism when they attributed institutional racism to the 'negative' public behavior of their people," Higginbotham writes, as if good behavior and proper decorum "could eradicate the pervasive racial barriers that surrounded black Americans."[5]

For my parents, advancing the race was about taking pride in our racial identity, not about achieving social status or embracing white middle-class mores and strict standards of decorum. Values were colorless as far as they were concerned. It was right over wrong that ruled, and there they—especially my mother—had a keen sense of what was right, at both the macro- and microlevels. Yet she never held herself above her society, and the only fellow blacks she looked down on were those who put on airs, even as she had high expectations for anybody on TV or otherwise in the public eye where the one would be taken for the whole. Hence, I am reluctant to encamp my mother or my father within the discourse of respectability politics, which has lost much of its original connectedness to the self-help ethos of black churchwomen and been appropriated into contemporary debates over personal responsibility tied to conservative critiques of the black underclass that focus on individual behavior rather than systems of power and structural barriers.

As a young family in the 1950s, we were definitely of the masses rather than to the manor (except in the original Shakespearean "manner," perhaps), yet my parents' hopes, ideals, values, and beliefs in higher education and property ownership were similar to those of the black bourgeoisie. They wanted to rear their children in a comfortable home in a quiet country neighborhood, away from the hustle, bustle, and blight of the inner city. But when the color of their capital wasn't green enough to overcome the color of their skin and house after house for sale in the suburbs suddenly would become unavailable, they finally settled for a half-acre plot in a rural white, blue-collar community in southeastern Massachusetts where a white man named Frank Connell was giving away free land to anyone who would build on it. Thus it was that my family began the nightmare of building "Mr. Blanding's dream house" (after the fashion of the 1948 Cary Grant film) from the foundation up with blueprints drawn from my mother's imagination, a set of do-it-yourself, how-to books, and absolutely no practical knowledge of carpentry or construction.

Building the American Dream house that ultimately would finish off the family before we finished it became our life's work. We all labored at it. My father was an excellent tailor but a slapdash block layer who didn't care about aesthetics as I did even as a child; so at some point in my girlhood, I started

FIG. 1.1 Little Adrian, Ann, and Danny at the building site in the summer of 1953.

FIG. 1.2 Danny, the cutest baby ever, on the front lawn of neighbors and long-term friends the Crockers, also 1953.

FIG. 1.3 A 1960s view of the building site with my neater masonry to the left and a family friend, Joanne Jackson (Spann), seated in the foreground.

FIG. 1.4 The "Three Ds," a little older in their Sunday best. I'm not mad, just squinting because the sun is in my eyes.

mixing concrete and laying cinder and cement blocks alongside him, trailing after him with a trowel to scrape away the excess mortar and point the seams between the blocks as I had watched Nat Williams, a black mason from our church, do at the brick house he was building for his own family down the street, over the line in Brockton, the hometown of Rocky Marciano and Marvelous Marvin Hagler.

Ours was a different but by no means difficult childhood. We worked harder than most kids we knew, but we played hard, too, in the surrounding woods that were our wonderland. I don't remember my parents reading us traditional fairytales and bedtime stories, though I suppose they did, because I have a vague recollection of thinking I was like the princess in "The Princess and the Pea" when I was put to bed atop several mattresses when we stayed overnight in Boston at the home of family friends while my mother was in the hospital giving birth to my baby brother. What I do remember clearly is my father reading us Bible verses and passages from Shakespeare and scaring us with duppy stories—ghost tales and other folklore from Africa and the Caribbean—and both parents reciting poetry to us. I walked around declaiming "Half a league, half a league / Half a league onward / All in the valley of Death / Rode the six hundred," parroting my father's British West Indian accent—"Theirs not to reason why / Theirs but to do and die"—loving the rhyme and rhythm of the words, knowing nothing of their meaning, and believing Dad's tall tale that he had fought alongside a guy named Tennyson at the Battle of Baklava. "Baklava" for "Balaclava" was one of many linguistic jokes my parents played on us that I didn't get until I was significantly older.

One of my mother's favorite tricks of tongue and ear was to say, "Desert the table," when we would ask her what's for dessert, a response that was a great mystery to me as a small child. "What does she mean, 'dessert the table'?" Her playful, homophonic retort was all the more confusing because she was as good at cooking and baking as she was at knitting, puzzle solving, and everything else she undertook; there were always lots of homemade desserts to be had. In fact, it was her pound cakes, pies, cobblers, fresh-baked breads, and other sweet and savory culinary delights that had helped win over the local residents when we first arrived and she cooked outside on a wood stove. Her "desert the table" play with words is all the more amusing now, considered in light of her reaction to the *Wheel* contestant's *dessert* versus *desert* faux pas.

But I digress. The main point I want to make is that my parents had the kind of grand scheme of the good life that is generally ascribed to the middle and upper classes. My mother stayed home with us kids when we were little, despite the fact that before marriage and children she had done everything from domestic labor in the homes of well-off whites to top-secret mechanical calibrations at Picatinny Arsenal where she received awards and commendations from the War Department for her service. For much of that time, my father, a tailor by trade, worked by the piece as a stitcher at New England McIntosh, a local garment factory, even though this single-income, sexual division of labor kept us near the poverty line. Somehow even on a tight household budget, my parents belonged to the Book-of-the-Month Club and built an impressive library of encyclopedia volumes, reference books, and literary classics. They paid for music lessons and new instruments for all three of us—clarinets for my brothers and an upright piano for me when I was eight, because they mistakenly thought they saw Beethoven-like genius in the way I moved my fingers up and down the keyboard of Great Aunt Alice's spinet instead of banging on the keys like other kids.

We did seasonal farm work and scooped cranberries in the bogs near Plymouth to make extra money and gardened, raised chickens for meat and eggs, farmed, fished, and foraged to economize in the early years. We used to fish from the pier at Plymouth Harbor, where when the fishing boats returned to port at end of day, they would give away bushel baskets of what I imagine must have been their less desirable catch. Between what we caught and what we were given, fish was a foodstuff we didn't have to buy in the grocery store. Still, how my parents managed to give us so many of what they considered the finer things in life on so little money still puzzles and moves me. Their poor man's enactment of racial uplift and respectability politics suggests how complicated and perplexing these concepts are and how much their so-called elite pretensions stretch across class lines.

In all corners of midcentury America, millions of poor black parents like mine moved heaven and earth and juggled meager budgets to give their children keys to the kingdoms of culture, class, and capitalism: not only the equal education fought for in *Brown v. Board of Education* (1954) but also the music lessons, dance classes, museum visits, silver tongues, and polished manners they believed were part of preparing us to lead ethical, examined lives of service and achievement rather than the quiet desperation Thoreau attributes to the masses. For them, racial uplift was nothing other than a black version of the desire—the determination—most parents hold for their offspring to do better than they. In this case, doing better wasn't simply for the sake of the individual or the family but, rather, for the race. My brothers and I and multitudes of black kids like us were reared under the colored kids' mantra that everything we did, anything we accomplished, was not

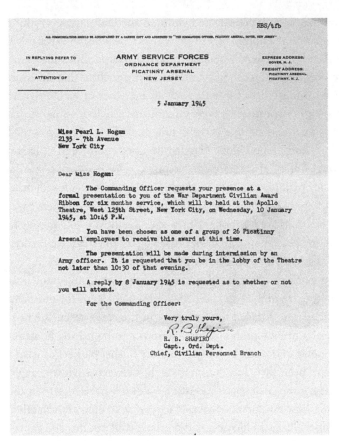

FIG. 1.5 A letter from the War Department announcing an award ceremony for one of several commendations that Mom received for her work at Picatinny Arsenal in New Jersey during World War II.

for our own aggrandizement but, rather, for the advancement of colored people.

As it began to enter American households in the 1950s, television, oddly enough, quickly became part of the master plan for that advancement, a new, thoroughly modern instrument of uplift that would show off African Americans at their most talented and accomplished. And black people were not alone in envisioning television's potential for progressive racial profiling. As the media historian J. Fred MacDonald establishes in his critical study *Blacks and White TV: African Americans in Television since 1948* (1992), white TV pioneers like Ed Sullivan and Steve Allen regularly featured black performers and celebrities on their variety shows.[6] They, too, viewed the emergent medium as a kind of great equalizer that would subtly contribute to the cause of civil rights by bringing the talents of "the Negro" into the living rooms of mainstream America, where, as Sullivan put it in 1950, "public opinion is formed" and hearts and minds are changed. Calling television "just what the doctor ordered for Negro performers," Sullivan optimistically declared that the new medium provided "ten-league boots to the Negro in his fight to win what the Constitution guarantees as his birthright."[7]

A forerunner and possible progenitor of the oxymoronic category of "reality TV," game shows may seem a less likely instrument of racial uplift than the variety shows that Sullivan and Allen hosted. I turn to these quiz and puzzle programs first both because they constitute my earliest experiences of television and because I have a theory that as game shows go, so goes the medium and perchance the nation. As game shows—one of TV's first integrated spaces—have changed from white to technicolored, so, too, has television as a form of home entertainment.[8] I am interested less in the shows themselves, however, than in what they may say about their moments—what they may tell us about the blackening and even the sexing of American culture. At the same time, I am well aware that, as Olaf Hoerschelmann addresses in his comprehensive study of the genre, within academia "quiz shows are generally regarded as a trivial cultural form that does not warrant scholarly attention."[9] Hoerschelmann's monograph, *Rules of the Game: Quiz Shows and American Culture* (2006), attempts to correct that perception, taking up the challenge of the media theorist John Fiske, one of the founding fathers of television studies and arguably the first scholar to take quiz shows seriously as cultural texts and to call for their critical examination.[10]

Part of what makes this "widely devalued" (Fiske's terminology) genre worth studying, in Hoerschelmann's view, is the extent to which "ideological formations manifest themselves in this seemingly trivial form." Rebutting the notion that TV audiences are "passive receivers of prepackaged media messages," quiz shows, according to Hoerschelmann, "create a discursive space in which a reversal of cultural hierarchies is possible and in which the audience is at least symbolically involved in the production of a program."[11] I have undertaken scholarly investigations of seemingly trivial forms and figures in the past: Barbie dolls, Shirley Temple, Martha Stewart, O.J. Simpson. In this instance, however, my interest is personal as well as intellectual. Largely in tribute to my mother's love of the game and the extent to which her expert, interactive participation in the quiz-show fad of the 1950s determined what these shows became to us as a double-edged audience watching her watching TV, I want to revisit this genre I grew up on within the context of my family's everyday experience as viewers and cultural consumers. At the same time, a long life as a scholar and my interest in reading icons and artifacts as cultural texts make it impossible for me to close the critical eye I have been trained to keep wide open, especially since what strikes me most immediately about the difference between these programs of my past and their revival in the present is the change in color and content—a subject neither Fiske nor Hoerschelmann addresses.

<hr />

My mother passed away in 2002 at the age of eighty. She lived to see her preferred type of TV programming come of age with its own network, GSN— the Game Show Network—but she missed by a few years the turn in the genre that seems to me symbolic of larger trends in television and popular culture. Once light, bright, and mostly white, game shows have gone over to the dark side. Not only are most of them liberally peppered with contestants of color, but several of them, including syndicated mainstays like *Let's Make a Deal*, *Family Feud*, *The Newlywed Game*, *To Tell the Truth*, *The $100,000 Pyramid*, and the newer network classic ABC's *Who Wants to Be a Millionaire?*, are now (or recently were) also hosted by black celebrities, most of them comedians, although the Best Actor Oscar winner Jamie Foxx and the rapper Snoop Dogg (who cohosts a variety show with Martha Stewart, *Martha & Snoop's Pot Luck Dinner*, on VH1) have assumed the helms of a *Name That Tune* update called *Beat Shazam* (Fox) and a reboot of *The Joker's Wild* (TBS), respectively. Moreover, since these shows went black, their ratings have soared. Since Steve Harvey took over *Family Feud* in 2010, for example, its ratings have skyrocketed, at times surpassing even the gold standard of game shows, the longtime favorites *Wheel of Fortune* and *Jeopardy*, and landing second only to what for some time has been the biggest daytime audience grabber and moneymaker of all, *Judge Judy*, although some reports even have *Feud* besting the Queen of Mean in certain demographics.[12]

Television's black gold rush doesn't start or stop with game shows, it seems. It has invaded almost every genre, from small-claims arbitration melodramas and tabloid talk shows like *Judge Judy*, *The People's Court*, *Maury*, and *Jerry Springer*; to soap operas, reality series; sitcoms like *Black-ish*, *The Carmichael Show*, Tyler Perry's *House of Payne*, and his quartet of series on the new Oprah Winfrey Network (OWN); and even hit prime-time potboilers such as *Empire* on Fox, which follows the drama and dysfunction behind a black family's hip hop entertainment enterprise built on drug money, and *Scandal* on ABC, which revolves around the love life and life's work of a high-powered former White House staffer turned D.C. fixer and her firm of misfit operatives she calls "gladiators." Created and produced by Shonda Rhimes, the same black woman showrunner behind *Grey's Anatomy* and *Private Practice*, *Scandal* is famously inspired by the life and times of Judy Smith, the black female former deputy press secretary for George H. W. Bush turned corporate crisis manager and PR consultant with high-profile clients ranging from the intern Monica Lewinsky to the actor Wesley Snipes.[13]

Daytime talk shows like those hosted by Queen Latifah, Wendy Williams, and, here again, Steve Harvey, as well as roundtable chat fests with multiracial casts of cohosts such as ABC's *The View* and *The Chew* and CBS's *The Talk* are all a part of the changing face of twenty-first-century television. The long-running morning show *Live! with Regis and Kelly* saw a surge in ratings across the demographic spectrum when the black former New York Giants defensive end and Hall of Fame inductee Michael Strahan succeeded Notre Dame's Fighting Irish favorite son Regis Philbin as Kelly Ripa's permanent cohost in 2012. During a high-profile, yearlong search for a second chair to complement Ripa, a petite blonde soap opera actress turned TV host, nearly sixty celebrities—including several white men of means with movie-star credentials like Alec Baldwin, Rob Lowe, and Matthew Broderick—sat in the coveted second seat that ultimately went to Strahan.

Although pleased with the element of diversity his new black cohost brought to the show, Michael Gelman, *Live's* longtime executive producer, denied that race had anything to do with casting Strahan. Kelly and Michael just happen to have "that x-factor," Gelman said, "a chemistry" that "just works."[14] Maybe so, but it's hard to see the two hosts together in the visual medium of television, especially standing back-to-back—as the *New York Post* captured them under the sexually provocative headline "Size Matters"—and not notice what one media analyst describes as the "very stark physical contrast" between "the NFL superstar with the monster build and America's tiniest sweetheart."[15] Even Gelman acknowledges that he finds the "great visual contrast" of "this big football player and this petite blond" to be "interesting."[16]

What hangs in the air but doesn't quite get said about this interesting mashup of beauty and the beast is that hiding there somewhere in the country's collective unconscious is that same lingering sense of tension and taboo that D. W. Griffith exploited a hundred years ago in his silent film that still speaks volumes, *The Birth of a Nation* (1915), and called up again in pairing the white, pint-size wunderkind Shirley Temple with the big black dance man Bill "Bojangles" Robinson in the four films they appeared in together in the 1930s.[17] The age difference and the dance man's cozy, affable Uncle Tom persona—Temple called him "Uncle Billy" in real life—effectively neutered Robinson and made him safe, a sign without signification, black and male without the threat of black masculinity.[18] But what of Michael Strahan? What makes this big black man with the "*monster* build" tame enough to go from gridiron to giggling gal-pal consort? Perhaps it is the willingness to giggle and gossip and be girl-friendly goofy with America's tiniest sweetheart in the safe space of the television studio—popping up onto the TV screen out of a Pandora's box of uniquely American contradictions.

As John Fiske (among others) has pointed out, "America has a long tradition of using the beauty and vulnerability of the white woman as a metaphor for its social order." He goes on to suggest that unless properly controlled and contained, the nonwhite male—especially the black male—"individualizes and sexualizes the threat of the other race."[19] That threat, at times, can be more titillating than terrifying. At 6'5" and 250-something pounds, Michael Strahan could easily pick up the 100-pound pixie Kelly Ripa and toss her around like Fay Wray in the arms of King Kong. I suspect it is at least in part this visual vulnerability that makes this particular white/black, beauty-and-the-beast pairing so interesting to Gelman, to TV critics, and to much of *Live*'s predominantly white audience.[20] And to the canonical tensions and taboos of black man/white woman, the former football star supplies the additional titillation of the sexual tease—literally. During one of Strahan's twenty-plus trial runs as Ripa's guest cohost, Channing Tatum visited the *Live!* set to promote his film *Magic Mike* (2012), loosely based on his own experience as a male stripper. In the midst of the actor's appearance, Strahan surprised Kelly and upstaged Tatum by standing up, ripping off his tearaway trousers, and performing his own bump-and-grind floor dance, including a drop split that he didn't quite complete.[21]

Even Strahan has suggested it was the striptease that finally scored him his new, hard-won day job as permanent cohost, as well as a near-nude cameo in *Magic Mike XXL*. What Uncle Billy Robinson lacked, which made him safe, Strahan has in affable abundance, which makes him—in the most literal sense—spectacular. That is, to borrow from the television theorist Lynne Joyrich, he is "constituted as spectacle," performing the "masquerade of hypermasculinity" that society particularly likes to project onto the African American male. According to Joyrich, a professor of modern culture and media at Brown University, "the interlocking issues of race and sex" are often

FIGS. 1.6 AND 1.7 The *New York Post*'s image of Michael Strahan and Kelly Ripa, with the caption "Size Matters," recalls the D. W. Griffith–inspired pairing of Bill Robinson and Shirley Temple in the 1930s.

"played out across the body of a black man—a man marked in our culture's racist discourses as little more than body."[22]

Television is seldom interested in the brains of black men. (The astrophysicist Neil deGrasse Tyson is a rare exception.)[23] TV is, however, extremely interested in the black male body. (Elsewhere I have dubbed this interest "Mandingoism," after Kyle Onstott's steamy 1957 novel and the equally trashy 1975 film based on it, and "Mapplethorpism," in honor of the white gay photographer Robert Mapplethorpe, whose studies of nude black men are legendary for their homoerotic fetishizing of the black male body.)[24] Repeatedly described as "charismatic," "warm," "personable," "affable," "endearing"—a "gentle giant"—amid endless notations of his monster build and super size, Strahan as a walking body of abundant black masculinity also embodies some of the classic contradictions underpinning othering and racialization

What's in a Game? 35

in the United States, including, in an odd simultaneity, hypermasculinization and its seeming opposite, feminization—a paradox that Joyrich argues "is the underlying logic of texts of male spectacle," especially black male spectacle.[25] It is "overdetermined," she says, that this sometimes "deadly conflation of excess and lack, threatening femininity and superabundant masculinity, would be projected onto an African American male." This conflation appears most alarming, she continues, in its "(imagined) relation to the white woman"; "it is because of the myth of the hypervirile black male rapist (used historically to justify lynch laws) that the symbolic castration of African American men became all too often realized in fact."[26]

In the case of Strahan, the symbolic castration or sexual containment is accomplished through the articulation of a feminizing counternarrative of charisma, charm, and self-effacing, goofy, grinning, giggling, girl-friendly good humor, which disrupts the historical threat of black masculinity and turns it into marketability. "Dark and handsome" to Ripa's "blonde and petite," in the words of one critic, "big and brotherly" to Kelly's "girlish and silly," according to another, Strahan is in fact so marketable and so much a ratings boost for *Live!* that he was promptly tapped to join the crew of ABC's eye-opener *Good Morning America* (*GMA*), sitting in with the anchors a few days a week, before jumping *Live*'s ship completely in the spring of 2016 for the catbird seat with *GMA*, along with hosting summer editions of the Dick Clark vehicle the *$100,000 Pyramid*, on top of his standing Sunday assignment with Fox Sports.[27]

Strahan is one of the newest faces of a technicolored turn in TV some media analysts consider part of the Obama effect. The election of an African American president in 2008, the argument goes, alerted television executives to the possibility of cashing in on the interests of an increasingly multiracial population and a changing national character that, before the Trump turn in 2016, seemed more open to diversity than ever before. By my reckoning, however, the roots of the trend predate the 2008 election and may actually have more to do with the Oprah effect—the tremendous power and influence Oprah Winfrey wields with her extensive, multiracial fan base and the American electorate—which some believe helped put Obama in office. Little or nothing in TV history has matched the stunning, megawatt, multimillion-dollar success of *The Oprah Winfrey Show*, which ruled the afternoon airways from 1986 to 2011, winning dozens of Emmy Awards during just the first fifteen years of its quarter-century run and becoming the highest-rated talk show of all time.[28]

Oprah and its namesake host and producer broke several glass ceilings, opened all kinds of doors, and changed the character and the color of daytime TV, paving the way for other black program hosts like Tyra Banks, Iyanla Vanzant, Wendy Williams, and best friend Gayle King, who describes herself as standing in Oprah's light rather than her shadow.[29] *Oprah* also can be credited with making television personalities out of the psychologist and former jury consultant or "courtroom scientist" Phillip McGraw, "Dr. Phil," and the heart surgeon Mehmet Oz, "Dr. Oz," and with helping to launch the TV careers of celebrity chef Rachael Ray, interior designer Nate Berkus, and financial analyst Suze Orman.[30] Oprah's Book Club, a virtual reading and discussion group launched in 1996, turned obscure titles into instant bestsellers and revived interest in old classics like Leo Tolstoy's *Anna Karenina*, catapulting the nineteenth-century love story to the top of the bestseller lists in 2004 when Oprah named it her book of the month.[31]

While no one has been able to fill Oprah's red-soled Louboutins since she shut down her show to build OWN, Steve Harvey, the increasingly ubiquitous black comedian, actor, author, radio talk- and game-show host, is wearing more and more hats on TV and may be poised to be the next big thing in daytime, although Strahan may give him a run for the money. Harvey, who played a godfather of 1970s funk turned high school music teacher in an eponymous sitcom on the WB from 1996 to 2002, helmed his own self-titled daytime talk show *Steve Harvey* from 2012 to 2017, along with hosting *Family Feud*, episodes of which are shown multiple times a day and night on GSN, CBS, and other networks, including a prime-time celebrity edition on ABC. Partnering with Ellen DeGeneres as cocreator/producer, he added yet another new program to his repertoire in the spring of 2016—*Little Big Shots*, a children's talent show on which kids not only perform amazing feats but also say the darndest things, after the fashion of the old Art Linkletter and Bill Cosby vehicles. A new L.A.-based, celebrity-driven talk show, *Steve*, coproduced and creatively controlled by Harvey, premiered in the fall of 2017, along with a throwback variety vehicle *Showtime at the Apollo*, also with Harvey as host.

Not restricting himself to mechanical media, Harvey has also published two bestselling advice books aimed at educating black women about black men: *Act Like a Lady, Think Like a Man* (2009), which was the basis for the 2012 similarly titled movie, and *Straight Talk, No Chaser: How to Find, Keep, and Understand a Man* (2010)—which perhaps is what qualifies the thrice-married comedian to dole out dating and matrimonial advice to the black female lovelorn. As Harvey mansplains the gender achievement gap to "Strong, Independent—and Lonely—Women" (chapter 13 of *Act Like a Lady*), the savvy route to a marriage proposal is through the male ego. For example, in a guest appearance on *Oprah* that went viral in 2009, he famously advised a group of successful, single, husband-hunting black women not to stop being successful but to hide a little of their light under a bushel in order to "make a space for [a man] to fit in so he can come in and do what men do"—that is, "profess, provide, and protect," what Harvey calls the "three Ps of love." "A man has got to see where he fits into the providing and protecting role," he advised.[32] As he explains even more explicitly in *Think Like a Lady*: "If we can't exercise two of the major components that make up who we are as men—providing and protecting—then we're not about to profess our love for you."[33]

There is nothing new about this type of old-school relationship advice, of course. Steve Harvey's guide to the single black female merely echoes familiar claims that black men have been deprived of their natural roles as providers and protectors, not only by the white man but also by the black woman, who is often better educated and otherwise better off than the brothers she outclasses, thereby leaving herself high, dry, and alone, by default—the fault of her own achievements. Lopsided male/female demographics and the much-reported dearth of black males who are marriage material and black female friendly may help explain why so many otherwise self-reliant, modern women take seriously Harvey's Me-Tarzan-You-Jane advice and counsel. What's harder to understand is why the television industry is buying and selling this particular Original King of Comedy as its picked-to-click technicolored king of daytime. But Harvey is definitely getting the "O" buzz—not Oscar but Oprah, with the *Hollywood Reporter* and other sources speculating that he is the next Oprah Winfrey, and Harvey himself saying that while there is only one "Big O," he wouldn't mind being called "the little 'O.'"[34]

My mother, who even found a bone to pick with Oprah, who she felt gave away too many secrets of the sisterhood (we straighten our kinky hair with hot combs and chemicals and grease our legs in the winter to ward off ash), wouldn't be impressed with Steve Harvey, no matter how much Hollywood is. She would hate what he does to the English language, for one thing, and his buffoonish brand of black performativity, for another, which has led some in the black community to dismiss him as a clown—and worse (even more so after his tête-à-tête with Trump). He, however, is laughing all the way to the bank, because millions of fans of all colors are feasting on Harveyism. Not only has *Family Feud* gone big-time since he took it over, but *Steve Harvey* beat out *Dr. Phil* and *Dr. Oz* for the Daytime Emmy for Outstanding Talk Show in 2014 and 2015, and again in 2017, and so outperformed much of its competition in its first two seasons that it more or less blasted off the air rival talk shows hosted by TV veterans like Ricki Lake, Anderson Cooper, Jeff Probst, and Katie Couric.

Even the seismic gaffe of crowning the wrong winner in his first outing as host of the sixty-fourth annual Miss Universe Pageant didn't burst Harvey's rising bubble or damage his hosting credentials, as some predicted. His talk show won its second NAACP Image Award in a row in 2016, as well as another Emmy in 2017, and he was back in 2017 as host of the sixty-fifth Miss Universe pageant. Of course, anyone familiar with Harvey's role-specific theories of gender relations or his work on *Family Feud*, where, as I am about to argue, Q&A has become T&A, might wonder for what reason other than a play for ratings is the current black golden guy the chosen emcee of a ceremony that celebrates intelligent, polished, empowered young women.

Likewise taking note of the diversity upturn in contemporary television programming, Emily Nussbaum, the *New Yorker*'s Pulitzer Prize–winning TV critic, has rightly pointed out that this wave of interest in all things black "could easily recede, as it has many times before after periods of progress." She points to the early 1950s when television was brand new, to the 1970s when *Roots* and Norman Lear productions were all the rage, and again to the early 1990s when the success of *The Cosby Show* set the stage for a host of other black sitcoms.[35]

Television is indeed a fickle lover where the Negro is concerned, but for however long it may last, this is a time when the industry is learning that it does well to cater to what it takes to be the tastes of black people. From our viewing habits and spending patterns to our conspicuous consumption of everything from hair products to smartphones, twenty-first-century African Americans are such obvious candidates for target marketing that many media analysts are surprised business and industry, especially the television and advertising industries, are not more attentive and responsive to the getting and spending, moving and shaking of black consumers and cultural producers. According to a 2013 report from Nielsen market research, the black population is younger and more media savvy than the populace at large and exerts tremendous influence on pop culture. In addition, African Americans, who have an escalating collective buying power topping the trillion-dollar mark, watch significantly more television than any other racial group—37 percent more, according to Nielsen—with a heavy preference for "programming that includes diverse characters and casts."[36]

First to get the market-share message, daytime TV has been eager to pick up and promote whatever black goose it thinks will lay the Oprah kind of golden eggs, even if the goose is a gander named Harvey. The only surprise is that prime time was slower to cash in on the same black gold. Cedric the Entertainer, who briefly helmed *Who Wants to Be a Millionaire?* (and turned it "ghetto," by some reports), has offered his own explanation for why prime time brought up the rear in the race for race.[37] He and fellow game-show hosts such as Steve Harvey and Wayne Brady of *Let's Make a Deal* are "allowed" to be themselves, he says, bringing their "true personalities" and humor to their programs, which represent an "authenticity" to which audiences respond. "But in prime time," he adds, "the perception of what black people and other minorities are like is still being filtered by the industry, who feel they know what's best."[38] In other words, at least according to Cedric the Entertainer, TV of the game-show kind allows black hosts to be their quintessentially colored selves while prime-time drama requires black actors to perform identities other than their own and limits who and what they can pretend to be.

This theory of theatrical identity politics ought to be nonsense, because it's all acting, all performance, all personas. Unfortunately, in Hollywood casting is still often typed according to fixed notions of what parts black actors appear culturally, phenotypically, and otherwise right for. I'm not convinced, however, that the Cedric the Entertainer or the Steve Harvey or the Wayne Brady or any of the other African Americans we see hosting game shows on both daytime and nighttime TV are any more real and true than the personalities who appear as themselves on so-called reality shows like *Married to Medicine* and *The Real Housewives of Atlanta* or the actors who perform for the cameras on prime-time dramas such as *Empire* and *Scandal*.[39]

What this new breed of black game-show hosts actually has in common is the fact that they are almost all stand-up comics. Humor is their stock and trade, part of the shtick they bring to the emcee role. This is the case with certain white game-show hosts as well—Drew Carey, for example, who replaced the venerable Bob Barker as host of *The Price Is Right*. But the difference between the black comedian turned host and the white funny man as emcee is difference itself. And while daytime TV may seem to be saying *vive la différence*, I would counter, cynically, that it is the same difference—that is, that "black" is not quite the new thing it seems. "Funny" has long been America's favorite way to see black people—the quintessential performative mode for people of color, whose job so often is and long has been to provide local color and comic relief.

Funny is a kind of typecasting that is good enough for the lower-brow brand of television most game shows are seen to represent. Accordingly, a black comedian fits the bill for most such shows. Cedric the Entertainer's homeboy humor may not have worked well for the upscale quiz show *Who Wants to Be a Millionaire?* and likewise wouldn't do for a higher-end puzzler like *Wheel of Fortune*, which enjoys a large following and doesn't need low-brow black humor to boost its ratings. One of the most upscale quiz shows of all time, *Wheel's* sister series *Jeopardy*, hosted by Alex Trebek since its return to television in 1984, is definitely not a candidate for black comedy. Billing itself as "the classic thinking person's answer-and-question quiz," *Jeopardy* boasts players (and presumably viewers) who are smarter than your average bear. Contestants have to compete to compete in this exclusive quiz bowl. They have to pass a written test before even being allowed to audition for the show. Smarter-than-average contestants need a smarter-than-average host, and Alex Trebek oozes erudition. Even though we know he has the correct responses in front of him, he still manages to come across as a bottomless fount of knowledge, regularly ad-libbing clarifications, corrections, and extra bits of trivia as if off the top of his head, reading answer clues in impeccable French when called for (he's half French-Canadian), and matter-of-factly correcting wrong responses (and pronunciations) in a way that makes it clear just how incorrect those wrong answers are. Not that his corrections and emendations are always accurate. Still, given the high standards Monsieur Trebek has established in more than thirty years at its podium, *Jeopardy* clearly is no country for droll black men.

But if *Jeopardy* and *Wheel* are beyond the pale of black comedians who would be hosts, there are some game shows whose success seems to depend on how low they can go. The newly popular Steve Harvey version of *Family Feud* is purposefully front-loaded with provocative questions designed to elicit scatological retorts—responses "over and above the nasty scale," as Harvey himself described one contestant's answers. High-fiving and otherwise posturing, Harvey then plays such retorts for all the laughs he can generate, often rolling his eyes and mugging for the cameras, sometimes strutting around or walking off the stage in mock surprise and feigned indignation that anyone would offer such a racy response on a family show.

FIG. 1.8 The game-show host Steve Harvey feigning shock at a contestant's answer in an episode of *Family Feud*.

The object of the game is for the five members of each of two opposing family teams to attempt to match the most popular responses to survey questions asked of one hundred people previously polled. The first team to accumulate three hundred points through matching the most survey answers wins the main game and gets to send two representatives to the Fast Cash bonus round to compete for $20,000. In one episode that went viral on the Internet, two sisters from a winning black family were posed the following Fast Cash question previously asked of one hundred men: "Name a part of your body that is bigger now than when you were sixteen." Predictably, one sister delivered the bidden response: "His penis." The audience erupted in wild laughter as Harvey stood by feigning shock, then dropped to bended knee as if in prayer, before making a show of chastising the woman for using "that word" in mock irritation, milking the moment for more laughs than it was worth.

It was happening upon a wee-hour rebroadcast of this episode of *Family Feud* one sleepless night that led me to start paying attention to the show. One need not sit through hours of the game as I have. YouTube has an extensive collection of the most suggestive questions and sexually explicit answers. A sampling: "Name something that pops up at the most inconvenient time." Response: "My quivering member." Another: "Name something a man might have in his pants when he's going on a hot date." Contestant's response: "A boner." And another: "Name something you feel self-conscious about doing alone" or, in other versions of essentially the same question, "doing under the covers" or what someone might be doing if in the bathroom for more than five minutes. The answers, of course: "touching yourself," "masturbating," or "playing with yourself." And still another: "Name something you put in your mouth but don't swallow." The response from a contestant who happened to be a pastor's wife: "His sperm." She was unashamed, though Harvey jokingly tried to convince her that she, a minister's wife, should be.

There was some pushback against the game's sexual content when the question "What's the last thing you stuck your finger in?" elicited the response "My wife," and again when a team's patriarch answered "vagina" when asked to "name the first part of a woman you touch to get her in the mood." Clips of both responses—and Harvey's high-fiving, preacherly play with them—went viral and drew a barrage of angry responses condemning the "downright vulgar" turn in what used to be a good family show. Some respondents blame Harvey for making *Feud* the "raunchiest show on TV," much as Cedric the Entertainer was accused of dumbing down *Who Wants to Be a Millionaire?*[40]

While female genitalia may suddenly be sacrosanct, the penis not only remains *Feud*'s favorite plaything, but from the thrust of many of the questions, it seems size does matter: "Tell me something that a bride wants to be huge"; "When people talk about 'the big one,' what do they refer to?" "Name something that can never be long enough"; "Name something you wish was a little bigger"; and, asked of one hundred men, "Name something Shaquille O'Neal has that's bigger than yours."[41] The answer to all of these questions and others like them is, of course, "penis" or some euphemism for the male organ. When the judges XXed-out a male contestant's answer of "junk" in response to the Shaq question on the grounds that "junk" was included in the previously given top answer of "body parts," Harvey begged to differ and offered up a nearly three-minute riff on men's separate and sacred relationship to their private parts, which they guard with their lives and even give names like "Russell, the Wonder Muscle," he said. "Mine is the GFS—Godfather of Soul," he added, cracking himself up and breaking into a few bars of James Brown's "I Feel Good," complete with a little leg shimmy.

Is this progress: a black man publicly playing with his penis for the pleasure of white women and men? Just as pornography is overwrought with bulging black members, *Feud* has its own penis fetish, it seems, colored by a black host's willingness to stand and deliver provocative one-liners. The raunchy expostulations and replies go on game after game ad nauseum, except audiences both in the studio and at home—if ratings are any indication—have been turned on rather than off by the program's penile puns.

Much the same is true for the new *Newlywed Game*, hosted by the black comedienne Sherri Shepherd from 2010 to 2013, with reruns currently airing on the newly launched black-owned and -oriented digital network Bounce TV, whose founders include Ambassador Andrew Young and Martin Luther King III.[42] Shepherd has bragged that her show is "more racy" than the original and boasted of having added to it not only comedy but also "sass," by which she seems to mean a heightened level of sexual content, "couched in innuendo." As an example of "the kind of thing" she brings to the series, she offered her willingness to go boldly where no host had gone before by sharing details of her own love life (she, too, has had sex in public, for example, even if in her own backyard). She also credits herself with frankly lifting the veil of ambiguity for clueless contestants who miss the point, such as the husband who apparently didn't understand that "package" is a euphemism for penis and needed her to spell out the fact that she was asking him the size of his. Shepherd is clearly willing to go to great lengths for her job. Meg Ryan made faking an orgasm famous in *When Harry Met Sally* (1989), but what other TV host has gone so far as to take the hand of an uptight contestant and lead him in simulating orgasmic noises, as Shepherd boasts of doing for and with a reluctant husband struggling with a question about what he sounds like when he makes love with his wife?[43]

To be fair, *The Newlywed Game* and some other shows like *Match Game* always played a little fast and loose with double entendre, but in the old days, the humor, even at its naughtiest, was subtler, smarter, dare I say more mature than the trite, predictable high school locker-room schlock of today. When my brothers and I watched *Newlywed* with our parents in the 1960s, we giggled whenever Bob Eubanks asked the couples a question about "making whoopee." Any reference to intercourse was racy stuff for family television even in the midst of the sexual revolution. I vaguely remember one episode where a husband answered a question in a way that implied that he and his bride had had sex before they were married. Mortified, or pretending to be for her parents back home, the wife whacked the husband with the answer card and declared something like, "Not before we were married, we didn't, stupid!" Today, the questions that Shepherd asks contestants unabashedly assume that husbands and wives have slept not only with each other before the wedding but also with multiple lovers of either or both genders. ("Will your wife say she has only visited the Eiffel Tower or also had her passport stamped at Girl-on-Girl Island?"—a question to which all the husbands confidently answered only the Eiffel Tower and all the wives said they had also visited Girl-on-Girl Island. Of course, if they are as clueless as some of the friends to whom I repeated this question, they may not have understood the metaphors.)

There is no fault in this frankness about a sexually active past, of course. I'm all for what used to be labeled disparagingly "premarital sex" (and wouldn't mind having some myself) and for consenting adults doing whatever with whomever, but I'm also a fan of age-appropriate TV programming. Late-night adult entertainment is one thing, but nothing is off-limits in these daytime and early evening shows where contestants are encouraged, if not required, to talk tits and ass and broadcast the most intimate details of their private lives, regardless of who might be watching—parents, children, bosses, students, neighbors. The hypocrisy is gone and with it, one hopes, the judgment, but one might well wonder whether oral and anal sex, the size of Shaquille O'Neal's penis, and the name of Steve Harvey's package are suitable subjects for what are still billed as family shows.

One might also wonder what in the culture accounts for this turn in TV programming in which the Negro is in such vulgar vogue and the black male pubic is so public. Should we forget Freud and simply take all these punch lines aimed below the belt as innocuous, lighthearted, all in good family fun? My own dirty mind defaults to *Black Skin, White Masks* (1952) and Frantz Fanon's claims about civilized white society's "irrational longing for unusual eras of sexual license, of orgiastic scenes, of unpunished rapes, of unrepressed incest" and that same society's propensity for projecting its own carnal desires onto black people who are "only biology," Fanon says, "fixed at the genitals."[44] If there is anything to Fanon's argument that the Negro male "is viewed as a penis symbol"—a walking phallus, *Homo erectus*—is there, then, some more sinister, salacious connection to be drawn between the bawdy nature of the game-show questions and the black bodies of the game-show hosts and many of the contestants?[45]

So, which came first? Did black people *blacken* (as in dumb down and dirty up) TV, or did the turn into this era of unusual sexual license open up a space for an always already sexualized black body to enter a once overwhelmingly white medium? Is television merely trending dark and dirty out of and in response to that license, playing to modern America's appetite for the sexually explicit in everything from commercials to quiz shows to soap operas and reality series where naked is the newest normal? (Examples include *Naked Vegas* on Syfy, *Naked and Afraid* and *Naked Castaway* on the Discovery Channel, *Dating Naked* on VH1, *Buying Naked* on the Learning

Channel, no less, naked shoots on *America's Next Top Model* and naked models on *Project Runway All Stars*, along with *Skin Wars* or what might be called *Painted Naked* on GSN, as well as prime-time dramas like *Empire, Power, Being Mary Jane, Scandal, Atlanta, How to Get Away with Murder*, and the raunchy TNT newcomer *Claws* where sex, drugs, and crime are the hot commodities that sell the shows.) Is our present preoccupation with the naked and the dark the sexual revolution turned revolting, or is it simply a new frankness about human sexuality and social reality that is to be celebrated—the long-overdue death of Puritanism that has more to do with sexual freedom as a contemporary societal phenomenon than with Frantz Fanon?

I raise these points as questions because I can't claim to know the answers. As troubled as I am by the dumbing down and sexing up of contemporary TV programming playing itself out in blackface, there may be other ways of reading this technicolored turn. It may be that vulgarity, like beauty, is in the eyes of the beholder, and I'm the one with tunnel vision. We have been a sexually repressed and repressive society for centuries, so maybe there is something to be said for an easier, breezier way of being with our bodies. In the second season premiere of *Celebrity Family Feud*, the first prompt Steve Harvey put to the teams anchored by the country music star Kellie Pickler and Lance Bass of the boy band *NSYNC was "Name something specific that only your man is allowed to do to your behind?" Pickler's sister, fifth in line to hazard an answer, sheepishly offered, "Doing the dirty from behind," with the caveat, "only when you're married." Although her answer didn't appear on the scoreboard, it was clearly the response everyone was waiting for. Amid a cacophony of hoots and howls of hilarity, Harvey paused, strode across the stage to a little white boy sitting in the front row of the studio audience, motioned for the child to stand up, patted him on the head, and proceeded to joke that this perhaps twelve- or thirteen-year-old boy was clapping louder than anyone else at the sexually explicit, married-adults-only response.

After milking the moment for a few more laughs, Harvey eventually moved on to the next question: "Name something Steve Harvey would look extra sexy in." I, however, haven't moved on. I haven't stopped thinking about that little boy in the front row. Why was he laughing and clapping so enthusiastically? Was he simply caught up in the excitement of being in the studio audience of the number one game show in town? Or was he genuinely tickled by a question and answer I would not even have understood at his age? It's not such a good thing that many girls of my generation grew up not knowing much about our own bodies. In *Go Set a Watchman* (2015), the controversial early draft of *To Kill a Mockingbird* (1960) published as its sequel, we learn from the narrator that at twelve a confused and misinformed Jean Louise Finch, who fans of *Mockingbird* know better as Scout, climbed to the top of the town water tank, intending to jump to her death because she was sure she was pregnant after being French-kissed by a boy and didn't want to bring shame on her family. Scout's misery resonated with the women in my reading group, because most of us had held similarly crazy ideas about s-e-x as girls, like the belief that you could get pregnant from a toilet seat. (I even thought at one point that a nosebleed meant I was pregnant, because I had overheard my mother telling a woman friend that the first sign she got with each of her three pregnancies was a bloody nose.)

Sex wasn't a topic of discussion in our household during my growing-up years. In fact, when a detective uttered the word "prostitute" in an episode of *The Naked City* circa 1958 or 1959, when I would have been nine or ten, our parents both gasped. Of course that made us eager to know what a prostitute was. They wouldn't tell us, which naturally set us on a course to find out for ourselves by looking up the word in the huge, heavy, two-volume dictionary that for some reason was kept high up on a shelf over the sofa in the den where the television also was. I remember Adrian climbing up, getting down the L–Z volume, and the two of us looking up the word by sounding it out. We found it, but the definition offered was no help. "Pros-ti-tute: a woman who practices prostitution; a harlot." That sent us to the A–M volume to look up "harlot": "a lewd woman; a prostitute; a whore," which also wasn't informative and sent us back to L–Z to look up "whore."[46] I don't remember at what point we got off this linguistic merry-go-round, but I don't think we succeeded in figuring out the meaning of prostitute and its synonyms because I went on to embarrass myself in front of my classmates some years later by declaring that the word "whorehouse" in *The Old Man and the Sea* was clearly a typo for "warehouse."

What stood in for sex talks around our house were salvos about purity and marriageability, such as "Why buy a cow if you can get the milk for free?"—the midcentury version of Steve Harvey's girl-friendly advice to "keep the cookies in the cookie jar"—and homilies about what nice girls did and didn't do. Nice girls didn't chase boys, for example, or call them on the phone. At least that was the Mother Law until I entered first my thirties, then forties and fifties without a husband, at which point Mom would invent reasons why I should call a particular man or invite a certain male being over for a seductive home-cooked meal of pan-fried aphrodisiacs. My nieces and nephews—my older brother Adrian's four children—growing up in the 1980s, were certainly far better informed about sex than we were, and I do attribute their awareness and comfort level, at least in part, to television. (My nephew David as a little boy at one point had me rolling on the floor laughing at his imitation of Eddie Murphy's "Popeil Galactic Prophylactic" skit from *Saturday Night Live*, in which Murphy mocks the inventor Ron Popeil hawking a condom guaranteed to last fifty years, along with the Dura-Fram Diaphragm.) Still, would I want *Family Feud* to be a part of my child's sex education? Would I want my son sitting in the front row of *Feud*'s studio audience or singled out on national TV for laughing at a crude allusion to anal intercourse as "doing the dirty from behind"?

Steve Harvey is well aware of but at the same time remarkably unconcerned with the lowbrow, bawdy nature of his family show. He jokingly complains that *Feud*'s founding host, Richard Dawson, never had to deal with the kinds of questions and answers he faces, and he occasionally makes would-be nervous noises about the show's getting booted off the air for indecency, but he knows as well as the producers and sponsors that the program is more popular now than ever. In fact, feigned concern aside, *Feud* was at one point apparently so proud of playing dirty that its official website provided links to clips of the show's most salacious moments. And playing funny, talking dirty has had its rewards: Harvey picked up a Daytime Emmy as "Outstanding Game Show Host" in 2014 and 2017, along with his wins in the "Outstanding Talk Show" category. But just as Michael Strahan's hypermasculinity is defused by a feminized affability, playing funny and merely *talking* dirty neutralize whatever sexual threat a big black man like Steve Harvey might otherwise pose. Rather than an instrument of seduction on the one hand and terror on the other that might either satisfy or rape a white woman, the penis in the pants of a black buffoon is limp and laughable.

Back in the day, my mother often joked that quiz shows were her classroom and crossword puzzles her lessons. Despite its fondness for risqué business, the Game Show Network plays with the same witticism by claiming the initials GSN actually stand for "get smarter now." I'm not sure exactly what my smart mother would make of today's dumbed-down and dirty TV programming that extends way beyond game shows, but I can say with some certainty that *Wheel of Fortune* would not be the only program turned down in the name of uplift. Mom would be excited by the fact that black people appear on television today with greater regularity and at times in better roles than in the 1950s, but she would be disappointed that the heroic characters she hoped to see portrayed are few and far between and that more often the lone black character is still the villain, the vixen, the victim, and the demeaned, disgraced, or disposable minority.

My mother, who had been a maid in real life and was tired of watching them in films and on television, would be thrilled to see a black woman like Kerry Washington, who plays the D.C. fixer Olivia Pope on *Scandal*, starring as a high-powered professional in a top-rated network drama created and produced by a black woman named Shonda Rhimes, founder of her own entertainment company, ShondaLand Productions, but she also would be scandalized by *Scandal*. She might even hum a few bars of the spiritual "Scandalize My Name" and question the show's choice of title. If, out of solidarity, she made it to the second season of the series, she most likely would not make it past the steamy flashback inauguration night episode where Fitzgerald Grant (Tony Goldwyn), the white, newly sworn-in president of the United States, slips away from his wife and children and the inaugural balls into the Oval Office for a session of horizontal balling with his black mistress atop a replica of the *Resolute* desk made famous by little John John Kennedy during his father's administration. My mother might put it more delicately, but pantyless, prone, and silent, save for the coital moans and groans of a late-night booty call, is not the position she would emplot for a twenty-first-century black female protagonist.

But it's not quite fair of me to upload onto my mother my own angst and ambivalence about this show and the culture of drugs, sex, and violence that permeates contemporary television, especially in shows with or about black people. In the case of *Scandal*, I understand the arguments about the campy tropes and over-the-top plot twists generic to the soap opera genre. I take, too, the point many *Scandal* fans and critics make that there is something subversive and appealing about a black woman's being passionately pursued by powerful white men and getting to twist that desire to her own advantage and pleasure, getting to be a sensual, multifaceted, fabulously flawed female, loved and in love, rather than a sexless stick-figure stereotype. The media theorist Kristin J. Warner admits that despite whatever misgivings she might have about the "completely unrealistic and often troubling depiction of a co-dependent interracial relationship" between Olivia and Fitz ("Olitz," as the couple is called in the *Scandal* fandom), she can't help "reeling with glee that a black woman is on the receiving end of someone who desires her that much on primetime network television."[47]

Beyond this pleasure principle, I also understand that late in the second decade of the twenty-first century, positively representing the race and defending black womanhood are old baggage no actor should have to carry onscreen. Still, for me, *Scandal* jumped the shark almost before it began, in part because it hooks itself on a great extramarital love affair, yet the how, why, when of a man and woman falling illicitly in love occurs before we meet the characters, outside the context of the televised narrative, and virtually doesn't exist. Even with flashbacks, what we actually see acted out amid incredible corruption, horrific violence, and brutal betrayals is lots of simulated sex in scene after steamy scene, which taken together (as you can find them captured on YouTube) play a lot like soft porn.

As Warner points out, "Olivia Pope receives more oral sex than anyone on network television, black or white," but as the "receiving end"—to use Warner's oddly appropriate phrasing—Olivia is indeed often taken, like a possession.[48] An uncomfortable level of male entitlement and sexual aggression attend liaisons marked by manhandling, with one lover or another grabbing or groping her, pressing the point of *his* desire. Missing in action, particularly with the president, is the throbbing, thwarted sexual tension wrought of impossible, improbable, frenetic yet unfulfilled desire, which, for me at least, makes for better TV. In prime time if not in real life, sexual tension often plays better than sex. (Think of *Moonlighting*'s decline and fall once Maddie and David [Cybill Shepherd and Bruce Willis] cut the sexual tension and consummated their relationship.) What if Olivia Pope, hotly pursued, desperately desired, just said a Nancy Reagan "no" to the world's would-be most powerful white man?

That, however, is not the way prime time wears basic black. Hypersexual and superbad are America's other favorite ways to imagine colored people. It's no accident that the best roles for black actors are some of the worst characters ever to grace the TV screen. Good black guys would finish last in the ratings. Who (except my mother) would want to watch a black female leading lady as squeaky-clean as, say, Téa Leoni's character Elizabeth McCord on the CBS political thriller *Madame Secretary*? This Madam doesn't even get to have simulated TV sex with her handsome TV husband (Tim Daly). When we do see the McCords in bed together, they're usually talking or texting, as they save the world from terrorists yet again.

Despite my upbringing, I thought I had evolved into a modern, liberal-minded woman and a theoretically sophisticated critic, but some old-fashioned part of me wants to see some semblance of the ethical lives—the uplifting racial profiling—that was the American Dream of black parents like mine at the dawn of television. I want the happily married black female secretary of state who gets to take care of husband, home, kids, and country and also keep her clothes on. I want the smart, sexy, ruthless black female criminal defense attorney who isn't a criminal like Viola Davis's character Annalise Keating on another ShondaLand production, the ABC legal thriller *How to Get Away with Murder.*

Et tu, Mater? You haven't really lived until you have been stabbed in the back by the most unkindest cut of all: the realization that you have become your mother. For good or ill, I am my mother's daughter, watching television much as she did—through the lens of race. I delight in the success of Kerry Washington and Viola Davis. I applaud Shonda Rhimes as the first black woman mastermind behind multiple award-winning TV series. I even salute Steve Harvey's success. I want to embrace the programs that my people have made hits. But my *jouissance* is, I fear, always and forever disrupted by its refraction through the prism of race. If these shows were not technicolored, I might not watch, but I also wouldn't care. My displeasure wouldn't be guilty. The shows and I could peacefully coexist in the same way I have gotten along without any number of "white" shows: *Seinfeld, Friends, Cheers, Frasier, Sex and the City.* "Black" makes all the difference. It carries me home to my mother's knee—or some other joint—and the sad, shameful, unspeakable question that haunts my own twenty-first-century TV viewing: was television in general—like my mother's forsaken game-show favorite *Wheel of Fortune*—easier to watch when it was all white? When there was nothing at stake other than cheap amusement and petty pleasure?

Chapter 2

"Those Thrilling Days of Yesteryear"

STIGMATIC BLACKNESS
AND THE RISE OF
TECHNICOLORED TV

The pioneer [TV] set owners found their lives profoundly
affected by the new medium. It kept them at home more, and
cut down on outside activities like visiting or attendance at
public events and meetings.

—LEO BOGART, "TV Viewing in Its Social Gathering" (1958)

Writing in 1956, the sociologist and cultural theorist Leo Bogart identified three major stages that characterize the nature of television viewing as it had advanced thus far. The first stage he calls "the tavern phase"—the early days when television sets were scarce and most often located in public settings such as city taverns where the communal audience was predominantly white, working class, and male. In the second "pioneer phase," TV sets moved into the homes of those few who could afford them and not only became an activity in which the entire family participated but also drew friends and neighbors without television sets into the homes of those who had them. In the third, but not necessarily the last stage—what Bogart calls "the mature phase"— "television ownership . . . spread to the point of virtual universality," and viewing became a family activity, although without commanding the dominant position in the household it had in the early days when conversation and all else ceased once the TV set was turned on. At this point, television programs "represent one of the family's principal shared experiences," he adds, "and as such are a subject for small talk and occasionally for real discussion." Bogart also correctly predicted that as they became lighter and less cumbersome, television sets would be dispersed throughout various rooms of the house, and viewing would become less a family affair than an individual activity.[1]

Bogart's analysis fits my own family experience of and with television almost too well, with the exception of his opening assertion that the first families to acquire TV sets were those with higher incomes. My family was one of if not the first in our blue-collar community to own a TV. But, with only my father working in the 1950s, we were far from well off. My mother was very good at stretching the small paycheck my father brought home each week from his garment factory job; even so I've often wondered how they afforded the console TV set that came into our home around 1953.

As Lynn Spigel demonstrates in her foundational study *Make Room for TV: Television and the Family Ideal in Postwar America* (1992), television sets were advertised early on as "the new family hearth," which would bring parents and children closer together, replacing the fireplace as the center of the warm, happy home.[2] It's true that in the beginning we gathered around the set—with and without friends and neighbors—and watched programs together as a family. But it's also true that television eventually changed the family dynamic in ways that were not all for the good. As Spigel also points out, coming together spatially around the TV set "did not necessarily translate into better family relations." In some instances, the intrusion of television even undermined patriarchal authority, Spigel says, and "threatened to drive a wedge between family members."[3]

Before TV got a firm grip on our family life, the five of us always ate dinner together, weeknights in the kitchen and in the dining room on Sundays and holidays, as well as breakfast together on the weekends, the preparation of which was often a collaborative culinary effort in which we children sometimes took charge. One or two of us would be making pancakes or waffles or muffins, while somebody else scrambled eggs (Adrian Jr. liked to jazz them up with additives such as Campbell's mushroom soup, but I was and am a purist, preferring my scrambled eggs unadorned) and another family member fried bacon or sausages. One of us kids was always assigned the task of mixing the Tang, after John Glenn took it into space in 1962, or defrosting the frozen concentrate—Minute Maid when it was on sale, the store brand when it wasn't—and adding the requisite three cans of cold water that transformed the condensed goo into orange juice. For poor people, we always ate well. My brothers and I used to feel sorry for the white kids at school for whom macaroni and cheese was a meal; for us it was a side dish—a complement

FIG. 2.1 Christmas dinner in the dining room, circa 1960.

FIG. 2.2 Danny surprised at getting the bicycle he wanted for Christmas. Mom and Dad purchased a cheap load of used knotty pine, which meant knotty pine ended up everywhere, even on the ceilings in the dining room and den. (I came to hate knotty pine.)

to roast chicken or pork or meatloaf or fried fish or chuck steak, always with at least one green vegetable. Often begun before we left for church in the morning, Sunday dinners were a feast only slightly less elaborate than holiday banquets, usually headlined by a pork roast, a leg of lamb, or a crispy-skinned capon.

Meals in those days were a time of laughter and lively conversation. Birthdays, like holidays, were major family events, boisterously celebrated over a special dinner at the dining room table followed by homemade cake and ice cream. I remember in particular Danny's second birthday on December 17, 1954. Since it was his special day, he was reigning from a booster seat at the head of the table at the end nearest the kitchen where my mother usually sat. Baby Danny had never been able to wrap his tiny little tongue around his big brother's name, which rolled off his lips sounding something like "En-der-in." As he was about to blow out the two candles on his birthday cake, he paused and said suddenly, seemingly out of nowhere, "Not En-der-in, Adrian." We all laughed, confusing him, I think. I guess it was a sign he was our baby no longer. If he was turning two, I would have been two months shy of six years old, but it's such a vivid memory, it seems like yesterday. Later, we took to eating in front of the television, mostly in hushed silence, and birthday celebrations became less exuberant. At some point, Mom even saved up enough books of S&H Green Stamps to be able to redeem them for a set of folding tray tables to facilitate in-den dining TV-side. Since the alternative name given to such portable tables is "TV trays," I know my family was hardly alone in moving the main meal from the kitchen or dining room to the den or living room, wherever the television set was located.

Then, too, before television took over, we went to the drive-in theater regularly as a cheap form of family entertainment, loading up the car with pillows and blankets, because one or both of my brothers would almost always fall asleep, which my parents encouraged since not all the movies were as child friendly as *Tammy and the Bachelor*, which we saw in 1957 with the Lynches, family friends visiting from Atlanta where the theaters were segregated. I was usually too mesmerized by what was happening on the screen to doze off. My mother would lean over the front seat and say something like, "Go to sleep, Big Eyes," but I didn't want to miss a minute of the action, especially anything starring Barbara Stanwyck, whom we called "Lady Rat Face," because she was so often the villain in her pre–*Big Valley* TV days. We generally took our own snacks with us to the drive-in: Mom and I would eventually perfect our own special sparkling fruit punch with pineapple juice, ginger ale, and orange sherbet, but in those days it was Kool-Aid in a big thermos jug with a spigot and a makeshift picnic basket full of better homemade options than what they sold at the concession stand. I, however, was completely susceptible to the advertisements that ran continuously during intermissions, often in cartoon form. I was a skinny kid and a bit of a picky eater, but somehow I always wanted whatever they were selling at the snack bar. Occasionally, my father would take one of the boys with him to get popcorn and maybe ice cream from the concession stand, but mostly we ate and drank what we brought with us to save money.

We also sometimes went to Fenway Park to watch the Red Sox play ball, again carrying our own vittles for the sake of economy, but our boxed lunches sometimes made us the envy of the fans seated near us, especially when we lived dangerously and dared to leave home with some of Mom's batter-fried chicken in the picnic hamper. It seems silly to say so now (like something out of Ralph Ellison's novel *Invisible Man*), but it was a very black thing in the 1950s and even into the '60s not to want to be caught being too colored by eating fried chicken or watermelon in the presence of white people. When we weren't in the stands at Fenway during baseball season, we were in front of the TV set watching the games at home. I'm not sure it was television alone that curtailed the Fenway Park outings or the vehicular pilgrimages we used to make back to Brooklyn on a regular basis and the weeklong trips to Long Island every summer to visit family friends we called Aunt Janie and Uncle Harold who had moved to a new, Levittown-like subdivision in Amityville. But card playing and other parlor games were definitely upstaged by the television set. I don't recall those days so well myself, but in later years I often heard my parents reminiscing with Cousin Emily and Cousin Percy about the good old days when they used to get together with other couples every week to play bid whist, gin rummy, and pokeno, and I do have vague recollections of trips to the city and playing with cousins and other kids while our parents socialized. (Some little boy at my Cousin Keith's birthday party when I was about seven proclaimed that he was going to marry me when he grew up. Just my luck that he hasn't been seen since.)

All of these outward-bound, shared activities likely disappeared at least in part because of the stay-at-home character of TV viewing, which transformed human interaction in the mid-twentieth century just as email, texting, Facebook, Twitter, and the like continue to affect how we communicate in the twenty-first. But our lifestyles were certainly also affected by other changes that came and went with the times, such as the civil rights movement and Lyndon Johnson's unconditional War on Poverty declared in his State of the Union address in 1964, which ultimately would alter forever the nature of my parents' home and work lives as they both became involved in Self Help, Inc., a local front of Johnson's War dedicated to improving the lives of "the disadvantaged residents of Greater Brockton."[4] Revolutions in consumer culture like the rise of suburban shopping malls, which took us out of the house for pleasures more commercial than social, also affected family life in the 1950s and '60s. And then there were the natural growing pains of maturing and drifting off into our own more individualized arenas of friends and sports and band practice, babysitting and other after-school jobs.

What may be most memorable in terms of my family's relationship to television, however, is how much watching TV became a sore spot in my parents' marriage, as the recliner in front of the set became a privileged domain my father occupied all too frequently, often falling asleep in front of some favorite program instead of working on the house, which my mother considered a sacred obligation. I would hear her on the phone complaining to her women friends—especially the one we called Aunt Gladys—about the slow progress on the house and my father's lack of ambition, often comparing his inertia to the industry and steady progress of Nat Williams, the deacon from our church who was building a lovely brick house for his family a few miles from us on the Brockton end of the same long street we lived on. Mom would repeat what Mrs. Williams had told her about the many nights her husband came home exhausted from his day job but still insisted on going to the building site, even when she encouraged him to lay off for a night and rest, because *he* (unlike my father) was determined to provide a decent home for *his* family. "Rest when it's finished," Mom would say into the phone, loud enough for her message to be carried to other ears. "Watch TV when it's over and done with." And usually ending with the coup de grâce: "When I have something to do, I finish it before I plop myself in front of the television."

I understood my mother's frustration, and in my own way took her side, as I always did. After all, she had been patient, living in a basement, first pregnant and then with a newborn, and helping to build the homestead up around us. (Aunt Janie and Uncle Harold would talk for years about coming to the building site early on and finding my pregnant mother up on the roof hammering boards into place.) What woman would want to live indefinitely in an unfinished structure in need of constant repair even before it was completed? And television made a bad matter worse in its own graphically seductive way, for what did we see depicted daily? Lovely finished, normal homes where lovely finished, normal white families lived. I wanted to live in a house like the Cleavers of *Leave It to Beaver* or like Bentley Gregg with his niece and manservant on *Bachelor Father*, especially after they moved

FIG. 2.3 Dad asleep in his recliner in front of the TV set (mid-1960s).

to the big house with the pool. My mother always wanted a breakfast nook with a banquette in the kitchen, which the Gregg house and other TV homes had. But more than anything, I wanted the residential address of the Rileys on *The Life of Riley*—1313 Blueview Terrace—which made California living sound so bucolic. So I, too, wasn't happy that my father's lack of industry doomed us to living within unfinished Sheetrocked walls.

More than a half century later with the wisdom of hindsight, I have greater sympathy for my dad's predicament and a fuller appreciation of what he did accomplish. He worked all day in a factory at a job that couldn't have been pleasant. And he was, after all, a tailor with no experience in carpentry or construction, unlike the skilled mason Nat Williams to whom he was so often unfavorably compared. Without any formal training or on-the-job experience as a contractor, he learned enough of the rudiments of masonry, heating, plumbing, drywalling, tiling, woodworking, electrical wiring, and such to put a roof over our heads—even if it did leak—and all in pursuit of a dream that I understood even as a child was more my mother's than his. The Motorola, then, helped fill our unfinished house with dramas, not all of which were on-screen. While it's not fair to blame all my parents' marital woes on the TV set, as I reflect on those days of yesteryear, I'm struck by how profoundly that box interceded in our everyday lives.

As a baby boomer whose early childhood spanned the decade of television's entry into American homes, my first encounters with what I call "stigmatic blackness" are closely connected to this evolving medium that brought the world to life before our eyes, even as it altered forever our ways of seeing and being in and of that world. By "stigmatic blackness" I mean mass-mediated representations of African Americans as what Peter Stallybrass and Allon White call the dominant culture's "low-Other": those constituted as racially distaff and disposable—"*socially* peripheral," they say, yet at the same time "*symbolically* central" to mainstream society as the often eroticized repository of its most salacious fantasies and darkest desires.[5] As the phenotypical embodiment of the low-Other, stigmatic blackness is the inverse of the normative, valorized, exulted whiteness in which the dominant culture has a "possessive investment," according to the historian and cultural theorist George Lipsitz. Whiteness, like all racial identities, is a socially constructed fiction with "no valid foundation in biology or anthropology," Lipsitz explains in *The Possessive Investment in Whiteness* (1998). Nevertheless whiteness has real "cash value" in the form of historically accrued assets and advantages, power and privileges, options and opportunities that (re)produce the racial hierarchies on which American society depends.[6]

By way of mass media in general and television in particular, the dominant culture secures and protects its possessive investment in whiteness and the privileges thereof through an equally possessive investment in stigmatic blackness—that is, in characters and caricatures historically demeaned and popularly represented as lazy, inept, ineffectual (except at sports, music, and dance), colorful, comical, criminal, crack-addicted; as Sambos, Sapphires, Mammies, Toms, Tricksters, Cons, Coons, and Jezebels; as servants, singers, and dancers; saints on the one hand or sinners on the other. Although these stigmatized figures and figurations have been the predominant representational model of blacks and blackness in mass media and popular culture for centuries, I am primarily concerned with what I have encountered in the last sixty years or so since we acquired that first TV set, including—in a few instances—films I have seen solely translated through the medium of television.

As it came into our living rooms and reshaped our lives in the 1950s, television dramatized racial, class, and cultural differences for mass consumption in broader terms and ultimately for a wider audience than ever before. Blackness was absent and present, present and absent; colored people were at once nowhere and everywhere. We were absent from popular all-American domestic series and sitcoms such as *Leave It to Beaver*, *Ozzie and Harriet*, *Lassie*, and *I Love Lucy*, but we were present in others, most often as domestics, comic relief, or musical entertainment.

Among the most-watched of the early shows, *I Love Lucy* might seem to upset the category of colored absence because of the revisionist history that now figures the show as groundbreaking due to what is touted as the mixed-race marriage (on-screen and off) of its costars, the white American comedienne Lucille Ball and the Cuban-born bandleader Desi Arnaz. Today's mixed-race is yesteryear's cross-cultural, at best. At a time when intermarriage was illegal in many states, midcentury audiences were primed to view Desi Arnaz and his *Lucy* persona, Ricky Ricardo, as culturally Latin, in an exotic, European, or Iberian sense, rather than racially nonwhite; the Desi-Lucy marriage was intercontinental rather than interracial. At the same time, Ricky's ethnic difference—especially his Cuban accent—was played for laughs, often with Lucy both mimicking and mocking his imperfect English or with Ricky demanding that Lucy "splain" herself as his hot, Latin temper flared and he regressed into rapid-fire *español* and *"¡Ay carambas!"* in exasperation at his wife's wild and crazy antics.

Some fans insist in Internet postings that there were black musicians in Ricky's band. If so, they were so far at the back of the bandstand as to be invisible. Multiple sources list Sam McDaniel (older brother of Hattie McDaniel) as the only African American to appear on *I Love Lucy*, where he had a bit part as Sam the Porter in "The Great Train Robbery" episode in 1955.[7] At midcentury, it was essential to keep the Ricardos as far removed from colored people as possible, lest anyone get the idea that Ricky was anything other than Caucasian. In his one quick encounter with color, the fact that he hailed Sam the Porter as "Boy," while Sam, of course, addressed him as "Sir," confirmed the proper racial hierarchy.

If *Lucy* and similar domestic sitcoms were short on racial variety, colored people added talent, comedy, cultural diversity, adversity, and what I call "debase relief" to a host of other TV programs, ranging from game shows like *Queen for a Day*, *Name That Tune*, and *Strike It Rich*; to westerns like *Zorro*, *The Lone Ranger*, *The Cisco Kid*, and *Gunsmoke* when Burt Reynolds, who is one-quarter Cherokee in real life, joined the cast as Quint Asper, the "half-breed" blacksmith, in 1962. Popular talent competitions such as Ted Mack's *Original Amateur Hour* (where a seven-year-old Gladys Knight was a winner) and variety shows like *American Bandstand* and the two eponymously titled programs hosted by rival emcees Ed Sullivan and Steve Allen rounded out early TV offerings.

American Bandstand (1952–1989), hosted by the former radio disc jockey Dick Clark for most of its long run, lives in the annals of television history as the show that helped make both rock and roll and black music "palatable to cynical and even fearful audiences," as one source put it on the occasion of Clark's death in 2012.[8] With teenagers dancing on stage to Top 40 tunes as vocalists lip-synced their biggest hits, *Bandstand* did indeed provide a national forum for hip, modern music and musicians, including Motown recording artists and other black performers. The show never quite caught on in our household, however, perhaps because it didn't seem to be for or about "us," as *Soul Train* would become in the 1970s. *Bandstand* may have helped make black music palatable to white audiences, but it didn't necessarily do the same for or with black people, at least not for the first decade or so when it was broadcast live from Philadelphia with a studio audience of white teens dancing to music that was only sometimes performed by black recording artists.

Dick Clark claimed credit and received considerable accolades for integrating *American Bandstand* once he took over the show in 1956. "As soon as I became host, we integrated," he told the *New York Times* as recently as 2011, echoing assertions he first made in his 1976 autobiography *Rock, Roll and Remember*, where he claims that making sure the show had black representation was something he elected to do because he understood that both rock and roll and *Bandstand* owed their existence to black music and musicians.[9] His claims appear praiseworthy and progressive for the historical moment; however, some critics and scholars have challenged the accuracy of Clark's activist assertions. Matthew F. Delmont points out, most notably, that while *American Bandstand* did indeed open its stage to a variety of black musical groups when it went national on network TV in 1957, the show also "regularly blocked black teenagers from its studio audience until it moved from Philadelphia to Los Angeles in 1964."[10] In his book on the subject, *The Nicest Kids in Town: American Bandstand, Rock 'n' Roll, and the Struggle for Civil Rights in 1950s Philadelphia* (2012), Delmont, who teaches history at Arizona State University, sums up this other Philadelphia Story as follows: "In the context of local and national mobilization in favor of segregation, underscored by widespread antiblack racism, integrating *American Bandstand* would have been a

bold move and a powerful symbol. . . . Clark and *American Bandstand*, however, did not choose this path, and the historical record contradicts Clark's
memory of integration. Rather than being a fully integrated program that
welcomed black youth, *American Bandstand* continued to discriminate
against black teens throughout the show's Philadelphia years."[11]

It wasn't that *Bandstand* operated under an official whites-only policy,
Delmont makes clear, but that it used dissembling strategies such as dress
codes and selective ticketing to limit access to the show, much as poll taxes
and loaded literacy tests were used to suppress black voter registration in the
South and redistricting and voter ID laws are used to the same end today. As
those of us from Greater Boston know only too well, it wasn't solely south-
erners who resisted integration, especially the implementation of the *Brown*
decision and subsequent state and local school desegregation orders. There's
an old saying—sometimes attributed to the black comedian and activist Dick
Gregory—that in the South, whites don't care how close blacks get as long as
they don't get too big; in the North, whites don't care how big black people
become as long as they don't come too close. White homeowners in certain
sections of the City of Brotherly Love had no desire to get up close and personal
with their black brethren and fought to keep them out of their communities
and their schools. *Bandstand's* discriminatory admissions practices, then,
were wholly in keeping with both "neighborhood and school segregation
in Philadelphia," Delmont explains, as well as with the "commercial pressures of national television and deeply held beliefs about the dangers of racial
mixing."[12]

And race mixing was very much the issue and the fear in the 1950s. The
wild abandon with which white teens were willing to rock around the clock
and across the color line caused commotions in dance clubs and concert halls
and chaos on the street corners of the white West Philadelphia neighborhood
where the TV studio that broadcast *Bandstand* was located. It was only logical
that Clark and his network compatriots would want to keep this kind of trouble off the air and away from sponsors.

There are at least two sides to every Philadelphia story, then, and I suppose
it's possible to put a kinder, gentler time stamp on Clark's airbrushed account
of his activist role in the desegregation of *Bandstand* and American pop culture. His mistake was in presenting himself as a heroic integrationist rather
than acknowledging "the immense economic and social pressures," which
Delmont says "made segregation the safe course of action."[13] The on-screen
image of black and white teens dancing together to music many adults dis-
trusted might have made for a progressive picture of a new world order, but

it also might have shut down the show. It is well known and much remarked that when little Frankie Lymon, of "Why Do Fools Fall in Love" fame, danced with a white girl on a live broadcast of Alan Freed's TV rock-and-roll show *The Big Beat* in 1957, the same year *Bandstand* went national, the spectacle so outraged network affiliates that Freed's program was promptly canceled. Integrating the artists and not the studio audience may have been a compromise that saved *Bandstand* from a similar fate. Midcentury audiences weren't ready for video verification that what many of them saw as "jungle music" could generate the "jungle fever" that Spike Lee would later immortalize in his 1991 film of the same name.

I have almost no recollection of Dick Clark in the 1950s and 1960s and certainly not as the clean-cut choirboy, angel face of the devil's music. When I consider who brought black performers into our home during that time, it's not the smooth-talking, forever young impresario Dick Clark I think of but a stiff-necked, tongue-tangled, old white guy named Ed Sullivan and the "really big shew" he put on every Sunday night. Originally titled *Toast of the Town* when it debuted on CBS in 1948, *The Ed Sullivan Show* was renamed after its host in 1955. As host, Sullivan made a point of featuring black celebrities like Joe Lewis and Jackie Robinson and showcasing vocal groups like the Temptations and Diana Ross and the Supremes, as well as a cavalcade of individual black entertainers who lit up my childhood: Mahalia Jackson, Sammy Davis Jr., Sarah Vaughan, Lena Horne, Pearl Bailey, Eartha Kitt, Nat King Cole, Louis Armstrong, Ella Fitzgerald, Harry Belafonte, and the comedian and impressionist George Kirby, among many other Others. For families like mine, *The Ed Sullivan Show* was the closest thing to a black performance hall of fame the 1950s had to offer.

The musician, composer, and comedian Steve Allen and his namesake show were popular in our household for much the same reason: they showed off people who looked like us. Unlike Clark, both Sullivan and Allen were vocal at the time, not after the fact, about their commitment to integration via video and to showcasing black artists on their programs. Both were quoted in *Ebony* and also contributed articles on the subject of race and TV to the magazine, then the nation's premier black publication and, along with *Jet*, a staple not only in the homes of African Americans across classes but in our barbershops and beauty salons as well.[14] In championing the racial integration of the airwaves in the pages of *Ebony*, Sullivan and Allen were in effect preaching to the gospel choir. This is not to suggest that they were less than sincere in their remarks; their actions in regularly presenting black entertainers, athletes, and other celebrities on their shows speak louder than mere words. But neither showman seemed eager to claim himself as a do-gooder or a crusader. Allen, in fact, described himself, perhaps somewhat disingenuously, as "accidentally doing what I guess is the right thing. I just hire the best singers and piano players and trumpet players and it just happens that a very high percentage of them are Negroes. It's about that simple."[15]

Of course it wasn't that simple, as Allen—and Sullivan—well knew. There was resistance, even hate mail, from white viewers and pressure from nervous sponsors who feared losing audiences and advertisers, especially in the Jim Crow South. Some southern affiliates did censor segments of shows with black performers and celebrities. In *Dreaming Me: Black, Baptist, and Buddhist— One Woman's Spiritual Journey* (2008), Jan Willis, a Buddhist scholar and professor of religion, writes compellingly of growing up in the segregated South in the 1950s and 1960s and never seeing a black face on the TV set that her father, like mine, somehow managed to secure for the household in the mid-1950s. She recalls in particular one Sunday evening when the family huddled around the television console hoping to catch Sammy Davis Jr. on *The Ed Sullivan Show*. "We leaned in close as stiff-necked Ed began his introduction," she writes. "But just as Sullivan threw wide his arms to greet Davis—like so many times before—the card came on, with its message of denial." The message: "Trouble along the cable." "Every time a black person appeared on television, we saw only this card," Willis says.[16]

Both Sullivan and Allen maintained at the time that the positive responses to black programming far outweighed the negative. But in the early days of black-and-white TV, there was something other than integration at stake. Nothing less than the fate of television itself rested, at least in part, on the talents and popular appeal of black entertainers and celebrities who were ready, willing, and able to step in front of the camera. "Television needs the Negro performer and benefits by his contributions to the medium," Allen wrote in *Ebony* in 1955.[17] Sullivan had been even more explicit in an earlier article, writing in May 1951 that "recognizing the place of the Negro in television is not generosity. It is just common sense and good business." That good business common sense literally could be calculated in dollars and cents, as Sullivan went on to explain: "generous" Negro performers, including high-profile headliners who had worked with him in vaudeville and were willing to "talk friendship, not money," brought big talent to the small screen for cheap in what Sullivan described as the "early, lean days when there wasn't much money in TV for any of us." To make his point stronger still, he added, "They didn't get much money—the Negro performers—very little, in fact, but when

I needed help—when the squalling infant industry of television needed help, the Negro star was loyal and considerate."[18]

In declaring in *Ebony* that television owed a debt to the Negro—that "you just can't have great programs unless you integrate the Negro performer into a show"—Sullivan spoke to an aspect of early TV history that the industry has little acknowledged.[19] The story more often told is of what J. Fred MacDonald describes as the emergent medium's "new fairness"—that is, television's "conscious effort" to use black talent fairly in keeping with "an atmosphere of postwar liberality."[20] Sullivan's inside scoop reveals, however, that the black presence in 1950s television wasn't simply a function of noblesse oblige on the part of progressive industry executives but, rather, a way to take advantage of the talents of the best available performers—"a very high percentage of [whom] are Negroes"—thus bringing needed star power to a fledgling enterprise that was unsure of itself and its future.[21]

Most African American performers, however, no matter how talented, had to settle for guest appearances on programs like *The Ed Sullivan Show* and *American Bandstand* in the early days of television. Eddy Anderson was one of the exceptions. He landed a regular gig as Rochester, the host's faithful, flippant, raspy-voiced manservant and chauffeur on *The Jack Benny Program* (CBS, 1950–1964; NBC, 1964–1965).[22] A carryover from the radio show where he first appeared as a Pullman porter, Anderson as Rochester successfully negotiated the giant leap from bit player to series regular, but he also brought to television elements of cinema's most enduring stock figures: the male mammy; the faithful racial retainer; the wily, wisecracking manservant; the bumbling, benighted, bosom buddy; and the colored sidekick who might be silly, saintly, sagacious, long suffering, superhuman, superbad, or all of the above.

Such roles have been reprised and to a certain extent recouped with dignity in recent times by veteran actors such as Robert Guillaume, who spun a smaller part as the wisecracking butler on the parody *Soap* (ABC, 1977–1981) into the title role of his own prime-time TV series *Benson* (ABC, 1979–1986), much as Esther Rolle had done a few years earlier with her character Florida Evans, the maid on *Maude* (CBS, 1972–1978), who became the star of her own Norman Lear spinoff *Good Times* (CBS, 1974–1979). In film, similar parts have often fallen to Morgan Freeman, who has acted as the faithful servant, suffering sidekick, or bosom buddy in several Academy Award–winning motion pictures, including *Driving Miss Daisy* (Best Picture, 1989), *Unforgiven* (Best Picture, 1992), and *Million Dollar Baby* (Best Picture, 2004), where the wizened black buddy role finally netted Freeman a Best Supporting Actor Oscar.

It isn't only black artists who have populated such parts, however. From 1949 to 1957, the First Nation actor Jay Silverheels (born Harold Smith) galloped alongside Clayton Moore (and briefly John Hart) as the "faithful Indian companion" of "the daring and resourceful masked rider of the plains" in ABC's hit western *The Lone Ranger*. Despite the dignity Silverheels brought to a part that was by definition a caricature, Tonto has become a trope epitomizing Hollywood's bad idea of the good Indian, even giving title to a vaudevillian, Wild West Show way of misspeaking English—like a Native—known as "Tonto talk" or "Tonto speak": "Me Tonto. You Lone Ranger." It was a problematic portrayal of the white man and his noble Native sidekick even in a less racially sensitive era, which makes it difficult to understand why Disney decided that *The Lone Ranger* should ride again as a twenty-first-century film starring the A-list Anglo actor Johnny Depp as Tonto. Depp, who claims distant Native American ancestry, has been widely quoted as wanting to help right the representational wrongs of the cinematic and televisual past by reimagining Tonto as a Comanche warrior and reconfiguring his relationship with his white kemosabe as one of equality and empowerment.[23]

I'm all for righting the wrongs of yesteryear, and I do believe it is a responsibility we all should share in, regardless of our race or ethnicity, but what Depp's good intentions needed was a rewriting—as in, a new narrative—not the resurrection of a cinematic relic repackaged as a New Age frontier farce that not only plunges an already problematic figure even deeper into debase relief but also gives him a backstory that makes him complicit in the slaughter of his own family and fellow Comanche. The fictional detail that this Tonto as a boy was duped into selling out his people for a cheap pocket watch from Sears makes the fact that his name means "dumb," "stupid," "crazy" in Spanish, Italian, and Portuguese historically resonant in ways it wasn't before. Rather than elevating him as an avenging warrior hero, this plodding emplotment potentially reduces Tonto to another dumb Indian, tricked into betraying his own people and giving away his birthright by fork-tongued white men much like those backward seventeenth-century savages who sold Manhattan to the Dutch for sixty guilders' worth of beads and trinkets. Moreover, in keeping with the same-old same-old of noble savage mythology, it is white people whom this reimagined Tonto rescues, while doing nothing to aid his Comanche brethren, masses of whom are once again slaughtered by double-dealing white men—this time with Gatling guns—and then disappeared from the narrative, save for a few feathers floating in what we can only imagine is the blood-red river.

Since Depp's "redface," dead-crow-wearing version of Tonto is theatrically crazy, driven mad by *his* historical guilt and impossible grief, the story he narrates of yesteryear is, it would seem, a tale told by an idiot, full of sound effects and fury, ultimately signifying nothing. Except—how we right/write history does matter. With all that frontier mythology and legends of taming the Wild West necessarily elide about genocide, exclusion, removal, and imperialism masquerading as Manifest Destiny, perhaps it's high time the Hollywood western rode off into the sunset with the minstrel show. "Hi-yo, Silver, away."

....

While depictions of Tonto, old and new, have generated endless discussion and debate, much less has been made of another white man/colored servant coupling that troubled me even as a child, although not necessarily for the right reasons: the hierarchical relationship between "Mr. Gregg" and the Asian manservant he relentlessly referred to as "my Chinese houseboy" on the sitcom *Bachelor Father* (1957–1962). As a series regular, the Chinese American actor Sammee Tong turned the traditional part of the retiring racial retainer into a supporting role as Peter Tong, the longtime manservant of a successful, decidedly single Beverly Hills playboy lawyer named Bentley Gregg (John Forsythe), who becomes the guardian of his orphaned niece Kelly (Noreen Corcoran) when her parents are killed in a car accident. Mr. Gregg, as Peter always called him, loves his niece and wants to be a good dad, but, distracted by women and work and women, he sometimes has to be coaxed into better parenting by his more maternal but often quite gullible and childlike Chinese houseman. The dynamic of this domestic arrangement, then, isn't only master and servant; it's also lord and little woman. One of the show's running jokes revolves around the fact that Mr. Gregg—father lawyer, if not Father Law— frequently has to save Peter from his own innocent, immigrant naïveté, as well as from the self-serving schemes of his entrepreneurial, Americanized conman Cousin Charlie (played by Victor Sen Yung).

As played, Peter is in some ways a postwar throwback to the Chinese minstrelsy that was almost as popular in the nineteenth century as its blackface counterpart—or even more popular, perhaps, in places like California. Though having lived a long time in America, Mr. Gregg's houseboy necessarily speaks the Pidgin English of the immigrant that is so basic to the minstrel routine and that performs a kind of cultural backwardness that is emblematic of being insufficiently or inappropriately civilized. In "The 'Heathen Chinee' on God's Free Soil," a critical, much-cited essay on yellowface minstrelsy, Robert Lee, a professor of American studies at Brown University, argues that the othering of the Chinese immigrant "relied on a trope of insurmountable cultural difference." Unlike the comparable characterization of black Americans, who Lee says were represented as "fraudulent citizens because they were supposed to lack culture," the Chinese, he explains, "were seen as having an excess of culture."[24] Not, it's important to understand, an ancient, honorable culture of the Greek or Roman kind but, rather, the backward culture and antiquated ways of the heathen and the improperly civilized. Peter has been around long enough to have picked up many of the bad points of being American and a few of the good but not long enough to have been fully divested of his backward Chinese ways.

In an episode from 1961 called "Peter's China Doll," the unenlightened houseboy brings home an adorable seven-year-old Chinese girl he won in a poker game at Cousin Charlie's club, which seems to him a perfectly normal turn of events. He's determined to keep the little China doll, even if doing so means quickly marrying any willing woman he can find in order to meet the American adoption board's two-parent requirement. Mr. Gregg, who, of course, immediately sees the impossibility of the entire scheme, saves the day as usual by finding a suitable Chinese couple to adopt the child. All's well that ends well, and the practice of gambling with or trafficking in orphaned or abandoned children is made to seem like business as usual among the insufficiently civilized Chinese, which seems an outrageously orientalist plotline even for the early 1960s.

But, then, Cousin Charlie and his fellow Asians don't just trade in children; they also merchandise adult China dolls through what is presented as the traditional Chinese custom of arranged, mail-order marriages in "Bentley and the Bartered Bride" (1960). This time Mr. Gregg intercedes to save Peter from a phony marriage arranged by his conman cousin and an equally cunning Chinese matchmaker, Mrs. Choo Lo Wing, who takes Peter's money and uses a picture of her niece to trick the gullible houseboy into thinking he's buying a beautiful, young bride from San Francisco named Precious Jade, instead of the much older, rounder, plainer partner the matchmaker actually has in store for him. Mr. Gregg, who has reluctantly agreed to act as the go-between in the transaction, realizes it's all a scam when he coincidentally encounters the lovely, young woman pictured in the photograph and learns she is Dolores Wong, not Precious Jade. He arranges a rendezvous with all the princi-pals, exposes the bait-and-switch bride-trading scheme, and saves Peter from his own naiveté and the conniving of his kin and kind.

Although easily taken advantage of and so silly he thinks the characters in his favorite TV westerns and soaps are real, Peter also has the sagely in-sight of Confucius. Like Hop Sing, the cleaver-wielding cook on the long-running western *Bonanza* (NBC, 1959–1973)—a part also played by Victor Sen Yung—he imparts simple fortune-cookie wisdom in stereotypical Pid-gin English. Today it is easy enough for me to say from my high horse that the injustice of these roles of yesteryear lies not only in the fact that Asian American actors like Tong and Yung had few options other than such pi-geonholed parts but also in the reality that they rarely received due credit for their acting abilities, for playing well who and what they were not: foreign, feebleminded, linguistically challenged. Both men were born and educated in the United States. Sen Yung, in fact, earned a bachelor's degree from the University of California, Berkeley, and fell into acting while pursuing gradu-ate studies at UCLA and the University of Southern California.[25] But like their African American counterparts, Asian American actors historically have been caught in that slippage between person and persona—so auto-matically and quintessentially typecast that their role-playing is read as real rather than as performance.

I was eight years old when *Bachelor Father* began its five-year run. I would like to say that I resented the terms and terminology of the show—"Mr. Gregg" and "my houseboy Peter" and the endless overlay of stereotypes—because of the colonial hegemony, paternalism, and orientalism they represent or because I understood what it meant for a black man to be called "boy" and didn't like hearing another Other so addressed. I certainly grew into such perceptions, but at eight, I suspect my motivation was closer to home and tied to my mother's apron strings, so to speak. While there was something endearing about watching two very different single men lovingly bungle and bumble their way through parenting a teenage girl, the comedy of *Bachelor Father* played out against the reality of my mother's oft-told tales of her days as a domestic, with an emphasis on how much she despised being called "girl" by her white employers and even more so being referred to possessively by them as "my girl." "My girl this, my girl that," my mother would say, mocking the pretentious tone of one particular Miss Ann for whom she had worked. "'My girl makes the best Welsh rarebit'—always Welsh rarebit and cheese fondue. That's what they insisted I serve whenever they had company: Welsh rarebit and cheese fondue."

I had heard the complaint for as long as I can remember, but it wasn't until I was a young adult that I fully understood the subtext of what my mother was saying about Miss Ann and her husband, Mister Charlie: they were nouveau riche and knew so little about fine dining that cheese fondue and Welsh rarebit were their idea of haute cuisine. I had no notion of what cheese fondue was, but, with my child's ear, I thought my mother was saying "Welsh *rabbit*," and I resented Miss Ann and Mister Charlie all the more because not only had they acted as if they owned my mother, but they also had made her serve them bunny rabbits. So, in what I'm sure a psychiatrist would diagnose as a clear-cut case of transference, every time Mr. Gregg referred to Peter as "my houseboy," I heard some mean-faced, bunny-eating Mister Charlie calling *my* mother *his* "girl."

To be clear, "Mister Charlie" and "Miss Ann" weren't the actual names of any of the white men and women for whom my mother worked as a maid in her youth. Mister Charlie and Miss Ann are black folks' code names for white bossmen and -women. Somewhat like "honky" and "cracker," Miss Ann and Mister Charlie are racial epithets for white people originally deployed by the enslaved to refer to the plantation master and mistress behind their backs or, in the case of Mister Charlie, to the white man who would be lord and master, also known as "the Man." Miss Ann can likewise refer to any white woman in a superior position—real or imagined—to the black people she treats as underlings or any white woman with an imperious, better-than-thou attitude.

Much to my personal chagrin, Miss Ann is also used pejoratively to refer to a black woman considered by other blacks to be uppity or self-important. I often overheard my mother and her friends who had also worked for white people—and some who still did—talking about their travails with Miss Ann and Mister Charlie. And, yes, if I misbehaved or was otherwise deemed to be acting too big for my britches, I would be called out either by my full name, which was bad, or by Miss Ann, which to me was much worse. "Who do you think you are, Miss Ann?" To this day, there is probably no appellation I dislike more than "Miss Ann." I would almost rather be called the N-word, because at least that puts me with my people, not against them. In other words, I hear "Miss Ann" as a slur. I understand that not everyone knows the history of those two words spoken together (or is familiar with James Baldwin's brilliant three-act play *Blues for Mister Charlie*). I get it that most people mean only to convey respect or affection when they put "Miss" before my name. Still, I suspect that somewhere in the white collective unconscious, the construction may be racialized for them, too, because, as far as I can tell, white women so named are not so impulsively (or maybe compulsively) called "Miss Ann."

In any case, the Mr. Gregg of *Bachelor Father* was actually a pretty nice guy, as lords and masters go, but he was still Mister Charlie in my mind. John Forsythe, both in real life and on-screen as Bentley Gregg (and later as the oil magnate Blake Carrington on the prime-time soap opera *Dynasty* [ABC, 1981–1989]), was white, well spoken, suave, and sophisticated, with the leading-man good looks of a Cary Grant but without quite the same level of tall, dark, handsome physicality, panty-dropping charm, and gift for humor that made Grant's screwball romantic comedies from the 1930s and '40s such fun to watch on television in the 1950s and '60s of my impressionable youth. Sammee Tong, short, balding, and almost always grinning from ear to ear, was the funny one who carried much of the show's comedy and had a lot to do with its success. Forsythe, who claimed top billing and earnings as the star of the show, readily acknowledged the importance of Tong's comedic talents and impeccable timing. The real joke behind the show isn't that a playboy bachelor has become father to his niece, Forsythe told *TV Guide* in 1960, but that "Sammee Tong behaves in all our family crises as if he were her mother."[26]

The feminizing of Tong as the Chinese houseboy was so deliberate and so essential to the show's sense of humor that Niece Kelly at times called Peter "Mother." In the "Kelly's Charge Account" episode, not only does she address Peter as "Mom," she also buys him a Mother's Day present, while Uncle Bentley, of course, gets the Father's Day gift. When a more grown-up Kelly becomes engaged in a later episode from 1962, it's Peter himself who delivers the punch line of the show's running joke about his gender role. He tells Mr. Gregg that Kelly's fiancé is lucky to be marrying into their family. "Where else he get package deal like this," he says, "pretty wife, rich father, and Chinese mother-in-law." The credits roll over the laughter of the studio audience.

It's not surprising that in the age of *Amos 'n' Andy* (a Forsythe favorite), actors and audience alike would take the terms and terminology of *Bachelor Father* for granted, but, unlike *Amos 'n' Andy*, which didn't survive its contemporaneous criticism, *Bachelor Father* lives on as another one of those programs considered by some to have been ahead of its time because Peter the houseboy wasn't simply the obsequious Asian manservant who exists only to do the bidding of his betters and is otherwise disappeared.[27] He was present in every episode and had his own story lines. But the fact that Forsythe and the show's producers were so comfortable with the British colonial term "houseboy" and with feminizing and infantilizing the male costar for laughs in such stereotypical ways should trouble us today, not only because *Bachelor Father* is still alive in reruns, but also because the lessons we might have taken from such a show haven't been learned.

FIG. 2.4 The cast of *Bachelor Father* on the cover of *TV Guide*: Noreen Corcoran as Niece Kelly, John Forsythe as Mr. Bentley Gregg, and Sammee Tong as Peter (1960).

For decades, Asian Americanists have criticized Hollywood's lingering fascination with Asian stereotypes, which Elaine Kim, a professor of Asian American and Asian Diasporic Studies at Berkeley, says fall into two basic categories in the Anglo-American imagination: good Asians and bad Asians. The "'bad' Asians" are "sinister villains and brute hordes," who she says can't be controlled and therefore must be destroyed, while the "'good' Asians" are either the "helpless heathens to be saved by Anglo heroes or the loyal and lovable allies, sidekicks, and servants."[28] Peter does double duty. While he isn't necessarily a heathen, he is constantly in need of being saved by his white boss, Mr. Gregg, to whom he is also the quintessential loyal, lovable sidekick, servant, ally, and wingman. (By prior arrangement, Mr. Gregg presses a buzzer with his foot signaling Peter to run into the room with a made-up excuse to end a date the moment any woman mentions marriage. In one episode, Peter is so caught up in his favorite TV program that he doesn't hear Bentley madly pressing the buzzer to be rescued from a husband-hunting blonde. Consequently, Bentley ends up presumptively engaged to a vamp whose parents already have the wedding planned—and a shotgun.)

Despite decades of such criticism, stereotype casting of Asian and Asian American actors remains alive in twenty-first-century Hollywood, where it still seems to be okay to portray Asians as walking clichés and the butts of racial jokes. Consider, for example, Lucy Liu as the Dragon Lady lawyer Ling Woo from *Ally McBeal*, Mark Dacascos as the Fu Manchu–ish supervillain Wo Fat resurrected from the 1960s to fight again in the twenty-first-century edition of *Hawaii Five-o*, and Matthew Moy as the pint-size, linguistically challenged Korean immigrant Han Bryce Lee on *2 Broke Girls*. The more Han Lee tries to fit in as a typical American, the more alien he is made to seem by bad jokes at his expense, including snarky one-liners from the white girls who both belittle and feminize him. When he stands up too quickly and whacks his genitals on the edge of the table, he grabs his crotch in pain, setting himself up for the girls' quip that, oh, poor Han hurt his vagina—and this is in the same episode with an equally tasteless racial joke about black mold driving the white mold out of the neighborhood (s3, e22).

Emily Nussbaum writes in her review of *2 Broke Girls* that the show's ensemble cast "is conceived in terms so racist it is less offensive than baffling." Indeed, the program's black cashier (Garrett Morris) and Ukrainian cook (Jonathan Kite) don't fare any better than their Korean boss. Nussbaum says Morris "should sue for the limp gags he's fed," and quotes one of the Ukrainian cook's typically off-color, immigrant-inflected lines: "Once you go Ukraine, you will scream with sex-pain."[29] Presumably the cook is attempting to riff the Aphro-ism, "Once you go black, you never go back," but of course, as immigrants are wont to do on television, he gets the saying wrong and the sentiment only half right, more or less. Somehow the show survived for six seasons.

Even putatively progressive programs many applaud for their diverse, multiracial casts, like *Glee*, *Fresh Off the Boat*, *Modern Family*, and *Black-ish*, still derive much of their humor from playing the race card in predictable ways, with characters conceived in stereotypes and dedicated to the proposition that there is no new thing under the sun. I didn't think it was possible, but *Modern Family* makes even more fun of Gloria's (Sofia Vergara) Spanish accent, mispronunciations, and malapropisms than *I Love Lucy* made of Ricky Ricardo's sixty years ago. Gloria's family, including the little kids, constantly correct her and translate into proper English what she's trying to say: "child drop-off," not "dropout"; "gargoyle," not "gargle"; "carpal tunnel syndrome," not "car pool tunnel syndrome"; "blessings in disguise," not "blessings in the sky"; "dog-eat-dog world," not "doggy-dog world." It's as if Hollywood writers and producers assume a stereotype that in other hands would be a slur is cleansed of its offensive properties when it's dealt by or with a person or persons of color. It's a version of what the cultural theorist Richard Slotkin calls the "race-face convention": film and television's use of a character of color—the black friend, the Asian mean girl, the Puerto Rican bully—whose inclusion in the dominant group okays and authorizes its otherwise racist gestures.[30]

USA's hit series *Royal Pains* (2009–2016) provides a useful example of the race-face convention doing its dirty work. Although the ensemble cast featured no black regulars during the show's eight-year run, the Tony Award–winning African American actress Adriane Lenox makes a pivotal cameo appearance in the pilot episode as the hospital administrator who fires the white male lead, a brilliant emergency room physician (Mark Feuerstein), sacked and blackballed for saving a poor colored "kid off the street" instead of the hospital's white billionaire trustee, Clayton Hale Gardner (John Farrer), who dies on the doctor's watch. The firing is the board's decision, but of the group assembled, only the black woman speaks, delivering the loaded line that the stabilized Mr. Gardner is the priority, not the crashing "basketball kid." Out of the mouth of a black character, who treats the triage tragedy as a financially consequential judgment error, the underlying message that a wealthy white man's life is more worth saving than a poor black kid's is depoliticized and divested of its otherwise startling racism.

If early sitcoms like *Bachelor Father*, *Father Knows Best*, and *Make Room for Daddy* focused on the happy, white, male-headed home, TV westerns like *The Lone Ranger*, *The Cisco Kid*, and *Gunsmoke* revolved around cultural conflict on the frontier. Not surprisingly, a frequently televised clash of cultures was between cowboys and Indians, settlers and savages (mostly white actors in redface), but African Americans, Asians, and Hispanics (mostly Mexicans, often played by white actors in brownface) sang and danced, shuffled and bowed, burned and pillaged across the screen as slaves and savages, sidekicks and servants, foils, fools, and desperados whose alternately comical or criminal antics peppered early black-and-white televisual narratives. Many of these narratives came to the small screen by way of other media—literature, film, radio, comic strips—and other times: the 1920s, '30s, and '40s, for example, when the nation was far less concerned about race relations and the politics of representation than it would become decades later in the face of civil rights, black power, and feminist activism.

Popular half-hour shows like *Gunsmoke*, *Hopalong Cassidy*, *Zorro*, *The Cisco Kid*, and *The Little Rascals* (*Our Gang* in the movies) had all had long lives in fiction and film before they morphed to TV in the 1950s. Like *The Jack Benny Program* and *The Lone Ranger*, *Amos 'n' Andy* and its sister series *The Beulah Show* came to television by way of radio, bringing with them an enduring, if not always endearing, cast of colored characters and caricatures. *Beulah* jumped from a long run on CBS radio—where white men voiced the title role before Hattie McDaniel took over the part in 1947—to television in 1950, where it lasted only three seasons. Dubbed "queen of the kitchen," Beulah was a warm and fuzzy, would-be problem-solving maid, first played on television by Ethel Waters and then by Hattie McDaniel when Waters quit, wanting out of the white folks' kitchen even as a TV role, and finally by Louise Beavers when McDaniel became ill, passing away from breast cancer later that same year.[31] (Beavers also had a recurring role as Louise the maid on *Make Room for Daddy*, later *The Danny Thomas Show*, from 1953 to 1955, when she, too, became ill and was replaced by Amanda Randolph.)

Reams have been written about *Amos 'n' Andy* and first the white men who voiced the characters on the radio (Freeman Gosden and Charles Correll), and then the black actors (Alvin Childress and Spencer Williams) who played them on TV, but, with few exceptions—Donald Bogle's careful, enlightening analysis in *Primetime Blues* (2001) and Aniko Bodroghkozy's similarly thoughtful, extended examination of both *Amos 'n' Andy* and *The Beulah Show* in *Equal Time* (2013)—Ethel Waters and the other actresses who played Beulah probably have not received due attention as the first black female stars of a television sitcom.[32] In many ways, Beulah was the prototype for *Hazel* (NBC/CBS, 1961–1966), a white iteration of the fix-it maid/mammy comedy vehicle starring Shirley Booth in the title role, and for other black maids to come, from Florida on *Maude* to Nell Harper (Nell Carter) on *Gimme a Break!* (NBC, 1981–1987) and Lilly Harper (Regina Taylor) on *I'll Fly Away* (NBC, 1991–1993).

The cultural anthropologist Oneka LaBennett even suggested to me that one could trace a line of descent (or is it ascent?) from Beulah to Kerry Washington's character, Olivia Pope, on *Scandal*.[33] Young, beautiful, sexy, slim, well educated, and powerful, Olivia might seem like the antithesis of the rotund, sexless colored maid/mammy of yesteryear, but she is, in the same instance, the supreme black female fixer of all time, queen not of the white folks' kitchen like Beulah, perhaps, but of two presidents' Kitchen Cabinets, "cleaning up other people's messes, fixing up their lives." Or so her own dead but actually alive traitor, terrorist mother tells her in an episode from season three, adding, "I'd rather be a traitor than what you are, Livvie. You think you're family but you're nothing but the help and you don't even know it" (S3, E15).

By the way, the often-repeated claim that Kerry Washington is the first black actress to star in a network series since Teresa Graves played the title role in the drama *Get Christie Love!* (ABC, 1974–1975) presupposes, incorrectly I think, that Sam Waterston was the star of NBC's *I'll Fly Away* in the '90s rather than Regina Taylor, who was nominated for a Primetime Emmy for Outstanding Lead Actress in a Drama Series for her role as Lily Harper the housekeeper, for which she won a Best Actress Golden Globe as well as an NAACP Image Award for Outstanding Lead Actress. In the finest tradition of the problem-solving, colored family fixer, Taylor as Lily carried the series as well as the southern white household she managed.

That said, the identification of Beulah as a problem-solving maid may be furthering a bit of a fantasy. It was certainly the show's tagline claim about its title character, in keeping with what a good colored maid of all work is supposed to be for the white family she loves more than her own. In actuality, from what I remember of the program from the reruns we watched in syndication in the '50s and from revisiting the few episodes currently available on YouTube and DVD, the problems Beulah solved were often of her own making, born of her proclivity for sticking her nose in other people's business, jumping to the wrong conclusions, and talking too much to her omnipresent handyman boyfriend Bill (played by Ernest Whitman, Bud Harris, and Dooley Wilson) and her ditsy, dumb-as-a-rock BFF Oriole, first played by Butterfly McQueen who famously knew nothin' about birthin' no babies as the slave Prissy in *Gone with the Wind* (1939), and then by Ruby Dandridge. When a baby carriage is delivered to the home of her employers, the Hendersons, in "The New Arrival" episode, Beulah decides on no other evidence that Mrs. Henderson is expecting, a conclusion she shares with Bill and Oriole in confidence, swearing them to secrecy. Of course the baby news is soon all over the neighborhood. That, coupled with the unfortunate fact that Beulah takes it upon herself to share Mrs. Henderson's "secret" with Mr. Henderson, results in all manner of chaos, confusion, and misunderstandings, including an overjoyed father to be who isn't and a flood of baby gifts sent to the expecting parents who aren't. Turns out Donnie, the son, ordered the carriage so he could use the wheels to make a go-cart.

Another time, Beulah reads a magazine article listing signs that a marriage is in trouble and decides she sees the signs in the Henderson union. Naturally she intercedes in a way that creates discord where there was none, driving the happy couple into separate bedrooms, before she fixes the damage *she* did by getting the Hendersons to renew their wedding vows, with Donnie acting as the officiant. Beulah uses the occasion to lobby Bill for a wedding of their own; he seems amenable but says they have to wait until Donnie grows up and can marry them for real. Of course, the joke the audience gets, even if Beulah does not, is that insisting they wait for Donnie to become a man is the same as saying never.

In "The Waltz" from 1952, the Hendersons are concerned because Donnie's dance instructor, Miss Matilda, says he is hopelessly clumsy on the dance floor and awkward with girls. Beulah decides to fix things by teaching Donnie how to dance herself, with help from Bill. She and Bill toss aside the waltz record Miss Matilda sent home for Donnie to practice with and instead teach him to dance their way, like colored people. When Donnie and his mismatched, much older, taller blind date—also courtesy of Beulah—break into the jive at the academy ball, Miss Matilda is appalled by the "barbaric exhibition" and banishes Donnie from her school. Mrs. Henderson is afraid that being publicly humiliated and expelled will scar her son for life and make him even more awkward with girls, which today is easily interpreted as a fear that Donnie will turn out gay. But Beulah tells her she needn't worry and takes her to Bill's Fix-it Shop where Donnie is holding court, surrounded by little white girls eager for him to teach them how to jump and jive. The colored maid saves the day this time, then, by teaching the white boy how to be black. And, in a comic reversal of the very thing that historically has been a death sentence for African American males, being "black" or at least performing blackness as a "barbaric exhibition" is the way to win not one white girl but a whole gang of them.

The funniest thing about *Beulah* may be that the title role was played by three different actresses in as many years, with the parts of Bill and Oriole experiencing similar cast changes. Both Bogle and Bodroghkozy maintain that Ethel Waters as Beulah and Ernest Whitman as Bill brought the most depth and dignity to their individual roles but, unfortunately, never shared the screen. As Bodroghkozy writes, "Waters was saddled with the clownish Dooley Wilson and Whitman with the weakened Hattie McDaniel and lackluster Beavers. Had Waters and Whitman been cast together," she continues, "*Beulah* may well have offered viewers a quite revolutionary representation of a loving black couple."[34] (While it would have been a treat to see these two talented actors command the screen together, even if cast opposite one another, Waters and Whitman still would have faced the limitations of the writing and directing.) The fact that so many different actors played the same three parts has led some to suggest that, since all black people look alike, the producers

FIG. 2.5 Hattie McDaniel as Beulah and Ernest Whitman as Bill, teaching little Donnie Henderson (Stuffie Singer) to jive dance in "The Waltz" from season 3 (1952).

thought swapping actors wouldn't much matter. I'm not sure what effect the cast changes had on the show's short run, but, *Beulah* ran afoul of the NAACP for promoting the mammy stereotype that Hattie McDaniel had made infamous in her Oscar-winning role in *Gone with the Wind*.

What I remember most and liked least about the show was Beulah's relationship with Bill, who even as a kid I pegged as a loser and a user. He always showed up at mealtime expecting to be fed—"trying to cop a meal," as Bogle puts it cleverly—and flattered and cajoled Beulah into serving him heaping helpings of the white folks' food.[35] Beulah would hint about marriage and sometimes outright ask him when they were getting hitched—just as she does in the vow renewal episode—and he always had some lame excuse that he would sugarcoat with sweet talk and the affectionate epithet "Baby" that rang hollow even to my child's ear. I used to wonder whether Laura Nyro had Beulah and Bill in mind when she wrote "Wedding Bell Blues," which the 5th Dimension made a hit: "Bill, I love you so, I always will / I look at you and see the passion eyes of May / Oh, but am I ever gonna see my wedding day / . . . Marry me, Bill, I got the wedding bell blues." I wanted Beulah to have more self-respect and kick Bill to the curb.

As a child viewer, I lacked the sophistication to interrogate my own resistance to a relationship that rankled my romantic heart. Bodroghkozy, however, offers a piercing analysis that dissects intellectually what I merely felt intuitively. This would-be love affair and Beulah's ever-imagined marriage and motherhood are narrative impossibilities, and not just because Beulah is obviously well past prime childbearing years, as Bodroghkozy notes, but even more so because the would-be bride is already spoken for. Beulah, the colored maid of all work and the mother of all white folks, can't be wedded to anyone other than the Hendersons; she can't possibly have a husband and a child of her own. To render the always already improbable televisually impossible, the show "undercuts and lampoons Bill as a romantic partner for Beulah," Bodroghkozy writes, ultimately "presenting viewers with a thoroughly desexualized as well as demasculinized figure."[36] Put another way, Bill is the bad joke everybody but Beulah seems to get.

....

Like the part of Beulah, the title roles of the Harlem-based black lodge brothers in *Amos 'n' Andy* were roles that also had previously been performed by white radio players speaking into microphones in would-be blackvoice. Hugely popular and long-lived on the radio, John Forsythe's favorite *Amos 'n' Andy*, which first aired on CBS in June 1951, had a significantly shorter initial run on television, where it was driven out of production in less than two years by protests over its stereotypical depictions of African Americans, although reruns aired well into the 1960s. In the same policing role that undermined *Beulah*, the NAACP was behind many of the protests that shortened *Amos 'n' Andy's* first-run TV life. J. Fred MacDonald points out, in fact, that the NAACP officially condemned both shows at its forty-second annual conference in Atlanta, June 26 through July 1, 1951, passing a resolution and enumerating the shows' crimes against black humanity, which included portraying Negro doctors as "quacks and thieves"; Negro lawyers as "slippery cowards, ignorant of their profession and without ethics"; Negro women as "cackling, screaming shrews, in big-mouth close-ups using street slang, just short of vulgarity"; and all Negroes as "dodging work of any kind."[37]

The amazing who's who of NAACP conference participants that year includes Ralph Bunche, the activist, diplomat, and Nobel Peace Prize winner; Roy Wilkins, the civil rights activist who would soon become executive secretary and then executive director of the association; Thurgood Marshall, luminary legal counsel and future Supreme Court justice; Mary McLeod Bethune, civil and women's rights activist and founding president of what is now Bethune-Cookman University in Daytona Beach, Florida; Dr. Benjamin Mays, then president of Morehouse College in Atlanta; and the southern white writer Lillian Smith, who presented that year's Springarn medal to the black activist and nursing pioneer Mabel Keaton Staupers.[38] But if Hollywood had the might of NAACP giants aligned against its racial stereotyping, *Amos 'n' Andy* in particular also had its champions within the black community, where some appreciated its ironic humor. Even the *Pittsburgh Courier*, which in the 1930s led a nationwide protest against *Amos 'n' Andy* and other shows it felt misrepresented African Americans and committed a cardinal sin in using white actors to play black characters, had somewhat of a change of heart once the programs came to television with black performers and even questioned whether the NAACP had the right to dictate the new medium's colored content and take jobs away from black actors who had few enough opportunities to ply their craft.[39]

Protests, petitions, boycotts, resolutions, and even a lawsuit—all of which made both networks and sponsors nervous—may have succeeded in getting the shows canceled, but the popularity of *Amos 'n' Andy* in particular carried it through the airwaves in syndication into the 1960s, until it was finally shelved in 1966. Bodroghkozy insists, however, that it wasn't protests from the NAACP and others that drove the cancellation of *Beulah* and *Amos 'n' Andy* in 1953. It was the fact that the networks were moving toward a different kind of programming featuring domestic situation comedies, focused, she says, "on blandly white, suburban, and consumerist families like *The Adventures of Ozzie and Harriet*" (ABC, 1952) and *Father Knows Best* (CBS, 1954), even doing away with their "'ethnic' and working-class comedies such as *Life with Luigi*, *The Goldbergs*, *The Honeymooners*, and *Life of Riley*."[40] Perhaps, but it's also the case, I think, that the networks' risk aversion and the sponsors' anxieties helped propel the broadcast industry toward replacing troublesome black programs with much safer white shows that also better fit both the consumer culture and the move to suburbia that even many black families like mine undertook in the '50s in pursuit of the white-picket-fence American Dream.[41] Not until 1968 with *Julia* would the networks take a chance on another black situation comedy.

In any case, the demise of *Beulah* and *Amos 'n' Andy* represented the end of an era that some race men and women considered more an error. The NAACP would take quite a different approach to the policing of black images some decades to come in not only a new century but also a new millennium, where the association would seem better able to distinguish between the part and the performance and more open to a cynical rather than uplifting representation of twenty-first-century African American life.

Unfortunately, in the 1950s, the same racial anxiety on the part of sponsors that sent them scurrying from colored comedies would become an impassable roadblock for black programming that tried to step outside the familiar stereotypes of *Beulah* and *Amos 'n' Andy* in the '50s, most notably *The Nat "King" Cole Show*, which aired on NBC from November 1956 to December 1957. The decade's most noteworthy attempt at presenting a TV variety series hosted by an African American, *The Nat "King" Cole Show* began as a fifteen-minute musical segment but was expanded to a half hour beginning in July 1957. At the time, Cole was already a musical superstar by any reckoning, with an international profile as a singer, pianist, and composer; an impressive list of radio, movie, and TV credits; numerous chart-topping recordings in multiple genres and different languages; and such staggering record sales on the Capitol label that the almost instantly iconic circular tower near Hollywood and Vine, which still serves as the record company's West Coast headquarters, was nicknamed "The House That Nat Built" when it opened in 1956.[42] Such an impressive dossier made Cole seem a better bet for pulling off a TV program of his own than either of the other black entertainers who had previously tried their talents at hosting network namesake variety shows: the pianist and vocalist Hazel Scott (*The Hazel Scott Show*, DuMont Television Network, 1950) and the singer Billy Daniels (*The Billy Daniels Show*, ABC, 1952), whose respective programs ran only a few months.[43]

Cole's luck held out a little longer, slightly over a year—sixty-four consecutive weeks, by his count.[44] His show debuted without a national sponsor, underwritten instead by NBC, with the belief that Cole's talent would attract autonomous commercial backing. Rheingold Beer, Gallo and Italian Swiss Colony wines, Colgate toothpaste, and Coca-Cola reportedly were among the advertisers who purchased airtime in certain regional markets like New York, San Francisco, Los Angeles, and Houston, but no national sponsor ever materialized.[45] Even the backing of Nelson Riddle and his orchestra and white guest stars such as Tony Bennett, Peggy Lee, and Mel Tormé, as well as a stellar roster of black entertainers, couldn't win over sponsors. Ironically, the show might have fared better had Cole been less talented and professional and his program less swank. It was the 1950s after all, and shucking and jiving, clowning and cooning were more in keeping with the stigmatic blackness Hollywood prized and promoted.

Unable to secure sustained backing for his show, Cole performed his TV swan song on December 17, 1957, Danny's fifth birthday. I don't think we knew it then, but it was the host himself, not NBC, who pulled the plug, as Cole details in the *Ebony* article "Why I Quit My TV Show," in which he credits NBC for backing him, even as he pointedly blames his show's demise on the Madison Avenue advertising industry and its big clients who "didn't want their products associated with Negroes." The same executives who "scramble all over each other to sign Negro guest stars to help boost the ratings of white stars," he says, "won't put money on a Negro with his own program." The failure was all the more acute because Cole, who called himself the Jackie Robinson of television, was well aware of his role as a pioneer in the fledgling TV industry and just how much was at stake with a program such as his. "On my show rode the hopes and fears and dreams of millions of people," he wrote in *Ebony*.[46]

Like his hit recording, the velvet voice of Nat King Cole is unforgettable; he lived on as a favorite in our household long after the demise of his show and his own death from lung cancer in 1965. A dozen years later in the latter 1970s, I took a job in Boston as a program director for the Massachusetts Council on the Arts and Humanities, where his widow, Maria Cole, was a member of the board. A talented jazz singer in her own right who had performed with the likes of Duke Ellington and Count Basie, Mrs. Cole would arrive at monthly council meetings in a chauffeur-driven Bentley, imposing in her chiseled beauty and haute couture elegance, yet down-to-earth and approachable. She was always kind to me—lowly staff person that I was—and supportive of the federally funded arts-in-education program I ran, which paired visual artists, writers, performers, and cultural institutions like the Museum of Fine Arts and City Stage with Boston public schools for short- and long-term residencies aimed at using the arts to facilitate the integration of the Boston school system in the wake of Judge Arthur Garrity's 1974 desegregation order.

Whenever I crossed paths with the glamorous Mrs. Cole during those council years, I struggled not to gush my admiration like a groupie, though I'm sure she was used to people—especially women—fawning over her late, great spouse. I held my tongue and never did say that, for my part, whatever the fame, fortunes, and accolades heaped upon other crooners of the day, nobody could turn out a tune like Nathaniel Adams "Nat King" Cole. The demise of his variety show is one of early television's saddest stories and biggest blunders. Ultimately, the case of Nat King Cole—and Hazel Scott and Billy Daniels before him—drives home the unfortunate fact that early television was not quite as welcoming to the Negro performer as Ed Sullivan suggested.

Chapter 3

The Shirley Temple of My Familiar

TAKE TWO

Frieda brought her four graham crackers on a saucer and some milk in a blue-and-white Shirley Temple cup. She was a long time with the milk, and gazed fondly at the silhouette of Shirley Temple's dimpled face. Frieda and she had a loving conversation about how cu-ute Shirley Temple was. I couldn't join them in their adoration because I hated Shirley. Not because she was cute, but because she danced with Bojangles, who was *my* friend, *my* uncle, *my* daddy, and who ought to have been soft-shoeing it and chuckling with me.

—TONI MORRISON, *The Bluest Eye* (1970)

Television in the days of my youth could be hazardous to the health and well-being of black people, almost nothing more so than Shirley Temple films, which were broadcast regularly on network TV from the 1950s through the 1980s and still make occasional appearances in weekend movie marathons and Shirley Temple film festivals. Their small-screen heyday was the 1950s when, in addition to variety shows and other programs produced specifically for television, the networks rounded out their lineups by endlessly airing old movies from the 1930s and '40s, none more frequently, it seemed to me as a child, than Charlie Chan movies and films featuring the white wunderkind Shirley Temple, whose charms Toni Morrison's nine-year-old narrator, Claudia

MacTeer, has the self-love to resist, unlike her older sister Frieda and the worshipful, ill-fated Pecola Breedlove in *The Bluest Eye.*

The Shirley Temple whom Frieda and Pecola so worship in Morrison's novel often was surrounded on-screen by black butlers and mammies and dimwitted colored kids blithely referred to as pickaninnies who also adored her. Black actors such as Hattie McDaniel, Willie Best, Stepin Fetchit (Lincoln Perry), and Bill "Bojangles" Robinson who did Temple's bidding on-screen, together with those who played Buckwheat (Willie Thomas) and Farina (Allen Hoskins) on *The Little Rascals* and *Our Gang* and Algonquin J. Calhoun (Johnny Lee), George "Kingfish" Stevens (Tim Moore), and his wife, Sapphire (Ernestine Wade), on *Amos 'n' Andy,* had representational superpowers in the 1950s when we came to know them. Their presence on-screen—their racial performativity, in today's parlance—validated and memorialized exactly the vernacular, vaudevillian view of black people that so concerned my mother's generation. The characters and caricatures these actors played didn't simply represent fictional figments of the Hollywood imagination; they offered up the facts of what was often taken to be real black life. With their mumbling, bumbling, broken English; slow, lumbering gaits; bulging black eyes; and quivering lips, these and other stigmatic characters were more than mere emblems of a black experience—they were *the* black experience for many segments of midcentury America.

Certainly they were so for many of the white kids my brothers and I went to school with. Beulah, Farina and Buckwheat, Amos and Andy, and Sapphire and the Kingfish were all our classmates knew and all they needed to know about colored people. If the protruding lower lip of Willie Best or Stepin Fetchit stammered through a Shirley Temple film on Sunday, it was a sure bet I would hear the words "liver lips" on the playground on Monday. Insults and slights—both deliberate and unintentional—were a way of life that took on their own normalcy. My big brother, Adrian, was the smart one—the brains of our bunch—but where he fought with his fists and Danny with a thicker skin, I fought back with wit and humor. Making other people laugh became both my modus operandi and my armor, as I learned to poke fun at myself before others could.

Some encounters with racism could be traumatic in ways no one understood or acknowledged at the time, such as the awful moment in my sophomore year (1964–1965) when someone at E. B. High got the bright idea of holding a slave auction as a fundraiser for a worthy cause like football equipment or band uniforms. Worse for me, as a class officer, I was among those slated to be sold along with all the other good sports—from the principal to the lunch ladies—sacrificing ourselves to the gods of good citizenship and school spirit. Crazy as it seems, such slave auctions—sometimes still so-called—remain a go-to form of fundraising for fraternities, churches, charitable organizations, and the like. But even as a kid I knew it was wrongheaded and wished in vain that someone else would see the folly of the plan.

I was no shrinking violet. I could have spoken up. I could have stopped the auction with a word to the unthinking but not unkind organizers for whom "slave" was merely a metaphor, or I could simply have told my parents, who would have put a stop to the event, just as they had years earlier when one of Adrian's teachers tried to mount a classroom production of *Little Black Sambo* starring you-know-who in the title role. But to kill it—to pull the plug on a rally the whole school was behind—would have called attention to my difference and made me a pariah among my peers at a time in life when, like most teens, I wanted nothing more than to fit in. So once more unto the breach I went, submitting myself to what I as a colored kid saw as a sin against the ancestors, but worse, still, was the awful, even uglier twin torment of hating the sale but wanting not to go unsold, to be left standing alone on stage, remaindered like a book nobody wanted to read.

In the end, I was sold and for the respectable sum of $35, as I recall, purchased by a favorite teacher I'll call Mrs. Jones, who promptly put me to work grading papers. But not before I tried to add a feeble little right to what I knew was wrong. Walking across the proscenium to join my buyer stage right, I stopped midway, turned to the audience, and said something close to "I thought slavery was abolished by the Thirteenth Amendment in 1865. What am I doing here?" I'm not sure what I expected: dawning lights rising over the auditorium like thought bubbles, perhaps, or a sudden, communal gasp of recognition or hush of regret. What I got was laughter. The audience may even have applauded. It was just another joke. I was fifteen, but I saw then the error in my ways and learned that laughter isn't always the best medicine. But sometimes it is. When I shared this story with my friend Iris recently, she said it could have been worse. Mrs. Jones could have taken me home and made me clean her house. It was the first time in more than fifty years that I laughed about this childhood haunt, which I suspect my classmates have long forgotten, if it registered at all.

Occasionally, the racism that hovered over our daily lives could almost be amusing, such as the absurd debate I once got into with a classmate I'll call James over whether a certain older black kid I didn't even know was my brother. For a short time in the mid-1950s, there was another black family in town. We didn't know them; I don't think our paths ever crossed, but once when James and I were sent on an errand, one of the boys passed by us in the hallway. "There's your brother," James said to me. "He's not my brother," I replied. "Yes, he is," James insisted. And we went back and forth like that, with him standing me down that this black stranger was my brother, until I gave up in frustration. Of course, James was the same kid who would turn around in his seat and stare at me whenever we came upon a section on the Civil War and slavery in our social studies books, with the inevitable pictures of happy darkies down on the plantation.

....

I was perhaps nine or ten the first time it hit me that we were less than a hundred years removed from slavery. But what did I know of slavery? What did any of us know of the plantation system, other than the portraits that our TV sets, history books, and songsters painted of a paternal institution, which brought savage heathens out of what our textbooks called the "Dark Continent," attempted to civilize them through the enlightenment of Christianity, and housed and cared for them "way down upon de Swanee River" until Abraham Lincoln, the Great Emancipator, freed this inherently lazy lot and turned them loose on civil society, leaving them longing for "de old plantation, and for de old folks at home."[1]

Unfortunately, the African American past wasn't the only history disparaged, distorted, and denied by what we were taught and what we were not. Native Americans, too, didn't exist except as savages to be moved out of the way, along with Mexicans, on the heroic march west to fulfill the nation's Manifest Destiny. There was no Trail of Tears in our social studies books, no Chinese Exclusion Act, no internment of Japanese Americans. And the closest we came to the horrors of the Nazi concentration camps was *The Diary of Anne Frank*. I'm not sure the word "Holocaust" was ever spoken in any of our classrooms. To my own great shame and embarrassment, I knew racism well enough, but I had no knowledge of anti-Semitism and didn't understand the prejudice against the one Jewish girl in our class, to whom small-town life also could be quite cruel.

Shirley Temple films and other similar televisual narratives graphically confirmed in black and white the tales our textbooks and Stephen Foster tunes told of happy darkies on the plantation. It was for this reason that watching TV in the early days brought both delight and dread: the thrill on the one hand of seeing black people on-screen and the anxiety on the other of knowing their blackface foibles would be taken for our own.

Charlie Chan, too, was televisually both friend and foe. I loved watching murder mysteries featuring the brilliant Chinese detective from Honolulu, though even as a child something told me I shouldn't. Chan was another Other, which made him a friend, and intelligent and heroic in ways the black characters on our TV screen were not, including Lincoln Perry in his controversial persona as the bug-eyed, scaredy-cat Stepin Fetchit, billed as "the Laziest Man in the World," and the equally problematic, jive-talking Mantan Moreland, each of whom appeared as Chan's colored manservant and chauffeur, respectively, at different times in various films. That Fetchit and Moreland, who as Birmingham Brown sometimes aided as well as drove the detective, were the same kind of stigmatic black caricatures in the company and command of Charlie Chan that they were with white folks, often serving as foils for the detective's superior intellect, made Chan a foe and watching his films on TV a kind of guilty pleasure. But there was something else bothersome about the Honolulu detective, who was world famous like Agatha Christie's Belgian sleuth Hercule Poirot. Chan delivered sing-songy aphorisms and fortune-cookie platitudes in a slower, more deliberate version of the same Pidgin English that Peter on *Bachelor Father* (and just about every other Asian or Asian American character on TV) performed.

The bigger deal, however, was that Charlie Chan was also the other kind of faux, as in phony. The would-be Chinese detective was actually played by the Swedish-American Warner Oland, the Missouri-born Sidney Toler, and the Bostonian Roland Winters, as well as a number of other Caucasian actors in so-called yellowface, including J. Carrol Naish in a short-lived TV series in the mid-1950s and Ross Martin in a made-for-TV movie in the '70s. I read somewhere that, even performed by white men, the Charlie Chan character—a character inspired by Honolulu's real-life, legendary Chinese American detective Chang Apana—supposedly was popular in China in the 1930s and '40s because he was wise, worldly, and honorable, unlike the evil Dr. Fu Manchu (also played in the movies by Oland) and similar stereotypical Asian characters.[2] However, from the collection *Charlie Chan Is Dead* (1993) to a long list of books and essays, numerous Asian American writers and scholars have debunked the Charlie Chan figure and interrogated the orientalist mythology the character represents.[3] In one of the earliest contemporary critiques, Frank Chin and Jeffery Paul Chan argue that each racial stereotype has its acceptable and unacceptable counterweights. For the threatening black brute, it's the buffoon; for the "savage, kill-crazy Geronimo," it's Tonto; for "the mad dog General Santa Ana there's the Cisco Kid and Poncho"; and for "Fu Manchu and the Yellow Peril," they write, it's Charlie Chan and his

Number One Son. "The acceptable model is acceptable," they say, "because he is tractable. There is racist hate and racist love."[4]

And sometimes the sight line between the two is blurred, the image double exposed. "To gaze upon a body in Blackface or yellowface or whiteface," Matthew Guterl writes in *Seeing Race in Modern America* (2013), is "to note the very obvious exterior façade and the supposedly just as obvious subterranean real."[5] My parents wanted us to see through such façades. They hated even the idea of blackface and anything resembling minstrelsy. Yellowface and the Charlie Chan series' obvious orientalism fared no better with my folks. Their racial politics didn't mean we couldn't watch Charlie Chan, however; it did mean we were not supposed to laugh at the othering of the Asian Others, which is oddly hypocritical in a way, since we could and did laugh at the antics of the Amos and Andy characters, behind the closed doors of our own home, even appropriating some of the Kingfish's malapropisms into our own intramural misspeak: "unlax" for "relax," for instance, and "jay-rage" for "garage." But *Amos 'n' Andy* was only funny as a private joke. When white people brought up the show or assumed that, of course, we loved it, we played dumb, as if we didn't know what they were talking about. It's a little like the old saying that a lady cannot be insulted because she simply doesn't understand (or so she pretends).

My own silent, secret pleasure in the texts of Charlie Chan was my crush on his bumbling but beautiful Number One Son, Lee Chan, played by the young, handsome Keye Luke, although my fidelity wavered from televised film to film, because I also thought Number Two Son was divine. It was a long time before I realized that Victor Sen Yung, who played Number Two Son, was the same actor who later played Peter Tong's conman Cousin Charlie on *Bachelor Father* and the cook Hop Sing on *Bonanza*. Keye Luke likewise later appeared as Master Po in the TV series *Kung Fu* (1972–1975) and any number of other roles where I didn't recognize him as my youthful heartthrob.

Whatever conflicts and contradictions Charlie Chan wrought in our household, Shirley Temple was by far the most monumental and paradoxical of my childhood guilty TV pleasures. With the possible exception of Michael Jackson, no other child performer achieved Shirley Temple's level of success and universal recognition at such a young age. As the star of more than fifty films—and later as a diplomat and politician—the former prodigy, who as an adult went by her married name Shirley Temple Black, reigned as a genuine American icon for more than eighty years. As she boasts in her autobiography *Child Star* (1988), at the ripe old age of seven, she had greater name rec-

FIG. 3.1 Roland Winters as Charlie Chan in the rear seat (*right*), with Keye Luke as Number One Son Lee, and Victor Sen Yung as Number Two Son Tommy (previously Jimmy) in front with their chauffeur Birmingham Brown (Mantan Moreland) behind the wheel in *The Feathered Serpent* (1948).

ognition than Amelia Earhart and Eleanor Roosevelt and bigger box-office receipts than leading men like Clark Gable, Robert Taylor, and Bing Crosby.[6]

As Temple tells it, age discrimination cheated her out of the Best Actress Oscar for 1934 when she was just six years old and "odds-makers had [her] an almost certain win," until a "vicious cat fight" over the Academy's failure to nominate either Myrna Loy (*The Thin Man*) or Bette Davis (*Of Human Bondage*) led officials to rescind Temple's nomination, awarding her instead a miniature special Oscar for "monumental, stupendous, elephantine achievements."[7] Her biographer, Anne Edwards, tells a slightly different story, pointing out that in the Academy's first and only experiment with write-in ballots, little Shirley Temple did receive an overwhelming number of votes for her performances in *Little Miss Marker* and *Bright Eyes* (both 1934), leading the Academy, which had never before honored a child performer with an Oscar, to present Temple with the special, miniature award.[8]

She may have lost the Best Actress accolade to Claudette Colbert (who won that year for *It Happened One Night*), but Temple went on to win the hearts of her country and the approval of presidents. In the 1930s, FDR praised her infectious optimism as the antidote to the Depression; in 1969 Richard Nixon appointed the forty-year-old Shirley Temple Black to the U.S. delegation of the United Nations; Gerald Ford made her an ambassador to Ghana in 1974 and Chief of Protocol in 1976. Ronald Reagan, her former costar in *That Hagen Girl* (1947), passed her over, probably because she endorsed George H. W. Bush in the 1980 Republican primary, but Bush made her envoy to Czechoslovakia when he assumed the presidency in 1988. In a two-hour segment of *A&E Biography*, former President Ford decreed that Shirley Temple "made all of America feel good about themselves." Other commentators, including Anne Edwards, attributed Temple's "universal appeal" and enduring popularity to the fact that the beautiful child seen singing and dancing on-screen is "everything parents want their children to be." "Everything about her was perfect. Perfect. Perfect 10."[9]

Outside academic circles, few have dared imagine that Shirley Temple may not have brought perfect joy to *every* American. Like Gerald Ford, most commentators simply assume all audiences have received the prodigy's fifty-six blonde curls and snow-white skin the same way. This assumption—that the perfect-10 white girl necessarily has a universal appeal—is a presumptive privilege. As George Lipsitz and other cultural theorists have shown, a silence about itself is the primary prerogative of whiteness, at once its grand scheme and its deep cover. "Whiteness is everywhere in U.S. culture," Lipsitz writes, "but it is very hard to see. . . . As the unmarked category against which difference is constructed, whiteness never has to speak its name, never has to acknowledge its role as an organizing principle in social and cultural relations."[10]

Historically, popular culture's silent affirmation of perfect whiteness often has occurred at the expense of those who fall outside the dominant blonde-is-beautiful, white-is-right construct. Like notoriously racist films such as D. W. Griffith's *Birth of a Nation* (1915) and Walt Disney's *Song of the South* (1946), Shirley Temple movies function within and further an ideology of white superiority, which equates beauty with whiteness and makes true white girl- and womanhood a prized domestic ideal, while stigmatizing blackness as blighted and deficient. That this simultaneously racial, sexual, and national narrative was written on the body of a white child in the 1930s might easily be misread as a troubling but not altogether surprising relic of our less sensitive past. But while the mass-mediated sexualizing of little girls may have begun in the early 1930s with Shirley Temple's debut as a pint-sized femme fatale in sexy one-reelers called Baby Burlesks that spoofed popular adult roles, it certainly did not end with the demise of her film career a decade later, as the 1996 murder of JonBenét Ramsey, the six-year-old child-woman the media dubbed the "Barbie-doll beauty queen," made tragically evident while calling attention to the scary world of little-girl glamour and child beauty pageants.

Most of the critical commentary and scholarly debate on Temple and her films and their long afterlife in television have centered on sexuality rather than race. In a review of *Captain January* published in *The Spectator* in 1936, the British novelist Graham Greene, then a freelance journalist and movie critic, infamously suggested that some of Temple's popularity seemed "to rest on a coquetry quite as mature as Miss [Claudette] Colbert's and on an oddly precocious body as voluptuous in grey flannel trousers as Miss [Marlene] Dietrich's."[11] A year later, in an even more explicit review of *Wee Willie Winkie* (1937), published in the British magazine *Night and Day*, Greene alluded to his earlier critique, calling Temple a "fancy little piece," and then went on to note "the way she measures a man with adult, studio eyes, with dimpled depravity" in her new film. "Her admirers—middle-aged men and clergymen—respond to her dubious coquetry, to the sight of her well-shaped and desirable little body, packed with enormous vitality," he concluded, "only because the safety curtain of story and dialogue drops between their intelligence and their desire."[12] So saying, Greene raised the safety curtain on the adult desire behind the child star's appeal. Shockingly bold for the 1930s, his critiques prompted Temple's parents and Twentieth Century Fox to file a libel suit. The British High Court found for the plaintiffs and ordered Greene and *Night and Day* to pay £3,500 in damages.

Although he paid a heavier price for free speech than some, Greene is by no means the only critic to comment on the bawdy nature of Shirley Temple's body language. As the film scholar Jeanine Basinger notes in *A Woman's View* (1993), much has been made of Temple's "sexy little body, her pouty mouth, her flirtatious ways"; there has been considerable flap over "smarmy scenes" in which the child star plays wife to her perennially widowed film fathers, sitting on their laps, nestling against their chests, stroking their cheeks, and, as in *Poor Little Rich Girl* (1936), Basinger points out, singing them alluring love songs with lyrics like "In every dream I caress you. Marry me and let me be your wife."[13] Basinger, however, views the sexing of Shirley as much ado about very little. Chiding Greene and other critics and scholars for their "sinister interpretations," she insists that all Temple "really did was tap her guts out in a series of well-made, unpretentious, and entertaining little films designed to lift a Depression audience out of its worries."[14]

There may be something sinister about removing cultural icons from their temporal context: we are certainly more aware of and self-consciously concerned with incest, child abuse, child pornography, and pedophilia than most audiences of the 1930s. But when the five-, six-, or seven-year-old Shirley Temple tapped her guts out, wiggled her baby bottom at the camera (Gary Cooper nicknamed her "Wiggle-Britches"), and sang her sexy little love songs to handsome male costars, she was under the direction of grown men. She may have been innocent, but that doesn't mean her films are. The Baby Burlesk shorts deliberately cultivated in the toddler the same erotic savoir-faire that made Marlene Dietrich the queen of sex, sin, and song in the '30s. In *Kid 'n' Hollywood* (1933), for example, Temple plays a bathing beauty reduced to a scrubwoman whom a Hollywood director discovers, dolls up in sequins and feathers, and transforms into a starlet suggestively named Morelegs Sweetrick, explicitly modeled after Dietrich, whom little Shirley Temple attempts to imitate to the tune of Dietrich's signature song, "Falling in Love Again" from *The Blue Angel* (1930).

Basinger insists that "Temple's films are actually women's films," with her "always the center of the universe in them," which is certainly one way to read them.[15] But on another level, it is most often men's fantasies that these vehicles engage. However cute and frilly, they still work to incite, excite, and satisfy a paternal white gaze, as cinema so often does. Sewing and scrubbing one moment, batting her eyelashes the next, Shirley Temple is at once a pint-sized purveyor of true-womanhood ideology and a make-a-blind-man-see femme fatale. A handsome, skirt-chasing Robert Young gives up his playboy ways for her in *Stowaway* (1936), and a jewel-thieving Gary Cooper attempts to go straight because of her in *Now and Forever* (1934). She is every man's white dream, the perfect embodiment of the virgin-whore that patriarchy loves to look at—simultaneously Snow White and Black Widow, albeit without the killer instinct. And while Temple may be the central figure in her films, as Basinger maintains, she is almost invariably the darling of men—and lots of them: a bunch of bookies and gangsters in *Little Miss Marker* (1934), a troupe of vaudevillians in *Little Miss Broadway* (1938), a squadron of aviators in *Bright Eyes* (1934), a British regiment in *Wee Willie Winkie* (1937), a troop of Royal Canadian mounted police officers in *Susanna of the Mounties* (1939), two crusty old sailors in *Captain January* (1936), and much of the

FIGS. 3.2 AND 3.3 Shirley Temple literally goes from rags to riches as Morelegs Sweetrick, in the 1933 Baby Burlesk short *Kid 'n' Hollywood.*

Union army—including the commander-in-chief, Abraham Lincoln—in *The Littlest Rebel* (1934). These films were successful not only because of Temple's talent but also because of a pliant, "innocent" white female sexuality that was indulged, petted, and, quite frequently, bedded.

Romantic comedies of the 1930s often feature bedroom scenes of some sort, even if the characters aren't shown between the sheets as they invariably are today. Getting the leading lady into bed in Shirley Temple pictures presents a seemingly more innocent iteration of the same suggestive signs and symbols of seduction common to 1930s cinema, including a coy, even coquettish resistance to the bedroom. "I don't wanna go up there," Temple's character, Lloyd Sherman, says to Walker (Bill Robinson), the house slave, backing away from his outstretched hand in *The Little Colonel* (1935), the first of four films Temple and Robinson made together. "Why everybody's gutta go upstairs, Miss Lloyd, if they wants to go to bed," Walker replies. The six-year-old is adamant. "I don't want to," she repeats, digging in her heels. The rhythmic seduction that follows—literally, a step dance—is actually the black butler's trickster way of luring the resistant white child up to bed. Dazzling as the duet was for most Depression audiences, the sight of a black male and a white female holding hands and heading for the bedroom intimated a relation so taboo that the dance sequence had to be cut from the film when it played in southern cities. "To avoid social offense and assure wide distribution, the studio cut scenes showing physical contact between us," Temple Black explains in her autobiography.[16]

She also reveals that it was none other than the aging D. W. Griffith who approached Fox executives with the "controversial idea" to add a transgressive black male presence to her films. "There is nothing, absolutely nothing, calculated to raise the gooseflesh on the back of an audience more than that of a white girl in relation to Negroes," Griffith is quoted as saying—a comment that is similar to what has been said about the pairing of the diminutive blonde beauty Kelly Ripa with the big, black former footballer Michael Strahan as cohosts of the morning show *Live!*[17] Temple Black ends her own commentary on her partnership with Bojangles by proudly proclaiming that she and "Uncle Billy Robinson" were "the first interracial dancing couple in movie history."[18] Yet, as James Snead points out in *White Screens/Black Images: Hollywood from the Dark Side* (1994), Robinson and Temple were never a "dancing couple" in the Ginger Rogers and Fred Astaire sense. Snead says, in fact, that in the stair dance and their other routines together, Temple is "not so much dancing with Robinson . . . as dancing like him."[19]

FIG. 3.4 Bill "Bojangles" Robinson and Shirley Temple in their famous stair dance from *The Little Colonel* (1935).

Rogers and Astaire were a sensual ensemble from the first time they danced cheek-to-cheek in *Flying Down to Rio* in 1933. Restricted to dancing toe-to-toe, Temple and Robinson, by contrast, had to work at avoiding the organic sensuality of the male-female pas de deux. The same little girl who spent most of her film career in the arms and laps of white men never got closer to Bill Robinson on-screen than a hand clasp. The popularity of the Temple-Robinson duo depended, in fact, on maintaining the distance between them as mistress and slave, on playing up what the folklorist Patricia Turner describes as the public's infatuation with Little Eva and Uncle Tom. "With laws against miscegenation on the books in many states," Turner writes, "the match between Shirley Temple and Bill Robinson was the only one that would be tolerated."[20]

In *The Little Colonel*, and elsewhere in their cinematic oeuvre, Robinson is so much more mammy than man that he seemingly poses no threat, sexual or otherwise, to innocent white womanhood. Rather, his gray hair and Uncle Tom devotion contest the very sexual menace his black male presence evokes. In this way, Hollywood gets to have its chocolate cake and eat it, too: to invoke the always already sexual black male and deny him at the same time. This strategy is less typecasting than castrating, but even as a metaphoric eunuch, Robinson doesn't actually get to put Shirley to bed.

The staircase foreplay interrupted by her crusty old grandfather (Lionel Barrymore), Uncle Billy rushes his charge up the remaining stairs and turns her over to Mammy (Hattie McDaniel), who picks her up and says, "Now, honey, we gonna go to bed," just before the camera shifts to Robinson dancing back down the stairs alone.

If Robinson's approach to his leading lady is necessarily hands-off in *The Little Colonel*, Adolphe Menjou's is decidedly hands-on in *Little Miss Marker* (1934), based on a short story by Damon Runyon. Temple plays Martha Jane, a fetching five-year-old whose father leaves her with bookies as collateral for a twenty-dollar bet. As a matter of strict policy, Menjou's character Sorrowful Jones doesn't accept markers, but after picking up the child and gazing into her eyes, the smitten boss tells his stunned underling to take the kid in lieu of cash: "Little doll like that's worth twenty bucks, any way you look at it." Predictably, the father commits suicide when his horse loses, and Martha Jane, whom the bookies dub "Little Miss Marker," becomes Sorrowful's property, his ownership confirmed by the cavemanly way he scoops her up under one arm and carries her off, exposing her bare legs and bottom to the camera.

The scene shifts immediately to the bedroom, where Martha Jane appears in a man's pajama top; Sorrowful, of course, is wearing the bottoms. "But I can't sleep in my underwear," she says when he asks if she's ready for bed. "Okay, well take 'em off," he replies. "They button up the back," she explains, lifting the oversized shirt and poking out her little derriere for him to see. He dutifully unbuttons the drop seat of the tattered undergarment and loosens the straps of the front bib, exposing Temple's bare chest just before she turns her back to the camera and steps out of her underwear, presumably leaving herself naked beneath the oversized pajama top.

The leading lady's bedding down or waking up in the leading man's pajama shirt is another staple gag of the romantic comedy genre that works to enhance the sexual tension around which such films revolve. Just what *isn't* Doris Day or Sophia Loren or Annette Bening in *The American President* (1995) wearing under the oversized man's shirt? Claudette Colbert wears a pair of Clark Gable's pajamas in *It Happened One Night*, which was released the same year as *Little Miss Marker* and won Colbert the Oscar Temple Black implies should have been hers. In one scene, Gable helps Colbert hurriedly button up her dress, as detectives looking for the runaway heiress pound on the door. But imagine Gable *undressing* Colbert. In 1934 a man couldn't remove a woman's undergarments on-screen, but he could, in an act of sexual displacement, undress a little girl playing at being a woman, because the child's flat chest deflates and purifies this otherwise risqué gesture, making it censorproof. Titillation without tits.

....

The columnist Walter Winchell once argued that the international popularity of film attractions like Shirley Temple, Charlie Chan, and Boris Karloff was evidence that "sex can't be important in films."[21] Winchell missed the undertones that a close reading can uncover. But, certainly, it was not just Temple's innocent sexuality and little-womanish ways that gave her such tremendous star power in the 1930s and beyond. The survival-of-the-pluckiest, rags-to-riches class narratives of her movies also played well with audiences in Depression-era America and around the world. In the mid-1930s, Shirley Temple films broke box-office records in India and Japan, as well as in the United States and Canada.[22] Bette Bao Lord's semi-autobiographical children's book, *In the Year of the Boar and Jackie Robinson* (1984), suggests the iconographical power of Temple in China, where she became a metaphor for quintessential Americanness. For Lord's young heroine, Sixth Cousin, who renames herself Shirley Temple Wong at the beginning of the book, "the most famous movie star in all the world" is not only a namesake but a lifeline that helps the small child bridge the gap between China, the land of her birth, and her new home in Brooklyn, New York.[23]

But if the most famous movie star in all the world has been a positive role model for many, she also for others has become the sign and symbol of impossible standards of beauty and perfection. The most powerful counternarrative to the popular reading of Shirley Temple as everybody's darling is almost certainly *The Bluest Eye*, where in the brown eyes of Pecola Breedlove, the homely black girl at the center of the story, Shirley Temple is indeed a blonde goddess who is everything she is not. But the price Pecola pays for her innocent adoration is a deadly one. The looming image of the perfect, beloved Shirley Temple is the embodiment of the white, Western standards of desirability that leads the unloved Pecola to believe only those with blue eyes and blonde hair are beautiful and worthy of affection. Raped and impregnated by her father and rejected by her mother, Pecola retreats into madness, first praying for and then believing she has acquired the blue eyes that will make her adorable and beloved like Shirley Temple. (Temple's eyes were actually light brown, by the way.)

FIG. 3.5 At Massasoit Community College circa 1985 with Nan Ellison, the hairdresser I asked to give me Shirley Temple ringlets, after a concert by Hallelujah Voices, the verse and vocal chair I cofounded and codirected with Dr. Julius Coles, under the auspices of the South Shore Conservatory of Music. I'm wearing a custom-tailored concert ensemble by Mom.

My own relationship to Shirley Temple is a vexed one. I didn't worship her like the ill-fated Pecola, but I didn't hate her either. The truth is, much of the time I wanted to be Shirley Temple. That is, I wanted that trademark Shirley Temple cuteness: the ability to charm the crust off old codgers—or, better still, handsome, virile young men whose mottoes seemed to be "Oh, come let us adore you." Once, when I was eight or nine, I asked Nan Ellison, the church lady who pressed and curled hair in her kitchen before opening a salon in downtown Brockton, to do my hair in ringlets like Shirley's. In those days, getting your hair done could be an all-day affair. I sat for hours anxiously awaiting my ascension into the ranks of the adorable, but when Mrs. Ellison finally put down the curling iron and handed me a mirror, the gap-toothed, black face that looked back at me from beneath a rat's nest of tight, greasy spirals was anything but cute. Yet however silly and absurd I saw myself as at that moment, I also understood that mine was a self-inflicted homeliness, begot of my own betrayal: in attempting to look like the white wunderkind, I had succeeded only in making my black difference ridiculous.

This, then, is what pained me about the Shirley Temple films that filled my girlhood: Temple's adorable perfection—her snow-whiteness—was constructed against my blackness, my racial difference made ridiculous by the stammering and shuffling of the "little black rascals," "darkies," and "pickaninnies" who populated her movies. In the opening moments of *The Littlest Rebel* (1935), one of Temple's most popular films, this distinction between perfect-10 whiteness and stigmatic blackness is played out in the contrast between Temple as Virginia "Miss Virgie" Cary, the light, bright, beautiful belle of her own birthday ball, and Hannah Washington as Sally Ann, the dark, dumb, plain pickaninny.

Called from the lavish festivities inside, Miss Virgie is met on the front porch of her plantation manor by a group of slave children who have come to the big house bearing birthday greetings and a gift for their little mistress. But Sally Ann, the designated spokesperson, can't manage to get out the simple salutation. Although older and much taller than the diminutive Miss Virgie, Sally Ann stumbles over a simple and presumably well-rehearsed greeting. "Miss Virgie. Please, ma'am," Sally Ann says. "We all done come here to wish you many happy . . . happy . . ."

"Returns," the bubbly, hyperarticulate Miss Virgie interjects.

"That's it," Sally Ann musters. "We all done made you a doll and here it is," she adds, holding out a black golliwog rag doll. "There was more I had to say, but, Mammy, I forgot it," she cries, dissolving into tears and burying her face in Mammy's skirt.

The magnanimous Miss Virgie, cradling the black doll against her white dress, tells Sally Ann not to worry: "This is the very nicest present I got. Thank you ever so much." She exits, promising over her shoulder to save Sally Ann and the other slave children some birthday cake, which makes all the darkies dance with joy. As a child watching the film on TV in the 1950s and '60s, I might have thought Miss Virgie's promise of birthday cake played like a modern-day version of Marie Antoinette's apocryphal pronouncement "Let them eat cake." But as a critic, I know the gesture is meant to make Miss Virgie loom all the larger for her largess to dimwitted darkies, who thrill at the thought of crumbs.

Commenting on this scene, James Snead argues that the "extreme self-effacement and awe" effected by Hannah Washington as the taller, older Sally

FIG. 3.6 Temple as Miss Virgie receiving a homemade golliwog ragdoll as a birthday gift from bashful, tongue-tied Sally Ann (Hannah Washington) and other slave children in *The Littlest Rebel* (1935).

Ann necessarily augment Shirley Temple's "mythic stature and the figure of leisure and beauty for whom blacks must work and to whom they also must defer."[24] The more subtle point, however, is not that the black slaves *must* defer to their white masters, but that they *want* to defer. The willing deference and submission of happy slaves are critical to the film's ideological scheme and wholly in keeping with how slavery was represented in our textbooks and on our television sets during the 1950s.

Like its cousin *The Little Colonel*, *The Littlest Rebel* offers such a benevolent portrait of the South's peculiar institution that Uncle Billy, the devoted house Negro and nursemaid (again played by Robinson), has no thirst for freedom. When Miss Virgie's birthday party is interrupted by news that the South is at war, she asks Uncle Billy what war is and why men kill each other. More than mere dialogue, the exchange between the two—between child and adult, mistress and slave—is pure plantation mythology:

> UNCLE BILLY: Seems like to me, honey, no one knows why. I hear a
>   white gentleman say dere's a man up North who wants to free da slaves.
> MISS VIRGIE: What does that mean, free the slaves?

UNCLE BILLY (walking away with a tray): I don't know what it means myself.

MISS VIRGIE (musing to herself): It's funny, isn't it?

Although Uncle Billy is more knowledgeable and articulate than his fellow slaves, his ignorance of freedom here is a narrative necessity, because it affirms the dominant belief that docile, devoted darkies need slavery to protect them from their own stupidity and helplessness. A war that will pit white brother against brother has just broken out, but the dumb Negroes for whom the nation is being torn asunder don't know or care what freedom is. In fact, Sally Ann and the even dimmer-witted James Henry (Willie Best) aid and abet the Rebels, who are fighting to keep them enslaved, but are so afraid of their Yankee liberators that they shake, shiver, and run whenever Union forces approach the plantation. At one point, James Henry says to Miss Virgie, "Dem Yankees is mighty powerful. Dey can even change da weather. Whenever dey come around, I never know whether it's winter or summer. I'm shiv'rin' and sweatin' at da same time."

If Sally Ann, Uncle Billy, and James Henry are good slaves with no desire for freedom, Miss Virgie makes a bad, rebellious would-be pickaninny a little later in the film when she poses as a slave to hide from the Yankees, blackening her face with shoe polish and tying up her blonde curls in a bandanna. When a disreputable Union sergeant orders her to remove his boots, she pushes his outstretched leg, sending him toppling out of the chair. Her defiance throughout the film (twice she shoots a kindly Union colonel with her slingshot and defiantly sings "Dixie" just to annoy him) stands in stark contrast to the cowardly acquiescence of the enslaved who have no stake in their own freedom.

The film's other ironic reversals have similarly charged political implications. Uncle Billy may not know what it means to free the slaves, but when Miss Virgie's father, Confederate Captain Cary (John Boles), is the one who needs to be freed from a Yankee prison, it's the loyal slave who devises a plan to raise the train fare for a trip to Washington, D.C., where he and Miss Virgie will plead for the captain's release: they sing and dance on the streets of Richmond until they have collected enough cash for the trip. Once in Washington, the two of them have an audience with Abraham Lincoln himself, who immediately succumbs to the irrepressible charms of the "littlest rebel." Over a shared apple, she explains to the doting president that her father and the kindly Yankee colonel imprisoned with him were only trying to get her to safety. As she sits on Lincoln's lap and snuggles against his chest, he assures

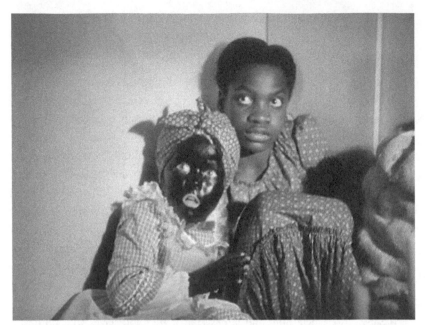

FIG. 3.7 Miss Virgie in blackface, hiding from the Yankees with Sally Ann.

FIG. 3.8 Defiant Miss Virgie pushing over the chair of the Yankee sergeant who, assuming she is a slave, orders her to pull off his boots.

her that she need study war no more: "Your father and Colonel Morrison are going free." Thus, the curtain closes on a new world order that looks remarkably like the old one: Lincoln has freed the white men, while Uncle Billy still proudly describes himself as one of Massa Cary's slaves.

First appearing as savages, maids, and missionary-eating cannibals in Baby Burlesk shorts like *Kid 'n' Africa* (1933), where tiny Madame Cradlebait is bent on civilizing the natives, casts of mostly anonymous black characters provided Shirley Temple with color, comedy, and companionship throughout her film career: they show her off; she shows them up. For example, when Temple as Martha Jane first sees Willie Best's character sweeping the floor in *Little Miss Marker*, she points a finger at him and says, "I know you. You're the black knight." "Go on child, I'm black day and night," Best replies, displaying his character's homophonic ignorance of the King Arthur legends with which the five-year-old is fully conversant. In *Just around the Corner* (1938), it is again Uncle Billy Robinson, this time a doorman, who plays the foil for the white child's superior intellect. When she asks him where Borneo is, he replies, "Borneo? Borneo? Oh, ah, he's moved up in Harlem." "Borneo isn't a man, it's a place," she corrects. "Where is it?"

Trying to save face, the doorman guesses again: "Oh sure, that's where that big light come from in the sky. Nights. The roar . . . borinelis," he adds, murdering "aurora borealis." "Everybody's heard of dat." When the trusting child says she hasn't, he proceeds to further miseducate her. "Well, it's sorta north. Way up north near the North Pole. That's where Borneo is." Sure of himself now, he goes on to describe a land of icebergs and people-eating polar bears, but, of course, the joke is that he couldn't be more wrong: lush with flora and fauna, with a mean temperature of seventy-eight degrees, Borneo is in the middle of the Indian Ocean.

I didn't always get the joke, but I knew my people were being made fun of, and I hated the recurrent episodes of black stupidity that were the brown bread and butter of these films turned TV texts. However much I might have aspired (both vainly and in vain) to a head full of Shirley Temple curls, it was not to her that I was blood bound, but to the celluloid mammies and minstrels who did her bidding, whose bowing and scraping across the screen affirmed her whiteness and superiority while putting my blackness in debase relief. No matter how well I might speak, how straight I might stand, I was those ignorant darkies and they were me.

It's that racial metonymy my mother understood so well: any black is every black. It's not just that we all look alike, but that we're all the same—guilty of the same sins, convicted of the same crimes. This awareness that we are always already guilty of blackness keeps us ever on the defensive, in perpetual pursuit of the elusive innocence that is Shirley Temple's birthright. The colored kid's code that we must go forth and do well—for our people—working twice as hard for half as much, may have been personally empowering for some of us, but such clarion calls to uplift are actually like spitting in a hurricane when it comes to combating what whiteness says blackness is. Tutored by our parents, my brothers and I could talk that *other* talk, a King's English more precise than that of our most articulate white classmates; we could hold our heads high in deliberate defiance of the bowed and bumbling blackness of fiction, film, and television. Yet no matter how perfect our diction or regal our carriage, we could not escape the shuckin' and jivin' of Algonquin J. Calhoun, Kingfish, and Sapphire on *Amos 'n' Andy*; the protruding lower lip and bulging eyes of Willie Best, Stepin Fetchit, and Mantan Moreland in the Charlie Chan and Shirley Temple movies on TV almost every Sunday; and the quintessential technicolored kidness of Farina and Buckwheat appearing daily in *The Little Rascals*.

As proud black children, we identified ourselves against these black caricatures, but for many of our white classmates, Farina and Buckwheat and Amos and Andy were the authentic coloreds. We were the exceptional Negroes—the abnorm to the stigmatic blackness that popular culture made normative. Whether we fought back with fists, wits, or witticisms, we paid a heavy price—or so I felt as a child—for the on-screen antics of our fellow African Americans, and we held them, not something called "Hollywood," accountable. Although the argument that it's better to play a maid for $700 a week than be one for $7 makes dollars and sense to me now, it wasn't good enough for me as a child, and like my mother I resented the black actors who I felt demeaned the race for the pleasure of white people.

That white people were watching was the heart of the matter. As I suggested earlier, at home, black families like mine could watch *Amos 'n' Andy* with amusement. None of my familiars at the time appreciated the skill underpinning the moronic, drooped-lipped performances of Willie Best and Stepin Fetchit (reprised in *Forrest Gump* by Mykelti Williamson as Bubba Blue, Gump's doomed and dimwitted army buddy), but even playing a slave or butler or doorman, Bill Robinson was still the best reason to watch a Shirley Temple movie—behind closed doors. Outside the home, in the real world whose power to define us seemed so much greater than our efforts to define ourselves, we knew the minstrelsy, mammyism, tomming, and buffoonery of black performers constituted authentic, true-blue blackness for most white audiences. Our own black lives were made harder by our need to live down what they played up.

But even greater trauma lay in the guilt that our own resistance and resentment produced. After all, for the racially proud, being ashamed of blackness—like speaking the King's English instead of the Kingfish's—is equated with wanting to be white. Both are sins against the racial self, assumed by many social theorists and child psychologists to be the result of internalized racism. Perhaps the most famous evidence of this condition is the Clark doll studies of the 1940s. Given a choice between a white doll and a black one, nearly 70 percent of the black children studied picked the white doll as the nice doll. This choice of white over black, Drs. Kenneth and Mamie Clark concluded, demonstrated the extent to which institutionalized racism and segregation had made black children reject their own color and kind.

Although the Clark studies, which played an important role in *Brown v. Board of Education*, have since come under fire, the concept of internalized racism remains compelling. This is especially true for middle-class black intellectuals, whose success is often regarded as an embarrassment of riches that separates them from the poverty of "the people." We damn such intellectuals and all those judged insufficiently black as "Oreos" and "Uncle Toms," while celebrating as "authentic" others we consider to be down with the people, "keeping it real." I don't mean to make light of the disturbing disparities between middle- and upper-class blacks and the masses of African Americans who struggle in not-so-quiet desperation, but it's a telling commentary on our understanding of class and cultural identity that "the people"—those who qualify as authentically black—are always and forever the folk, "the Negro farthest down," Zora Neale Hurston called them: Sally Ann, James Henry, Uncle Billy. Setting yourself apart from them and the vernacular tradition they represent is the same as denying your own black soul.[25]

I came to consider it so myself and was embarrassed by the uplift philosophy of my parents and my own youthful rejection of the minstrels, mammies, maids, coons, and toms by whom popular culture demarcates and stigmatizes blackness. For some time, my attempts as a child to define myself against such images haunted me as a kind of double fault, a shameful shame that ate at the core of my black identity and challenged my credibility as an authentic African American. Revisiting Shirley Temple, Sally Ann, and Uncle Billy later in my intellectual life, I came to a different conclusion, however. To identify resistance to mass-mediated blackness as internalized racism is to complete the racist move television and popular culture enact. Such a diagnosis confuses the reductive fictions of the screen with the complicated, contradictory lives of real black people. It implicitly accepts the assumption that "black" is only one thing, an essence that is at its heart stigmatic, criminal, comic: Stepin Fetchit but not Paul Robeson; or Young Thug but not Jessye Norman; or Bojangles tap dancing for massa as a house slave on film but not Misty Copeland leaping across the stage at the Metropolitan Opera House as a principal dancer with the American Ballet Theatre.

The real power of whiteness—the actual evidence of internalized racism—is how readily many of us accept the notion that authentic blackness is first and finally vernacular, stigmatic. For every other racial or ethnic group that has come or been brought to these shores, surviving in America, succeeding in America—indeed becoming American—has meant embracing the American Dream of life, liberty, and the pursuit of wealth and property. For blacks, however, buying into the American Dream is considered selling out. Unfortunately, this understanding of authentic blackness depends on an essentialism as pathological as the ridiculous, stigmatic blackness used to affirm Shirley Temple's whiteness, beauty, and superiority more than three quarters of a century ago.

Hollywood's habit of using stigmatic blackness to brighten whiteness is such a permanent fixture, such a basic trick of the trade, that one hardly has to turn to the fictions of yesteryear to find black people laid low or to see the Shirley Temple kind of technicolored coding written on the bodies of children. Just the other night, I happened upon an episode of the TNT drama *Major Crimes*, with the trendy title "#FindKaylaWeber" (air date December 14, 2015). As ripped-from-the-headlines police procedurals are inclined to do, the show appropriates an all-too-terrible true story about a five-year-old black girl in Des Moines, Iowa, who overdosed on morphine belonging to her mother's drug-dealer boyfriend. The TV rendition moves the tragedy to Los Angeles, melodramatically embellishes it to make it even more appalling and sensational, and presents it to the viewing public as prime-time holiday entertainment.

In the TNT dramatization, the Los Angeles police department's Major Crimes squad (the successor to *The Closer*'s Priority Homicide Division) finds the dead body of the five-year-old daughter of a black professional baseball player (Kamal Angelo Bolden) stuffed in a garbage bag inside a cardboard box in the refrigerator of a black drug dealer's den of iniquity, located, of course, in Compton, the heart of the gangbanger ghetto. Reported missing by her mother (Daniella Alonso) and presumed kidnapped, the child, the detectives determine, actually died at home of a cocaine overdose after she ingested some of "mama's special sugar," which the mother inexplicably kept hidden from her clueless husband in, of all places, her five-year-old daughter's bedroom closet. The kidnap scenario is a ruse concocted by the family's loyal black bodyguard with the aid of the equally loyal drug dealer—both child-hood friends of the dad, who evidently got straight outta Compton thanks to the baseball-pitching arm that carried him from the hood to the Majors. His two homeboys conspired to cover up the daughter's awful but acciden-tal death because, as the bodyguard explains, the mother begged him to help, and he thought a kidnapping would play better than the truth that the daughter ODed on her mother's drugs, and the mother was too stoned and inebriated to notice until it was too late.

To make the already unspeakable even more so, the writers add the telling detail that it's not the first time the five-year-old ingested her mother's dope: once before she had sprinkled some of mama's special sugar on her cereal. That time, the bodyguard rushed her to the team doctor, who pumped her stomach. In California and every other state, doctors are mandatory report-ers of suspected child abuse and/or neglect, but the writers don't bother with such a detail. Their fictional physician apparently didn't report the overdose to the authorities or even to the father. In fact, as written, all of this—the wife's drug use and criminal child neglect, the overdoses, the stomach pumping, the death, the cover-up—all occur unbeknownst to the paterfamilias, who functions in the narrative much like the traditional absent black father. He's not the classic hit (that)-and-run baby daddy, but the reason given for his absenteeism isn't exactly noble either. He was hiding out in a hotel room the night his daughter died, after secretly undergoing surgery on his pitching arm, which he wants kept under wraps so as not to jeopardize his marketability as a free agent. In other words, he plans to defraud whatever team attempts to sign him.

When the whole truth comes out about his daughter's death and his wife's role in it, the pitcher dad is so distraught and enraged that he slaughters his junkie spouse. The detectives find her dead body sprawled on the back patio of the couple's rented mansion, her left hand covered with a white powdery substance and resting in more of the same scattered on the concrete beside her bloodied body. No doubt we are meant to surmise from this final scene that the grieving father snapped when he came upon his wife sneaking yet another snort of the nose candy that killed their kid.

Lauding the show as well-done high drama, viewers gave "#FindKay-laWeber" high ratings online. As TV shows go, the acting may deserve the applause, but the episode as a whole left me sick to my stomach and sleepless in Providence. I know it was inspired by actual events. I know we can't bury our heads in the sand about the terrible things done unto children by adults, but what's the point of a plot that puts a black girl in a garbage bag and throws her away, denying her any semblance of loving care or dignity even in death. Typecast with characters of color as the villains and victims, the episode doesn't just say keep your drugs out of the reach of children but, rather, you can take the folk out of the ghetto, but you can't take the ghetto out of the folk. Even rich and famous and living well among the civilized, colored people are animals who kill their own.

A black friend of mine who also saw the show read the mother as a white trophy wife and said she therefore wasn't troubled by her depiction as a deceitful, drunken, drug-addicted Medea figure. That may be exactly the kind of misreading the producers angled for in casting the light-skinned, racially ambiguous Latina, Daniella Alonso, as this worst of all possible monster moms, rather than an actress as phenotypically "black" as the other characters, including the dad and the dead daughter. I suspect the showrunners had some sense of the racial politics in play in such a dark drama with dark principals and what a dark-skinned black woman in such a contemptible role would mean on the screen. Alonso is a beautiful, smart, talented actress, to be sure, but here she is deployed as the default repository of a racialized, overwrought, overwritten depravity so terrible that Hollywood didn't quite dare give it a politically incorrect blackface. Brown, then, becomes the safe black.

I think we need to question the racial and gender politics of the texts and subtexts and the color-coding with which television bombards us—all the more so when Hollywood deliberately blurs the lines between fact and fiction, real and reel, including the law-and-disorder, get-away-with-murder implication that the mother couldn't be punished by the courts for her heinous crime. The drug-dealer boyfriend in the Iowa case pled guilty to multiple charges, including child endangerment resulting in death, and was sentenced to sixty-five years in prison; the mother also pled guilty and was sentenced to forty years. Terrible as the true story is, "#FindKaylaWeber" goes over the top and out of its way to ugly-up and blacken a tragedy it turns into entertainment. If I blogged or tweeted or posted on Facebook, I would be railing online about this episode instead of just talking back to my TV set, not least because at a time when we are insisting to the world that Black Lives

Matter, and critical race theorists like Kimberlé Crenshaw are spearheading national campaigns to improve the lives of black youth through initiatives such as #BlackGirlsMatter, we cannot afford to abide in silence televisual narratives that make a mockery of those efforts and suggest that black communities don't take care of their children.[26]

But the issue for me isn't just one episode of a single series, which, after all, I do understand is fiction. It's the pattern; it's popular culture's propensity for using blackness as a kind of bleaching agent that makes white bright, beautiful, benevolent, heroic, even (or perhaps especially) in narratives that are putatively about the lives and lived experiences of black people: *The Cotton Club, Mississippi Burning, Glory, Ghosts of Mississippi, Driving Miss Daisy, The Blind Slide, The Help.* I was struck—stricken really—by how much "#FindKaylaWeber" reminds me of a troubling tale about another disposable black daughter that haunts me anew every time I see it listed in the onscreen TV guide: the 1996 film *A Time to Kill* (based on John Grisham's 1988 novel).[27] In its underlying message that even in the new Old South a blue-eyed blonde girl is worth more than a brown-eyed black one, the motion picture delivers its message through an opposition of light and dark—Shirley Temple and Sally Ann—that revisits, revises, and perhaps critiques the stigmatic color-coding of its celluloid precursors.

At the outset of the film, Tonya Hailey (played by RaeVen Kelly), a ten-year-old black girl, is brutally raped, beaten, and left for dead by two good old boys of the Confederacy. The rapists are caught and due to stand trial, but afraid they'll get off lightly, the girl's father, Carl Lee Hailey (Samuel L. Jackson), shoots and kills them in the courthouse, also unintentionally wounding a white deputy (Chris Cooper), who loses a leg as a result. Predictably, the ensuing drama revolves not around the brutalized black child, left sterile by the assault, or even her father who is tried for murder before an all-white jury, but around the trials and tribulations of Jake Brigance (Matthew Mc-Conaughey), the young white lawyer who agrees to represent Carl Lee. For defending a Negro who dared to kill two white men, Brigance and his family and his white law student associate (Sandra Bullock) have visited upon them all manner of Klan-inspired plagues, from death threats and attempted assassinations to a flaming cross on the lawn and the loss of the Brigance home to arson. Carl Lee and his family, meanwhile—the more likely victims of Klan violence—are left alone to their own devices.

But if it is the white man of courage and conscience who holds the lion's share of heroism in the film, it is his white daughter, Hannah, who ultimately, if subliminally, serves as the film's cause célèbre. We see remarkably little of Tonya, the black girl whose rape merely advances the plot, and we hear almost nothing of her voice beyond her screams of "Daddy, Daddy" as she's being raped and tortured at the beginning of the film. She is local color, as mute yet meaningful as Sally Ann in *The Littlest Rebel*. And as with Sally Ann, her narrative significance lies in the contrast she provides between deficient, stigmatic blackness and perfect-10 whiteness, between the sullied, peed-on black daughter, whose very survival annuls her rape, and the pure, true-woman white daughter, whose rape (by black men) is ever threatened in the southern white male imagination but is always forestalled by her own virtue and her father's protection. Tonya's relative absence in the film is complemented by Hannah's "ain't-she-the-sweetest-thing" presence. When Tonya's assault is referred to, it is often Hannah's blonde hair and blue eyes to which the camera shifts.

The purpose of the shifting subject comes fully into focus in the final moments of the trial and the film. On the eve of what looks like a conviction, Carl Lee tells Brigance that in order to save him, he must think exactly like what he is: a white man. It's good advice, but the strategy that ultimately wins the case comes from Brigance's estranged wife, who has come back to town to tell her husband that she no longer blames him for bringing the wrath of the Klan down on the family, putting their lives in jeopardy and leaving them homeless. "It's not your fault," she says. "You didn't kill those boys. You were trying to make it right. I know that now. . . . You took this case because if those boys had hurt Hannah, you would have killed them yourself."

Inspired by his wife's words and the visage of his own angelic daughter, Brigance asks the members of the jury to close their eyes as he describes in lurid detail how a little girl walking home from the grocery store was dragged into a field by two men, tied up, raped repeatedly, pelted with full beer cans thrown so hard they tore her flesh to the bone; how she was beaten, urinated on, and hung by the neck from a tree; how when the hanging branch broke under her weight, she was picked up, thrown into the back of their truck, and then tossed from a bridge into the creek thirty feet below. The unspeakable things done unto this little girl can only be spoken because she is nonwhite, but as Grisham brilliantly frames the tale, even all this violence visited upon such a child is not enough to justify a black man's killing two white men. The secret to winning the case lies in what Jake Brigance and all the other men, including the black father, share with the wounded white deputy who, despite his amputated leg, magnanimously bears Carl Lee no malice, because, as he tells the courtroom, "He did what I would have done. I have a daughter." What the men share are the property rights and responsibilities of patriarchs, which *seem* to trump race. The daughter is property, and she must be protected, avenged. This, after all, is what white men like the deputy—sons of the South—have done for generations: protect their women. In the daughter's name, black men have been lynched, castrated, and burned alive. (One thinks of the torture and terrorizing of fourteen-year-old Emmett Till in the name of a white woman.) But what constitutes "a time to kill" is not the brutal violation of a living, breathing, feeling black girl but the imaginary assault on a mythic white one.

Close your eyes and see all the horror done to Carl Lee's daughter, Brigance instructs the jury in his summation. "Can you see her? Her raped, beaten, broken body—soaked in their urine, soaked in their semen, soaked in her blood. Can you see her?" The camera pans the courtroom, pausing on face after face, as all await the lawyer's last words: "I want you to picture that little girl," he says. "Now imagine she's white." All eyes snap open, as if suddenly called to attention. *Now imagine she's white.*

The invocation of the white child, who is Shirley Temple perfect, accomplishes what the image of the imperfect, violated black daughter—Tonya, Sally Ann, Pecola—could not. In a calculated way that doesn't have to speak its name, the film embeds Carl Lee in a master narrative of female protection and makes him complicit with the Klan in defending *white* women against what traditionally has been the sexual threat posed by black men. In other words, *A Time to Kill* uses a black man to justify lynch law and the very white male vigilante justice of which black men have been the most frequent victims. What or, rather, who gets lost in this translation is the black girl whose badly abused body is erased even as her story is appropriated by men. The substitution of a white daughter for colored is a historical necessity, of course, because, despite the irony of her married name, Shirley Temple can never be black.

Chapter 4

Interracial *Loving*

SEXLESSNESS IN THE SUBURBS OF THE 1960S

To get to a place where you could love anything you chose—
not to need permission for desire—well now, *that* was freedom.

—TONI MORRISON, *Beloved* (1987)

June 12, 2017, marked the fiftieth anniversary of *Loving v. Virginia*, the landmark U.S. Supreme Court case that nullified Virginia's antimiscegenation
statutes, including the "Racial Integrity Act" of 1924, along with similar laws
banning intermarriage in fifteen other states. The Racial Integrity Act, which
the court ruled unconstitutional, not only prohibited but also criminalized
marriage between persons the Commonwealth classified as "white," in this
case the plaintiff Richard Loving, and those it defined as "colored," Mr. Loving's African and Native American wife and coplaintiff, Mildred Jeter Loving. Operating at the intersection of racism and eugenics, the Virginia act
under which the Lovings had been snatched from their marital bed, tried,
convicted, and sentenced to a year in jail (suspended on the condition that
they leave the state for twenty-five years) fell back on the "one-drop rule" in
defining "colored" as "every person in whom there is ascertainable any Negro
blood," as well as "every person . . . having one fourth or more of American
Indian blood."[1]

As one of the last strongholds of *de jure*, or state-sanctioned, segregation, miscegenation laws like Virginia's, some dating back to the seventeenth

century, were enacted not simply as a "statutory scheme" to prevent inter-marriage, the Justices concluded, but specifically "as a measure designed to maintain White Supremacy." Speaking for a unanimous court in *Loving* in 1967, as he had in *Brown* thirteen years earlier, Chief Justice Earl Warren once again affirmed the unconstitutionality of "measures which restrict the rights of citizens on account of race." "Under our constitution," he wrote, invoking the due process and equal protection clauses of the Fourteenth Amendment, "the freedom to marry, or not marry, a person of another race resides with the individual and cannot be infringed by the State."[2] So saying, the Warren court delivered another in a series of civil rights rulings that tore at the foun-dations of Jim Crow segregation.[3]

Although inspired by the Civil Rights Act of 1964 to seek their own legal remedy in what became *Loving v. Virginia*, the plaintiffs in this momentous case were by no means civil rights activists like Rosa Parks. They were simply a white man and a black woman who had grown up together, dated, and fallen in love in a rural part of eastern Virginia, where race mixing, intermarriage, and multiracial families were a far more typical and established part of south-ern country life than in my own northern, much more segregated hometown. Herein lies the ironic distinction between the de jure segregation of the South and the de facto segregation of the North. An interracial union like that of the Lovings, who had married in 1958 in the District of Columbia where they could do so legally, would not have been a felony in the Commonwealth of Massachusetts as it was in the Commonwealth of Virginia, but in the small, overwhelmingly white town of my youth, where segregation was custom rather than law, the intimate mixing of the races that *Loving* sanctioned was all but unheard of.

Save for the color of my skin, I was the quintessential New England coun-try girl next door in the 1960s when the Lovings were fighting for the right to live together as husband and wife. There have been times I've wished for and even invented a more exotic past, claiming my birthplace Brooklyn as home or Boston rather than the tiny town of East Bridgewater, with one traffic light and almost no black people. But whenever I see the hood dramatized and demonized on TV and contemplate what my own life in the inner city might have been, I'm grateful for the move to the country my parents made in 1952, although it thrust us into a lion's den of a different kind and color.

Growing up as lone black spots in a sea of whiteness wasn't easy. I think it may have been even harder for my brothers than for me, especially for Adrian, who was the first to enter the small-town school system where in 1952 no one looked like him and who not only paved the path for Danny and me but also literally fought his way through years of bullying and racist taunts with his fists. I wonder now how much of what would trouble my big brother later in life and leave him dead of a heart attack at forty-six stemmed not just from the Du Boisian double consciousness of always seeing yourself through the jaundiced eyes of the dominant culture but from living the literal trauma of difference, from being, even as a small child, ever under assault. For decades I have gazed with tearful sympathy and admiration at the iconic photographs of little six-year-old Ruby Bridges being escorted by federal marshals to and from the William Frantz Elementary School in New Orleans, which she single-handedly integrated in 1960. But until recently, I hadn't thought nearly as much about what it must have been like for my own seven-year-old brother sent off alone to a white elementary school where some were welcoming but many were not. I have never forgotten the crushing blow my own happy little soul sustained when a white girl named Cookie called me a nigger on my first day of school in 1955. I didn't know what the word meant, but from the reaction of the other kids—some of whom quickly came to my defense—I knew it was bad and dreaded going back to school.

"Sticks and stone may break my bones," my mother would tell us, "but names will never hurt me." I'm not so sure, but one way or another, my brothers and I rolled with the punches, throwing one every now and then but mostly taking the consequences of our suburban existence on the chin. But dating and certain other normal aspects of teenage social life posed a particular set of problems for black kids living in isolation in small towns like ours. I was popular enough in high school to be elected class treasurer three years in a row, but my popularity was to the playground born and rarely saw the parlor. On the spicier side of sociability, I collected my share of wolf whistles, catcalls, and sexist taunts, sometimes with a decidedly racial edge, especially from older boys who didn't know me and were prone to being crude and disrespectful in ways my own classmates after a time never were. One afternoon when I was shooting hoops in the gym by myself before basketball practice, I took the lady's way out and pretended not to hear an older kid up in the balcony above the bleachers follow up a wolf whistle with the quip to his buddy, "She almost makes me wish I was colored." As insults and lefthanded compliments go, it was rumored that some of the boys in my class year were—shall we say—studying the female form and had voted on which girls had the best figures. I never did know whether there really was such a poll, but supposedly I fared in the top five—a dubious honor at best and one that did me absolutely no good. I could have been crowned Miss America, and I still wouldn't have been a date-worthy object of desire to the white male student body at a time when and a place where big hearts were ruled by small-mindedness, and interracial dating wasn't even within the realm of the conceivable, on either side of the color line.

Although both my brothers would eventually date—and in Adrian's case marry—outside the race, I was no more interested in dating white boys in the 1960s than they were in dating me. Even in those states where interracial romance wasn't illegal, as it was in about a third of the country during my high school years, it was the ultimate not-in-my-backyard of race relations for most segments of the populace and a topic TV didn't dare touch in black and white. Occasionally in westerns, a white frontiersman might deign to homestead with a Native woman invariably called a "squaw," which turned the term pejorative. And an episode of *Perry Mason*, "The Case of the Blushing Pearls" (1959), proposed but promptly derailed the union of a white man and a Japanese woman, shifting the would-be bride into a more suitable relationship with a man of her own kind (played by the Japanese American actor George Takei, the future Lt. Sulu on *Star Trek*).

According to the social historian Renee Romano, opposition to black-white intermarriage was almost universal among white Americans. "At the beginning of the 1960s," she writes in *Race Mixing: Black-White Marriage in Postwar America* (2003), "perhaps 5 percent of whites nationwide claimed to favor interracial marriage," which little changed with the decriminalization of such unions in 1967.[4] Among African Americans, the idea of mixed marriages received mixed reviews. Many blacks supported intermarriage in principle as a civil right, Romano explains, but were often less enthusiastic about it in practice.[5] My parents believed in live and let live—even live and help live—where other people's lives were concerned. They would have sided with the Lovings if they had paid attention to the case, but at the same time, it was so well understood within our race-proud household that my brothers and I would partner with our own that interracial dating wasn't even a topic of discussion. What was a colored boy or girl of courting age to do, then, when race-appropriate options of the opposite sex were few and far between or nonexistent?

Well-meaning parents in black families like mine, dotted throughout the predominantly white suburban hamlets of southeastern Massachusetts, attempted to solve the dating dilemma for their offspring by organizing their own informal escort service. Parents with boys would lend out their sons to accompany the daughters of families with girls to various functions and vice versa. Tall, dark, and handsome, Adrian was in high demand for escort duty in the early '60s. How Danny—quite a catch as well—managed to escape

FIGS. 4.1–4.4 Six-year-old Ruby Bridges with her U.S. Marshal escort; Adrian, about eight, integrating EB Central Elementary School circa 1953; Ann about seven, circa 1956, with flyaway pigtails that fascinated her classmates and wearing a sweater knitted by Mom; Danny in the first grade at Central Elementary School.

being similarly deployed neither of us is certain. He entered high school in 1967, the fall after I graduated. By that time, there was a handful or more of colored kids in the school system—a couple of whom did not so identify and avoided us like the plague, because we knew their relatives with the same surname who considered themselves very black. Danny, then, was the only one of us to have a few other black kids in his class year, as well as in the other grades, so perhaps the lending practice had outlived its necessity by the time he came of an age to be pressed into service.

Much to my humiliation, my parents insisted on securing escorts for both my junior and senior proms. I didn't know the handsome young man dispatched by prior parental arrangement to accompany me to my junior prom in the spring of 1966, but he was older—a sophomore or junior at Boston University. The fact that my "date" was not only a college man, but also elegantly outfitted in a cool Madras tuxedo that made the other males in plain white dinner jackets seem underdressed, elevated me from wallflower to femme fatale in the wide eyes of classmates who had never before seen me with a male being. Me, it merely made so nervous and self-conscious that I could barely speak, let alone dance and be charming. With all due respect and gratitude to the very nice guy who was stuck with a nervous kid on his arm for an evening, the only thing worse than going to the prom with a stranger your parents picked out for you would be going to the prom with your parents. Oh, yes, and there was that, too. It was the school's practice to invite the parents of the class officers to the proms. Some parents had the good sense to decline politely. Mine did not. There's a picture in the yearbook of the two of them in tuxedo and gown, happily chatting with a group of my classmates who were no doubt thrilled to be talking with my parents rather than their own.

Everything TV tells us about the generation gap dictates that I have to hate the fact my mother and father crashed my junior prom. I didn't. I was proud of them, glad to be their daughter, and thrilled by the chance to show them off to my classmates. They were the belles of the ball—the most glamorous couple on the dance floor. My mother often said that as a small child I had once asked her, "Mummy, why did you marry Daddy? You're so different." I don't remember posing the question out loud, but it's true that I used to wonder why my mother—so strong-willed, level-headed, and independent, with a dowry wrought of her own hard work and economy—succumbed to the charms of Adrian duCille of all men, a Jamaican immigrant in the United States on a temporary work visa, with no money and no particular prospects. The match was all the more mysterious to me because my mother talked all the time about the man she said she should have married—Johnny Davis, the

FIG. 4.5 My arranged "date" and me at the senior prom in 1967.

FIG. 4.6 Yearbook photo of Mom and Dad at the junior prom in 1966.

soldier she was engaged to when my father swept her off her feet and rushed her to the altar. She talked so much about this other man, in fact, that I do remember saying to her once, "But Mummy, if you married Johnny Davis, we wouldn't be your children." She dismissed my interjection as nonsense and insisted that, of course, we would still be her children. I was a little girl and trusted my mother in all things, but somehow I knew that couldn't be right. It couldn't be true that I would be the same person if I had a different father.

Then one day I came across my parents' wedding picture and my father's passport in the top drawer of the dresser in their bedroom. I know it sounds shallow, but once I found the wedding portrait and the passport with a photo of my father as the devastatingly handsome young man he was when they met shortly before Christmas 1944, I wondered no longer. I had always thought my mother remarkably beautiful, but it hadn't hit me until then what a handsome man my father was. He was also charming and funny, well read and well spoken; so suddenly their spontaneous combustion made a certain kind of quixotic sense. Their wedding picture, which had been water damaged during the months we lived in the damp basement of our homemade house, was never displayed, never seen outside their dresser drawer, but I was fascinated by it, especially by the curious look of almost sad uncertainty on my mother's shyly beautiful face. She seems so much more vulnerable in that wedding portrait than I ever saw her in my childhood. I would peek at the photograph every chance I got, and years later I would use it as the cover of my first book, appropriately titled *The Coupling Convention* (1993). Oddly enough, I hadn't really thought about it before, but it seems obvious to me now that my almost lifelong fascination with the institution of marriage began with my curiosity about my parents' union and the secrets that lie hidden within that picture taken February 18, 1945, less than two months after they met.

Patty Wilson, who sat in front of me in sixth grade, often paid me the great compliment of telling me I was pretty. Once when my parents came to our classroom to pick me up for an early release, Patty turned around and said to me, "Your mother's so pretty—but not as pretty as you are." I didn't believe her. No one was more beautiful to me than my mother, but, still, living so far outside the dominant standards of beauty as I did as a lone colored kid among comely, datable cheerleaders and majorettes, Patty's compliments were a kindness that meant more to me than she could have imagined. It was something I didn't hear often and certainly not at home where the rule was "pretty is as pretty does," and the word itself was never to be said to me or about me. If someone made the mistake of suggesting I was pretty or some semblance thereof, a correction would immediately ensue: "She's *nice*," my

FIG. 4.7 Mom and Dad's 1945 wedding portrait as the cover of my first book, *The Coupling Convention* (1993).

mother would say pointedly. "She's a *nice* girl." "Nice" was good, pure, and safe; "pretty" was a vanity and a vulnerability from which my mother was determined to save me.

For my mother, vanity—primping, preening, trying to be cute—was the road to perdition, the pathway to seduction and sins of the flesh. More than once I was told to stop primping in front of the mirror when I was merely brushing my teeth at the bathroom sink or combing my hair. Harsh as it seems, I understand now what I didn't then: it was my mother's way of promoting qualities other than the physical and of protecting me from the gaze of men and what she knew too well went with it.

She need not have worried. Her de-vaining strategy was aided and abetted by location, location, location. In a land without temptation, I didn't suffer the classic tensions of teenage girls torn between the nice of their home training or religious teaching and the naughty of their hearts' desires. Nice was my only option. I wore well "the mask that grins and lies," always ready with a joke or a pun, yet undercover carrying my own blackface version of the body baggage that troubles far too many teens.[6] Tall, lean, and fit, I imagined myself large, heavy, and awkward—mortified since eighth grade that at upward of 5′8″ I weighed the same 140 pounds as Bobby Demers, the white boy alphabetically ahead of me in line for the school's annual weigh-ins. In actuality, I was at the time the ideal weight for my height and frame, but I was impervious to my own perfection. When you're a lone black girl in a small white town and you don't get to have the normal experiences of dating and the like that everyone else is having, you don't necessarily own the intellectual wherewithal to chalk it up to circumstance. Rather, your exclusion becomes your fault, a sign of something wrong with you. You internalize your isolation, in other words, and become ugly in your own eyes.

But, oddly enough, not consciously unhappy. My erotic life was well lived within my adolescent imagination. Desire was displaced onto TV characters and the star-crossed lovers of Jane Austen and the Brontë sisters. I saw through Darcy's pride and fell for his better self long before Elizabeth Bennet strolled the halls of Pemberley thinking, "And of this place . . . I might have been mistress!" And I was far more carried away with wondering whether the TV detective Joe Mannix would fall for his faithful Girl Friday, Peggy Fair, than with who would fall for me, knowing all the while that since Mannix was white and Peggy was black, there was little hope Hollywood would let love happen.

At almost exactly the same moment that I was graduating from high school in June of 1967 and *Mannix* was in production for its fall debut, Richard and Mildred Loving were winning the lawsuit argued on their behalf before the highest court in the land and finally securing, eight years after their marriage, what should have been their inalienable right to live together in their Virginia home as husband and wife. Although soon and very soon, a drunk driver would rob them of the chance to grow old together, this fatefully named couple felled one of the last standing giants of Jim Crow segregation and changed the course of American history with no larger weapon than their love for each other.

Inspired, perhaps, by the couple's love story and legal victory, television made its first furtive forays into black-and-white romance in the fall of 1968 with a lip smack heard round the world. The now famous mixed-race kiss wasn't between Mike Connors and Gail Fisher as Joe Mannix and Peggy Fair, which I was waiting for, but between William Shatner as Captain James T. Kirk and Nichelle Nichols as Lieutenant Uhura of the starship *Enterprise*, which I missed entirely. So it is that these two characters from the short-lived but still enduring NBC science fiction series *Star Trek* (1966–1969) became the odd couple credited, rightly or wrongly, with sharing the first interracial kiss in U.S. television history.

Although I can't cite chapter and verse, I suspect a few other performers of color—Asians, Hispanics, and Latinos—may have shared onscreen salutations with white actors before Kirk and Uhura smooched, and '60s television (especially westerns) definitely depicted intimate relationships between white men and women of Native or Mexican ancestry. Much of the tension of the border drama *The High Chaparral* (NBC, 1967–1971), for example, revolves around the arranged marriage of convenience between the recently widowed white settler Big John Cannon (Leif Erickson) and Victoria Montoya (Linda Cristal), the beautiful, headstrong daughter of the powerful Mexican ranchero Don Sebastián Montoya (played by the Jamaican-born, mixed-race actor Frank Silvera). Today I see glaringly obvious issues of race, gender, and nation in the way notions of property and peace are negotiated through the bartered body of a Mexican woman, but in 1967 tracking whether Big John would ever get over his first wife's death and fall in love with Victoria who, like Madame Butterfly, of course, loves the white man who scorns her, was the only reason to watch the show, as far as I was concerned.

As kissing the Othered goes, British television has staked an earlier claim than American TV with the rediscovery of *You in Your Small Corner*, the Jamaican playwright Barry Reckford's sensual drama about an intimate relationship between a middle-class West Indian student and a white Cockney factory worker, which aired live on ITV in 1962. CNN aired a clip of the black male and white female leads sharing what is now believed to be the first interracial kiss in TV history worldwide when footage of the televised play was found in the British Film Institute's National Archive in 2015.[7] As more lost or forgotten footage is uncovered, this claim, too, may be upstaged by earlier examples.

Back on the home front, YouTube's candidate for first interracial buss is a clip of Sammy Davis Jr. and Nancy Sinatra exchanging a quick, friendly peck that just grazes the lips during a variety show, *Movin' with Nancy*, that aired in December 1967, almost a full year before Kirk and Uhura famously locked lips in the "Plato's Stepchildren" episode of *Star Trek*, which first aired on November 22, 1968.[8] Nevertheless, their out-of-this-world *beso* is generally

FIG. 4.8 William Shatner and Nichelle Nichols as Capt. Kirk and Lt. Uhura, puckering up in the "Plato's Stepchildren" episode of *Star Trek* (1968).

recognized as the first interracial kiss in the annals of American television history.

By their own accounts, Shatner and Nichols were so ready and willing to go boldly where no white TV actor and black actress had gone before that they fought for the scene over the objections of nervous studio executives, even though the two of them would later disagree about whether their lips actually touched in the scene that aired. Nichols claims they did; Shatner swears they did not, insisting in his autobiography that "the network got their way" and it was the "no-contact kiss" that made it to the airwaves. "For that reason," he writes, "the widely held assumption that *Star Trek* features the first interracial kiss in the history of television is absolutely untrue."[9]

What are we to make of Shatner's denials, especially since he says that when asked whether he would *mind* kissing Nichols, he replied, "Mind? What, are you kidding? You're gonna *pay* me to kiss Nichelle? What a job!"[10] (What a question.) Shatner's contradiction is all the more confusing because Nichols makes him the hero of the encounter, crediting him with passionately kissing her in the first shot—to the shock of the director and horror of the studio executives looking on—and then outsmarting the "suits" by wasting time and takes and then sabotaging the final no-contact take by crossing his eyes in a way that only the cameraman could see during the shoot but which showed up in the dailies when it was too late to correct without the expense of reshooting the entire scene.

Perhaps Shatner is just being a gentleman who doesn't want to kiss and tell the world. But whether or not their lips touched, plotwise kissing each other—as any true Trekkie or media student knows—was not something their characters did voluntarily. Rather, as per the story line, Kirk and Uhura are under the influence of mind control, telekinetically manipulated like marionettes by the alien inhabitants of a distant planet. Seen in its true light, the famous, daring kiss actually came with the not-so-subliminal message that even in the distant future, in a land far, far away, a white man would have to be out of his mind to kiss a black woman.

No fan of science fiction at the time, to my great shame, I missed the famous Uhura-Kirk kiss during *Star Trek*'s original broadcast and had to wait for reruns. As I revealed earlier, the black-and-white TV duo I rooted for on a show I did watch regularly was the team of Peggy and Joe in the detective drama *Mannix*. Peggy Fair, a police officer's widow and single mother with a young son, was dedicated, efficient, and as loyal to her boss Joe Mannix, a private detective and friend of her late husband, as Della Street was to Perry Mason. And like Della, Peggy ran her boss's office, did his legwork, and even patched him up when he got hit on the head and knocked out or otherwise beaten up by bad guys, as he did in almost every episode. Hopeless romantic that TV made me, I saw or perhaps imagined meaningful, admiring, loving looks flash from faithful Peggy to her seemingly oblivious boss. But if one can be both a romantic and a realist simultaneously, I understood that erotic love between black and white was as unlikely on network television as it was in my hometown, even in the age of *Loving*.

I would discover decades later when perusing *Primetime Blues* that I was hardly alone in reading an undertone of interracial desire into the detective drama. Donald Bogle also notes "romantic undercurrents" floating between Peggy Fair and Joe Mannix and points to a particularly suggestive episode from 1970, "The World Between," in which each character exhibits jealousy over the other's love interest.[11] But since the new woman in Joe's life is also in his office attempting to fill Peggy's secretarial shoes while she's in the hospital, and the new African man in Peggy's life would take her away to the Motherland, there are certainly less starry-eyed ways viewers could interpret the characters' possessive, petulant behavior.

Similarly, when a private plane carrying Mannix to meet a client goes down in the wilderness in "Climb a Deadly Mountain" (s7, E3), an episode from 1973 guest-starring Greg Morris as an escaped convict who saves Joe's life, Peggy acts and is treated like the worried wife in waiting. Joe's police detective friend appears with airline tickets for the two of them to fly to the crash vicinity, correctly assuming Peggy will of course lock up the office, leave her young son behind, and rush off to be near her imperiled employer. When Joe is found alive and reunited with Peggy at the search party's base camp, there are tears aplenty from her but no kiss or comforting embrace—just Joe's reassuring hand on Peg's heaving shoulder and his tongue-in-cheek apology for not phoning home as he earlier promised the "little mother" he would. Of course, the very fact that Joe refers to Peggy as the "little mother" rather than the wifely epithet "little woman" again allows the viewer to see the character as mammy rather than mistress and the relationship as maternal rather than amorous. Whatever romantic undercurrents the showrunners might flirt with, Joe Mannix would remain as impervious to any deeper feelings for or from Peggy Fair as Perry Mason was to those of Della Street.

Despite the *Loving* decision in 1967 and *Star Trek*'s star-studded, if not star-crossed kiss in 1968, it was not until the mid-1970s that prime time dared to tackle even a tame version of the erotic black-and-white relationships that are everywhere on TV today. In 1975, Norman Lear's colored offspring George, Louise, and Lionel Jefferson (Sherman Hemsley, Isabel Sanford, and Mike Evans/Damon Evans), the black family first introduced as the Bunkers' next-door neighbors on *All in the Family* in 1971 (although George Jefferson wasn't seen on-screen until 1973), left Archie and Edith behind in Queens and moved on up to their own show *The Jeffersons* and a deee-luxe apartment on the Upper East Side.[12] Their upscale high-rise residence came with a doorman and new neighbors, Tom and Helen Willis (Franklin Cover and Roxie Roker), whose mixed-race marriage and biracial offspring become fodder for George Jefferson's black version of Archie Bunker bigotry. One of the show's signature gags, especially in the earlier seasons, involved George's tormenting the Willises over their not only mixed but in his view mixed-up marriage, throwing around racial slurs like "honky" and "Oreo" and calling the Willis children "zebras," despite the fact that their daughter, Jenny (Berlinda Tolbert), is engaged to and later marries his son, Lionel.

I appreciate the fact that the legendary producer Norman Lear may have wanted to experiment with the blackface of bigotry through the creation of a colored character as ignorant and intolerant as Archie Bunker, but the unfortunate takeaway that white racism and black racism are somehow the same flies in the face of centuries of American history and misrepresents the patriarchal performance of white privilege and power. Only in the Hollywood imagination could these bigotries be covalent. I understand also that, like *All in the Family*, *The Jeffersons* attempted to redress and ridicule racism by reducing ignorance and bigotry to laughable absurdity, but George Jefferson's nouveau riche or, in my father's Jamaican parlance, "never-see-come-see" malapropisms and small-minded, loudmouthed buffoonery were too much in the tradition of *Amos 'n' Andy* for my willing enjoyment of what often seemed to me more silly than funny.

As played by the talented comedian Sherman Hemsley, George Jefferson represents the well-dressed, classed-up side of stigmatic blackness. Like a pig in lipstick, however, Jefferson in an ascot and smoking jacket is still at heart just another low-Other living high off the hog in a luxury apartment with a doorman and a maid. Show after show, the point of the plot is to put the little man back in his place, to bring him low for laughs. The *New York Times* said as much of the "high-strung, irrepressible" George Jefferson, "one of America's most popular television characters," in its obituary for Hemsley who played him: "Each week, his wife or their irreverent maid, Florence (played by Marla Gibbs), would step up to scuttle his wrongheaded schemes or deflate his delusions of grandeur."[13] And grand he is or tries to be. George Jefferson is never humble but often humbled; he perpetually tries to show off but invariably is shown up; he sometimes does the right thing but usually only after the wrong thing backfires in his face. More bluster than brains, he is a mighty mouse of a bop-walking, big-talking black brother man, but he rarely knows what he is talking about. He is, as one of the 1970s' first African American headline characters of a technicolored sitcom, a lovable, laughable twist on the traditional black trickster figure, safe for prime-time public consumption not least because the joke is always on him.

Much as I didn't take to George Jefferson's fish-out-of-water cultural illiteracy and his honky talk and name calling (including dropping the N-word unbleeped), I also couldn't warm up to the favorite targets of his racialized bullying, the Willises—not because Tom Willis is white and Helen is black, but because they didn't work for me as a couple. They have no chemistry and very little character, seeming to exist only as foils for George Jefferson's racial jokes, which is quite different from their promising first appearance as the Jefferson's interracial in-laws-to-be in the engagement party episode from season four of *All in the Family*, where a different pair of actors (Charles Aidman and Kim Hamilton) played the Willises, in my opinion, to greater effect.

Having been insulted by George, who refuses to shake his hand when they're introduced at the party, Aidman as Willis diffuses a tense and potentially volatile confrontation not by trading racist epithets as would come later in *The Jeffersons*, but by simply and graciously asking Mrs. Jefferson to dance, leaving George and Archie Bunker standing alone at the bar, looking like the two racist chumps they are.

If the story line behind *Star Trek*'s famous interracial kiss implied that a white man had to be off his rocker to kiss a black woman, Franklin Cover's Humpty Dumpty portrayal of Tom Willis up against Roxie Roker's more robust performance as his black wife, Helen, suggested that a white guy had to be a wimp to marry a Negress. *The Jeffersons* took the bold step of bringing forth television's first black-white mixed-race couple, but by making Tom Willis the butt of George's barbs (about his waistline as well as his skin color) and the Casper Milquetoast of his marriage, the show made interracial wedlock a cliché-driven punch line. That's the downside of reducing racism to the ridiculous antics and aberrations of a foolish few, as both *The Jeffersons* and *All in the Family* attempted to do: a slapstick or satirical approach to showing up individualized racism offers society an easy way around the larger, deeper, systemic but unacknowledged features of structural racism that cannot be laughed away.

Of course, as the groundbreaking cultural texts they are, both *All in the Family* and *The Jeffersons* necessarily are the subjects of a wealth of rich critical readings that probe the deep structures of the shows' identity politics and racial performance. Lisa Woolfork argues quite rightly, for example, that debates about race staged in these shows "are not just displays of bigotry, they are also ways that each man [Archie Bunker and his son-in-law, Mike Stivic; George Jefferson and his son, Lionel] simultaneously configures boundaries around (and shores up from within) whiteness in *All in the Family* or blackness in *The Jeffersons*."[14] Woolfork's provocative essay, "Looking for Lionel: Making Whiteness and Blackness in *All in the Family* and *The Jeffersons*," uses the figure of Lionel, who is a mediating force in both shows, as "the lens through which to witness the conversations that are a part of racial identity formation" in each series. The ongoing arguments between and among these characters "are not just about racism as a social problem," Woolfork asserts. "They also become a method by which each man . . . as a member of a social group, configures his racial image of himself."[15]

Indeed, but what of the way the audience and the viewer configure or read this racial self-making? Self-making for George Jefferson, it seems to me, is a kind of almost anti-American othering, while for Archie Bunker it's all-in-the-family working-class Americanness. We see just how much this is the case and the consequence in the meteoric rise of Donald Trump as a self-proclaimed man of the silent majority, the beleaguered white people—the Archie Bunkers who, unlike the George Jeffersons and even, in their view, *because* of the George Jeffersons, are denied their piece of the pie. (This dichotomy in temperament is reflected even in the different tempo of each show's theme song: the nostalgia for the past when white "Guys like us we had it made / Didn't need no welfare state / Everybody pulled his weight" of *All in the Family*'s "Those Were the Days," as opposed to the buoyant, upbeat "Movin' on Up" success story of *The Jeffersons*.)

Henry Louis Gates Jr. has suggested that George Jefferson—whom he describes as "pure street, draped in a Brooks Brothers suit"—epitomizes Richard Nixon's "bootstrap variety" of black capitalism, that is, upward mobility born of hard work.[16] Seemingly on the surface, perhaps, but not quite so much if we look closely at Jefferson's carefully crafted Hollywood "blackstory" and interrogate the trickster-like way this struggling, barely blue-collar high school dropout working as a janitor in Harlem became a white-collar millionaire with a penthouse apartment on Park Avenue and a colored maid he treats with as little dignity as the most clueless of his white male counterparts.[17] He parlayed a lucky accident with a city bus into a dry-cleaning empire. His nouveau riche success is achieved, then, less through the bootstrap variety of hard labor we don't see than through the pure street cunning we do. The big break that buys George Jefferson a piece of the pie and enables his American Dream is a lawsuit settlement from the city funded by the tax dollars of the left-out Bunkers, quite literally left behind in Queens.

That said, the miscegenation taboo, which *The Jeffersons* was arguably the first show to challenge, slowly began to be lifted in the latter 1970s, as interracial sex—so long a reality of American life—became a subject to toy with in prime time beyond the crass jokes of George Jefferson. In 1977, ten years after *Loving*, CBS turned to the topic in *A Killing Affair*, a Wednesday night made-for-TV movie, which cast O.J. Simpson and Elizabeth Montgomery as Los Angeles detectives who fall in love and quickly into bed while investigating a series of robbery-homicides. We are supposed to believe they feel deep and abiding affection for each other, I think, but the narrative devotes little time to the development of that affection. Simpson, as Woodrow "Woody" York, a black trigger-happy, "cowboy" beat cop, who shoots a fleeing suspected rapist in the back in the opening scenes of the melodrama, is disciplined for his history of excessive force—four fatal shootings in twelve years—by what plays more like a promotion to plainclothes investigator and a transfer to the Robbery-Homicide Division, where he is partnered with the white, sexy, and sexually liberated veteran detective Vikki Eaton (Montgomery).

Somewhat surprisingly for the times, the couple's racial difference isn't the looming obstacle to coupling that it was in the Stanley Kramer film *Guess Who's Coming to Dinner* (1967) a decade earlier. What makes York and Eaton's sexual relationship illicit isn't so much that he's black and she's white, but that he's married with a twelve-year-old son. His black wife, played by Rosalind Cash, who had shared her own interracial kiss with Charlton Heston in *The Omega Man* in 1971, and his son (a young Todd Bridges) are ultimately the insurmountable obstacles that racial difference is not. Realizing that Woody's wife has a thirteen-year claim on him with which she says she can't complete, Nikki nobly ends the affair and transfers to a precinct in the Valley.

A Killing Affair, with its double entendre title, may have been daring back in the day, starring as it does the beautiful blonde-haired, green-eyed Elizabeth Montgomery, late of the popular sitcom *Bewitched* (ABC, 1964–1972), and the African American football hero and Hall of Fame inductee turned pitchman and actor O.J. Simpson. Beyond the two big names—only one of whom could act—the TV movie is slow, uninspired, and otherwise forgettable. Indeed, I had forgotten it until it was alluded to in the 2016 ESPN miniseries *O.J.: Made in America*. Returning to the forty-year-old made-for-TV movie recently on YouTube, I found my judgment completely undone by my inability to muster the necessary willing suspension of disbelief to see its black male star as anything other than an accused, if acquitted, double murderer, which gives the title, *A Killing Affair*, a bitter irony too terrible to contemplate.

In "A Painful Case," a powerful but disquieting short story from *Dubliners*, James Joyce writes, "Love between man and man is impossible because there must not be sexual intercourse and friendship between man and woman is impossible because there must be sexual intercourse."[18] The first interracial relationship to flourish on TV in the '60s did so precisely because it was between man and man, and there was no sexual intercourse—at least not between the principals. I'm thinking of the adventure series *I Spy* (NBC, 1965–1968), which paired the white actor Robert Culp and the black comedian Bill Cosby as TV's first successful, happily hooked-up, mixed-race couple. Culp and Cosby played secret agents posing undercover as a white touring tennis pro and his black trainer. Cosby's character, Alexander "Scotty" Scott, a Rhodes Scholar, was the brains of the coupling; Culp as Kelly Robinson the tennis jock was the brawn. The actors shared equal billing as costars, and Cosby actually beat out Culp for the Emmy Award for Outstanding Lead Actor in a dramatic series three years in a row, although some might argue that Culp was the better actor—certainly the more experienced.

The show was a hit with my parents, who appreciated Scotty's multilingual, calm-under-fire intelligence. I don't much remember what I thought of the program at the time, except that as a fan of the rising African American tennis great Arthur Ashe, I wanted the roles reversed, with Cosby playing the tennis star and Culp the trainer. But Culp's character, Kelly Robinson, was figured as a player off the court as well as on, and—whatever sexual outrages Cosby is now alleged to have committed—in the 1960s it would not have worked for a brother to play a ladies' man, using his James Bond charms to seduce white women. When Hollywood did reverse the roles in a 2002 movie remake, with Owen Wilson as the white trainer and Eddie Murphy as the black athlete—a boxer in this incarnation, perhaps because, as Roger Ebert quipped at the time, the filmmakers hadn't heard that "there are black tennis stars"—the new *I Spy* was a multimillion-dollar flop, and Murphy and Wilson were nominated for a Golden Razzie for Worst Screen Couple but lost to Adriano Giannini and Madonna for *Swept Away*.[19]

Finally, it's important to note that daytime, too, tested the waters of interracial romance in the 1970s. In the '60s, daytime soap operas—and even the prime-time soap *Peyton Place* (ABC, 1964–1969)—had lived dangerously in casting a few black actors as something other than servants and criminals. The deep-voiced James Earl Jones played a doctor on at least two soaps in the mid-1960s: *Guiding Light*, where first Cicely Tyson then Ruby Dee played his wife, and *As the World Turns*. He also appeared as Dr. Lou Rush in a few episodes of the prime-time medical drama *Dr. Kildare* (NBC, 1961–1966) in 1966. But in the latter 1970s, *Days of Our Lives* (NBC) added a black family, the Grants, to its regular cast and then went rogue with a romantic relationship and eventual engagement between the black daughter, Valerie, and David Banning (Richard Guthrie), one of white Salem's favorite sons of wealth and privilege. In a story line laughably counter to the extreme bed-hopping characteristic of the genre, the betroths were more friends *without* benefits than lovers, barely touching each other in the course of their courtship and saving sex for marriage.

Tina Andrews, the black actress who played Valerie Grant, the bride to be, has said that "scripts would arrive with stage directions like, 'They look at each other warmly—but they do not touch,'" even as a related story line has the celibate, saving-it-for-marriage fiancé deflowering a white gal pal he knocks up.[20] Yet even though the interracial coupling was hands-off, hate mail flowed in. Andrews had read a letter with a hateful message: "'I hope you're not going to let that nigger marry that white boy.'" "Apparently they are not," she added in an interview. "I'm being canned." Guthrie, her costar and onscreen fiancé, also attributed the demise of their romance to negative mail.[21] Not surprisingly for 1977, the wedding was called off four days before the ceremony was to take place, and the bride was packed off to medical school at the historically black Howard University with a full scholarship as a consolation prize for giving up the white guy. NBC claimed the breakup was a predetermined "plot twist" that had nothing to do with the hateful response from viewers.[22] I didn't buy it and in my youthful militancy wrote a fiery op-ed in protest for some local rag. (A few years hence, Dr. Valerie Grant, then played by Diane Sommerfield, returned to Salem for her medical residency and began a relationship with the black police detective Abe Carver [James Reynolds], before being written out of the show in 1982, only to be dramatically resurrected in 2016 as a renowned cardiologist, now played by the veteran actress Vanessa Williams, returned to Salem to save the life of her old flame Abe Carver, while hiding the fact that, despite their presumably celibate relationship, she somehow secretly gave birth to a son by her white former fiancé all those years ago.)

Those were the days. There is plenty of evidence that *Loving* did not quite conquer all. It wasn't until the year 2000 that Alabama, the last state in the Union with antimiscegenation laws still in its constitution, finally lifted its prohibition against interracial marriage, but with more than 40 percent of the voters electing to retain the ban.[23] And Alabama's 40 percent are hardly alone in hanging onto segregationist sentiments. A sweet Cheerios TV commercial featuring a mixed-race couple and their adorable biracial daughter, who covers her father's chest with heart-healthy Cheerios while he's napping, drew such vile, racist responses on YouTube and Facebook when it first aired in 2013 that the comment sections of both sites had to be disabled.[24] Still, given the abundance of much-watched, highly rated shows depicting mixed-race couples, biracial children, multiracial families, and households with two dads or two moms of different races or a mom who used to be a dad—not to mention the graphic, explicitly sexual, extramarital antics of black-and-white intimate pairings like the black crisis manager Olivia Pope and the white Republican president Fitzgerald Grant on *Scandal*—it's hard for me to believe I lived through an era when black and white TV characters could not even touch each other.

Chapter 5

"A Credit to My Race"

ACTING BLACK AND
BLACK ACTING FROM
JULIA TO *SCANDAL*

I sincerely hope I shall always be a credit to my race
and to the motion picture industry.

—HATTIE MCDANIEL, 1940

Although I was neither a hippie nor a New Age flower child in step with the sex, drugs, and rock 'n' roll counterculture of the times, I nevertheless consider the Age of Aquarius—the 1960s and '70s—my era. I came of age in the '60s and into my own in the '70s. And, in its way, so did television. By the end of the first of these two decades, my family was nothing like the tightknit fivesome that had first gathered around the TV set in the early 1950s. My parents' marriage had fizzled, Adrian had been drafted by the army but had joined the air force instead, and I had gone off to college, though not exactly away from home. But the changes wrought within the Sheetrock and knotty-pine walls of our still unfinished homestead were nothing compared to what was happening across the country as the world we knew was turned upside down and inside out, into a new age at once a Great Society and a House Divided. Television helped the country turn the corner into this new age. More than merely an instrument of lighthearted family entertainment, TV became a social and political force that helped the nation develop both political consciousness and social conscience.

When Richard Nixon broke into a sweat facing off against a young, handsome, cool, calm, and collected John F. Kennedy in the first presidential debate ever televised on September 26, 1960, it altered how the American public viewed the incumbent vice president and may have helped lose him the election.[1] When Police Commissioner Eugene "Bull" Connor and the Birmingham Fire Department sicced police dogs on civil rights activists and turned fire hoses full-force on youthful, nonviolent protestors, the broadcast images of black children knocked off their feet and carried flying into the air by the water pressure sent shockwaves across the country and around the globe and generated sympathy and support for what television helped the world see was a movement whose cause was just and time was now.

TV news coverage of the chaos and calamities of the times, from civil rights sit-ins to Black Power protests and cataclysmic events like the bombing of the 16th Street Baptist Church in 1963 and the Watts uprising of 1965, helped liberal Hollywood come alive to the existence and both the plight and the pocketbooks of black Americans. Negroes were a misused and abused people, but we were also audience, consumers, and market shares. Television, arguably for the first time, began to consider the tastes, interests, and spending power of black people as well as the talents and entertainment value the industry had drawn on since its inception, in the ways Ed Sullivan described in the '50s.

A variety of black actors began appearing as guests on many of the mainstream TV dramas and westerns my family and I watched in the 1960s and '70s. One of the most memorable was the "Goodnight Sweet Blues" episode of *Route 66* (1961), guest-starring the incomparable Ethel Waters as Jennie Henderson, a dying jazz singer who convinces the white costars Tod Stiles (Martin Milner) and Buz Murdock (George Maharis) to round up her six former bandmates and bring them to her bedside to play together one last time. It's a crazy, impossible mission, but unable to refuse such a sweet old lady's dying wish, the guys set out crisscrossing the country on Jenny's last dime, trying to round up her old gang. One of the members has died, they find, but his son, who remembers Jennie as the only person who ever really cared about him, is eager to fill in for his father. A second bandmate—a lawyer in the middle of trying a case—requests a continuance, while another has to lie his way out of prison on a furlough. No matter what the obstacles, the band members all show up just in time to play Jennie out, in one of the greatest tearjerkers of my childhood.

"Goodnight Sweet Blues" seemed rather corny when I screened it as a jaded adult (not that I wasn't still moved), but I don't think there was a dry eye in the den when we watched it together in 1961. Of course, just about any outing of a black actor that wasn't some slapstick farce was a treat in those days, and this particular musical melodrama had and retains a certain mesmerizing charm, not only because of Waters in an Emmy-nominated role—the first such nomination for a black female performer—but also because the musicians playing her bandmates, including Coleman Hawkins on the saxophone, were some of the best jazz artists in the country. As Donald Bogle writes of the episode and its luminary star, "Ethel Waters was once again something of an all-knowing, all-hearing, all-seeing Black earth mother, who refuses to judge those who stand before her. It's a very seductive, double-edged fantasy, both pleasurable and dangerous."[2] An article in the *Saturday Evening Post* by the white writer and TV critic Richard Lemon offers the unhappy footnote that while the main cast of this breakout episode was all black—save for the two series stars—the production crew was all white as usual, and Ethel Waters had to suffer the indignity of being told how to sing "Goodnight Sweet Blues" by one of the writers, amid an atmosphere that made it clear the show was taking a risk on her, so she "better be good"—an observation that definitely makes the memory less sweet.[3]

A small band of black actors had recurring, supporting roles in other shows we watched: Cicely Tyson with George C. Scott in the short-lived series *East Side/West Side* (CBS, 1963–1964), Ivan Dixon in *Hogan's Heroes* (CBS, 1965–1970), Greg Morris in *Mission Impossible* (CBS, 1966–1973), Hari Rhodes in *Daktari* (CBS, 1966–1969), Robert Hooks in *N.Y.P.D.* (ABC, 1967–1969), Don Mitchell in *Ironside*, with Raymond Burr in the title role (NBC, 1967–1975), Clarence Williams III in *The Mod Squad* (ABC, 1968–1973), my particular favorite Gail Fisher as the title character's Girl Friday in the private investigator (PI) drama *Mannix* (CBS, 1967–1975), and, of course, Nichelle Nichols as communications officer Lt. Uhura on *Star Trek: The Original Series* (NBC, 1966–1969), who in 1968, as discussed in chapter 4, joined William Shatner in what's touted as network TV's first interracial kiss on the "Plato's Stepchildren" episode.

From the beginning of their work in television, black actors faced a challenge virtually unknown to their white counterparts: the pressure to represent their race in a positive light. What perhaps hasn't been given enough attention is the toll that this burden of representation took on earlier African American performers in particular. Lincoln Perry's Stepin Fetchit persona may have made him Hollywood's first black millionaire in the 1930s, but in later years his lazy-man, shucking-and-jiving routines—along with his own fight for parity with whites within the motion picture industry—also netted him the career-killing ire of both his people and his employers, reducing him to bankruptcy by the latter 1940s and derailing later attempted comebacks through the new medium of television. Some contemporary scholars, including his biographer Mel Watkins, have offered a compelling reappraisal of Stepin Fetchit as the consummate trickster figure, who put one over on Hollywood, and even Perry's old nemesis the NAACP honored him with an Image Award in 1976. But at the height of the civil rights movement and Black Power militancy, Perry was so maligned by criticism not only of the stereotypical characters he played but also of him as an Uncle Tom, who had set back the race, that he sued CBS (unsuccessfully) for the televised documentary *Black History: Lost, Stolen, or Strayed* (1968), which he claimed defamed him personally—costing him a costarring role with the comedian Flip Wilson in a new TV series—while also "slurring an entire generation of Negro Americans as inept."[4]

Perry was hardly alone in facing intense criticism and even condemnation from the NAACP, the black press, and much of the black community for institutionalizing demeaning images of African Americans. There was a heart-tugging tremor in Hattie McDaniel's voice, as well as tears in her eyes that February night in 1940 when she accepted the Academy Award for her controversial supporting role as Mammy in *Gone with the Wind* (1939). "I sincerely hope I shall always be a credit to my race and to the motion picture industry," she said, swallowing the myriad indignities that followed her onto the stage at the Cocoanut Grove nightclub in the segregated Ambassador Hotel (the same L.A. landmark where Bobby Kennedy would be assassinated twenty-eight years later).[5] The producer David O. Selznick had had to call in favors just to get McDaniel into the hotel, where she was seated not with him and her white costars Olivia de Havilland, Vivien Leigh, and Clark Gable, but at a booth in the back in a corner in the dark, as Flip Wilson used to say.[6] She and the other black stars of *Gone with the Wind* had not been allowed to attend the Atlanta premiere at the segregated Loew's Grand Theater two months earlier. (It's widely claimed that Gable threatened to boycott the premiere because of McDaniel's exclusion until she talked him out of it. I would think a lot more of Gable if he had boycotted the premiere or left the *Gone with the Wind* table to sit with his colored costar at the Academy Award ceremony, as his character Rhett Butler likely would have done.)[7] Yet for McDaniel, who, like Lincoln Perry, was criticized by much of the black press and all but condemned by the NAACP for playing roles that furthered negative stereotypes, the biggest hurt was no doubt winning the enmity rather than the admiration of the community she wanted to count her as a credit.

One of three black actresses to play the title role of Beulah in the TV series, McDaniel fared no better in this new medium. *The Beulah Show*, as discussed in chapter 2, was driven off the air in 1953 in part by the efforts of the NAACP, which publicly challenged the demeaning representations of colored people the title character typified. Although not subjected to the same kind of formal protests, the 1960s comedy *Julia* (1968–1971), with a decidedly middle-class heroine about as far from Mammy or Beulah or Sapphire as one could get, nevertheless met with criticism of a different kind throughout its historic three-year run on NBC. The title character Julia Baker, played by Diahann Carroll, was a nurse rather than a maid or mammy, a fact that has led many to call *Julia* groundbreaking, because it "challenged stereotypes and changed perceptions," but that didn't save the series or its leading lady from censure.[8]

I was an all-knowing nineteen-year-old college sophomore when *Julia* first appeared. Perhaps it was my budding feminism coupled with the revolutionary spirit of the day, but I remember proclaiming to classmates that the show would be more groundbreaking and progressive if Julia were a doctor like the titular heroes of my favorite medical dramas *Ben Casey* and *Dr. Kildare*. I was blind to my own shortsightedness at the time, but it seems absurdly paradoxical to me now that I wanted a black female character to be more like the white men I had grown up watching and wanting to emulate just as I did Perry Mason. And while I was enough my mother's daughter to appreciate the fictitious detail that Nurse Julia was an independent, self-supporting, middle-class African American woman, I was less enamored of the idea that she was a single mother—a Vietnam War widow—rearing a young son on her own (like Peggy Fair from *Mannix*). Her polished, poised persona and single-parent status fed into the findings of the *Moynihan Report*, which we were deconstructing in my sociology courses, and seemed to sanction the reigning stereotypes of black women as ball-busting matriarchs and black men as ne'er-do-well, absentee sperm donors.

It's somewhat mind-boggling to me today that *Julia* began its well-intentioned run in 1968 with a black female lead who was figured as a single mother, given the fallout from the *Moynihan Report* published just three years earlier and what many perceived as the report's attack on both black women and the black family. Compiled by then Assistant Secretary of Labor Daniel Patrick Moynihan, *The Negro Family: A Case for National Action*, as the report was officially titled, was a government-sanctioned study of "the

Negro problem" that attributed poverty, unemployment, crime, juvenile delinquency, illegitimacy, and everything else said to ail the black community to an alleged preponderance of female-headed households, which the report billed as a holdover from slavery that had forced the black community into a matriarchal structure dangerously out of line with the male-headed nuclear-family model of white society. Even as a war widow presumably made single through no fault of her husband or her own, Julia symbolically fit the bill of black women who do better without the good-for-nothing black men who knock them up and then disappear.

If holding a fictional character accountable for furthering a stereotype seems silly, Julia had plenty of detractors on other grounds as well. Many of the show's most severe critics maintained that with straightened hair instead of an afro (before she went natural with a short-cropped fro) and a bourgeois demeanor instead of an activist or Black Power persona, Carroll's character was too tame, too apolitical, too far removed from the civil rights movement and what was happening in the real world. It was the '60s, after all, and the sitcom hit the airwaves just five months after the assassination of Martin Luther King Jr. And although the show was set in Los Angeles, devastating life-and-death events like the Watts riots that rocked South Central L.A. in 1965 were outside the scope of its camera lens. I can't say for certain how much of this criticism I indulged at the time, but I'm somewhat ashamed now that my youthful brand of Black Powerism kept me from fully appreciating what Diahann Carroll and the show brought to television at a time when nuanced roles for African American women were virtually nonexistent.

In *How It Feels to Be Free: Black Women Entertainers and the Civil Rights Movement* (2013), Ruth Feldstein, an associate professor of history at Rutgers University, offers a compelling reconsideration of the political contributions black women entertainers like Carroll, Lena Horne, and Nina Simone made to both the civil rights and women's movements in the 1950s and 1960s. Carroll not only "lent her name, home, and money to SNCC [Student Nonviolent Coordinating Committee] and other civil rights organizations," Feldstein explains, but she also testified before Congress about racial discrimination within the entertainment industry.[9] Christine Acham, who likewise offers an extended rereading of *Julia* in *Revolution Televised: Prime Time and the Struggle for Black Power* (2004), points out that Carroll's critique of Hollywood racism included publicly taking exception to the racial politics of her own show, especially the absent father as a misrepresentation of black family life. She felt the writers created what she called "the white Negro" with "very little Negro-ness."[10]

It should also be noted that Carroll marched and protested and raised funds for the civil rights movement through concerts and benefit performances. But her contributions to the cause of equal rights and social justice were not limited to what we readily recognize as traditional modes of political activism. Rather, her persona itself functioned as a form of what Daphne Brooks, a specialist in black performance studies at Yale University, identifies as the "imaginative activism" of "artists who performed progressive representations of black womanhood."[11] Carroll as a public figure and *Julia* as a purveyor of wholesome, middle-class values and respectability performed the integrationist move that Ed Sullivan and Steve Allen, along with race women like my mother, envisioned for the medium in the earliest days of television. "To some extent," Feldstein writes of *Julia*, "the series sought to integrate" the living rooms of middle-class whites "by bringing fictional middle-class blacks into them." This was the good intention behind the show, according to its creator and producer Hal Kanter, who reportedly wanted to deploy comedy in the cause of civil rights through black characters whom white audiences would laugh with rather than at.[12]

Comedy can certainly be political and transformative. Some of the most biting social commentary that has ever found its way to television has come from black comedians like Moms Mabley, Redd Foxx, Dick Gregory, Flip Wilson, Richard Pryor, Eddie Murphy, Dave Chappelle, and, more recently, Wanda Sykes, Issa Rae, Larry Wilmore, Trevor Noah, and Keegan-Michael Key and Jordan Peele of *Key and Peele*, many appearing regularly on Comedy Central. Key and Peele's satirical comedy sketches with the character Luther (played by Key) as Barack Obama's (Peele) "anger translator" caught President Obama's attention. He invited Key up on stage in character as Luther during his speech at the White House Correspondents' Dinner in 2015 for a skit featuring the two of them.

In general, however, the situation comedy—for some time, arguably the primary televisual medium for black entertainers—has not been the place for hard-boiled black history or hard-core racial politics. In a perfect world, it wouldn't matter what form black programming takes, because it's all make-believe anyway. Christine Acham reminds critics who would be hard on shows like *Julia* of the parodic power of characters and images too easily praised or panned as positive or negative. She suggests that it is often our own class pretensions and biases that underpin our views and reviews.[13] Thinking of my mother and of my own race-, gender-, and class-conscious way of watching TV, I can hardly deny the claim. Yet and still, the problem of black television and blacks on television is a problem the medium shares with other African

American expressive forms, especially literature: playacting blackness is not just acting, not simply representing something out of the imaginary; rather, it's taken to present something in the social real—the facts rather than the fictions of real black life.

....

As my family's favorite TV dramas unfolded in the 1960s, Ivan Dixon as Staff Sergeant Kinch Kinchloe on *Hogan's Heroes* was the gallant prison-camp captive whose mechanical genius, communications, and foreign-language skills masterfully aided and abetted his fellow POWs' subversive work against the Nazis during World War II. Much the same is true of Greg Morris as Bernie Collier, also an infinitely inventive mechanical genius and the linchpin of a force of secret government agents, whose wizardry made the team's assignments doable on *Mission Impossible*. Clarence Williams III as Lincoln "Linc" Hayes, one of three hip, young undercover cops on *Mod Squad*, and Robert Hooks as Detective Jeff Ward on the crime drama *N.Y.P.D.* were all on the right side of the law, fighting for truth, justice, and the American Way, like Superman.

Cicely Tyson, too, played a do-gooder on *East Side/West Side* (CBS, 1963–1964). Her underexposed, short-lived role as the young, gifted, and black social service worker Jane Foster on the edgy, socially progressive series was overshadowed by the larger, luminary, leading-man presence of George C. Scott and the meatier, more poignant parts played by black guest stars who appeared in two of the series' most acclaimed and defamed episodes: "Who Do You Kill?" with James Earl Jones and Diana Sands as desperately poor black parents forced to live in a vermin-infested Harlem tenement where their infant daughter dies after being badly bitten by a rat; and "No Hiding Place," guest-starring Ruby Dee and Earle Hyman (Cliff Huxtable's father on *The Cosby Show*) as an "intelligent, well-educated" Negro couple whose arrival in a suburban Long Island neighborhood sets off a chain reaction of blockbusting and white flight.

Still discussed in media studies as a tour de force of '60s TV programming, the "Who Do You Kill?" episode broke my fourteen-year-old heart and gave me nightmares for weeks.[14] The crippling despair of the once optimistic mother and the anger and anguish of Jones's character, a young husband and father shut out of every decent job by discriminatory labor practices, are well played and palpable. The scene where Jones rushes into the street, clutching his rat-bitten baby and begging for help getting her to the hospital, only to be passed by cab after cab, is so horribly haunting it seems it was excised from the videos of the show available online. (Either that or the scene is an invention of the fog of memory, which is entirely possible. I once fell asleep after watching the 1935 version of *Mutiny on the Bounty* and dreamt a sequel set on Pitcairn Island. I'm only certain it was a dream because all the characters were from *Star Trek*, with Captain Kirk in Gable's role as Fletcher Christian, but it lives in my memory as if it's something I actually saw.) At the time, some affiliates refused to air the episode, which won rave reviews in many circles and eight Emmy nominations (winning for best director) but also generated bags of hate mail and even some death threats.[15]

I hadn't remembered the connection until now, but I think the second memorable episode from the series, "No Hiding Place," which originally aired on December 3, 1963, may have inspired one of the few frank classroom discussions we had about race in high school. In the episode, the white residents of Maple Gardens, "A Friendly Community," as the welcome sign says, hold a neighborhood meeting to discuss what to do after a cultured, middle-class black family moves into their midst, and corrupt real estate developers begin buying out nervous homeowners among threats of drastically declining property values. One of the terrified residents who has decided to sell out and run voices exactly what everyone else is afraid of: "I don't want to live in a colored slum," she says. Tough words to hear, but it wasn't the story line or the "oops-there-goes-the-neighborhood" presumptions of the good white people of Maple Gardens that broke my heart. It was that same favorite teacher Mrs. Jones who shared with our class the personal detail that the homeowners in her neighborhood had held just such a community conference to talk about what they would do if a colored family moved into their midst. Their conclusion, according to Mrs. J., was that a black family who could afford to buy a home in their neighborhood would "probably be all right" and, therefore, they would do nothing. For the more than fifty years that I have stewed over this remark, I've never been sure which troubles me more—that my favorite teacher, who would buy me at a slave auction fundraiser the following year, shared the racial fears of the nation or that I was silenced by that knowledge and offered no challenge or rebuttal.

Cicely Tyson wasn't silenced in *East Side/West Side*, but she was treated like little more than a token by the network executives, who reportedly wanted her character out of the picture to soften the program's hard edge. She was given little screen time and few opportunities to strut her big talent. Yet, as Bogle says so well, even underutilized as she was in *East Side/West Side*, Tyson had a "glowing intensity," which let viewers know that herein lies "a remarkable actress who was bigger and better than the part she played."[16] Even deliberately minimalized to appease sponsors and affiliates, Tyson's role as a series regular drew bags of hate mail about miscegenation and race mixing, especially if Scott's character so much as suggested walking his black female colleague to the subway stop after a late night at the welfare office where they both worked.[17] In the end, all the accolades the show received for its frank treatment of pressing social issues were not enough to counter the low ratings; the show was cancelled after a single season.

With the possible exception of Tyson's role in *East Side/West Side*, it generally didn't matter to the plots of these mainstream dramas that some of the regular characters were black, but in the 1960s it made all the difference in the world to us as African American viewers. Nichelle Nichols as Lt. Uhura, for example, was seen as such a positive role model that, by her own account, no lesser force for uplift and progressive racial profiling than the Rev. Dr. Martin Luther King Jr. personally pleaded with her to remain on the show when she was about to leave *Star Trek*, largely because of the racism she says she experienced, not from the series creator Gene Roddenberry or her fellow actors but from studio executives who wanted her gone and took every opportunity to insult her, even keeping her fan mail from her so she wouldn't know how popular her character was.[18] Dr. King convinced her of the broad importance of her groundbreaking position. "You are a role model for everyone," she quotes him as saying, important not "in spite of your color" but "*because of your color*."[19]

To a certain extent, TV news coverage of the real life-and-death dramas that accompanied desegregation in the South in the 1950s and '60s and in northern cities like Boston, Chicago, and Philadelphia in the 1970s, set the stage for the proliferation of black programming in the '70s and '80s. Historical dramas, documentaries, and miniseries notwithstanding, it's worth noting that most of this programming avoided calling a spade a spade like *East Side/West Side*. Rather, it played its race cards through comedy, from *Room 222*, which ran on ABC from 1969 through 1974, to the first *Bill Cosby Show* on NBC (1969–1971), in which Cosby played a gym teacher named Chet Kincaid; *Sanford and Son* (NBC, 1972–1977); *That's My Mama* (ABC, 1974–1975); *Good Times* (CBS, 1974–1979); *The Jeffersons* (CBS, 1975–1983); *What's Happening!* (ABC, 1976–1979); *Diff'rent Strokes* (NBC, 1979–1985; ABC, 1985–1986); and, of course, in the land of cartoons *Fat Albert and the Cosby Kids* (CBS, 1972–1984).

In his 2014 autobiography *Even This I Get to Experience*, Norman Lear, the legendary white creator and executive producer behind *All in the Family* and

The Jeffersons, as well as many other successful sitcoms, details the "joyful stress" of developing and sustaining black shows like *Good Times, Sanford and Son*, and *What's Happening!* Lear's motivation to go black stemmed from his belief that television should reflect the real-world life experiences of its audience and his conviction that black people are an important part of that reality or, as he puts it in his autobiography, "a strong presence in my mind."[20] Shonda Rhimes, by the way, has cited Lear as a model in addressing her own commitment to putting gay characters and gay intimacy front and center on TV as Lear showcased black characters and African American actors in the 1970s.[21]

In explaining his interest in black life, Lear recalls taking the train into New York City as a teenager and looking through the windows of tenements at "all kinds of activity" inside, as the train traveled along the elevated tracks, slowing down for its first stop at 125th Street. What he saw as he peered through windows was "family after family—almost all Negroes, as we referred to them then," he says—"living their lives."[22] He would imagine their stories, assigning a hero here and a villain there and at points inserting himself into the narratives he invented for them—a creative process to which I can relate, since I used to do much the same thing as a child, riding in the backseat of the family car. I always fought my brothers for the right-side window seat, directly behind my mother riding shotgun while my father drove. (That was before Mom got her driver's license in the early 1960s and took to the open road at eighty miles an hour, so much so that we nicknamed her "Colonel Glenn" after the astronaut.) I wanted that seat so I could peer out at the houses we passed, trying to catch a glimpse of the people inside, as I invented not only lives for them but also furniture arrangements. (I was a born interior decorator.)

Considerably more came of Norman Lear's Peeping Tom ways than of my own. His autobiography recounts how it was that *Good Times* came into being as "the first full black family on television," spun off from *Maude* (CBS, 1972–1978), largely because of the talent and acting chops Esther Rolle displayed playing Bea Arthur's maid, Florida Evans, during *Maude's* first two seasons. Rolle's dynamic on-screen presence led Lear and the network executives to believe she could carry her own series; when she and the black actor John Amos—brought on to play her husband for a single episode—"clicked loudly together," the foundation for *Good Times* was laid.[23] But, here again, as Lear goes on to explain, carrying a history-making, first-of-its-kind urban sitcom also meant carrying the burden of the race for Rolle and Amos, both of whom were of my mother's mind-set regarding TV's obligation to present positive black family values. Even though only Rolle, who was almost twenty years older than Amos, was actually of my parents' vintage, both actors felt "a personal responsibility for every aspect of TV's first black family's behavior," Lear writes.[24] That same old ideology of respectability politics led them to resist and at times outright refuse scripts about topical but typical, ghetto-fabulous subject matter such as drugs, gangs, teenage sex, and even the color of Jesus, until Lear put his foot down and respectfully established himself as the Decider.[25]

Still, in Lear's assessment the adult stars' preoccupation with perception haunted and hurt the show, especially their open antipathy toward their eldest TV son, James "J.J." Evans Jr., as played clownishly by the nightclub comic Jimmie Walker. From the veteran stars' perspective, it was stereotypically colored enough that the impoverished Evans family lived marginal lives of desperation in Chicago's infamous Cabrini-Green housing project or a fac-simile thereof, barely getting by, even with the chronically underemployed James Sr. working two and three menial jobs. In an episode in which the family is about to be evicted, James comes home after having worked all night with only six dollars to show for his labors, after all the withholding, includ-ing, he explains, a deduction for his dishwasher's uniform. (When he was in-troduced as Florida's husband on *Maude*, James was named Henry and was employed as a firefighter.) But the fact that increasingly the show revolved around the buffoonish antics of their jive, womanizing, artistically talented but barely literate firstborn was a source of bitter discontent.

Both Rolle and Amos were vocal about how they believed Walker's antics as J.J. and his endlessly repeated catchphrase "dyn-o-mite" dumbed down and negatively transformed a show that was supposed to uplift the race with posi-tive images of hardworking black people struggling to make a way honestly.[26] Rolle complained in *Ebony* that the part of the younger son Michael (Ralph Carter), the "bright, thinking child," was diminished in favor of Walker's role as the eighteen-year-old ne'er-do-well offspring who "doesn't work," "can't read and write," and "doesn't think." John Amos has voiced a similar criticism, pointing out that the writers "blew right by" Bern Nadette Stanis who played his "beautiful daughter, Thelma, who aspired to become a doctor," as well as Ralph Carter who played his younger son, the militant intellectual. Rolle punctuated this critique by making clear how much she resented the nega-tive imagery slipped into the show by way of Walker's character, which she felt conveyed to black kids the message that "standing on the corner saying 'Dyn-o-mite!'" is the way to get ahead.[27]

My mother was with Rolle and Amos; she would kiss her teeth in annoy-ance every time J.J. let loose with his trademark utterance, and while Walker's character was supposedly popular with younger viewers, I wasn't a fan of his antics either. It's no secret, however, that my early experiences with stigmatic blackness made situation comedies a hard genre for me to embrace, but *Good Times* and especially J.J. had much weightier detractors. Lear says he was visited by members of the Black Panthers who called the show "garbage"—"nothing but a white man's version of a black family"—and the character of J.J. "a fucking put-down."[28] Moving the Evans family from upstate New York to a Chicago ghetto, shifting the father from a gainfully employed firefighter to a poorly educated, perennially down-on-his-luck dishwasher, day laborer, sometimes pool shark who hustles for the rent money when the family is about to be evicted (S1, E3), and making a juvenile neo-minstrel the main character seemed to suggest someone indeed had a particular agenda and a certain view of blackness and how to make it funny.

Lear, however, lays whatever onus there might be for the ghettoization of *Good Times* squarely at the feet of the program's black cocreators. The Evans family lived and struggled in the ghetto, he claims, because that's where the show's young black quasi-creators placed them in the pilot episode that the two were entrusted with scripting. Declaring that the story of the program's genesis falls under the heading "no good deed goes unpunished," Lear recounts how it was that two black scriptwriter-wannabes were credited with creating the show that became *Good Times*. Michael "Mike" Evans, who played Lionel on *The Jeffersons*, wanted to write for TV, and Lear gave him a chance to do so by letting him "take a crack at the *Good Times* pilot script."[29] Evans teamed up with Eric Monte, a young black scriptwriter who had contributed to *All in the Family* and was himself a product of the real Cabrini-Green housing project; together the two "had the opportunity to be the first" black writers to create a TV show.[30] I guess what Lear claims happened next was predictable:

"They blew it creatively with a poor copycat of a script," he writes in the "Joyful Stress" section of his autobiography, leaving it to him and the other more experienced showrunners to step in and save the pilot, the series, and apparently the writing team of Evans and Monte, who, despite blowing their big chance, have nevertheless gone down in television history as the creators of arguably the 1970s' must groundbreaking black show. As Lear explains, "But even though what they [Evans and Monte] wrote was a far cry from what we shot, we did not seek to change their credit as the sole cocreators. I could be confessing to a bit of inverse racism here," he adds, "when I admit that it even pleased me to see them credited and paid." Just so there is no doubt, he goes on to spell out what he means by "inverse racism": "That would not have happened, at least not gratuitously, if they were white."[31]

In other words, white men, unlike soul brothers, aren't given credit for what they didn't do and money they didn't earn.

Since Lear says Monte later sued him for a gazillion dollars, perhaps being outed as an incompetent poser is no more than Monte deserves, but it seems an unkind cut at the late Mike Evans who can't counter the claim. Monte, however, does tell a different tale in a 2006 National Public Radio interview, where he claims not to have received due credit or compensation for his work. He also claims *Good Times'* producers pushed him to make J.J. Evans "more of a clown than a person" and to get rid of the James Sr. character, because a strong black man in a sitcom isn't funny.[32] Who knows the full truth of the matter, but in 1977, Monte—pretty undisputedly the writing genius behind *Cooley High* (1975)—successfully sued Lear, CBS, ABC, and others for "using his ideas in sitcoms like *Good Times*, *The Jeffersons*, and *What's Happening!* without giving him credit." His was at best a Pyrrhic victory, however, or maybe a nuisance kiss-off. He didn't get anywhere near the $185 million he supposedly sued for and claims to have been blacklisted for his troubles.

Whether by long-term design because his character was too strong to be funny or because he had become "so glum and dispirited" he did the show no good, as Lear maintains, John Amos was indeed written out of the series after the third season, killed in a car accident off-screen during the summer hiatus.[33] Rolle, who had said from the beginning that she would not play an unwed or otherwise single mother, wasn't far behind in leaving the show, although her exit at the end of season four, unlike Amos's a year earlier, was entirely her choice and tied to her sense that *Good Times* wasn't what she thought it should be. She was persuaded to return for the show's concluding season, however, when the matured Evans family, like the Jeffersons, is poised to move on up and out of the projects, but the final curtain closes before we actually get to see them established in their new settings.

....

While the thrust of black programming remained largely comedic, if not outright clownish, even where it attempted to recognize racism by satirizing bigotry with shows like *The Jeffersons*, television of the 1970s also sought to connect to the black historical experience through the new genres of the made-for-TV movie and the miniseries, with adaptations of Ernest Gaines's bestselling novel *The Autobiography of Miss Jane Pittman* in 1974 and Alex Haley's Pulitzer Prize–winning masterwork *Roots: The Saga of an American Family* in 1977 and its sequel, *Roots: The Next Generation*, in 1979. These were

FIG. 5.1 Uncle Danny (aka "FUNcle") with Adrian's kids, from left to right: Dave, Beverly Ann, Marie Louise, and Adrian III (in the latter 1970s).

major televisual events, stretching in the case of *Roots* over eight nights on ABC and drawing in more than one hundred million viewers across the color line, while *Miss Jane Pittman*, appearing three years earlier on CBS, raked in nine Emmys, bringing unprecedented national and international attention to the black American experience.[34] We watched both the TV movie and the miniseries obsessively, including reruns, although by the mid-1970s, who "we" were had changed dramatically and was no longer the five of us, who had lived together and watched TV as a young family in the cinderblock house on Thatcher Street.

"We" now included grandchildren (Adrian's offspring) and a daughter-in-law. "We" did not include my father. Nor were we all living under the same leaky roof. Danny was still at home, but I had gone to graduate school in Rhode Island and, after a year of teaching as one of three black women pioneers at Hamilton College in upstate New York, was shuttling between Boston, Brockton, and Providence where, among other things, I taught creative writing at the Rhode Island state prison for men (the ACI) and hosted two talk shows—*Not for Black Only* and *We, the Women*—on the local public television station, WSBE, channel 36. Adrian, after a brief stint in the air force and a few years in Connecticut, had come home with a German wife four-

FIG. 5.2 My own publicity head shot from my brief career in front of the TV camera as a talk-show host on local PBS (mid-1970s).
PHOTO CREDIT: BERT WADE, *PROVIDENCE JOURNAL.*

teen years his senior and (eventually) four kids, as well as three stepchildren and two stepgrandsons. He had expanded the two-car garage I helped build into another never-quite-finished home for his growing family. Gathered around a different set in the same spot, this new and expanded "we" still often watched television together as a family.

Hokey, whitewashed, and watered-down as they may have been, these Hollywood adventures of the 1970s still had the capacity to move us to tears over the horrors of our own history. But we also howled with cathartic release at some rather inappropriate moments, because my mother—who often seemed not even to be paying attention—suddenly would interject into the poignant drama some Gramma Pearlism that would crack us up. As always she watched with either knitting needles in hand or a pen and crossword-puzzle book, but a new creative diversion had been added to her repertoire: dress-making. Throughout all the years my parents were married, I had never seen my mother do anything more with a needle and thread than mend, hem, and embroider. But the moment my father the tailor left the house, Mom began sewing up a storm, even making dresses and selling them to friends and family. Her best customer was Cousin Emily, who had moved with Cousin Percy and their kids Keith, Joy, and foster daughter Shirley first to East Bridgewater at some point in the 1960s and then to Brockton.

If Cousin Emily was Mom's best customer, I was either her practice dummy or her fashion model, outfitted for college almost literally from head to toe by the mother I had no idea even knew how to sew. Thrifty as always, she bought most of her material on sale from remnant tables at Safler's, an iconic textile store nearby in Whitman, so there could be a little or a lot of any given fabric. I had been the beneficiary of my mother's phenomenal knitting skills all my life; now I was outfitted in custom-tailored cloth garments, including at one point a multipiece ensemble—skirt, vest, pants, jacket, topcoat, and hat—all in the same charcoal-gray windowpane plaid. (I might have ended up with a windowpane-plaid purse and booties, too, if she had put her mind to it.)

I think she was sitting in her rocker-recliner, hemming a dress, probably for Cousin Emily, when Mom began what became a running critique of the way those white Hollywood makeup artists aged Cicely Tyson, who was play-ing the title character in *Miss Jane Pittman* and who supposedly reaches 110 by the end of the saga. "Don't they know black people don't wrinkle up like that?" Mom was such a grammarian that she couldn't bring herself to utter the appropriate aphorism, "Black don't crack," so Danny and I would say it for her, the grandchildren joining in like a chorus. And this was no singular comment. Mom was genuinely indignant about this makeup anachronism; for the next quarter century or so, anytime we watched reruns of the TV movie or Tyson appeared in anything else or was mentioned anywhere, my mother would revisit how Hollywood had turned her into a prune in *Miss Jane Pittman.*

And then there were Leslie Uggams's fingernails, which became more fodder for streaming Gramma Pearlisms. Uggams was playing Kizzy, Kunta Kinte's daughter in *Roots*, who at one point is cruelly wrenched from the loving arms of her parents (John Amos and Madge Sinclair), her plantation home, and the white childhood playmate, Missy Anne (Sandy Duncan), she naively thinks of as her best friend, and sold down the river into an even harsher form of slavery as punishment for the high crime of literacy, which she uses to forge a traveling pass for the slave boy she loves. Amid Kizzy's

FIG. 5.3 Cicely Tyson too aggressively aged as the title character in *Miss Jane Pittman,* drinking from the white water fountain in a climactic scene from the made-for-TV movie.

kicking, screaming, crying, and fighting as she is being dragged off, my mother was the first to spot Uggams's long, beautifully sculptured, perfectly manicured fingernails, which gave rise to a series of bad jokes about stopping off at Miss Anne's Nail Salon on the way to them old cotton fields back home.

Kizzy's fate, which includes being raped and impregnated by her new master, is no laughing matter, unfortunately, but for good or ill, we were not the only ones who noticed the nails. For us, the polished talons were a source of comic relief. For some of the series' doubters and detractors, however, Kizzy's perfect manicure symbolized the extent to which the miniseries was a commercial contrivance of the Hollywood kind, meant to appeal to white audiences more so than black. For one set of viewer-critics, Alex Haley's rich exploration of African American history had been whitewashed by Hollywood in an effort to make slavery palatable for white viewers. For another, it was an eight-night shame fest, designed to make white Americans feel guilty about their sins of the past and present. For some, it pulled its punches; for others, it sucker-punched below the belt. Either way, television had never seen anything like it before. Nor, I think, has anything since had quite the same impact. I tried to watch the 2016 remake, but sitting

FIG. 5.4 Three generations of duCilles and a family friend at Thanksgiving in the knotty-pine dining room in the 1980s. (Adrian III is taking the picture and Beverly is obscured by Mom standing.)

through it in solitude, without the old gang that once gathered around the TV in Gramma's den and around the dining-room table in the old homestead, summoned ghosts of days gone by and a personal pathos that had little to do with the story at hand.

<hr />

At a critical moment in the season three opener of *Scandal*, after news breaks (the first time) of Olivia Pope's affair with President Grant, her black father, Rowan Pope (Joe Morton), suddenly appears on the scene—all knowing and all powerful—and belittles her for giving herself away so cheaply to a white man who only thinks he is the leader of the free world. "Did I not raise you for better?" Papa Pope asks before reminding his daughter of the colored kids' code under which she was raised: "You have to be twice as good as them [*sic*] to get half of what they have," he says, in words so similar to those under which I, too, was reared that I could have written the dialogue. "You know to aim higher," he adds. "Do you have to be so mediocre?" (S3, E1).

Black kids raised under the code do know to aim higher, but there is a certain irony, if not a false note, in the arch-evil head of a covert government agency speaking these words in a show billed as postracial to a character whose color, critics say, is a "nonissue." And Kerry Washington channeling Olivia Pope has had the luxury of playing the part without fidelity to the colored code of conduct governing her every move, unlike her predecessors a few decades earlier. Whether or not they wanted to be a credit to their race—and many of them did—black actors who appeared on television in the 1950s, '60s, and '70s were, as MLK said of Nichelle Nichols, "role models," representative bodies.

It's more difficult today and maybe even ill advised to turn to black TV characters for role models. Writing about Kerry Washington for *Marie Claire*, the white actress Lena Dunham gushed her admiration for the way Washington, as a black woman in a position of power on television, has "redefined identity and visibility for so many women." "Representation is what we all crave," Dunham says, and millions of women, across color lines, see themselves in Washington's *Scandal* persona Olivia Pope, whose "strength, power, and complexity are something rare in a network heroine."[35]

Dunham is unquestionably right about the inspiration and possibilities Washington's portrayal represents for many viewers, but Washington herself is quick to point out that Olivia Pope "is nobody's role model," not least "because she's having an affair with a married man, who is president of the United States. And a murderer."[36] Nor is President Grant Olivia's only bed partner who also happens to be a cold-blooded killer. Her sometimes lover Jake Ballard (Scott Foley), the brainwashed right-hand henchman who her evil-doing dad calls his "son," is also a murderer several times over. Her sexual relationship with her black father's white surrogate son adds yet another taboo to the show's soap operatic twists, turns, and tropes and may remind the more cynical among us that "unrepressed incest" is one of the irrational longings or sexual fantasies that "the civilized white man" projects onto the Negro, according to Frantz Fanon.[37] Kerry Washington says that while there are things to admire about the character she plays, Olivia Pope, like other Shonda Rhimes creations, is purposely and purposefully "complicated"—one of the many "three-dimensional, messy human beings" who inhabit the piece of Hollywood that is ShondaLand Productions.[38]

In the of-course of ShondaLand events, it was only a matter of time before the messy human being Olivia Pope moved from sleeping with murderers to becoming one, as she does in *Scandal*'s fifth season in an episode tastelessly titled "Thwack!" in onomatopoeic tribute to the brutal, hands-on nature of the deathblow Washington's character wields. It's no delicate, ladylike extermination by poison or proxy with which this (anti)heroine dispatches her victim, the villainous, wheelchair-bound former vice president, Andrew Nichols (Jon Tenney), whom she clubs to death with a metal chair. Back in season four when Nichols had his full faculties, he had Olivia kidnapped, leading to her being sold in a darknet auction. Now that she has been rescued and is back to her powerful, take-no-prisoners self, and the former VP is the one held captive by his own broken body, Olivia is not about to let herself be victimized again by the demeaning, sexually explicit trash talk with which Nichols foolishly taunts her.

Although paralyzed and speech-impaired, the former VP has no trouble verbally assailing the black woman he calls "just another cheap slut" under her designer clothes and threatens to auction again. He continues to berate and belittle Olivia in sexually and racially loaded language in much the same way that Annalise Keating's Caucasian husband will berate and belittle her in *How to Get Away with Murder*. "Do you talk this much in bed?" Nichols quips, cutting off Olivia mid-sentence. "Are you this chatty on your hands and knees? Does that big mouth of yours work as hard as it does right now? Tell me, I'm curious" (S5, E17).

ShondaLand Productions seems to have a penchant for subjecting black women to this kind of sexually explicit verbal assault, as if the racial dimensions of such discourse from the lips of white men don't matter beyond whatever cheap amusement they provide. (I discuss this issue in greater detail in chapter 7.) In a bitter confrontation with his onetime lover, the white former First Lady turned senator (and eventually president), Nichols merely suggests he now finds her "disgusting," without resorting to obscene, assaultive language. By contrast, the trash talk he unloads on Olivia, whom he labels a "cheap slut," is a form of sexual violence that attacks her below the belt and linguistically places the black female fixer on her knees ready for lip service.

In black culture, it's a criminal offense for a man to talk about a woman "all up under her clothes," as the old people say; so perhaps Nichols deserves what he gets. The earlier trauma and present taunting are supposed to justify the vengeful rage with which the usually cool, calculating Olivia Pope picks up a metal chair and bludgeons her "helpless" (her word) tormentor to death in a gratuitously gruesome murder scene set underground in a secret White House bunker. The slaughter leaves Olivia blood-spattered but unbowed by remorse, regret, or fear of retribution, because—in the spirit of the show's sister series—she knows how to get away with murder. After a few moments in the consoling arms of the president, who suddenly arrives on the scene, followed shortly by the White House press secretary, Olivia is back to conniving, calculating business as usual. In fact, the first words out of her mouth are decisive instructions to the press secretary, her former best friend and gladiator, on exactly how to cover up her crime, punctuated with a meaningfully delivered threat: "Never cross me again."

As I suggested earlier, *Scandal* long ago jumped the shark in my view, and this twist in which its black female protagonist viciously murders a defenseless, if evil, person in a wheelchair seems to me to submerge that character in waters so foul I don't see how to decontaminate her. Some viewers are more sympathetic, however, attributing Olivia's actions to posttraumatic stress disorder or insisting Nichols got what he deserved. The show invites such responses to hot-blooded murder, but what I find even more unredeemable is the fact that in this same episode Jake, who supposedly loves Olivia, is forced by Papa Pope to marry another woman, while Roberta Flack's signature song, "The First Time Ever I Saw Your Face"—a personal favorite since a real, rather than arranged, date took me to a Roberta Flack concert at Symphony Hall circa 1969—plays in the background of a ceremony that gives new meaning to the term "shotgun wedding."

To be clear, the outrage here isn't that Papa Pope has threatened to slit Jake's throat if Olivia interferes with the nuptials as she and Jake had secretly planned or that the groom will shortly murder his new father-in-law. No, the real crime is that here, as in episode after episode, season after season, murder and other high crimes and misbehaviors are staged to the dulcet tones of *my* favorite soul music. Like other members of *Scandal*'s ensemble cast, Motown and other black artists make weekly appearances through their music: Gladys Knight, Stevie Wonder, Diana Ross, Marvin Gaye, Aretha Franklin, Nina Simone, and as the entertainment reporter Mike Ayers has noted, Otis Redding, whose soulful rendition of "Try a Little Tenderness" plays as the accompaniment to a montage of gruesome scenes of murder, torture, and other cruelties in a cliff-hanger episode from season three (s3, e8). "If you caught the show on a whim, it might be an alarming pairing," Ayers writes. "But from the very beginning, Rhimes has mostly honed in on classic soul and funk from the late '60s and early '70s." Such music "has quietly become one of the show's trademark characteristics," Ayers adds, "along with the cheating, betrayal, murder, backstabbing, and rapid-fire plot twists."[39]

Also commenting on *Scandal*'s musical sensibility, Oneka LaBennett maintains that the Motown-era soundtrack is wholly in keeping with the show's "dark sense of nostalgia for a time when the only hope a Black woman had of being the president's partner would be as his mistress"—an illicit, backstairs relationship that LaBennett says is "belied by the legitimacy of

Michelle Obama's historic role." Both the show's soundtrack and its central premise transport audiences to "a pre-Obama White House," she writes, offering "Americans a nostalgic fantasy world" in which they can attempt to reconcile their "disbelief at Michelle Obama's presence as 'Mom-in-Chief.'" In this regard, *Scandal* is at once "avant-garde and a throwback," LaBennett concludes. The series takes the bold step of featuring a black female protagonist in the figure of Olivia Pope, but at the same time it bypasses Michelle Obama's real-life historic role as First Lady in favor of a black presidential mistress and what LaBennett rightly labels a "blast-from-the-past plotline that smack[s] of Thomas Jefferson and Sally Hemings."[40] Put another way, televisually, a colored mistress spread-eagle on the *Resolute* desk in the Oval Office is more appealing to audiences than an African American missus planting a vegetable garden on the South Lawn.

To LaBennett's provocative analysis, I would add the minor musical note that the televisual use of Motown-era soundtracks predates Rhimes's deployment and has a resonance that is not only nostalgic but also appropriative. From the variety shows of yesteryear to contemporary sitcoms and dramas, the television industry has used black music and musicians as both attention-grabbing, money-making vehicles and colorizing additives with which to nod at diversity, even or perhaps especially as theme music for otherwise white shows. *Murphy Brown* (1988–1998), for example, which was short on black characters but big on black music, drew on Motown's greatest hits as blackup throughout its ten-year run, even going so far as to produce a CD, *The Sounds of Murphy Brown*, featuring fifteen tracks of tunes by black artists ranging from Aretha Franklin and Stevie Wonder to the gospel group Take 6.[41] What is especially amusing or annoying about *The Sounds of Murphy Brown* is the fact that reviews on Amazon attribute the music to the show: "Although Murphy Brown ended, her music lives on? Relive those moments and ones of your own with this nostalgic CD."[42] Preceding *Murphy* by four years, *The Cosby Show* (NBC, 1984–1992) used black music—jazz, R&B, hip hop—as a safe way of playing the race card in a show whose winning hand was class. So even with her avant-garde African American leading lady and multiracial ensemble cast, Shonda Rhimes is nevertheless following a familiar pattern in using soul music to sign blackness in her would-be postracial televisual world.

While the number of black characters on TV has grown exponentially since the 1950s and '60s and even the 1980s and '90s of *Cosby* and *Murphy Brown*—

thanks in part in recent years to ShondaLand Productions—roles and narratives are only beginning to render complexities beyond the colorful antics of comedic characters and the traditional, one-dimensional good/bad, angel/demon, villain/victim formula of dramatic offerings. Complexity, along with variety, would surely be a welcome turn in technicolored television, but characters and plot twists like those of *Scandal*, *How to Get Away with Murder*, *Empire*, *Power*, and, heaven help us, as of 2017, *Claws* on TNT, leave me wondering whether Hollywood isn't merely dressing up old stereotypes in the emperor's trendy new clothes that make familiar, fixed, stigmatic properties less recognizable—so much so that the NAACP now gives Image Awards for parts it once would have panned, as it did *Amos 'n' Andy* for depicting Negro lawyers as "slippery" and "without ethics" and Negro women as "cackling, screaming shrews . . . using street slang, just short of vulgarity"—words from the 1950s that could just as well have been written about shows like *Empire* and *How to Get Away with Murder* today.[43] Certainly the successful, well-heeled drug dealers, murderers, and shady music moguls; well spoken, well-dressed deceitful doctors, unethical lawyers, and ruthless power brokers; or conniving, college-educated conmen, crooks, and criminals, who populate many of today's most celebrated shows, do not project more praiseworthy images of colored people than the TV characters of yesteryear. Rather, the difference in reception seems to be the maturing of the NAACP, which has learned to appreciate acting, to separate person from part, to acknowledge how well a black actor plays the role of demon without demonizing him or her for doing so.

It is, of course, a catch-22 to try to codify the black actors' performative condition: if they're very, very good like Diahann Carroll as Julia Baker (a name Olivia Pope uses as an alias at one point, clearly in a nod to Carroll's pioneering portrayal), they engage the saint or savior stereotype and are called out for acting white; when they're very, very bad, well, they are not only horrid, they're black—stigmatically so. Ideally, a black actor should be able to play any part without carrying the weight of the race on his or her shoulders. Yet history makes blackness mean on the screen in ways that whiteness does not. Imagine *Scandal* with a white woman in the role of Olivia Pope. Gone is that pulsating sense of black-and-white sexual tension and taboo that has swirled around the show ever since trailers began hyping the coming attractions of its first season. Disappeared is all concern that one white woman's sleeping with the president reduces, damages, and demeans all white women. Lost is the lurid detail to any critique larger than its lurid, little self. It's Olivia Pope's gorgeous black female body that encodes a grammar of racial meaning that American society clearly has not yet lived long enough to have outgrown.

Scandal is a quintessentially sexy show. Set against the backdrop of the ultimate Big House, even its title suggests the black-and-white intercourse of its human events. After all, America's premiere presidential scandal is the interracial coupling of Thomas Jefferson and his slave Sally Hemings (his dead wife's half sister), to whom Olivia cheaply likens herself in a one-liner in a flashback episode in season two—"I'm feeling, I don't know, a little Thomas Jefferson–Sally Hemings about all this" (S2, E8). Critics may say color is a nonissue in *Scandal* and other so-called postracial series, but the optics alone say race matters; the body language speaks sex, the bawdy dialogue screams difference. Technicolored has never looked so black and white. Nor has television ever before accomplished such fantastic feats of racial role reversal. Incredibly, within the anything-goes, all-things-are-possible soap operatic realm of the *Scandal* imaginary, it's not actually Olivia Pope's on-again-off-again lover, the white Republican president Fitz Grant, who is the master of the universe; it's her own black founding father, Rowan Pope, who suddenly enters the narrative in season three as the most immoral, evildoing black trickster of all time. Only Hollywood could turn white patriarchy black—and, if we add Olivia's similarly evil mother, female.

White slavery is a real and present danger, but selling a black woman on the auction block in the twenty-first century, as the show does in season four, has an entirely different historical resonance. When black actors perform for the camera, they almost inevitably function as deeply politicized foreign bodies whose screen presence upsets the very inbreeding Hollywood has been bred on. But they also almost always either challenge or confirm conventional class and color-coding, often serving as a repository of the nation's worst fears and darkest desires in the distaff position I spoke of earlier. Kerry Washington's role as Olivia Pope both confirms and denies conventional, stigmatic coding and caricature. It takes on and takes over such stereotypes as the strong, independent black superwoman; the hypersexual, easily-had Jezebel; and the domineering, ball-busting Sapphire, but herein lies the grand contradiction: it also fights for the right to *act*, to play a part against the grain of racial uplift and respectability politics—to perform not an identity but a role.

Chapter 6

A Clear and Present Absence

PERRY MASON AND
THE CASE OF THE
MISSING "MINORITIES"

Perry Mason went on the air when people were first buying
television sets. A lot of people in this country didn't know what
their legal system was all about. I'm sure just from the people
who have watched the show over the years, particularly the
minorities, they found out the system of justice was for them.

—RAYMOND BURR, Associated Press interview

Perry Mason, the stalwart criminal defense attorney played convincingly on
the small screen by the veteran movie actor Raymond Burr, was a respected
figure in our household. The whole family loved the *Perry Mason* series and
watched every episode, from the premiere in September of 1957, when I was
eight years old, to the finale in May of 1966, when I was seventeen, as well as
decades of reruns. Although we found an admirable model of integrity in
Mason's vigorous defense of the wrongfully accused, the show itself did nothing to convince us as black viewers that the American criminal justice system was on our side, the effect Raymond Burr seems to have imagined that
Perry Mason had on "minorities." The series was, if anything, yet another site
in which we felt keenly the presence of our own absence as human beings
worthy of a Perry Mason defense. Mason did handle a few cases that put
him in contact with Asian and Asian American characters, clients, and cul-
prits, including "The Case of the Caretaker's Cat" (1959), where he defends a

Chinese manservant (Benson Fong) accused of murdering his employer and benefactor, and "The Case of the Weary Watchdog" (1962), where an older edition of my former heartthrob Keye Luke—Charlie Chan's Number One Son—appears as both the owner of Mason's favorite Chinese restaurant and a killer whom he exposes.[1]

Black actors, however, appeared on *Perry Mason* only a handful of times during the series' nine-year run, almost always in decidedly minor roles and, in at least one case, a nonspeaking part. In addition to the various Asian characters who populate "The Case of the Blushing Pearls" (1959), the African American actor William "Bill" Walker has a minuscule part as a night watchman in the episode. Paul Winfield, who would go on to star on stage, film, and TV in Emmy Award–winning and Academy Award–nominated roles (for *Sounder*, 1972), began his acting career in 1965 with a small part as Mitch, a race-car mechanic, in "The Case of the Runaway Racer." To the best of my knowledge, such bit parts were the most *Perry Mason* offered black actors, with three notable exceptions.

In the first noteworthy appearance, an unknown, uncredited black actor presides over the trial in "The Case of the Skeleton's Closet" (May 2, 1963), but as if portending Clarence Thomas's judicial style, the black judge simply sits on the bench mute throughout the proceedings. He makes no rulings, issues no orders, holds no sidebars, and doesn't even bang a gavel. He is the perfect example of an absent black presence; even so there were complaints about an African American judge in Perry Mason's courtroom. According to J. Fred MacDonald, Gail Patrick, the movie star turned producer, responded to the complaints by citing realism, since at the time there were black jurists serving on the bench in Los Angeles County.[2]

L.A.'s actual integrated judiciary notwithstanding, this nod toward diversity is not sustained in subsequent shows, but blackness effects an absent presence of a different kind in "The Case of the Fancy Figures" from 1958, where the versatile character actor Frank Silvera has a pivotal role and guest-star billing as a successful white businessman Mason reveals as the killer. What is particularly noteworthy about this case is the fact that Frank Silvera was not himself white like the actors who play his daughter, son, son-in-law, and all the other characters in the episode. Born in Kingston, Jamaica (like my own dad), mixed-race, and light-skinned, Silvera played just about every race and ethnicity imaginable. In the 1950s and '60s, he was a fixture in both film and television, most of the time playing anything except what he was—a black man—not because he hid his racial identity but because he didn't look like what he was. He was Hollywood's Everyman, known in some circles as "the

FIG. 6.1 Perry Mason questioning a witness before the mute black presiding judge.

FIG. 6.2 Close-up of an unnamed, uncredited black actor as the judge in "The Case of the Skeleton's Closet" (1963).

man with a thousand faces," which is not to say he didn't encounter obstacles and limitations.[3] With his talent, versatility, and matinee-idol good looks, he could have been, should have been a leading man, instead of a visibly invisible one—a face without a name. He appeared in numerous motion pictures opposite the likes of Marlon Brando, Anthony Quinn, Charlton Heston, Telly Savalas, and Paul Newman, but he may be best remembered or least forgotten for his recurring TV role as Don Sebastián Montoya, the powerful Mexican ranchero on *The High Chaparral.*

Mexican, Italian, French, Spanish, Native American, Puerto Rican, Portuguese, Polynesian—whatever Silvera was on camera, off-screen he identified as black, fiercely so. He was active in the civil rights movement and not at all shy about confronting Hollywood heavyweights about their penchant for demeaning portrayals of African Americans. He was a member of the American Negro Theatre of Harlem and as a director and producer as well as an actor he fought for better roles for black performers, founding the Theatre of Being in Los Angeles in 1964 as an outlet and workshop for black actors and playwrights committed to progressive performance. At a time when few Hollywood agents handled black clients, the Theatre of Being served as a kind of repository of black talent that became the go-to place for casting directors looking to fill particular parts.[4]

Alison Mills (Newman), who as a child actress had a recurring role on *Julia* in the '60s, describes the Theatre of Being as a training ground and sanctuary for black artists and credits Silvera, who she says was "devoted to black people," with fostering the nascent careers of a number of actors and artists whose names are better known today than his: Beah Richards, Yaphet Kotto, Isabel Sanford, and Don Mitchell, who went on to work with Raymond Burr in his second successful television series *Ironside* (NBC, 1967–1975). Even Maya Angelou came through the Theatre in the early days, according to Mills.[5]

How Frank Silvera ended up on *Perry Mason* playing a white businessman is a perplexing question. Alison Mills mentions Burr's name in conjunction with Don Mitchell and the Theatre of Being, so that could be the connection. Another possible explanation may be a shared background in radio. Burr and Silvera both worked as radio players early in their careers, and Burr reportedly saw to it that radio actors were employed in his series.[6] Of course, the generous, if naive, explanation for Silvera's getting the part of a white man is that talent rather than race ruled. But then as now, race was and is reducible to and readable as skin color—what the eye sees and the camera captures. Radio, yes, but no dark-skinned actor—no matter how talented—

would have won the TV role of a wealthy white businessman in 1958. The optics just wouldn't compute in such a visual medium.

....

Interestingly enough, the pantheon of *Perry Mason* includes one episode— "The Case of the Nebulous Nephew" (1963)—in which *only* a phenotypically colored actor could perform a particular part critical to the plot, even as a largely absent presence. At first the episode seems classic *Perry Mason*, with the usual white cast of characters (including the servants) and a familiar story line built around ne'er-do-well relatives plotting to do each other out of the family fortune. The action begins with Ernest Stone (played by Hugh Marlowe, another veteran radio actor in one of six appearances on *Perry Mason*) schooling his handsome, young conman accomplice on the details of how to trick Stone's elderly aunts into believing that he, John Brooks (Ron Starr), is their long-lost nephew Caleb Stone IV. Ernest's scam is brilliantly conceived because Brooks is to present himself to the aunts as himself—that is, as John Brooks, a friend and former shipmate of their nephew Caleb, bringing them sad tidings of Caleb's death, while at the same time demonstrating an insider's intimate knowledge of the Stone mansion, saying and doing things only the real Caleb could.

The scheme works perfectly and soon both sisters are completely convinced that, no matter how much he denies it or what name he calls himself, John Brooks is Little Caleb, grown up and returned to the great aunts who loved him dearly but weren't strong enough to stand up to their tyrannical father—Caleb Stone, the Patent Medicine King—when he had their dead nephew Caleb III's marriage to the housemaid declared null and void and sent the young woman packing along with her son, Little Caleb IV, who was declared illegitimate and disparaged in the press as the "Patent Medicine Baby." Just as Ernest knew they would, each aunt rushes to her lawyer, Perry Mason, to have her will changed, naming John Brooks the beneficiary. But hanging around the Stone estate has consequences for his accomplice that Ernest didn't anticipate. In spite of himself, John becomes genuinely fond of the aunts who are nothing but generous, loving, and kind to him, while he also learns from the butler that it was actually Ernest Stone, his own silent partner in crime, whose specious claims of fraud did Caleb and his mother out of heritage, home, and inheritance.

Predictably, the two partners come to blows when John tries to back out of their deal. When Ernest, just as predictably, turns up dead, Brooks, of course, is the prime suspect, and the aunts implore Perry Mason to defend him. Key to Mason's defense and to the plot is determining who John Brooks is and what he has to do with Caleb Stone IV. Toward that end, Mason and his private detective aide-de-camp Paul Drake (William Hopper) make a red-eye trip to the Catholic orphanage in South Carolina that was Caleb's last-known residence, where they learn from the head nun, Sister Theresa, that Caleb, whose dying mother brought him to St. Mary's at age six, became fast friends with a nameless foundling, a "doorstep baby" the nuns dubbed John Brooks. The two boys ran away together when they were sixteen, after a tabloid exposé about the illegitimate Patent Medicine Baby resurrected the whole nasty scandal. Shown a picture of the man Mason knows as John Brooks, Sister Theresa will neither confirm nor deny that he is who he says he is; she merely smiles at the thought that the aunts are content to believe the young man calling himself John Brooks is their long-lost nephew Caleb Stone IV.

At trial, District Attorney Hamilton Burger (William Talman) attempts to one-up his perennial adversary by calling to the stand the counselor's own surprise witness—the long-lost Caleb Stone IV—whom Della and Paul have found by phone alive and well, living in Albany and only too eager to catch the first flight to L.A. to testify on behalf on his old friend. Once again, however, the joke is on Burger, because when Caleb Stone walks into the courtroom, Caleb Stone is black, played by the brown-skinned African American actor Ivan Dixon (Kinch of *Hogan Heroes*). No one says the word "black," "colored," "Negro," or "African American." It is a case of *res ipsa loquitur*: the thing speaks for itself.

Indeed, the racially marked body speaks volumes. Caleb Stone can no more be black than Shirley Temple. On the stand, Ivan Dixon's character, who of course is the foundling from St. Mary's, clarifies the relationship between Caleb Stone and John Brooks: "The color of a person's skin doesn't mean much to six-year-olds," he says, "so, we became friends, Caleb and I—brothers, really." He goes on to explain that when Caleb left the orphanage after the tabloid exposé, he joined him, and the two decided to exchange names, knowing that despite calling himself Caleb Stone no one would ever accuse him of being the Patent Medicine Baby. He also reveals that he received a letter from John Brooks, aka Caleb Stone IV, saying he had been approached by a relative who, not recognizing him, oddly enough wanted him to impersonate himself in a scheme to do the elderly aunts out of the family fortune. He had decided to go along with the plan in order to get even with the Stone family for what they did to him and his mother.

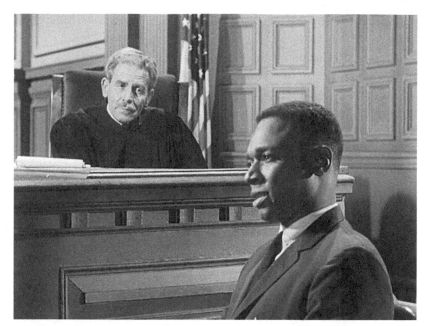

FIG. 6.3 Ivan Dixon as Caleb Stone (aka John Brooks) on the witness stand in "The Case of the Nebulous Nephew" (1963).

FIG. 6.4 The two Calebs shaking hands after the trial with the Stone aunts looking on.

Mason goes on to reveal the real killer—the deceased's lawyer friend and covert co-conspirator—but here the classic Perry Mason moment of exposure is insipidly anticlimactic, coming as it does on the heels of the colored Caleb's dramatic appearance and revelations. Black Caleb, the real John Brooks, who is on-screen for fewer than ninety seconds, speaks his lines and gets a warm handshake from White Caleb once the trial is over but then is absented from the narrative. "Brother" though he said he is to White Caleb, he's not present for the family reunion back at the Stone estate, where Perry Mason explains how he figured out who was who—that is, how he knew the young man calling himself John Brooks had to be the real Caleb Stone IV. The attitude of Sister Theresa was the first clue, he says, the fact that she would neither affirm nor deny that John was Caleb. She would have been honor bound to identify an imposter, Mason explains, but could see no harm in keeping the exchange of names a secret and letting Caleb be accepted by the aunts as himself, albeit by a different moniker.

Mason doesn't say whether he deduced the racial identity of the real John Brooks. In fact, other than what Ivan Dixon's character says on the stand, no one mentions the nonwhite elephant in the courtroom, but there are some clues along the way that encode the race trading on which the plot turns. First, two columns of black and white children file through the front doors and down the steps of St. Mary's Orphanage just as Perry Mason and Paul Drake are arriving in a cab. Mason pauses for a moment, glances back over his shoulder, and gives the children a pensive second look, almost as if he has never seen such a sight before or as if some germ of an idea is gelling. There is no logical reason for such a scene except as an objective correlative evoking an integrationist sensibility, symbolizing St. Mary's as a safe house where black and white children live and play in proximity and become best friends like Caleb and John.

Second, we might wonder why this fictional orphanage is set all the way on the other side of the country in Charleston, South Carolina. "The Case of the Nebulous Nephew" aired on September 26, 1963—a month almost to the day after Martin Luther King's March on Washington on August 28. While the episode doesn't make any overt allusion to the march or the civil rights movement, the location of the orphanage behind the Cotton Curtain and its population of black and white children at this moment in history again evoke the specter of integration. Compton or Harlem would have been too black, too obvious; locating St. Mary's in and tying Caleb to an obviously colored enclave might have upstaged the show's absent presence and stepped on the program's visually clever climax.

Third, Sister Theresa, who is otherwise circumspect and reticent, volunteers more than is necessary or seemly of John Brooks's personal history as a nameless, mother- and fatherless foundling, left on St. Mary's doorstep at five days old by an unknown nobody who presumably didn't want him. Being thrown away anonymously, without so much as a nametag, is a plausible backstory for a Negro. (So quintessentially so, in fact, that more than fifty years later, Dan Fogelman, the creator and producer of the NBC drama *This Is Us*, would hitch his new series to precisely the same blackstory of a colored newborn left at a fire station with nothing but a raggedy blanket and a dirty diaper.)[7] These elements combine to make the colored Caleb's climactic courtroom appearance surprising but not shocking. On a less dramatic scale, it's like the surprise ending to M. Night Shyamalan's supernatural thriller *The Sixth Sense* (1999) (or the premiere episode of Fogelman's series): it's only after the climactic twist has been fully turned that the clues register and we realize we should have seen it coming, but we didn't.

But there's something else curious about the color of the show's climax and its September 26 airdate. *The Dick Van Dyke Show* (1961–1966) uses exactly the same kind of sight gag as the punch line of an episode known as "That's My Boy??," which aired the night before "The Case of the Nebulous Nephew," on Wednesday, September 25, 1963, also on CBS. Yet, as much as the shows' airtimes were a month after the March on Washington, they were also only ten days after the bombing of the 16th Street Baptist Church in Birmingham, Alabama, which killed four young black girls. Was a grieving nation ready for the levity of the racial gag that the "My Boy??" episode enacted? And did "My Boy??" have a double meaning? In a flashback to the birth of the Petries' son, Ritchie, Rob (Dick Van Dyke) recounts for dinner guests his growing conviction that his boy isn't his—that he and Laura (Mary Tyler Moore) were given the wrong baby at the hospital, where the staff repeatedly confused Mrs. Petrie in Room 208 with Mrs. Peters in Room 203, who also delivered a baby boy the same day.

Just as an anxious, overwrought Rob is trying to decide what to do, the other new father, Mr. Peters, calls to say he has something that belongs to the Petries. Rob, now fully convinced he's right about the mix-up, cuts him off before he has a chance to explain what it is he has of the Petries. Jumping to conclusions, Rob quickly declares into the phone that, yes, you have our baby and we have yours, whereupon the as-yet-unseen Mr. Peters agrees to rush right over to make the exchange. Now thoroughly convinced he's right about the mix-up, Rob finally breaks the news to Laura, who he believes is simply in shock and denial when she insists the baby they have is theirs and stands ready to guard her son with her life when the doorbell rings, announcing the arrival of the Peters. When Rob opens the door, he and the studio audience are surprised to see that Mr. and Mrs. Peters are black, played by Mimi Dillard and Greg Morris (who would be cast as Barney Collier on *Mission Impossible* three years later). The Peterses enter laughing because, of course, they know they are walking proof of just how wrong Rob is.

White audiences have long loved sight gags, but the fact that the colored players here aren't minstrels or the butt of the racial joke may have helped the gag go over in households like mine. Carl Reiner, who created *The Dick Van Dyke Show*, has said that the executive producer Sheldon Leonard and some members of the cast and crew were concerned that the play on race might backfire and offend black viewers. He had no such concerns himself, Reiner says, and believed instead that introducing a black family into the all-white world of New Rochelle and the show was a baby step in the right direction. But the gag itself wasn't the show's most subversive gesture as far as he was concerned. The bigger coup came a little later in the episode, after the flashback bit, when Rob tells his guests that the two babies in the story—his son and the Peterses' son, Jimmy—now go to grade school together where Jimmy earns straight A's and Ritchie barely scrapes by. "I still think we got the wrong kid," Rob says. It's that little tagged-on dig—"that [the Peterses'] kid was in the top of the class and Ritchie was in the bottom"—that Reiner says he is most proud of.[8]

Baby steps indeed. The *New York Times* generously calls "That's My Boy??" an "expertly rendered joke" and applauds the show for striking a blow for integration. "If the March on Washington a month earlier had put race on top of the national agenda," the *Times* columnist writes, "'That's My Boy??' perhaps gently inserted it into the living rooms of suburbia." The columnist goes on to note the overwhelming whiteness of the Petries' world during the first two seasons of the show and seems to suggest that the "My Boy??" episode marked a turning point. "Now here was a new idea," he says, "middle-class blacks, having a baby just a few hospital rooms away from America's most prominent and whitest sitcom couple."[9] The episode was well received. In fact, the studio audience laughed so hard and cheered so enthusiastically that Greg Morris couldn't keep a straight face, which is wonderfully evident in the videotape. Fifty years later, it remains one of the series' best-remembered, most-discussed episodes. As I address in more detail in chapter 9, Sheldon Leonard, the producer, has said that the positive response to "That's My Boy??" in 1963 helped green-light the casting of Bill Cosby in *I Spy* in 1965. Given such a positive reaction and the supposed goodwill of the producers, *The Dick Van Dyke Show* might have made the Peterses regulars or at least brought them back a time or two. But as the one-off it was, the localized color in "That's My Boy??"—like its counterpart in "Nebulous Nephew"—is more correctly read as a comedic play on race as skin color that had bigger payoffs for the program than for "the people."

That is to say, the sudden, back-to-back appearances of black characters as plot twists and sight gags in two all-white shows on the same network one month after the March on Washington and just days after the Birmingham church bombing had less to do with an effort to insert race into the living rooms of suburbia as an aid to integration than with market share. This was a moment—not unlike our own—when Hollywood woke up to the existence of black people not simply as athletes and entertainers, mammies and maids, butlers and buffoons, but as consumers and as subject matter in which the entire world was suddenly very interested and to which it was also largely sympathetic. Nothing showed masses of black people to the world in a more positive and sympathetic light than the widely covered, well-received March on Washington and the unspeakably tragic deaths of four innocent colored girls.

Cynicism aside, "The Case of the Nebulous Nephew" is among my favorite episodes in a series I loved watching with my parents as a child. The episode is well plotted and better acted than many, although the narrative itself runs along lines similar to other tales in the oeuvre, such as "The Case of the Borrowed Baby" (1962), also featuring a boy foundling—this time left in a basket on Perry Mason's desk—with the radio actor Hugh Marlowe again playing a conniving relative trying to do an infant heir and his mother out of the family fortune. The "Nebulous Nephew" plot of mistaken identity and the twist on one character's passing for another also bear no small resemblance to the encounter with the Wilks family in *Adventures of Huckleberry Finn*, where Huck becomes too fond of the three lovely, kind, trusting Wilks sisters to stand by and let a conman king and duke bilk them out of their inheritance.

But if, as they say, we are most easily hurt by those whom or that which we love, there is also something troubling to me about *Perry Mason* that "The Case of the Nebulous Nephew" drives home: race was of no matter except where it could be played for plot and profit in a series that otherwise all but ignored black difference at a critical moment in American history. But I'm surprised at myself by how much this perception is an afterthought and not something that troubled me at the time.

With the hindsight of half a century, *Perry Mason* seems to me oddly out of step not with TV of the times but with itself in its black absence. Airing as it did from September 1957 to May 1966, the series ran directly alongside the civil rights movement, yet there is no sign in it of what was happening at that time, not only across the country but in its own backyard, from the infamous, deadly, destructive Watts riots close by in South Central L.A., to the local battles over restrictive housing covenants and segregated schools, including the American Civil Liberties Union's 1963 lawsuit against the Los Angeles Unified School District, which encompasses Hollywood High. Unlike today's law-and-order courtroom dramas and police procedurals, *Perry Mason* in the '50s and '60s didn't rip its plotlines and story arcs from current events and newspaper headlines. (Thirty years later, its successor *L.A. Law*, for example, would go out of its way to build several episodes around the Rodney King beating, the acquittal of the police officers involved, and the subsequent Los Angeles uprising of 1992.)

Hollywood at midcentury was racially risk averse, and *Perry Mason* was hardly alone in turning a blind eye to the plight of black America and the raging campaign for freedom and equality that dominated the news. But Erle Stanley Gardner, who created Mason first as the hero of a series of novels (six of which were made into Warner Brothers films in the 1930s), then as the star of a television series, honed his own considerable legal skills defending members of the Chinese communities of Southern California against discrimination and police harassment. Some sources even describe him as a civil rights attorney. Moreover, as a writer, he went to great lengths to fashion Perry Mason as a champion of the underdog, finely concerned with justice and equity. So where are the black minorities, the colored masses, yearning for the equal protection of the laws that both Gardner and his hero Perry Mason so esteemed? I'm not sure how much I countenanced my own absence at the time, but what was missing on the screen I made up for in my imagination.

To me, Perry Mason was a (capeless) crusader like Superman, Mighty Mouse, and Wonder Woman, committed to righting wrongs wrought of man's inhumanity to man. Lying awake in bed at night, I scripted episodes of my own version of the show in which my intrepid champion of the people flew to the defense of colored characters wrongly accused of capital crimes, which sometimes included doing in adversarial public figures from the front lines of the raging war on Jim Crow such as Alabama's "segregation now, segregation tomorrow, segregation forever" Governor George Wallace and his henchman police commissioner, Bull Connor. Even in my early teens, by which time I should have put away my childish things, I imagined Perry Mason shuffling off to Birmingham to get Martin Luther King out of jail. Sometimes I would be the Mason-like figure, presenting some brilliant oral argument before the bench. (I once turned a Freshman Comp essay assignment on argumentation into a polylogue in which Socrates, Stokely Carmichael, and H. Rap Brown debated the relative merits of nonviolence and Black Power.) Television made me the insomniac I am today, I think, because night after night I would fight sleep, not wanting the narratives in my head to end. I suppose I put too much stock in fictional characters, but I also worshipped the ground the black civil rights attorney and future Supreme Court Justice Thurgood Marshall orated on. Hero worship being the crazy thing it is, sometimes Mason and Marshall would merge into the same beatified being, instilling in me a fervent desire to become a lawyer.

I have always wished and will always wish as a child of the '50s and '60s that my own activism had been more, that I had been a Freedom Rider, journeying into the segregated South with John Lewis, now a Georgia congressman, then head of the Student Nonviolent Coordinating Committee and one of the original thirteen black and white activists who set out from Washington, D.C., in May of 1961, when I was twelve, bent on integrating bus terminals en route to New Orleans and who met with all manner of Klan violence along the way, especially in Wallace's Alabama. Lewis was also one of the activists leading the first march from Selma to Montgomery who was beaten by state troopers and gassed at the site of the Edmund Pettus Bridge in Selma on what became known as Bloody Sunday, March 7, 1965—another day that lives in infamy for the police brutality that left Lewis with a fractured skull and enduring scars still visible today. According to my parents, I was too young to go south as a Freedom Rider or otherwise actively participate in the campaign for voter registration and equal rights, even though children younger than I did do so.

Although the chickens would come closer to home to roost in the 1970s with the violent response to the court-ordered desegregation of Boston area schools, our town was a little like the land the times forgot where the civil rights movement was concerned. I think most white townies at the time, if they thought about it at all, saw segregation as the South's problem. East Bridgewater had been integrated since the early 1950s, after all, even if only by one or two black families who didn't make waves and were more like "us" than like those rabble-rousers down south. That doesn't mean, however, that the campaign for social justice left my family behind untouched. We were at best armchair activists compared to those who risked and in some cases lost their lives, but we were caught up in the tempo of the times in other ways, with both of my parents going to work for Self Help, Inc.—my father in the

Neighborhood Youth Corps and my mother in Head Start, both local flanks of the War on Poverty.

....

We had gone south for the first time in the summer of 1960—not to integrate lunch counters or register voters, I'm sorry to say, but for a family excursion that would take us across the Mason-Dixon Line, along the southeastern coast to Florida and eventually land us even farther south, in the Caribbean in fact. We packed up the car and left our home in the wee hours of the morning when the roads were near empty, planning to drive straight through to Miami, where we would stop overnight and then board a plane bound for my father's hometown of Kingston, Jamaica. We were flying to Kingston from Miami rather than from Boston because the flight was so much cheaper— only $49 round-trip—at a time when air travel was prohibitively expensive.

The trip had been well planned, months in the making, and funded in part, like George Jefferson's dry-cleaning enterprise, from an insurance settlement from a car accident my parents had been in where they, again like Jefferson, were rear-ended, although not by a city bus. The small cash settlement—even smaller after the lawyer's cut—was hard earned because my father was seriously injured in the accident and out of work for weeks, which was tough on a family for whom money was already tight. (We had a small, old-fashioned record player with a crank that my brothers and I loved playing with. It disappeared, and none of us kids could figure out what became of it. Years later Mom and Dad admitted they had pawned it during that tough period to help put food on the table. We were completely oblivious and, as I said, always well fed.) My mother made it clear that she would have preferred to use the insurance settlement to pay bills or to put toward finishing the house, but even her most practical side couldn't argue too strenuously against my father's desire to go home for the first time in more than fifteen years and to introduce his American family to their Jamaican relatives, especially since his father had died in the interim and been buried without his knowing anything about it. His mother had written after the fact explaining that she hadn't let him know of his father's passing because she understood what a hardship it would have been for him to come home for the funeral.

Mom, who had had a difficult hysterectomy some months earlier and said she didn't feel up to the trip, urged Dad to take us kids and go without her. He wouldn't hear of it; so, even though I'm inclined to think my mother got her way about most things in our family autocracy, off we all went somewhat against her wishes, with our new five-piece, graduated set of matching blue luggage full of new summer clothes, gifts for relatives (including hats for Grandma), and two new cameras—a Brownie still and an 8mm Bell & Howell movie camera—to document our journey. With my father as the only driver at the time, we still made our way south pretty much nonstop, save for a few rest periods, following the route that AAA had mapped out for us. We had an agenda, however, that AAA hadn't considered and that took us down backcountry roads through the middle of nowhere. We had packed plenty of provisions, but my parents refused to stop for water, ice, gas, or bathroom breaks anywhere advertising separate facilities for "colored" and "white."

My parents' refusal to play by the rules of segregation—with which we were all in accord—made us uniquely dependent on the kindness of colored strangers who gave us water and let us use their bathroom facilities, such as they often were, and a few white merchants who didn't care whom they sold gas to. Our relatively passive resistance to Jim Crow was a luxury we could well afford, since we were merely passing through the inhuman conditions people who looked like us were forced to live with day in and day out. I've said that just a year or two earlier, as a child of nine or ten, it had hit me for the first time that the country was less than a hundred years removed from slavery. Traveling through the South that summer of 1960 was like stepping back a hundred years into a world time had forgotten, the vestiges of slavery painfully evident in miles upon miles of ramshackle slave cabins and share-cropper shanties surrounded by cotton- or canefields.

I'm reminded of our southern sojourn, the miles of canefields, and my first taste of the stalks in Jamaica that we would learn to cut, strip, and chew in order to get their juice every time I watch Ava DuVernay's beautifully shot series *Queen Sugar* (based on Natalie Baszile's novel), which debuted on OWN in the fall of 2016, with Oprah Winfrey as one of its executive producers and a much-lauded, all-woman directorial team. Although the three siblings who inherit an eight-hundred-acre sugarcane farm in Louisiana learn to love and fight for the land their ancestors once worked as slaves, they live in far better conditions in the today of the TV series than the black farmers and share-croppers we encountered in 1960 still living and working like the enslaved. I am and I imagine forever will be haunted by the acres of shacks and the sad eyes of small children already shorn of hope and possibility. The sight—the grotesque American gothic—of how others like us were forced to live jarred me and woke me up to real poverty and misery wrought of racism. I told myself that I would never again complain about our unfinished house or think of myself as poor.

We reached Miami safely and by prior arrangement stayed overnight with a black family we didn't know who let us use their home as a way station where we could bathe, rest, and change into our Sunday best in the morning for the plane ride. They also fed us, took us to the airport, and kept our car for us for the three weeks we were gone. It's an odd thing to think about today—strangers taking in strangers—but it's how black people traveled through Jim Crow America not just in the nineteenth century as you might read about in history books but in my own lifetime. The great Jackie Robinson, who famously broke the color barrier in Major League Baseball, wasn't as successful with hotel accommodations. As captured in the 2013 biopic 42, in 1946 Robinson couldn't be lodged with his white teammates at the Mayfield Hotel during his first spring training in Sanford, Florida (the same town where more than a half century later Trayvon Martin would be killed). Instead, he and his wife were put up at the home of a local black doctor.[10]

Fourteen years later, race relations in Florida and the rest of the Deep South had little changed. Even if we could have afforded the luxury, a hotel would likely have meant racially segregated accommodations at best, unacceptable to our family. As a matter of both economy and conviction, my parents had arranged through friends of friends to stay with that wonderful black family who opened their home and their hearts to us, in much the same tradition as the informal interfamilial escort service that would provide my prom dates a few years hence.

There was even such a thing as *The Negro Motorist Green Book*, a published travel guide that listed Negro-friendly places at which to stay throughout the United States.[11] The realities of racial discrimination and segregation that made the *Green Book* necessary for colored travelers and the kind of homegrown bed-and-breakfast network my family participated in (we, too, opened our home to strangers) were also what led to the establishment of a number of black resorts dotted across the country, including Highland Beach, Maryland, founded by Frederick Douglass's son Major Charles Douglass, a Civil War veteran, and his wife, Laura, in the early 1890s after they were turned away from the Bay Ridge Resort in Maryland.[12] Other popular, once primarily African American resorts such as Sag Harbor in the Hamptons, Idlewild in northwestern Michigan, and Oak Bluffs on Martha's Vineyard have similar histories and reasons for being.

We flew to Kingston aboard KLM Royal Dutch Airlines: I'm not sure why. I wish I knew whether the choice to fly foreign rather than domestic had anything to do with racial discrimination or was merely a function of affordability and convenience. Airlines, unlike buses and trains, were never officially segregated as far as I understand, but airports often were; de facto discrimination was as real in and around air travel during the Golden Age of Flying in the 1950s and '60s as it was elsewhere in the country. In addition to tales of their troubles with lodging, Jackie and Rachel Robinson were also bumped from flights and refused service in airport restaurants in the South.[13] Of our own experience in 1960, I can say that to the best of my recollection we were the only black people on the plane, which was continuing on to Caracas, Venezuela, after the stop in Kingston, Jamaica. We were in economy or what they used to call tourist class, but we were treated like royalty. Part of it was the luxurious nature of air travel during the industry's Golden Age when airlines went out of their way to attend to the care and comfort of their passengers and travelers dressed to the nines in suits and ties, hats and gloves to fly from here to there. But the other part of it, I'm convinced, was the special attention the flight crew showered upon us as a family of five traveling together by air for the first time.

Even in economy, we and the other passengers were served filet mignon going out and lobster coming back, although the lobster was just for us—that is, solely for our family. Our return flight had been delayed leaving Kingston due to a threatened hurricane. The pilot announced that there would be no inflight meal service due to the late departure and invited passengers to dine at the airline's expense in either Havana, Cuba, where we were laying over, or Miami when we reached our final destination. Despite the announcement, however, the stewardesses served our family three-course lobster dinners, which they said they happened to have just enough of for the five of us. People sitting nearby eyed our food with an envy that made me feel guilty and self-conscious, even as I heard some mumbling that we must be dignitaries. I tried to sit up straighter in my seat and stick out my pinky finger whenever I picked up my cup.

The other passengers received some pretty impressive refreshments as well, much closer to a meal than the peanuts served today as snacks. Included with their boxed lunches were packets of pilots' wings for the few kids onboard, which we didn't get with our lobster dinners. I really wanted a set of those wings, but since the crew had already been so kind and accommodating, I didn't think I should ask. I learned my lesson from an incident in my toddler days that I barely remembered but hadn't been allowed to forget or live down. The owner of the Crescent Bakery in Brockton had given me a brownie. I had said, "Thank you," politely enough, and even added the compliment, "You a nice lady," but had also promptly appended the demand, "Now gimme one for my brother." The baker laughed and said it showed I wasn't a selfish child, but Mom and Dad were mortified that not only had I demanded a second freebie brownie but I also hadn't said "please." They never failed to point out in telling the story, as they did for decades, that the truly unselfish gesture would have been to share *my* brownie with Adrian instead of asking for a second. Danny was just a baby or I suppose I would have demanded a brownie for him, too.

The duCille family's excellent adventure that summer was a compendium of firsts: first trip behind the Cotton Curtain, first flight, first time out of the country (for all but my father), first time in Jamaica, first and last in Cuba (since this was just before the travel ban that would last more than fifty-five years), and, of course, the first time meeting most of our Jamaican relatives. For my mother, it was the first and only time she had to acquiesce in her maternal authority and perform the persona of the dutiful daughter-in-law. Although Mom hadn't wanted to make the trip, I remember feeling comforted by the happy, excited smile on her face as the plane took off from Miami, which had convinced me that she was as caught up in the adventure as the rest of us. Not surprisingly, her smile was even brighter when we took off from Kingston three weeks later, even if she was upset about having to travel bareheaded (and therefore not properly dressed), because, along with the gift chapeaux we brought her, Grandma Florence had literally taken Mom's last hat right off her head.

For me, it was the first and only time I was in the mesmerizing presence of the strong, powerful paternal grandmother after whom I'm named, even though what I inherited is the first name I use only where officialdom requires. My father's oldest brother, Uncle Hampa (Hugh), took us through the sugar refinery where he worked, where we experienced firsthand how the cane stalks we had seen growing tall during our trip south are transformed into the refined commodity we sprinkled on our cereal. A younger brother, Uncle Frank, and his wife, Aunt Pincie (Lolita), had five sons. I spent a lot of time with the baby, Houston, coaxing him in his first steps, and I still hear in my mind's ear the cadence of little Cousin Oliver's complaint that one of his brothers was messing with the pair of pants my father had made for him: "Uncle Ever! Uncle Ever! Donovan troublin' me trousers!" ("Ever" being short for Everard). Frank Jr., called Sammy, was the oldest.

But the boy cousin I remember most from that trip and would come to know best in later years is then four-year-old Michelangelo Everard duCille,

FIG. 6.5 Grandma Florence with assorted children: Adrian standing, Danny sitting on step, and Ann sitting on a porch wall in Jamaica; the girl in the foreground with her arms crossed is Cousin Dimples, the daughter of Dad's sister Aunt Tiny (Enid) (1960).

FIG. 6.6 Uncle Frank and Aunt Pincie with their five sons and Aunt P's aunt Ethel Clark in Jamaica in the early 1960s. From left to right: Aunt Ettie holding Oliver, Frank Jr. ("Sammy"), Donovan, Michelangelo ("Mikey"), and Houston.

to whom this book is dedicated. Little Michelangelo was so particularly memorable both because he bore my father's middle name and because even as a child he emitted a certain light that anticipated how well he would live up to the promise of his name as a three-time Pulitzer Prize–winning photojournalist, humanitarian, and artist who sought with each image to capture the struggles, dignity, and perseverance of the human spirit, whether his subject was what he himself called "the ravages of the [Ebola] virus" in Liberia, the crisis of crack cocaine on the streets of Miami, the devastation of a volcano eruption in South America, the desolation of war in Afghanistan, or the treatment of veterans at the Walter Reed Army Medical Center in Washington, D.C.—the site of an investigative series for which Michel (as he called himself) won his third Pulitzer Prize, shared with fellow *Washington Post* reporters Dana Priest and Anne Hull.[14]

At some point in our adult friendship, I took to teasing Michelangelo that I had to Google him before each phone call to see how many Pulitzers and other prizes he had won since our last conversation. He was kind enough to claim he kept track of me the same way, but I knew, of course, it wasn't true—just a joke between first cousins who liked and admired each other but never saw enough of one another, always thinking there would be time: time to connect, time to visit, time to collaborate on imagined projects. But there wasn't time. Michelangelo died of an apparent heart attack in 2014 while on assignment in Liberia, covering the Ebola outbreak for the *Washington Post.* It is only small comfort that he died doing the work he loved, writing life in a foreign land with the light of his camera lens.

Sad memories aside, of all the delights, discoveries, and dangers of our trip in the summer of '60, the most formative facet of the journey for me was the glimpse of the southern side of Jim Crow and the cruel legacies of slavery. I returned home wanting more than ever to be a lawyer, to be that cross between Thurgood Marshall and Perry Mason I imagined in my day and night dreams. In keeping with the spirit of the times, I wanted not only to rescue the perishing but also to save the world from the worst of itself.

While most television series of the '50s and '60s contributed little or nothing to the cause of civil rights as such, many Hollywood personalities were visibly present in the movement. Actually working closely for and with Martin Luther King—as I only dreamed of doing—they risked their livelihood and in some cases their lives both because they believed in the cause and because they were corralled by fellow artists and dedicated black activists like Dick Gregory, Sammy Davis Jr., Sidney Poitier, Ossie Davis, Ruby Dee, and especially Harry Belafonte—what Emilie Raymond calls "the Leading Six" in *Stars for Freedom: Hollywood, Black Celebrities, and the Civil Rights Movement* (2015). This gang of six knew star power would attract media interest and national attention and therefore worked at drawing some of Hollywood's biggest celebrities into the movement. Marlon Brando, whom Raymond identifies as "the first major Hollywood star to join demonstrations in Los Angeles," lobbied to bring more black actors and crewmembers into the film industry and became a big presence in the fair housing campaigns in Southern California (a cause Hattie McDaniel had championed two decades earlier). His participation in the movement brought unprecedented media attention to the cause but also got him branded a "nigger-loving creep," which Raymond says Brando simply brushed off and kept on marching and protesting.[15] He and a retinue of actors, directors, producers, and performers would be with Dr. King at the March on Washington for Jobs and Freedom in 1963. In addition to marching, others like Diahann Carroll would perform at benefits to help fund the movement. Still others, also like Carroll, would testify before Congress about limited opportunities and discriminatory practices within their own industry.

Charlton Heston stands tall among the many Hollywood supporters, not just because of his height. Long before he became president of the National Rifle Association, he was an activist of a different kind, picketing segregated lunch counters and standing up for equality. Asked why he was among the many marching in Washington in 1963, Heston gave a response less well remembered than the famous fighting words he uttered in 2000, "From my cold, dead hands," but more potent: "Two years ago, I picketed some restaurants in Oklahoma," he said, "but with that one exception—up until very recently—like most Americans I expressed my support of civil rights largely by talking about it at cocktail parties. But like many Americans this summer, I could no longer pay only lip service to a cause that was so urgently right, and in a time that is so urgently now."[16]

The little black girl who so admired Perry Mason would have been thrilled to hear such words from the lips of Raymond Burr or to see Mason—I mean Burr—marching alongside Belafonte and the star-studded group *Variety* dubbed the "show biz contingent," many of whom flew to D.C. together on a chartered plane.[17] But the aged, jaded black woman I am today has learned that it's hard to say where rhetoric ends and action begins, especially action that effects real change. Looking at Hollywood then and now, one could say,

FIG. 6.7 Harry Belafonte, James Garner, Marlon Brando, Frank Silvera, Charlton Heston, and other Hollywood stars arriving by chartered plane for the March on Washington in 1963. Frank Silvera is the black actor who played both a white businessman in "The Case of the Fancy Figures" and a Mexican ranchero in *The High Chaparral*. PHOTOGRAPH BY THOMAS J. O'HALLORAN, COURTESY OF LIBRARY OF CONGRESS, LC-DIG-PPMSCA-37249.

"Physician, heal thyself." To those who called for a boycott of the 2016 Oscars after no artists of color were nominated for awards for the second year in a row, the white, mostly male power structure that was Hollywood in the 1950s and '60s doesn't look that different from the powers that be today. In fact, in February of 2016, the *New York Times* published an exposé titled "The Faces of American Power, Nearly as White as the Oscar Nominees," an interactive graphic depicting 503 of the most powerful captains of industry, culture, government, and education, only forty-four of whom are minorities. Of the twenty-nine executives the *Times* lists as the "people who decide which television shows Americans see," only two are flagged as minorities, both black women: Shonda Rhimes and Channing Dungey, the head of ABC Entertainment, who became the first black network president in February of 2016.[18]

Perry Mason, at least in the 1950s edition of the series, never rose to the defense of a black man, woman, or child in distress like the capeless crusader of my imagination, but I have no idea where his alter ego Raymond Burr stood on civil rights. His later TV outings—the detective series *Ironside* (1967 to 1975) and the thirty made-for-TV *Perry Mason* movies (1985 to 1995)—were more ecumenical than the original show, with Don Mitchell cast as Ironside's ex-con caregiver and minordomo Mark Sanger, and Al Freeman Jr. and James McEachin, African American actors, as the Lt. Tragg equivalents in the Mason movies, as well as the black actors who guest-starred in each of the two later series. Although still played by Burr, the Honorable Judge Perry Mason who resigns from the bench in order to defend Della Street against a murder charge in the first of the TV movies seems little like the Perry Mason of my youth; I never warmed up to him in the same way I admired his 1950s incarnation. Nor did I care much for Burr as Robert T. Ironside, who seemed to me more despot than detective, with a looming presence from a wheelchair that dwarfed the rest of the ensemble cast. Then, too, by 1967 Don Mitchell's role on *Ironside* wasn't the benchmark it would have been a decade earlier. Here was that missing black presence, but why did he have to be not only the lone Negro minority in a subservient position but also an ex-criminal among good cops, effectively rescued by the Man and transformed into a law-abiding citizen and eventually a lawyer under the white man's wing? I didn't much cotton to seeing Burr as Big Daddy Bountiful.

In real life, Raymond Burr was by all reports a kind and generous man, who didn't necessarily flaunt the philanthropy he practiced and the good deeds he did. Briefly married and divorced in his early thirties, he also lived in a closet that could not have been comfortable, covering over his homosexuality with imaginary dead wives and even an invented son he claimed died of leukemia. Like many gay actors of the era, in the public eye he lived the lie that the times demanded. In private, however, in the early 1960s he found a life companion in Robert Benevides, with whom he seems to have lived happily until the end of his days in 1993.

Many of Burr's obituaries quote his claim from an Associated Press interview that *Perry Mason* educated midcentury audiences—"particularly the minorities"—about the American legal system and demonstrated that "the system of justice was for them." On its own, the assertion seems oddly anachronistic in singling out minorities, since in the 1960s the term typically included and most often specifically encoded African Americans—the very people never seen served by the justice system the series depicts and the same group who continue to see themselves as ill served by the rule of law in real life. Nevertheless, the *Baltimore Sun* goes Burr one better, speculating that the civil rights movement "never could have held the commitment of its followers nor won the sympathy of the American people without the reminder of the ideal of impartial justice beamed into the nation's living rooms each week on *Perry Mason*."[19] Raymond Burr might be thrilled to find his little show credited with enabling the big civil rights movement, but Perry Mason would surely object: overreaching; assumes facts not in evidence; incompetent, irrelevant, and immaterial.

Chapter 7

"Soaploitation"

GETTING AWAY WITH
MURDER IN PRIME TIME

This is Criminal Law 100, or, as I like to call it, How to Get
Away with Murder. I don't know what terrible things you've
done in your life up to this point, but clearly your karma's
out of balance to get assigned to my class.

—PROFESSOR ANNALISE KEATING, *How to Get Away
with Murder* (S1, E1)

Watching the balloon-drop on the closing night of the 2016 Democratic
National Convention, at which Secretary of State Hillary Clinton became the
first woman nominated for the office of president by a major party, I was
reminded of the excitement I had felt a half century earlier at another historic convention, where I had been one of the lithe, young campaign workers
running around in a blue dress and straw hat, carrying a placard and chant-
ing, "Go, Brooke, go! Go, Brooke, go!"

In 1966, Edward William Brooke III, the first black attorney general not
only of the Commonwealth of Massachusetts but of any state in the union,
was running for the U.S. Senate as a Republican. My parents leaned left, but
politics wasn't nearly as divisively partisan in the mid-twentieth century as
it has become in the twenty-first, so Brooke's party affiliation little mattered
stacked up against his other credentials. At an all-knowing seventeen, I wasn't
certain about his stance against Black Power and his open condemnation of

Stokely Carmichael, but he was otherwise on the right side of history and the social justice issues I cared about. He had even bucked the GOP in refusing to back Barry Goldwater, who was no friend of civil rights (and he would go on to become the first Republican to call for Richard Nixon's resignation in 1974). Then, too, there were personal connections that tied my family to Brooke and his senatorial campaign. He had been Great Aunt Alice's lawyer long before he entered politics and became an attorney general. In fact, if I remember correctly, Aunt Alice was still represented by his former law partner, whom he had chastened to take good care of her.

I'm not sure we had actually met Ed Brooke before joining his campaign, though we traveled on the fringe of some of the same circles—most notably the South Shore Citizens Club, a black social and political organization of which my parents were members. The organization was wholeheartedly behind sending Brooke to Washington as the first black senator since Reconstruction and the only African American to be popularly elected to the Senate rather than appointed by a state legislature. I don't know how my classmates spent that summer of 1966, but along with my part-time jobs first at that same Crescent Bakery of brownie fame, then at Sears, I got to be a "Brooke Girl"—one of several dozen teenage volunteer campaign workers. Dad got to ply his expertise as a tailor in service of the campaign. With a little help from my mother and me as cutters and hand sewers, he made all of the white bolero jackets the Brooke Girls wore with the blue sleeveless sheaths that were the official outfits we donned for campaign events, most notably the State Convention at the Hynes Auditorium in Boston on June 25. Brooke went on to win the election by a landslide in 1966 and again in 1972. The rest is history, although not what it might have been.

A moderate, even liberal Republican, Brooke is widely credited with trying to steer the party to the left rather than the right. More than once he was touted as a viable candidate for the vice presidency, including as a possible replacement for Spiro Agnew in 1972. On the occasion of Brooke's death in 2015, John Nichols, the national affairs correspondent for *The Nation*, speculated about what a different turn history and the Republican Party would have taken if the senator had been Richard Nixon's running mate in either 1968 or 1972 or if he had ascended to the vice presidency after Agnew's resignation in 1973, as some camps lobbied for. Then, "upon Nixon's resignation in 1974," Nichols writes, "Brooke would have been positioned to become the first African-American president"—thirty-four years before Barack Obama.[1]

It didn't happen that way, of course, and it is important to note as well that Brooke had his detractors, particularly among African Americans where, as

THE COMMONWEALTH OF MASSACHUSETTS
DEPARTMENT OF THE ATTORNEY GENERAL
STATE HOUSE, BOSTON
June 20, 1966

EDWARD W. BROOKE
ATTORNEY GENERAL

FIGS. 7.1 AND 7.2
Mom and Dad with
Ed Brooke in 1966,
and a thank-you letter
from the senator.

Mr. Adrian DuCille
560 Thatcher Street
Brockton, Massachusetts

Dear Mr. DuCille:

Winona Fredie and Sally Saltonstall have
told me of your kindness in offering to make fifty
jackets to go with the dresses for the "Brooke girls"
to wear at the Convention and throughout the campaign.

Although I know Winona and Sally thanked you
for taking on such an enormous task at the last minute,
I did not want to let another day go by without putting
into writing my own appreciation.

I look forward to meeting you and your wife,
Pearl, and thanking you in person for this valuable
contribution to my campaign.

With warm regards and appreciation, I am,

Sincerely yours,

Edward W. Brooke

EWB/ss

the Harvard political scientist Leah Wright Rigueur points out in her master-ful monograph *The Loneliness of the Black Republican* (2015), more militant voices "pilloried Brooke's middle-class respectability politics and integration-ist philosophies."[2] There were times when I, too, in my youthful exuberance clamored for Brooke to do more, be more. Still, his role in the Senate for the two terms he served and in American politics in the 1960s and '70s was remarkable, and I'm proud of the minuscule part my family played in the historic campaign that first put him in national office. Some pundits have claimed that the support of African American constituents had little bearing on Brooke's initial Senate win, because blacks represented less than 3 percent of the Commonwealth's electorate in 1966.[3] Perhaps, but the election of Ed-ward Brooke III was another one of those milestones that meant a great deal to people like us in the 1960s. It was one small step in our own revolution against taxation without representation.

With my budding love of the law, part of what I admired about Ed Brooke was the simple fact that he was a lawyer—the first attorney I saw up close and personal, as opposed to on TV. Watching *Perry Mason* had made me fantasize about becoming a lawyer as I played out murder mysteries in my head. Even with a very active imagination, however, I never went so far as to envision a legal thriller like ABC's *How to Get Away with Murder* in which the actor play-ing the wily, winning criminal defense attorney isn't a white man like Ray-mond Burr but a black woman like Viola Davis. Of course, Mason as played by Burr was a man of integrity who would go to almost any lengths within the law not simply to win the case but to prove his client's innocence. And, as fans know, Mason's clients were (almost) always innocent, as he would demonstrate at the climax of each trial or preliminary hearing by exposing the actual perpetrator in the usual "Perry Mason moment."

By contrast, Annalise Keating, as played brilliantly by Viola Davis in *How to Get Away with Murder*, is not above throwing ethics out the window in order to win an acquittal for a client she knows is guilty. A professor of law at a prestigious, fictional Philadelphia university as well as a ruthless, even unscrupulous, defense attorney, Keating specializes in teaching first-year law students the fine art of getting killers off. Her pupils learn their lessons well, it seems. We know almost immediately from flash-forwards in the opening episodes of the first season that four of her five best and brightest chosen disciples become embroiled in covering up the murder of Keating's own philandering, Caucasian husband Sam Keating (Tom Verica), a professor of psychology at the same university, but for much of the season we don't know who killed him; nor do we know who murdered the pregnant undergraduate with whom he was having an affair. The double-barrel whodunits—who killed the coed and who offed the faithless husband—splay out over other story lines and other murder cases, but much of the sustaining suspense of the first season turns on the possibility that when the Perry Mason moment arrives and Sam Keating's killer is finally revealed, the murderer just might be the law professor herself. By the time we learn that Attorney Keating engineered the cover-up but did not actually kill her husband, there's another dead body in her basement whose blood may be on the professor's hands and enough flashbacks and flash-forwards for us to know there are acres of scorched earth under Annalise Keating's stilettos.

Nobody has clean hands in this complex ShondaLand drama, created by Peter Nowalk and executive produced by Shonda Rhimes. Annalise Keating has a lover of her own—a black police detective she both screws and screws over, humiliating him on the witness stand and even framing him for her husband's murder. Even so, she is outraged by her spouse's lies and philandering, and at one point she confronts him with an accusatory query that became a tagline: "Why is your penis on a dead girl's phone?" Perry Mason never would have spoken the word "penis," of course. In the nine years he practiced law in our living rooms, the only briefs we ever saw him take off were the handwritten arguments he tore from a legal pad and passed to his confidential secretary, Della Street, to type. And the most physical he and Della ever got with each other or anybody else was a demure kiss on the cheek and a turn on the dance floor.

Conversely, explicit simulated sex is everywhere in *How to Get Away with Murder*, and the cheeks and lips that get kissed on-screen are just as likely to lie below the belt as above. In the series premiere, Wes Gibbins (Alfred Enoch), Annalise Keating's favored law student and the resident young black man of slowly unfolding mystery with a simian-sounding surname and past ties to the professor, walks into her office unannounced and interrupts her being pleasured from below by her bare-chested, outrageously ripped whipping-boytoy, whose wife is home alone dying of ovarian cancer. ShondaLand Productions is committed to equal-opportunity sexual representation, so in an ensuing scene, another law student, Connor Walsh (Jack Falahee), the resident gay guy, takes one for the team, blithely bedding an IT geek to get the goods he needs to curry favor with his mentor. It's a stroke of good luck that the hookup on the fly develops into a serious relationship, especially because a similar hookup *of* the fly with another gay guy bedded for evidentiary purposes ends in the screwee's suicide.

When I first started watching TV in the 1950s, Lucille Ball and Desi Arnaz, even though married in real life, could not be shown on-screen reposing together; the bedroom of their TV apartment was famously furnished with twin beds separated by a large nightstand that might as well have been the Berlin Wall. The same is true of Dick Van Dyke and Mary Tyler Moore as Rob and Laura Petrie in the 1960s. (Lucy, by the way, reportedly was not allowed to say the word "pregnant" when she was "expecting" both on the show and in real life.) For most of TV's near seventy-year history as home entertainment, black sexuality—especially black female sexuality—was either wanton or wanting. Gay, lesbian, and trans sexuality didn't exist to be televisualized.

Given this history, there's a lot that's refreshing about ShondaLand's mature representations of hetero-, homo-, and bisexuality. I'm less comfortable with the detail that this sexual freedom is so often expressed as promiscuity and infidelity in both *How to Get Away with Murder* and *Scandal*, frequently edged as well by elements of rage, revenge, manipulation, betrayal, and even force, which trouble the waters in ways that may be more prescriptive than progressive, perhaps interpretively in league with easy readings that claim Annalise Keating and Olivia Pope as "feminist heroines" and applaud both shows for their bold feminist politics. Certainly, one reason for these labels is the number and prominent positioning of strong, complex female characters—especially black female leads. But feminism isn't just a body count, female figures by the number, or simply powerful women in high places. Is female agency "feminist" if it's used to manipulate, maim, and murder in the same destructive fashion as male authority? Annalise Keating and her *Scandal* counterpart Olivia Pope are the kind of formidable, liberated black females the civil rights and women's movements made possible. At least they start out that way. Their existence in fact and representation in fiction are conceivable largely because of feminism, which untethered female sexuality from reproduction and marriage, and black female sexuality from the iron girdle of racial respectability.

I want to suggest, however, that in a close reading of *Scandal* and *Murder* what we get might actually be interpreted as an undoing of a black feminist heroics—a slow, season-by-season, frame-by-frame dismantling and disintegration of the fierce, feisty, take-no-prisoners personas that many viewers found so appealing and liberating. So that by the seventh and final season of *Scandal*, Olivia Pope has devolved into a power-mad, Oval-obsessed White House chief of staff, doing double duty and killing left and right as her father's

FIGS. 7.3 AND 7.4 Lucille Ball and Desi Arnaz as Lucy and Ricky Ricardo, mid-1950s; Dick Van Dyke and Mary Tyler Moore as Rob and Laura Petrie, mid-1960s.

successor as Command, even as she has left her namesake fix-it firm Olivia Pope and Associates (OPA) to her gladiators, in the swan song of a show taken over by fantastically violent, preposterously twisted narrative arcs and criminally bad storytelling.[4] Similarly, Annalise Keating, by the end of season three of *Murder*, has gone from a tough but esteemed lawyer and law professor at the top of her game to a sloppy mean drunk, accused of and jailed for murder and arson, who has lost her teaching job, her law license, her lover, her house, and the respect and admiration of her student disciples who once wanted to be her.

And in what is at once a brilliant turn and the most unkindest twist of all, this formidable, fallen, onetime "queen" of the courtroom—in the words of her cellmate Jasmine (S3, E10)—ultimately will upright herself and get her and her killer cohort off the hook and primed to reinvent themselves for season four by blaming their collective crimes on the dead black regular Wes Gibbins, the closest thing the show had to a cause and a conscience. Wes, who incidentally if not accidentally struck the blow that finished off Sam Keating, becomes the series' scapegoat or—in keeping with his surname one letter shy of "gibbons"—perhaps its signifying monkey. That is to say, Professor Keating, Esquire, cleverly, like a true trickster figure, saves herself and her students by betraying yet again the very black male protégé from her past she supposedly has risked so much to save and protect but, as plotted and played, somehow has been failing since he was twelve years old and she fled the scene of his mother's suicide, leaving a little boy to discover the only parent he had ever known bleeding to death before his eyes.

As with what happened to that little boy and his mother, much of what we come to know about Annalise we learn from flashbacks. Annalise is from Memphis, Tennessee, went to Harvard Law School, made her way into a prestigious professorship and a successful law practice, married her therapist and lives with him in his family home near the university where they both teach. Beyond this basic backstory, we initially don't know much about how Professor Keating came to be the powerhouse professional she is when we first meet her. We do know that she has a penchant for putting to practical use what traditionally have been called "feminine wiles," perhaps not typically a feminist means to an end, but all's fair in love and litigation. The counselor is quick to instruct her female protégées to use their bodily endowments to get her whatever she needs to win a case: "What's the matter? You don't know how to use your boobs?" she asks Michaela Pratt, the black female intern she sends to gather information about a black male client in an episode titled "Skanks Get Shanked" (S2, E4). "You've got boobs," she quips. "Any brother not screwing his sister should respond to them." No matter: the client in question turns out to be a killer several times over.

This use of the body is a plot point that has raised eyebrows in *How to Get Away with Murder*'s online afterlife. Some fans while loving the show have posed questions about what they see as its contradictory feminist properties and troubling sexual politics, particularly given the #MeToo and Time's Up movements. Some viewers even suggest that the show romanticizes rather than challenges the rape and sexually coercive culture prevalent on college campuses and common to many workplaces. It's established early on that

Professor Keating's right-hand henchman Frank Delfino (Charlie Weber) is a womanizer with a penchant for bedding coeds. Annalise acknowledges as much with a snide, knowing quip: "What about you, Frank? What slutty undergrad spread her legs and made you forget your job this time?" It's snappy dialogue, but the choice of the word "slutty" would seem to put a moral judgment in the mouth of a character presented as largely unconcerned about morals, even as it puts the onus for male behavior on younger women denigrated as skanks with the power to seduce and distract the weaker male sex. "This time" implies Delfino is habitually set upon by these promiscuous coeds. But "slutty" has another level of racial resonance that may make it hard to hear out of the mouth of a black woman for those who remember how that label was used to denigrate the black female law professor Anita Hill as "a little bit slutty and a little nutty" in 1991 when she was called upon to testify before the Senate Judiciary Committee about having been sexually harassed by her former supervisor Clarence Thomas, who was being vetted for the Supreme Court seat he currently occupies.[5]

Although perhaps too young to have lived through the infamous Thomas-Hill hearings, a blogger who describes herself as an activist and "victim of a professor's sexual harassment and emotional abuse" likes the series but cautions viewers to consider what she sees as "the show's glaring feminist shortcomings," namely, the uninterrogated abuse of power hierarchies. "I can't make it through an episode of *Murder* without feeling triggered and like my experiences with Professor/student-induced trauma don't matter," she writes, specifically referencing the "slutty undergrad" line from the pilot episode, although "skank" might also give some viewers pause.[6]

I hate to think of any television show as triggering trauma in its viewers, but it's also possible to see *Murder* as calling attention to the very issue that so concerns this blogger. A number of the characters, including Annalise, have rape and molestation in their pasts. In a generous interpretation, one might argue that the series explores how different individuals respond to sexual trauma. The problem is that it's not only Hollywood but also ShondaLand, and the viewer's personal ordeal really doesn't matter. Although not unconcerned with issues of race, gender, and sexuality, *Murder* is more plot driven than politically impelled. Accordingly, it has a kind of fast-paced hit-and-run approach that presents and perhaps even exploits hot-button issues but has no obligation to probe them in the thought-provoking, psychoanalytic ways of feminist discourse.

For example, Lila Stangard, the white undergraduate whose affair with Sam Keating leads to pregnancy and murder amid false promises of love and marriage, is nothing more than an already-dead, stick-figure straw woman, barely seen or heard from in flashbacks. Her murder merely advances the plot, and even though her character exemplifies the ultimate extremes of seduction, sexual violence, and betrayal, we know next to nothing of her story. Sam tells her he loves her and is leaving Annalise for her and the baby she's carrying, just before he orders her murder. She, too, is just some undergrad slut who spread her legs for a married man and got knocked up and bumped off.

There's little or no moral compass or conscience in *Murder*'s self-presentation, no reason or *raisonneur* in its narrative scheme, and seemingly no race or racism in its worldview. Bad stuff happens, often ostensibly without consequence of the crime-and-punishment kind, despite an early episode titled "Hello Raskolnikov" (S1, E10) after Dostoyevsky's guilt-ridden protagonist, also a law student with murder on his conscience. More often in *Murder*, morality and ethics are made fun of or disciplined. Emily Sinclair (Sarah Burns), for example, or "sin clear" in the show's epithetical surname game, the determined assistant district attorney bent on bringing down Annalise and the Keating Five, is repeatedly referred to as a bitch and eventually run down by one of the five and her dead body thrown off a roof by others in the group at Professor Keating's instruction. (*Murder*'s Keating Five shares a nickname with the quintet of U.S. senators involved in a savings and loan scandal in the late 1980s and early '90s.) Getting away with murder is a common soap trope, but usually it's a self-defense, temporary-insanity, heat-of-passion, or some other justifiable homicide plea or odd extenuating circumstance like a brain tumor that gets the killer off, especially when he or she is a regular member of an ensemble cast. A lawyer and law professor advising her students to burn one dead body, toss another off the roof, or slit a client's wrists to keep him quiet is a plot twist of a different kind and color.

There is the old saying "murder will out," but in this series, the protagonists—the regulars we traditionally root for—get away with so many homicides that the group is known as "Murder, Inc.," in some corners of the show's fandom. Who knew the title would be so literal? Killing and copulating are the show's version of action and adventure. When Annalise wants to get her lover Nate Lahey (Billy Brown) off the hook for the homicide she framed him for, she calls in—and of course beds—her sister Harvard Law alum Eve Rothlow (Famke Janssen), the lesbian lover she left behind twenty years earlier when she married her therapist, the same late Sam Keating. Sam wasn't the love of her life apparently, but Eve, who is still in love with her, may be. After a night of renewed passion, Annalise admits to Eve that she left her all those years ago because it was "good" and "too real" with her. "So I got scared and I left," she says, "but you're the most beautiful thing that ever happened to me" (S2, E2). Eve believes her and wants to nest with her in New York, but by now we know we can't take Annalise at her word, given the way she wields those wiles and that devious mind. And besides, as she says to Eve in a flashback to another time, "I'm not a lesbian"—another easily tossed-off line that carries with it the potential danger of presenting lesbian, gay, and bi sexualities as frivolous choices, a matter of sensual gratification rather than sexual orientation.

Annalise's hot, passionate, sexy lesbian love scenes with Eve are worlds apart from any encounters with her husband, especially their final bitter confrontation the same night he's killed. Convinced he did away with Lila Stangard, Annalise confronts her predatory spouse, less over the presumed murder of a young girl with child than over lying to her about his latest peccadillo. Her revenge is to taunt him with the dirty details of her own torrid affair with a man she says knows how to make her scream and groan and sweat and has taken her on the kitchen counter and everywhere else in Sam's house, even in the marital bed. But Sam gives better—or worse—than he gets. With her slammed up against the wall and his hands closing around her throat, he tells her she's a "monster" and "nothing but a piece of ass," who he knew would put out the first time he saw her, he says. "That's all you're really good for: dirty, rough sex that I'm too ashamed to tell anyone about. That's how foul you are, you disgusting slut" (S1, E9).

Annalise's words are nothing *any* woman should ever say about herself to any man. And Sam's words to Annalise are nothing I want to hear *any* TV husband say to his TV wife. In one of its finer gestures, *Murder*, like *Scandal*, naturalizes interracial relationships just as it normalizes same-sex coupling. Even so, I don't think we're postracial enough for the technicolored graphics of this couple's grammar not to matter. With a white man speaking such words to his black wife, whose own vile diatribe invites a vulgar response, it's all but impossible to escape the weight of race and history. That this white man says the only thing this "foul," easily had "piece of ass" is good for is dirty, rough sex too shameful to tell anyone about (as if a husband would/should) carries such heavy historical resonance that I am again disarmed by the seeming ease with which such haunting words are dropped in as dialogue and left dangling. These are the same words—lyrics of licentiousness—that were used to justify the rape, concubinage, sexual coercion, and reproductive exploitation of black women throughout the long life of slavery and beyond. The piety and purity of white women were preserved and protected by the easy availability and presumed hypersexuality of black women to whom white men like Sam Keating could do anything they wanted and with whom they could take all those too-dirty-to-tell sexual liberties that pristine white womanhood was spared.

My mother, as I suggested earlier, was perfectly open to interracial marriage for other people but always said she wouldn't wed a white man herself, because in a heated argument, he might slip and say the N-word, and then she'd have to kill him.[7] The heated argument between Annalise and Sam teaches me that there are worse things a white man can say to a black woman than "nigger." A history lesson at such a moment might not make good TV, but the fictional fact that Annalise is worse than silenced by her husband's physical assault and racist verbal rant is a short-stopped dramatic moment, a missed opportunity. "Well, at least we're finally able to tell the truth," she says with insufficient sarcasm and walks away, effectively giving the white male sexual predator the last word and allowing his perception of who she is to hang in thick air. Sam will shortly turn up dead; plotwise, the argument succeeds in setting up Annalise as the likely suspect, even as it undermines her authority as a technicolored character.

This scene and a somewhat similar one in *Scandal* where Olivia Pope is verbally assailed and sexually demeaned by the former vice president raise the stakes on what it seems to be okay to say to and about black women on prime-time TV. Elsewhere in ShondaLand, white women characters—Bellamy Young as Mellie Grant on *Scandal* and Ellen Pompeo as Meredith Grey on *Grey's Anatomy*, for example—are not subjected to the same level of demeaning dialogue routinely directed at black women leads, which might be a provocative plot point if both shows took more trouble to address the real-world distinction, disrupting rather than pretending to the postracial. *Scandal* attempts just such a move to mixed effect in one episode from season five, where Pope's team mounts a PR charm offensive to expose the racist, sexist subtleties of the coded language with which the media demean Olivia after she admits to the press that, yes, she is the president's mistress. Rushing to her defense, the OPA gladiators take to the airwaves as talking heads, crying microaggressions and repeating the buzzwords "dog-whistle politics" (also the title of the episode), which the black male mastermind directing the damage control campaign defines as "bigotry in the form of language coded so that only the person it's targeting is insulted by it," as only a dog hears the ultrasonic sound of a certain whistle (S5, E4). Played as a race card here, however, dealt from the bottom of a deck we witness being stacked, a hard fact of black women's lives becomes a ploy—a contrivance of convenience—used by

FIG. 7.5 Annalise in a cage- or cell-like bathroom stall (*How to Get Away with Murder*, S1, E10).

tricksters to turn a bad girl good in the court of public opinion. Black Twitter loved it, but elsewhere it may have been its own dog whistle.

Beyond the transparency of this single episode, I'm not sure most audiences catch the color-coding and internal contradictions of the series' plotting. As much as Annalise and Olivia are peddled in their respective programs as brilliant professional women of agency who have achieved tremendous power and success in male-dominated arenas, without attention to their racial difference, they are also regularly not only represented but also demonized in racially inflected terms. Annalise, in particular, is grammatically constructed not as superwoman—itself a stereotype—but as subhuman.

She's "not like you and me," one of two white women courtroom observers says of Attorney Keating in a scene in the courthouse restroom, just after she has, in their view, "sold out her husband" as the murderer of his pregnant mistress in order to win the case. "She's not a person like the rest of us are people," the observer adds. The second woman asks, "What is she then? An animal?" and the first replies, "Not even an animal is that heartless" (S1, E10). Annalise, who has retreated into a stall where she overhears herself gossiped about and reduced to less than an animal, emerges from the stall, which shot from above looks all the more like a cage or a cell, but again is given no dialogue that might humanize her or put her detractors in their place. Instead, the white witnesses again get the first, last, and only word.

To me in fact, these courtroom gossips function in this drama like a two-person Greek chorus, guiding the audience in decoding and *mis*interpreting Annalise. If you believe your husband murdered his pregnant mistress, exposing him, especially to exonerate an innocent party, is the right thing to do, not the heartless, subhuman action the chorus, if not the show's ideological scheme, wants us to believe. In considering these women's words and Sam's and other dialogue like the sexually explicit assault on Olivia Pope, I find myself skidding headfirst into what in literary theory we call an intentional fallacy: trying to assess the author's—or in this case, the writers'—intent. Are these characters incidentally voicing some subliminal belief about or attitude toward black women that the writers can't restrain themselves from (in)scribing? (Like the epithetical unconsciousness of naming a black character "Gibbins.") Or are the words put into the characters' mouths a critique of the very racialization they seem to represent?

Some viewers see such raw, racially ripe moments as "authentic storytelling," pointing to similarly troubling scenes like one from the first season finale of *Queen Sugar* in which a white off-duty cop demeans one of the black female leads as her white married lover's "piece," spits in her face, and grabs her under her skirt Trump-style, reducing her to tears and silence and a second season of mad, mindless bed-hopping and one-night stands. I'm concerned, though, that there is more going on in such scenes of black female degradation than simple storytelling that we swallow with a gulp and go past. It matters that showrunners decide to depict a black woman being spit on and sexually assaulted and demeaned by a white man as twenty-first-century entertainment. It matters that Sam Keating speaks with the forked tongue of a white man. And when the courtroom chorus says of Annalise, "she's not like you or me," it matters that the two women speaking this loaded judgment are white. Otherwise, given the show's claims of color-blind casting, why not give these bit parts to a couple of Other extras? The optics and the implication would be different, and that difference matters.

I have to be careful in raising this point about image, race, and meaning. I'm not concerned about the ghosts of Jezebel and all the other stereotypes that haunt black women, real and imagined. And I don't care whether Annalise Keating as a character is "likable," which the black feminist writer and critic Roxane Gay rightly argues is a false standard for fiction.[8] I can accept and enjoy Annalise as a powerful, brilliant, complicated character, messy human being, or a good old-fashioned bad girl to the bone. I'm concerned about language and what lives in it that belies the myth of the postracial, the color-blind, and even the feminist. Whether deliberate or inadvertent, the showrunners and writers repeatedly stage scenes and frame dialogue in racially loaded language, and we can't pretend it doesn't matter. We can't let our excitement and delight at seeing black women in leading roles beyond maids, mammies, and matriarchs blind us to stigmatic inscriptions of race and gender masquerading as feminist freedom, racial neutrality, and progressive programming.

The Italian American mobster Tony Soprano (the late James Gandolfini) was one of television's first truly over-the-top bad-guy antiheroes, though Emily Nussbaum cautions us not to ignore what female characters like Carrie Bradshaw (Sarah Jessica Parker) of *Sex and the City* have contributed to the category.[9] Although *The Sopranos* (HBO, 1999–2007) didn't escape complaints that it negatively stereotyped Italian Americans, the series' popularity and critical acclaim helped usher in an era of complicated bad guys making good TV. Forget inner demons and feet of clay; cruelty and corruption, murder and mayhem, meth cooking and drug dealing are in vogue in contemporary television's increasingly dark vision of how the world turns. In fiction as in real life, to be human is to be flawed. In fiction perhaps even more so than in life, human failings are a necessity; they build character and create complexity. Where would the Greek tragedies and most great works of literature be without the hero's tragic flaw?

Annalise Keating is a deeply flawed character, which is exactly what many viewers—and Davis herself—say they like and appreciate about a figure they find refreshing in her unlikability, her defiant departure from the sterile, one-dimensional roles that have too often boxed in, contained, and controlled the big talent, as well as the bold sexuality, of black actresses. The part of Annalise Keating is a Scarlett O'Hara role of a lifetime, the likes of which has never before come the way of a black female performer on television, and Viola Davis, the consummate Emmy- and Oscar-winning thespian, plays the part with an artistic intensity that elevates the show above the pedestrian melodrama it might be with a less talented lead. Exquisitely dressed, coiffed, and cosmetologized, she appears rock hard and invincible in one scene; in another, seated before a dressing-table mirror, stripping herself of makeup, wig, false eyelashes, and polished persona, she is momentarily undone. No longer Annalise, the larger-than-life lethal lady lawyer, she is Anna Mae, violated, vulnerable, wounded seemingly beyond repair by what turns out to be the worst of all possible poverties, not poverty of dollars and cents, we learn in

FIG. 7.6 Annalise removing her wig, makeup, and seemingly a tough-broad persona in a pivotal scene from the first season.

a later episode, but of the soul. For at the heart of this character's vulnerability lies a little girl, abandoned by an absentee father, sexually molested by a predatory uncle, and further hurt and haunted by the belief that her mother knew about the abuse and did nothing. In one of the last episodes of the first season, we discover along with Annalise/Anna Mae that her mother Ophelia (played by Cicely Tyson) did know, and far from doing nothing, she did at once the best and the worst a mother could do to protect her daughter from a predator: she killed the bastard, burning him alive in the little house she loved but sacrificed to the flames of child protection and retribution.

Motivation is an important ingredient in character development. Does this horrible, haunted, and haunting past explain and perhaps justify this character's cutthroat, criminal, maybe even homicidal state of being in the present? The show seems to suggest it does. In a kitchen confrontation with her mother over what she believes are the unacknowledged, unrecompensed crimes of Uncle Clyde, Annalise spits out that Sam, her dead psychologist husband, diagnosed the cause of her inhuman condition immediately. He knew the first time she walked into his office that she had been abused (and that she would put out, apparently). "[Sam] said this thing that happened to me, what you ignore," she tells her mother and the audience, "is why I am the way I am" (S1, E13). Ophelia's get-over-it response that women give and men take, that men "have been taking things from women since the beginning of time," matter-of-factly punctuated by her narrative of her sister's rape by a teacher at a very young age and her own repeated sexual violations, seems a cavalier endorsement of rape culture until we hear the rest of the story of house and human burning, quietly told as she combs her daughter's hair.

With two powerhouse performers facing off in such scenes, Ophelia's tale of maternity turned murderous is particularly poignant and pathetic, if "pathetic" can mean full of pathos. But it's also familiar. It's a lot like the story of her daughter's rape, also by a schoolteacher, and her own defilements that Nanny tells her granddaughter Janie in Zora Neale Hurston's master novel *Their Eyes Were Watching God* (1937). And Ophelia's observation that men take women and take from women is reminiscent of Nanny's pronouncement that black men use their womenfolk as dumping grounds in a way that makes them mules of the world. Then, too, burning the bed or burning down the house is the go-to trope of troubled domesticity in American, African American, Latin American—indeed, in world—literatures: Eva's burning alive her drug-addicted son in *Sula*, for example. When it comes to the plot of sexual abuse, Uncle Clyde might just as well be Jim Trueblood in *Invisible Man*, or Cholly Breedlove in *The Bluest Eye*, or Celie's (step)father in *The Color Purple*. Are we to assume that incestuous rape and other haunts and hurts of childhood have driven Anna Mae/Annalise out of her mind as they do Pecola Breedlove (or into a vodka bottle, as Annalise devolves into a self-described functioning alcoholic)? True to form, there was no father present in the home to offer his daughter the appropriate paternal protection. Indeed, what we learn about Annalise's dad in the second season finale—that he was an absentee husband and father, who left his family to fend for themselves—is yet another cliché of black familial pathology.

The familiarity of what are, unfortunately, common historically resonant narratives doesn't make the retelling here bad story, but where does one draw the line between common occurrence and cliché, between trope and formula? In this instance, the mother-daughter, Ophelia–Anna Mae blackstory of abuse and the father-daughter tale of abandonment and resentment play for me like clichés that make the characters less complex rather than more so. This is a personal rather than probable or perhaps even reasonable reaction, refracted through my ever-present racial lens. I have already confessed the difficulty I have digesting representations of racial and sexual violence acted out as entertainment. I have a similar lack of patience with the plot of paternal abandonment, especially uninterrogated. After all, the black father as absent, alcoholic, abusive, or all of the above is the facile, default paternal pathology.

It's not easy for a TV show to be original, compelling, poignant, and powerful—all those things good drama is supposed to be—week after week, year after year, but TV in general has a hard time sustaining credible story arcs for formidable female characters, who it seems are allowed only just so much power and control. Series that begin with a bang and a forward-moving, female-centered premise like *Scandal* and *Homeland* (Showtime, 2011–), for another example, have little place to go once the inaugural plot plays itself out. Showrunners don't seem to know what to do with the badass broads they create, except undo them with a man (even an all-powerful papa like Rowan Pope) or a baby—a consequence of fraternizing with the opposite sex that male leads rarely have to deal with, unlike *Homeland*'s crazy Carrie Mathison (Claire Danes), who gets knocked up by her foe's friendly fire. And there's no escaping the pregnancy plot even all alone in space for a year, as the black female astronaut Molly Woods (Halle Berry) discovers in the short-lived sci-fi thriller *Extant* (CBS, 2014–2015).

How to Get Away with Murder hit the airwaves as a high-flying legal thriller, soaring to the top of the ratings in the fall of 2014, propelled by the superb acting of Viola Davis and a provocative, if not entirely unfamiliar premise (I think *Perry Mason*; critics referenced *The Paper Chase*): a powerful black female Harvard-trained law professor and criminal defense attorney litigating a case a week with the aid of two associates and a multiracial team of bright, beautiful, ambitious student interns, operating against the backdrop of ongoing mysteries, which seemed a winning formula. It didn't take long, however, for the show to slip into the wild and crazy antics and over-the-top twists and turns of soap opera, like its ShondaLand predecessor *Scandal*, and to begin undoing itself and its black female star power.

I read in an interview from 2013 that predates *How to Get Away with Murder* and is principally about *Scandal* that Shonda Rhimes hates to see her shows described as "guilty pleasures" and cast into the category of soap operas, which she views as a gendered dismissal.[10] But if it quacks like a duck, what else should *Scandal* or *Murder* be called? Despite their early twentieth-century origins as serialized radio melodramas sponsored by Procter & Gamble and other product manufacturers, soap operas, especially as prime-time evening ware, have lost their lowbrow patina and become the model form for TV drama and the prevailing alternative to the old self-contained, episodic format, as the networks have gone from series to serials in an attempt to keep up with the freewheeling, often more sexually explicit, narratively adventurous offerings of cable and digital TV.

Conceding that Rhimes may be getting a bad rap with the soap opera label, Willa Paskin, *Salon*'s TV critic, argues that the plot points of *Scandal* (and I would add *Murder*)—passionate extramarital affairs endangering careers and national security, murder made to look like suicide, false identities, and the offing of associates who know too much—are the same as those of "prestige dramas" like *Homeland, House of Cards, Mad Men,* and *Breaking Bad,* each of which critics have at some point labeled a soap opera.[11] Even the elegant PBS series *Downton Abbey* has been so-called. Yet, because most prime-time dramas are serialized these days—or what Robin Nelson calls "flexi-narratives," a hybrid of the series and the serial, derived from the soap form—it may indeed be time for a new designation that better reflects the growth and development of the format.[12] The Colombian American writer Daisy Hernández suggests, in fact, that ShondaLand dramas are more like telenovelas, Spanish-language soaps that, like *Scandal* and *Murder,* are the "cash cow[s]" of prime-time programming, with fantastic plot twists and crazy characters, including strong female leads. Also as with telenovelas, American prime-time soaps attract large followings of devoted fans who constitute a virtual community afterlife for the shows, whose twists and turns are tracked in the Twitter- and blogospheres, especially, in the case of ShondaLand dramas, the virtual network known as "Black Twitter."[13]

The technicolored corner of the genre that has taken the prime-time market by storm with hit series like *Scandal, Murder, Empire,* and *Power* seems more like soap opera meets blaxploitation or what I have taken to calling "soaploitation": shows with black leads and predominantly black and/or multiracial casts doing all manner of mostly nefarious, often over-the-top deeds, mainly set to black music. In the case of *How to Get Away with Murder,* the soaploitation label seems a clean fit, especially as the show moves further away from its original premise, and Keating and crew are no longer professor and pupils teaching and studying law and barely criminal counsel and college cohorts defending clients. They are themselves the evildoers, partners in crime, killing at will and covering up their murders and misdeeds with outrageous abandon. If thy client offends thee, suffocate her. If the prosecutor insults thee, run her over, then toss her body from the client's roof and frame the client. If the client you got off by framing his sister turns out to be a psychopathic mass murderer ratting you out to the authorities, get your fixer to slit his wrists and make it look like suicide.

Even Omar Little (Michael Kenneth Williams), the fearsome, shotgun-toting stick-up man from *The Wire,* operated under a strict ethical code. Ethics are harder to find and fathom in *Murder,* even as the show invites and incites us to accept the improbable premise that Professor Keating's outrageous antics, foolish choices, and (il)legal counsel—from "burn the body" to "shoot me"—are motivated by good will and a material, if not maternal, desire to protect her collegiate coconspirators, especially Wes Gibbins, from the criminal justice system that eats black men alive. Not that Wes's race is ever overtly made a motivation in the program's presumptively postracial panoptics. And not that it makes any sort of sense for a hot-shot, highly skilled, hugely self-confident defense attorney to protect one black man from the racial injustices of the justice system not by the most artful lawyering of her career but by framing another utterly innocent brother—her detective lover, no less, for whom a turn in the tank among felons he has put away could well amount to a death sentence. (Of course, the arrest, hose-down, and strip search of Nate Lahey allows for a gratuitous nude scene and a near full-frontal view of Billy Brown's amazing body.) It turns out, perhaps unsurprisingly, that what Wes and his peers (not to mention the beleaguered boytoy) really need protection from is Annalise Keating. If only they had known the prescience of the professor's opening remarks that first day of class, when there was still time to drop the course: "I don't know what terrible things you've done in your life up to this point, but clearly your karma's out of balance to get assigned to my class" (S1, E1). How much better off would these first years be if they had not enrolled in Criminal Law 100 with Annalise Keating?

Although Counselor Keating is capable of pro bono beneficence—early on she reaches deep into her bag of tricks to exonerate a black man wrongly convicted of killing his girlfriend—by season two, she has emerged so corrupt, calculating, and manipulative and made so many enemies that when flash-forwards show her sprawled on the floor obviously gutshot and bleeding out, the question isn't whether she will survive—she's too essential to the show to kill off yet—but who among a legion of suspects pulled the trigger. The controlling question therefore becomes "Who shot Annalise?" just as "Who shot J.R.?" became the catchphrase query of the 1980 season for the prime-time soap opera *Dallas* (CBS, 1978–1991).

Bad, like greed, is good on TV today. But unlike J.R. Ewing, who was just an oil baron, or Tony Soprano, who was only a mobster, or even Carrie Bradshaw, who was merely a writer and fashionista, Annalise Keating is a teacher—a profession and a duty some of us hold sacred, even though she does not, which may be her biggest crime. Still, as the dead bodies mount, it occurs to me that *Murder* might be amusing in all its killing, conniving, and copulating if it took itself less seriously, like, say, John Waters's all-white black comedy *Serial Mom* (1994), where the homicidal housewife Beverly Sutphin (Kathleen Turner) gets away with multiple murders, manipulating witnesses and the judge and jury at her trial and then, once she is acquitted, killing Juror No. 8 (played by Patty Hearst) in the courthouse restroom for wearing white shoes after Labor Day.

But there may also be a lesson for me in the "if" of my own observation: perhaps I would do well to take myself and the show less seriously and to see *How to Get Away with Murder* for what it is, rather than wishing for a modern-day, black female Perry Mason or even Johnny Cochran or a black feminist, antiracist intervention in technicolored TV programming. Imagine a black woman defending the exploited and oppressed, challenging police brutality, the practice of racial profiling, and the criminalization of black youth, crusading against mass incarceration and the prison-industrial complex like Angela Davis, Kimberlé Crenshaw, and Michelle Alexander. The African American actress Lorraine Toussaint came close to playing such a part as Shambala Green, a badass Legal Aid defense attorney in seven episodes of the original *Law & Order*, but she had little screen time and was portrayed as an adversary, a thorn in the sides of the good white-guy prosecutors Ben Stone (Michael Moriarty) and Jack McCoy (Sam Waterston). Would anyone watch a show where such a black female character was the protagonist and the victor?

As a child so invested in television and in TV characters and wanting to be a lawyer, without black female models I could only imagine myself grown up and professional through the heroism and achievements of white men. If there are young, impressionable viewers out there watching TV today like the little black girl I once was, I would hope they take away from this and other ShondaLand dramas a sense of the possibilities a black female character like Annalise Keating represents rather than the ethical collapse the show presents.

The same night I finished this chapter, as above, *Downton Abbey* ended its phenomenal six-year run on PBS. I wept through the Sunday night finale, texting and talking on the phone with black female friends who were in a similar state of bereavement. My reaction created in me a small crisis of conscience. How in the world could I, a mature, racially chauvinistic, black feminist critic, possibly be bawling over the demise of a historical drama about the wealthy white British aristocracy and their white servants? Yet there I sat, tears welling in my eyes at every turn, as the finale neatly tied up all the lingering loose ends, bringing peace and joy to almost every character. It seems I was in good company in both my *Downton* devotion and my despair at its end. During its reign, the series attracted something like 270 million viewers worldwide, including the future king and queen of England, Prince William and Princess Kate, the Duke and Duchess of Cambridge, according to the Prince himself, who taped a salute to the series for a televised tribute. What strikes me, however, and what brings me back to this chapter is the great, glaring distinction between my pleasure in the soap operatic text of *Downton Abbey* and my, at best, ambivalence and, at worst, antipathy toward my own subject, *How to Get Away with Murder.*

Even as *Downton* was winding down and striking the set forever, *Murder* was wrapping up its second season with plot twists and turns that placed Annalise in grave danger. I cried when Sybil Crawley Branson died in childbirth and when they killed off Matthew Crawley, Lady Mary's first husband. But I had no tears and even less sympathy for Annalise Keating after finally learning through flashbacks the nature of her past connection to the black law student Wes Gibbins, the one whom the Keating cohort call "the puppy," but whose birth name we learn was actually Christophe Edmunds. Ten years earlier Annalise, who was pregnant at the time, hid out in the hallway and let little twelve-year-old Wes go into an apartment alone and find his dying mother, bleeding out from a self-inflicted fatal knife wound to the jugular.

And as if it weren't bad enough that Annalise fled the scene instead of dialing 911 and hanging around to help, if not the mother, then the traumatized child, she also was the force that drove Wes's Haitian mother, Rose Edmunds (Kelsey Scott), to take her own life in order to save her son from the white man Annalise assumes is his father—the wealthy client whose grown son she is defending—Rose's employer (Alan Arkin), a ruthless businessman Attorney Keating believes violated and impregnated his colored help. We will eventually learn that Annalise jumped to the wrong conclusion in blaming the father for a rape his son actually committed. But while this terrible turn speaks to the vulnerability of the poor, colored immigrant domestic, once again the pathos isn't quite there, perhaps because of the flashbacks and fast cutting that make the segmented medium even more so, propelling the viewer in and out of time and frame before details register and characters matter, while also creating oddly incongruous juxtapositions of past and present, dead and alive: horrific, blood-spurting death one minute and gratuitous, casual sex the next; a gruesome, charred body on a slab in the morgue in one scene, and the character alive laughing and playing Frisbee in another.

We learn in yet another flashback that Annalise, who had decided to tell the authorities the truth about the coercion that precipitated Rose's suicide, was T-boned in a car accident—that wasn't an accident—en route to do so and lost the baby boy she was carrying. It's another terrible turn of events, but the graphic hospital birth and death scene somehow didn't induce in me the sympathy it was supposed to, perhaps in part because the beautiful stillborn baby boy they show us looked a little too much like the silicone "reborn" doll one hopes it was, especially when Annalise suddenly declared, "I'm done," thrusting toward the nurse like a football the swaddled bundle she couldn't wait to be rid of and then screaming "Take him away" when the stunned nurse didn't approach fast enough.

As presented, the double death backstories—Wes's dead mother and Annalise's dead baby—demonstrate another problem with the show's heavy dependence on flashbacks: Rose Edmunds and Baby Sam are reduced to disposable plot devices, where Rose cries out to be a person rather than a prop and the dead baby doesn't cry at all. Moreover, because we know what wretched partners Sam and Annalise are in the present, it's difficult to feel for them in the past the sympathy that losing an infant ought to command. I suppose we are meant to surmise that this past tragedy put a crack in the Keating marriage and helped make them the miserable couple they are in the present. But flashbacks to Sam rubbing Annalise's baby bump and trying to talk her out of traveling to take the murder case so late in her pregnancy can't counter the fact that we know Mr. Keating best not as the attentive husband to an expectant wife or the grieving father of a stillborn son but as the heartless bastard who coldly ordered the murder of his pregnant undergraduate girlfriend, without a second thought to her or the fetus she was carrying.

A similar problem arises from the flashback hospital scene where Sam Keating learns from a desperately guilty Frank Delfino the awful truth that the car crash was actually a hit arranged by Annalise's client to silence her. The scene attempts to cast Sam as a caring husband, insisting his wife must never know the truth of her loss, for the sake of her sanity. "I lost my son; I can't lose her, too," he says (s2, e15). Knowing what we do about Sam in the present, however, his concern for the wife we watched him choke, demean, and belittle as "nothing but a piece of ass" is hard to swallow. In other words, this flash to the past that would have us see Sam the predatory, racist, womanizing murderer as a caring, loving husband is undone by all we have seen him do in the present. Much the same is true for the grief of the hard-hearted, hard-edged Annalise, who appeared ambivalent about the pregnancy her own mother knew nothing about.

....

Analepses and prolepses are essential devices in nonlinear storytelling, but *How to Get Away with Murder*'s overdependence on them undermines their effectiveness. The show's internal scheme—not to mention its incessant scheming—upends its own narrative and undercuts the suspension of disbelief that the viewer needs in order to indulge the program's fantastic fictions. It's possible to see the serial's topsy-turvy super-segmentation as deliberately contesting theories of flow and sequence that have long been advanced, revised, and debated in television studies, but, for me as a viewer, the less chaotic, if more familiar, narrative unfolding of *Downton Abbey* is far more appealing.[14]

Still, how can I be so easily driven to tears over the fabricated foolishness of characters in a dandy dramedy of manners that has nothing to do with me—in a time and place that has no space for anyone who looks like me— and yet be so mostly unmoved by that which and those who ought to be my own? *Downton Abbey* spilled a little blood and took more than its share of outrageous twists and turns: Matthew Crawley comes back from the Great War paralyzed and impotent but then suddenly pops up from his wheelchair like a jack-in-the-box, to pilfer the description of his miraculous recovery Dame Maggie Smith offered at the BAFTA tribute to the series.

Oddly enough, what struck me as *Downton*'s one true false note was the introduction of a lone black character in the fourth season—a jazz singer named Jack Ross (Gary Carr)—who has a romantic dalliance with fun-loving, forward-thinking Cousin Rose. A young, titled aristocrat in post-Edwardian England might lose her head over a handsome black man, but I doubt that the couple could have cavorted in public, dancing, dining, kissing, and merrily rowboating down the river as Rose and Jack do without white society taking more hostile notice and levying heftier social sanctions than Aunt Rosamund's horrified gasp. But while there may be some truth to my sense of what the times would not have tolerated, Julian Fellowes, the creator, writer, and executive producer of *Downton Abbey*, based the fictional Jack Ross on the real-life black bon vivant Leslie "Hutch" Hutchinson, a notorious satin-voiced cabaret singer, pianist, and high-society favorite who reportedly had his way with upper-class white women all over Europe in the 1920s.[15]

Whether it was realistic or far-fetched, I appreciated *Downton's* effort to address what Lady Rose refers to as that "imperialist nonsense about racial purity" (S4, E7). The final exchange between Jack Ross and Mary Crawley when she confronts him about his relationship with her young cousin may be my favorite bit of dialogue in the entire series. He tells Mary he's giving up Rose because he loves her too much to spoil her life and make her the subject of ridicule. But that doesn't mean he thinks it's right, he says. "I wouldn't give in if we lived in even a slightly better world," he adds. "It may surprise you, Mr. Ross," Mary replies, "but if we lived in a better world, I wouldn't want you to" (S4, E7).

There is nothing so high minded about the lowbrow banter that functions as dialogue in *How to Get Away with Murder*: "What's the matter? You don't know how to use your boobs?" Or "Don't tell me you two are boning." Or "If you all had balls, you'd be drunk, too." Or "Stop apologizing. We're all bad people. That's the only thing we have in common." But the idiomatic difference only partly explains my fondness for the foreign of a bygone era that didn't and couldn't include me (except as a singer, slave, or servant) over the familiar of my own times. Perhaps that is precisely what troubles me about *How to Get Away with Murder*: how much it is a sign of these times.

If *Seinfeld* (NBC, 1989–1998) was a show about nothing, *How to Get Away with Murder* is a show about nobody—that is, a show about nobody we should ever want to know. According to one of the lead characters, Bonnie Winterbottom, Annalise Keating's associate counsel who committed one of the murders attributed to Wes Gibbins and has enough blood on her own hands to know, *Murder* is a show full of "bad people"—bad people who, she suggests, have nothing in common other than their individual and collective depravity. That we eat it up—that even the NAACP, once the black image and propriety police, applauds and rewards these twenty-first-century versions of stigmatic blackness gone madly sociopathic—may say something about contemporary society's slow slide into either the darkness of ethical collapse or the enlightenment of no-holds-barred imagining, depending on one's point of view.

Like *Scandal*, *Murder* had greater potential to deliver a broader representation of blackness than just about anything that has ever appeared on television, certainly anything with a black woman lead and a multiracial cast. What the showrunners have given us instead is a rogue's gallery of murderers, cons, crooks, criminals, traitors, and terrorists—a retinue of some of the most over-the-top messy human beings of all TV time. My critique of the shows' depraved indifference to human life little matters in the face of their resounding success. Just the same, both shows underplay their potential, taking the safer, more sensational, and no doubt more salable route. It's too late to save either series from killing its better self, unless *Murder*, for one, were to posit its past episodes as Annalise Keating's nightmare or vodka-induced hallucination, after the fashion of its predecessor *Dallas*, which brought Bobby Ewing (Patrick Duffy) back from the dead by writing off the entire 1985–1986 season as his wife's bad dream.

Some see great hope in new shows like Ava DuVernay's serial *Queen Sugar*. I, too, am excited by new voices and different visions and extra-televisual options like *Master of None* on Netflix, but I haven't given up on the Rhimes revolution, which, after all, has placed black women and other actors of color, as well as gay characters, in unprecedented positions in prime-time TV. With three hit network serials flowing back-to-back, Shonda Rhimes clearly has a formula that works, but it is exactly that: a formula. As the head of her own television empire and the go-to producer everybody wants to work with in twenty-first-century Hollywood, Rhimes has the clout to shape truly different narratives. The question is whether she has the audacity to use that clout in other-than-predictable ways.

Chapter 8

The Punch and
Judge Judy Shows

REALLY REAL TV
AND THE DANGERS
OF A DAY IN COURT

What you are witnessing is real. The participants are not actors.
They are the actual litigants with a case pending in a California
Municipal Court. Both parties have agreed to dismiss their court
cases and have their disputes settled here, in our forum—*The
People's Court.*

—One version of the opening monologue for *The People's Court*

One of the first things I did when I retired in 2011 was cancel most of my
magazine subscriptions in the interest of economizing. It seems counterintu-
itive to me today that despite the shoestring budget we lived on in my youth,
the coffee table was lined with magazines that would arrive monthly and
even, in some cases, weekly. *Ebony* and *Jet* were staples of black households
no matter what the income level, but *Reader's Digest, The Saturday Evening
Post, Ladies' Home Journal, Redbook, Family Circle, Woman's Day, Good
Housekeeping, Popular Mechanics, Popular Science, Life, National Geographic,*
and one or two children's magazines whose titles I've forgotten seem like
an extravagance, though very much the way of mass media and family life
in the 1950s. I can't swear that we subscribed to all of these periodicals simultaneously, but this is the assortment I most remember being around the
house in the 1950s and '60s. It does seem to me, though, that the more TV

we watched, the fewer subscriptions we had, so that by the 1970s and '80s there were only the few women's magazines my mother picked up now and again at the supermarket.

When I helped Mom change the linens on the bed she and my father shared back in the day, I would see copies of *Ladies' Home Journal* on her nightstand, usually opened to the popular column "Can This Marriage Be Saved?" The column presented case studies of troubled marriages from the points of view of both wives and husbands, with a summary judgment for each case from "Mr. Marriage," Dr. Paul Popenoe, an old-school eugenicist who refashioned himself into America's premier marriage and family expert in the 1950s.[1] Although he called himself "Doctor," Popenoe's only academic degree was honorary, but more concerning than his inflated credentials is his belief in compulsory sterilization and the racial inferiority of Negroes and other Others. He had numerous irons in the fire in the 1950s and '60s but is probably most commonly remembered for creating and editing the phenomenally popular "Can This Marriage Be Saved?" feature in *Ladies' Home Journal*, along with appearing regularly on *Art Linkletter's House Party* and other TV shows, including a stint as the host and presiding judge on the reality series *Divorce Hearing*, which featured actual couples whose distressed marriages got the once-over from the nation's leading authority on this other peculiar institution.[2]

Had my mother known more about the man behind "Can This Marriage Be Saved?" she would have burned the column instead of reading it. It's easy to understand why such features were popular with women of her generation. They were trying to gain insight into their own marriages and family lives. Along with the other women's magazines my mother subscribed to, she also regularly watched the original *Divorce Court*, which aired from the latter 1950s into the early 1970s (counting reruns and a hiatus in the mid-1960s) and was among the first of the many courtroom dramas that are all over TV today. Couples with serious marital woes sought legal ends to their misery, battling over property, alimony, child support, custody of minors, or sometimes contesting the divorce altogether. Mom admired the *Divorce Court* judge, who seemed wise and kind and offered thoughtful words of wisdom at the end of each hearing. The original *Divorce Court* put forth the same "real people, real cases" promotional puff we hear today, so it was a big blow when we learned the whole thing was fake. The wise judge, warring litigants, and concerned court reporter were all actors, and the cases were scripted reenactments. My mother wasn't happy with the deception, but she would soon enough have her own day in a real divorce court.

During my sophomore year in college (1968–1969), my parents finally called it quits after almost twenty-five years of marriage. We had all heard my father say to my mother during an argument that he was tired of living her kind of life. My mother retaliated by letting it be known far and wide that my father had also told the judge he didn't care to be in the home and didn't even care if his soon-to-be ex-wife had custody of the children. Danny was technically the only minor child by then, but since I was in college, the judge decreed that my father had some fiscal responsibility for my health care and maintenance until I finished school. I was pretty determined not to be a financial burden on either of my parents and had chosen to live at home and attend the local state college where my part-time job at Sears could cover the tuition of $100 per semester, rather than go to a school of journalism in Boston where I had won a year's tuition as second prize in an essay contest. First prize was a full ride, so coming in second was a real miss. But I never regretted going to Bridgewater State, where I received a superb education without going into debt and where the quality of my English professors in particular turned my head from law to literature.

My parents had always preached the importance of higher education, harboring hopes that my brothers and I would become doctors, lawyers, scholars, but my father saw only dollar signs my senior year when I was accepted into a master's program at Brown University; fearing an extension of support payments, he promptly complained to the court that I was a "professional student." He needn't have embarrassed himself before the judge, who reportedly was annoyed that a father would make such a complaint about a kid who had worked her way through college in four years and received a prestigious scholarship for further study. I was fortunate enough to have been awarded a University Fellowship that not only covered tuition but also included health benefits and a living stipend. Some years hence in the latter 1980s, my mother would put my father further to shame, rushing to lend encouragement when I again had the colossal good fortune to be offered a fellowship to pursue a doctorate at an age well past any whiff of parental obligation. She even insisted on floating me a loan every now and then when living on a student stipend got tough. Once I was again gainfully employed in an assistant professorship and attempted to pay back the loans, she refused to accept a penny. It was money she had put away for my wedding, she said, a disclosure that left me feeling, PhD or not, without a husband to my credit, I would always be to

FIG. 8.1 With Mom in Middletown, Connecticut, after my PhD
commencement in 1991. The Hawaiian lei around my neck
is a gift from my Brown grad school classmate Tersa Bill.
PHOTO CREDIT: LAURA SANTIGIAN.

some degree a disappointment. It was the DNA of my mother's way of seeing
gender relations and what women were supposed to do and be.

Today *Divorce Court* is the longest running of the many reality courtroom
shows that populate daytime television. The current African American host,
Judge Lynn Toler, holds an undergraduate degree in English from Harvard
and a JD from the University of Pennsylvania Law School. After practicing
law in Cleveland for a decade, she was elected to the Municipal Court Bench
in 1993 and took over *Divorce Court* in 2006.[3] Despite her bench experience,

her version of the show, unlike the original we watched in the 1950s and '60s, makes no pretense of granting actual divorces. Rather, Judge Toler arbitrates debates between couples sparring over property, child support, and other monetary matters and sometimes gives courting or engaged couples compatibility tests, weighing in on whether the two are temperamentally suited to go forward with wedding plans and even tearing up the marriage license if she believes they are not. In one of the oddest forms of TV courtroom theatrics, Toler occasionally brings in a makeup artist to age the prospective husband and wife, giving each the opportunity to see what the other might look like once the bloom of youthful attraction has faded.

In a *Divorce Court* case from 2013 much discussed on the Internet, Nathaniel Smith, a thirty-nine-year-old black man from Dayton, Ohio, was accused of cheating on his twenty-three-year-old wife and fathering a child outside their marriage. Would that were all there was to the case. When Toler asked Smith how many children he had, his answer drew gasps from judge and audience alike: twenty-seven by sixteen different women. This is the stuff of which tragedies are made. First there is the fate of the twenty-seven kids— twelve boys and fifteen girls, whom Smith, an underemployed former barber turned poet, can't possibly support adequately and parent effectively—and the sixteen women dumb or desperate enough to bed down with this serial philanderer. Then there is the unfortunate fact—painfully evident in the flood of online commentaries—that many viewers come away from such tabloid tableaus convinced this "ghetto mess" is evidence of how black people live, swelling the welfare rolls and ruining the country.[4]

Indeed, a few days after his *Divorce Court* appearance, Smith was arrested for missing a court date pertaining to child support. Not only was his arrest widely reported in the tabloids, but even more legitimate media outlets like CBS News, the *Los Angeles Times*, and the *Huffington Post* used the occasion to revisit other notorious cases of deadbeat black dads with hordes of kids they can't take care of, including the infamous Desmond Hatchett, a thirty-three-year-old, often unemployed, minimum-wage worker with twenty-four children by eleven women, and Orlando Shaw, another unemployed thirty-three-year-old single sperm donor with twenty-two children by fourteen woman to whom he owes tens of thousands of dollars in unpaid child support.[5] Shaw has bragged publicly that women love him and claims abound all over the Internet that Hollywood has approached him about his own reality show.

The sex and violence, outrages and affronts to ethics and integrity highlighted in legal thrillers like *How to Get Away with Murder* are, thankfully, all make-believe—fiction, farce, and some would even say fun. As these samples from *Divorce Court* suggest, however, twenty-first-century television offers an abundance of real-life courtroom and conflict dramas that may actually be dangerous in the racial spectacles they present and the stigmatic blackness they seem to authenticate and normalize. Courtroom arbitration series, so immensely popular today, cut their teeth on claims of "reality"—real people seeking real justice with real judges. Though not nearly as long-lived as *Divorce Court*, another long-running program, *The People's Court*, which originally aired from 1981 to 1993 under the gavel of a former Los Angeles Superior Court judge, the Honorable Joseph Wapner, has always presented its reality bona fides at the start of each episode with a version of the voice-over monologue in the epigraph. A more recent incarnation of the show added a jazzy but oddly injudicial introduction to the authentication: "Everybody's talking about the Honorable Marilyn Milian, the hottest judge in town. Real cases, real litigants, here in our forum—*The People's Court*."

I'm not sure why even a TV judge with a Georgetown law degree and an appointment to the Florida bench from Governor Jeb Bush would want to be described as "the hottest judge in town" in the intro to her show, but the claims of authenticity are necessary, I suppose, because much of what happens within these TV courtrooms and on the sets of similarly "real" reality series and even more animated and outrageous tabloid talk shows is beyond belief. Indeed, courtroom dramas like *The People's Court* and *Judge Judy*, along with tabloid talk shows like *Jerry Springer*, *Maury*, and *Lauren Lake's Paternity Court*, seem to me to exist for no higher purpose other than to rake in millions of advertising dollars by exhibiting people of color and the white lumpenproletariat at their worst, most outrageous, and, in some instances, most vulnerable and pathetic. The danger of such shows is the extent to which they contribute to class and color warfare and fuel anti-immigrant, antiminority animus by dramatizing the depravity and dependency of those already disparaged as alien and Other. Every time Judge Judy berates a defendant for not paying child support; every time Maury Povich or Lauren Lake rips open an envelope of DNA results and tells some deadbeat Doubting Thomas dad, "You are the father," what the hooting audience hears is, "You are the problem," part of an army of serial dads, who don't support the children they father, among whom Nathaniel Green of Brooklyn, New York, is another classic example.

Green appeared before Judge Judy in a case that aired February 26, 2016, brought to court by his twenty-year-old daughter, Anissa Williams, one of Green's ten children, none of whom receive financial support from their forty-year-old father, an often unemployed day laborer. His daughter, who supposedly has legal custody of her three younger brothers, was suing him because she claimed he stole expensive Air Jordans she purchased for the boys for Christmas and also failed to pay the rent he agreed to when he begged her to take him in because he had nowhere else to go. Green denied taking the sneakers, and Judge Judy sided with him when the testimony of the oldest brother seemed to contradict his sister's claim. The judge also dismissed the pleading for back rent, ruling that the daughter could have no reasonable expectation of receiving money from someone with no job, who, by her own testimony, laid around all day doing nothing. But the deadbeat dad, who made the mistake of snickering when asked how many children he had, wasn't let off the hook easily. He was stupid enough to ask Judge Judy how he is supposed to support his ten kids when he doesn't have a job, unleashing even more of the judge's wrath and inviting one of her most frequent rants about the criminal irresponsibility of having children you can't support.

The riot act read Green was surely deserved, but not even a kind, encouraging word or anything else was offered the plaintiff, the defeated daughter who at twenty is caring for and supporting herself and her three younger brothers, while working part-time as a server, aided only by the SSI checks the two youngest boys receive (assuming what she testified to in court is true). Nor were any questions asked about the mother(s) of these four kids who might as well be orphans or the fate of their other six siblings. Considerably more patient and compassionate (and curious), Judge Marilyn Milian of *The People's Court* would have asked more questions and gotten the fuller story, but Judge Judy is quick to say she's not Dr. Phil and has no time for or interest in details of woe. Once accused by an interviewer of barely containing her contempt for "the carnival of humanity that files through [her] courtroom," Sheindlin took exception and insisted she actually does feel sorry for "people who become involved in the meshed minutia that ruin their lives," such as "having too many kids that you can't take care of."[6] But what if the humanity before you are some of those uncared-for kids? There was no sign of any sympathy for Anissa Williams and her band of brothers.

Off camera, Judith Blum Sheindlin is a wife (to her second husband, Jerry Sheindlin, also a former jurist who briefly presided over *The People's Court*), mother of five, and loving grandmother to a dozen, with progressive views on gay rights and same-sex marriage. In front of the camera as Judge Judy, she is the granddame of TV jurists, with more than two decades on the bench of the number one show in daytime and another twenty-five years in the New York family court system, fourteen of them as a judge whose tough talk and rapid rulings brought notoriety and a turn of good fortune that took her from an interview segment on *60 Minutes* in 1993 to her own nationally syndicated reality series in

1996. I've logged a lot of hours studying Judge Judy's show, and I've pretty much only seen her display the quality of mercy to dogs and distraught dog owners.[7] She once resolved a dispute over a cherished family pet by leaving the bench and returning with an irresistibly adorable lookalike pooch purchased in advance for a divorcing couple warring over custody of the furry friend they both loved. Since she couldn't split the dog in half, she did Solomon one better and replicated it. Of course, her final words to the couple after she dismissed the case were something to the effect of "You owe me $400 for the dog."

In cases like *Williams v. Green*, the ice-cold shoulder and flagrant lack of sympathy for the young plaintiff may have to do not only with the notoriously fast-paced, assembly-line nature of Judge Judy's courtroom style but also with a suspicion that the case was phony, made up by the litigants to get on TV and get money out of the producers who pay off cash judgments—to scam the show, in other words, in much the same way that Sheindlin believes many of the litigants devote their "energies to scamming the system rather than . . . to figuring out how to make a positive life for [themselves]."[8] Judge Judy has been played before, including famously so by a group of friends who posed as foes in a silly case over a cat supposedly crushed by a falling television set. The cohort in cahoots won a $1,200 judgment, plus the appearance fees, per diems, and the free trips to L.A., and then went public with the deception.[9] This cat-astrophe went viral as one of the greatest public punks since a group of activist artists calling themselves the Barbie Liberation Organization switched the voice boxes on several hundred talking G.I. Joes and Barbie dolls in 1993 and then returned the altered dolls to toy-store shelves, setting up a scenario in which unsuspecting children ended up with Barbies that said things like "Eat lead, Cobra" and action figures that just wanted to have fun shopping.[10] (I actually had the pleasure of once meeting one of the artists involved in the great doll switch of 1993.)

I don't know that fraud was suspected in the Williams lawsuit, but it's obvious the judge has such suspicions about a number of the cases she promptly dismisses. It does seem that there was something not quite right about this particular lawsuit, because these same litigants—Williams and Green—also appeared on the May 12, 2016, episode of *People's Court* in a case nearly identical to the one that aired on *Judy* three months earlier. Judge Milian was indeed more sympathetic and not only found for the plaintiff to the tune of $2,975 for back rent and stolen sneakers, but she also expressed concern for Anissa's welfare and advised her to seek help from social services. Milian did ask whether Anissa and the three younger brothers in her custody have the same mother, to which the plaintiff replied affirmatively and explained that their mother had abandoned the family. Having been chastened by Judge Judy, Green claimed to have a job and to be saving money to get his own place. There was no mention of the other six children he admitted to fathering in the *Judge Judy* edition. Nor was there any acknowledgment that the case had previously been adjudicated on a rival show. I don't recall whether the earlier case was dismissed with or without prejudice, but I smelled a rat and emailed *The People's Court* about the duplication, never receiving a response.

The *Judge Judy* production staff solicits and vets the cases brought before the bench and, at least according to the myriad complaints from disgruntled participants, tells prospective litigants anything to get them on the show. Sour grapes aside, I wonder how thorough the vetting is if obvious whoppers can make it on air and the same litigants can get away with presenting the same pleading on two different programs, each claiming to feature real cases. For me the fact that the producers effectively put forth bogus claims for the sake of making a television show and then watch the judge kick complainants to the curb is just another example of what's wrong with would-be reality courtroom TV.

And it isn't only on *Judge Judy* that the cases sometimes feel too far-fetched and fantastic to be anything other than phony: a young man claiming mechanophilia who sues his ex-girlfriend for taking a hammer to the beloved Volkswagen Bug with which he regularly had sexual intercourse (the true meaning of autoeroticism); a son who sues his mother for destroying his $5,000 anatomically correct inflatable girlfriend; a black woman who sues her eighteen-year-old son for rent to teach him a lesson after he asserted his manhood and took up with the white twenty-five-year-old high school English teacher who gave him a birthday lap dance in front of the class. Indeed, such cases appearing on shows like *Justice for All with Judge Cristina Perez*, *Justice with Judge Mablean*, and *Supreme Justice with Judge Karen*—all creations of Byron Allen's production company, Entertainment Studios—are often staged, as revealed in the fine print of disclaimers that speed-roll by with the credits explaining that issues and events depicted "are either presented by the actual litigants or may be re-enactments for entertainment purposes only. Wherever applicable, any resemblance to real persons, living or dead, is purely coincidental." The resemblance is often more than "coincidental," it seems, with story arcs ripped from the headlines, like *Law & Order* and other TV dramas. The case of Edward Smith, a self-described mechanophile in love with his VW Beetle, has been much reported in the tabloids, as has the case of the black middle-school teacher in Texas who was fired for giving a student a lap dance on his fifteenth birthday. It's not clear how viewers are supposed to tell the difference between real cases with the actual litigants and scripted stage productions with actors.

The case of the actual litigants Williams and Green aired on *Judge Judy* in February during a long run of shows in which all but a handful or so of complainants were African American or Afro-Caribbean immigrants in what played like a backhanded tribute to Black History Month. Other small-claims series like *The People's Court* and *Hot Bench*, a three-judge newcomer created and produced by none other than the Honorable Judy Sheindlin, likewise primarily air the dirty laundry of colored people, immigrants, and poor whites daring or desperate enough to suffer the minimal mercy of some of the more patient TV jurists and the fiery contempt of the irascible Judith Sheindlin, who presides over the *Judge Judy* courtroom set with an iron fist and a hard heart, often telling litigants how dumb they are and how much adjudicating their petty problems is a waste of the postgraduate education her dentist daddy paid for. With huge, multicarat diamond studs sparkling in each earlobe and a diamond wedding band of similar wattage glistening from her ring finger, a private jet, multiple residences, and an estimated net worth of $250 million, Sheindlin delivers such salvos without the slightest hint that she has given a moment's thought to how much more privileged she is than any of the unfortunate and often downright pathetic souls who appear before her, such as the white defendant the judge repeatedly called "a moron" and "a fool," even after noting from the bench that the woman was "mentally impaired" and had "a certain mental infirmity."

Judging Others and the othered is clearly a profitable enterprise for daytime TV. *Judge Judy* alone reportedly rakes in over $200 million annually in advertising revenue for CBS while costing $10 million or so to produce, which adds up to a huge profit share, even figuring in Sheindlin's $47 million salary, which she earns for working a mere fifty-two days a year.[11] It ought to be a crime but of course it isn't that TV judges like Sheindlin earn their bread and butter beating up on those who sometimes cannot afford bread and butter. Welfare moms with multiple kids by different men, tenants who don't pay rent, unlicensed drivers who crash uninsured borrowed or stolen vehicles, and similar examples of failed citizenship are the favorite fodder of an ever-expanding docket of courtroom reality shows, many with black judges, a disproportionately high number of whom are women of color, which Taunya Lovell Banks of the University of Maryland School of Law argues belies the fact that "women judges, especially black and other non-white judges, are still the exception in real courts."[12]

These TV arbitrators—some former jurists like Sheindlin, Milian, Toler, and the retired Michigan Superior Court judge Greg Mathis; others, Hollywood appointees—adjudicate disputes over dog bites, fender-benders, broken leases, and bad loans to deadbeat boyfriends, baby daddies, and sugar babies. Men, women, and children (and their pets) who have been attacked by dogs—especially pit bulls—are arguably the most common kind of litigants, although in a reversal of headline-making proportions, Judge Judy actually heard a case recently in which a black man had bitten a dog. In fact, she awarded $5,000 to the dog-biting plaintiff who had broken his own front tooth rescuing his pet from the jaws of a pit bill.

I'm not the first to point out the obvious fact that racial minorities are overly represented on *Judge Judy* and other similar programs, all of which seem to have a penchant for characters who are not only colored but colorful and put on a show. So many of the black complainants who appear on *Judy* and the other courtroom and conflict melodramas are such imperfect manifestations of conventional stereotypes of blacks as loud, lazy, oversexed, uneducated, unemployed, on welfare, and grammatically challenged that I hope the producers do go out of their way to find the most down-and-out of all possible black people in the name of making what somebody thinks is good TV. If not—if the litigants are to any degree a legitimate sampling of black America—we are in serious jeopardy. And this time I don't mean the game show.

But, of course, that's the point. The improperly civilized characters of color who perform for the cameras on these shows are not merely everyday people with everyday problems; they *are* the problem—a kind of cancer on the country. They cause accidents, property damage, and personal injury by recklessly driving uninsured vehicles, as the lawsuits daily demonstrate. They use their welfare checks and other government handouts (including federally funded grants and student loans) to bail out the same loafing losers who beat them up. They fail to pay rent to hardworking, tax-paying landlords whose properties they damage and destroy. They reproduce like rabbits but don't cough up a carrot of child support for the little black bunnies they drop here, there, and everywhere.

And who pays for what they do not? "Byrd and I pay," Judge Judy often decrees from the bench, strategically drawing her black bailiff, Petri Hawkins-Byrd, into what otherwise might be heard as just another recitation of the white taxpayer's burden. (Given that reported base salary of $47 million a year, the Sheindlins presumably pay a lot of taxes, unless they play the loopholes like Donald Trump.)

So why do millions tune in daily to watch hanging judges like the Honorable Judith Sheindlin mete out what the Honorable Marilyn Milian calls "rough justice"? It can't or shouldn't be to learn lessons about the law. Scores of lawyers, judges, and the American Bar Association itself have raised questions about the injudicious misrepresentations of reality TV courts and Hollywood-appointed judges, especially Judge Judy whose decisions some experts say are more about personality, behavior, and hard-hearted neoliberalism than about the law as such. The legal profession has even coined the term "syndi-courts" to describe this TV genre of syndicated pseudo courts with sets dressed to look like courtrooms and robed benchwarmers who look and act like judges but in actuality are merely arbitrators whose authority rests in the fact that the plaintiffs and defendants who appear before them have signed binding arbitration agreements to abide by the TV judges' decisions.[13]

Certainly to me as a law-loving viewer of long standing whose experience with such shows dates back to the original *Divorce Court* of the 1950s, televised court cases rarely seem to be about genuine jurisprudence. I remember a case in which a certain TV judge declared from the bench that she didn't care what the law said, in response to the pleadings of plaintiffs suing a couple who had rescued, cared for, but also neutered and thereby devalued the plaintiffs' lost purebred pooch. Judge Judy says that her show is intended to entertain and inform, but her rushed judgments often seem to be based more on her personal rules of life than on the rule of law. She sometimes tells litigants that because they agreed to binding arbitration, she is not bound by any county or state regulations and can use "common sense," which is what she says the law is supposed to be about.

Nor do these televised court cases necessarily deliver justice or even conflict resolution. Many, perhaps most, of Judge Judy's cases are promptly dispatched and dismissed; browbeaten, belittled loser litigants are sent packing with nothing more than a lecture and fifteen minutes or less of infamy, plus a small appearance fee and a free trip to L.A. If there is a judgment, the producers foot the bill for the penalty assessed, which can be as much as a $5,000 win for the losers who don't have to pay their own debt, despite the judge's rants about how the lack of personal responsibility is ruining the country. More often than not, however, the petty problems of her courtroom combatants go unresolved, while the larger problems that are the complainants themselves get publicly ridiculed in what might better be called *The Punch and Judge Judy Show*.

Is this then the great attraction behind these broadcasts: the ways in which they offer the white poor and the colored unwashed not their day in court but their televised comeuppance? In *Communication Ethics, Media and Popular Culture* (2005), Debra Japp, one of the coauthors, argues that the implicit message of *Judge Judy* in particular "is that it is acceptable to treat those one believes to be socially or morally inferior with condescension at best and rudeness at worst." Because the litigants "are often dysfunctional, under-educated, or under-employed," Japp writes, "they become legitimate targets for the host's chastisement" and the disdain of audiences who apparently find it "entertaining to watch Judge Judy berate people she considers marginal or unworthy members of society."[14]

Online commentaries from viewers seem to bear out Japp's perceptions. Even many of the comments that rail against Sheindlin's arrogance and impatience and the Hollywood hypocrisy behind the show's footing the bill for any and all cash judgments nevertheless express delight in seeing those they consider deadbeat litigants—and what the judge herself calls "marginal human beings"—endure a kind of verbal assault and battery from the bench. One posting in particular sums up the many: "The cases are real—but the judgements and the protests about paying are fake. The bad guys get away without any skin off their noses. But I still watch because sometimes I just like to see someone yell at these deadbeats the way I wish I could. It's cathartic. And I hope it humiliates some of these losers. Even if they do cry themselves all the way to the bank."[15] In other words, much as the Romans supposedly enjoyed watching captives and slaves eviscerated for their amusement, viewers today derive a degree of personal pleasure from seeing the racially, culturally, economically, and even mentally othered metaphorically slaughtered as a form of public spectacle.

What may be worse, however, is the extent to which some viewers buy into the metonymy of race and class that turns the part—the few bad apples—into the whole bad bunch, just as my mother predicted. One black welfare cheat becomes the entire black race, even reaching all the way to the Obama White House and its "Head Negro in Charge," in exactly the way my mother anticipated in the early days of television. One has only to spend a little time listening to conservative talk radio and TV or visiting websites online, reading virtual publications, or perusing the posts of good, common, everyday citizens to see and hear this racial metonymy at work.

In an infamous episode from 2011, Judge Judy lambasted and threatened to report to Congress the welfare fraud of an obnoxious young black male defendant named Duane Brooks Jr., who blithely pocketed the $437 monthly student stipend he received from the county for housing, while living rent-free with his girlfriend. As if that were not affront enough, he had the additional gall to argue with the judge about his right to do whatever he wants with *his* money, while also claiming that the pleasure of his company was payment enough for the ex-girlfriend suing him for back rent. Repeatedly noting that she and Byrd, as taxpayers, also waste $22,000 a year on his tuition, Judge Judy raked the would-be college student over the coals. I wanted to slap some sense into him myself, but online the case not only went viral, it also went racial and political, laid at President Obama's doorstep. At politicalinsider.com, for example, the case was written about under the headline "Judge Judy DESTROYS an Obama-Supporting Welfare Cheat" and punctuated with the inflammatory claim that "in Barack Obama's America, it's clear [Brooks] had a sense of entitlement to abuse that government program anyway [*sic*] he saw fit."

Lots of mostly hateful comments ensued, blackening and condemning the entire welfare system and racializing the people it aids, although a few respondents rightly pointed out that more white people use and abuse public assistance than any other group and that neither welfare nor welfare fraud began with the Obama administration. One respondent suggested that the complainers would do better to blame FDR. Truer to form, however, were comments like the following: "This is why I LOVE Judge Judy! Whenever these parasites (Oh, I mean 'valuable contributors to society') come in looking to win the ghetto lottery, she shoots them down"—ending with a stunning bit of trumped-up wisdom: "Imagine how much better our country would be without the sub-population of blood-suckers we're constantly being forced to support."[16] Again, such commentaries are all over talk radio and the Internet about this case and others with similar taglines like "Judge Judy Unloads on Obama Welfare Moocher Mom," Judge Judy reveals "the Entitlement mindset of Obama's America," "Obama-Voting Welfare Queen Mouths Off to Judge Judy—HUGE Mistake."[17]

Unfortunately, this line of thinking has big guns behind it. During the 2012 presidential campaign, Mitt Romney, a former governor of Massachusetts and a Republican candidate for the Oval Office, was caught on videotape complaining to wealthy donors about the presumed welfare state of alleged Obama supporters:

> There are 47 percent of the people who will vote for the President no matter what. All right, there are 47 percent who are with him, who are dependent upon government, who believe that they are victims, who believe the government has a responsibility to care for them, who believe that they are entitled to health care, to food, to housing, to you-name-it—that that's an entitlement. And the government should give it to them. And they will

Judge Judy DESTROYS an Obama-Supporting Welfare Cheat: I'm Sending This Tape to Congress! (VIDEO)

Archives

By Thomas

The welfare system, in theory, is supposed to be temporary and help people when they are down on their luck. But in practice, it has created an entire class of citizens who refuse to work and live off the work of others. In many minority communities, with the number of single-parent households skyrocketing, the state often takes the place of the father.

FIG. 8.2 A viral scene of Judge Judy with a defendant labeled a welfare fraud.

vote for this President no matter what. . . . These are people who pay no income tax. . . . My job is not to worry about those people. I'll never convince them they should take personal responsibility and care for their lives.[18]

Some bloggers and posters actually cite Romney, saying that he and Judge Judy have it right. In actuality, substantial portions of Romney's 47 percent are elders and retirees who receive senior tax benefits and a plurality of whom tend to vote Republican, as well as the working poor who contribute payroll taxes but unfortunately earn so little that, after standard deductions, they have no income left to tax. But the 47 percent also incorporates a sizable chunk of high earners, including—as we learned about Donald Trump during the 2016 presidential campaign—some millionaires and billionaires who through one loophole or another pay little or no federal income tax and who also are more likely to vote Republican. According to the Tax Policy Center and any number of other sources, there is no evidence to support Romney's claim that even a small percentage of those he pigeonholed as deadbeats are in fact government-sustained moochers with no sense of personal responsibility or that they are Obama supporters.[19]

Ironically, a young black slacker like Duane Brooks would find no more quarter with Barack Obama than with Judge Judy, not least because the forty-fourth president has made a point of calling out and calling on his black brethren to "step up" as men and as fathers, urging African Americans across the board to take personal responsibility for themselves, their families, and their larger communities. Linked to respectability politics, this position, too, has brought the president considerable criticism, this time from progressives who feel his "My Brother's Keeper" self-help initiative, which identifies failures of personal responsibility and missing father figures as part of the pathology haunting black America, effectively blames the victim rather than the barriers of structural racism and racial inequality that conspire to keep the underclass under. In other words, the president and the TV judge would be beating the same drum or banging the same gavel in this regard.

Judge Judy is fond of calling herself an ecumenical or equal-opportunity abuser, who beats up on the deserving without regard to race, class, or gender. I'm not at all convinced, however, that her courtroom set is a den of egalitarianism. Regardless of what a given case might be about, she almost always asks the litigants whether they are employed and if not why not, trailed by equally inevitable questions about the number of children they have and whether they support them financially. Her train of thought isn't hard to follow; neither are the presumptions of right and wrong, worth and worthlessness that attend the answers she receives and sometimes seem to shape her decision making more so than whatever evidence the petitioners present. That is to say, joblessness is prima facie evidence of poor character and questionable credibility; so is appearance. Judge Judy loves to say, "You look like a nice lady," or some version thereof to litigants whose self-presentation meets her approval. Those she finds slow, backward, or—her favorite word— "marginal" she is likely to ask whether they're on medication or take any psychotropic drugs, in effect mocking mental illness and the millions of sufferers who depend on medication therapy to survive in a world not as kind to them as it is to her and evidently also not realizing or not caring that such drugs are routinely and legitimately prescribed to treat neuralgia, fibromyalgia, and other forms of chronic pain. "Looks like" is a powerful simile, but a highly prejudicial standard even for a TV court of law.

Clothes make the man, they say, and it isn't only on the *Judge Judy* set that complainants with the goods and the good sense and sensibility to dress up and put their best foot forward sometimes fare better than those who simply come as they are, warts and all. To be fair, I must acknowledge that the poor, the infirm, the uneducated, and the unemployed are not the only types of real people who populate TV courtrooms. Doctors, dentists, lawyers, teachers, business executives, and plain old average, everyday Joes and Janes also appear, although much less regularly than the wild and crazy colored characters and poor white caricatures the producers appear to recruit.

From what I've seen of their relatively rare participation in televised lawsuits, MD-eities fare a little better that JD-eities. TV judges don't seem to like having other lawyers appear as litigants in their small-claims courtrooms. And while I can't say for certain that well-educated, well-spoken, well-dressed professionals necessarily come out ahead of the downtrodden and the tongue-tied in terms of actual dollars and cents, they often make better sense and generally seem to receive more of what might be called "professional courtesy," unless they aggravate the judges in some way, like the white male defendant in a tenant/landlord dispute who claimed to be both a lawyer and a doctor and asked Judge Milian to address him as "Dr. McCaffrey," although only after she cut him off and told him to "hold on a second, honey . . . counselor, I am directing these proceedings." McCaffrey, who clearly took umbrage at being hailed by a saccharine epithet, said, not incorrectly, that addressing him as "doctor" rather than "honey" would "create a tone of respect." Judge Milian countered with, "Guess what? Where I come from you sort of gotta earn that." Without missing a beat, McCaffrey trumped her counter with his own, "Guess what? Where I come from, you're born with it."

"Honey" is not a proper form of professional address, even by TV courtroom standards. It would surely be considered sexist, if not sexual harassment, if a male judge so addressed a female litigant. I don't usually stand on ceremony myself, but, with all due deference to the court, I, too, might be tempted to pull out my credentials if I felt diminished by someone flaunting an upper hand. McCaffrey's uncivil disobedience only succeeded in getting him thrown out of court, however, after he pushed the judge too far, shaking his head and telling her, "Watch yourself, your honor," when she implied he had "jerk[ed] around" the plaintiff for a year. Video of the contretemps went viral, as they say, and even had an airing on *Jimmy Kimmel Live*.

TV jurists demand respect, but contrary to Judge Milian's contention, they don't necessarily have to earn it. Because litigants sign waivers agreeing to abide by the judge's ruling, there is no recourse in small-claims arbitration TV other than to grin and bear not only the bench's ruling but also any mistreatment leading up to it, including what elsewhere might be considered slander. Civil courts have held—including in a libel suit brought against former mayor Ed Koch in 2000 when he presided over *The People's Court*—that even TV jurists have "arbitral immunity" and are "absolutely immune from liability for all acts within the scope of the arbitral process."[20] McCaffrey merely ended up on the Internet and *Jimmy Kimmel* for his run-in with Judge Milian. I have often thought that I would end up behind bars if a judge called me a liar in open court, as Judge Judy often does with litigants she doesn't believe based on no evidence other than her own look-me-in-the-eye truth meter or her oft-repeated commonsense conviction that "if it doesn't make sense, it isn't true."

As courtroom courtesy comes and goes, the one thing that may be more annoying to some TV judges and their audiences than a self-important white man like Dr. McCaffrey, Esq., or a lowlife, no-account Negro like Duane Brooks the welfare cheat is a well-off, uppity Negro with an attitude. The judicial atmosphere turned cold, catty, and cantankerous almost the moment Bishop Otis Craig Pringle walked onto the courtroom set in his tailored suit and faced the three-judge panel on *Hot Bench*. Pastor Pringle and his wife, Tiffany Anisette Pringle, described in an online tribute as "Atlanta's black power couple," were being sued by a young black clothing designer who claimed they breached a contract granting her the use of their home for a swimsuit fashion show.[21] Pastor Pringle countered that he had never given permission for the event to be held in his home because the plaintiff wanted to accommodate more than two hundred people on the premises, including what he unfortunately referred to in a text as "half-naked N-people."

The case was about a contract and should have been a simple matter, but the judges' first comments were about Pringle's watch, as the court took undue, injudicial notice of the large, fancy, diamond-encrusted bling around the pastor's left wrist. The watch had nothing to do with the case, yet its untimely presence on the arm of a too-well-dressed minister, who clearly had not taken a vow of poverty, seemed to offend the bench and set the tone for the hearing, which moved from snide remarks about the bedazzled timepiece to equally sarcastic comments about the couple's home. Judge DiMango, who is the only one of the original triumvirate with actual judiciary experience, asked for evidence. "Let's see some pictures of your house," she said, holding up a photograph of the dwelling in question. "I'm looking at your watch. . . . You must have some

FIGS. 8.3 AND 8.4 Close-ups of Pastor Pringle's diamond-encrusted watch and white-pillared mansion that so fascinated and annoyed the *Hot Bench* judges.

house." The camera zoomed in first on the watch, then on the house, with the image of a white-pillared mansion filling the screen, looking every bit like Tara in *Gone with the Wind*. "That's quite a house," Judge DiMango sniped in a voice thick with both annoyance and incredulity. "I'm coming back in my second life as a minister. . . . This is the house in which you two live?"

Watching at home as always through the prism of race, I could see the defendant's lips purse, body tense, and arms cross, which I read as a black man's response to microaggression at the macro level of public shaming but which the bench took as signs of a bad attitude, leading the lone black judge, Tanya Acker, to "jump down [the defendant's] throat" (to quote Judge DiMango), calling him out for arrogance and accusing him of trying to stare her down. "'This is not your church," she yelled (and she really was yelling). "This is not some place where you can tell people to give you offerings to buy you that watch"—that was followed by a lecture from DiMango about the evils of hypocrisy, especially for someone holding himself out as a man of God, while acting in a way "opposite to what a holy man or anyone living a decent life should do." DiMango rightly chided Pringle for his choice of words but not so rightly for choosing to come to court wearing "the most elaborate diamond watch" she's ever seen. Tensions had been high up to that point, but when the third judge, Larry Bakman, the token white male on the bench, demanded Pringle read out loud the hateful text message he had sent to the plaintiff, the contest between the two men became so explosive that without retiring to deliberate as usual or even consulting his two colleagues, Bakman screamed out, "$5,000, verdict for the plaintiff," and effectively threw the defendant out of court.

Please understand that I have no love for or patience with the kind of disorganized, if not dishonest, religion Pastor Pringle seems to me to represent. I don't know enough about him to conclude definitively that he fits the category, but preachers who get rich preying on the poor are among my least favorite beings in the world. The last time I went to a house of worship for other than a wedding, funeral, christening, or community event, friends dragged me to hear their choir sing at a Baptist church in Boston, where the black preacher bragged from the pulpit about the generosity of his congregants who buy him a new Cadillac every other year and had just sent him and his family of eight on an all-expenses paid trip to Hawaii. Such beneficence might not represent a hardship for a church located in the Hamptons or Beverly Hills, but this church draws its congregation from the poorer communities of Roxbury and Dorchester.

I was about as appalled by Pastor Pringle as I was by that Boston preacher, but even more inappropriate in my view was the behavior of the *Hot Bench* judges who set out to put the too-well-dressed, too-well-heeled, too-well-housed defendant in his place. The case was more a hanging than a hearing and did remind me of a verbal equivalent of what traditionally has been done to black men judged too big for their britches. There is such a thing as courtroom demeanor, which jurists may legitimately consider in decision making, but in what courthouse is it appropriate to chide a litigant for being *over*dressed and to snark repeatedly about his diamond watch and big house? It's beyond my heathen way of thinking, but there are those who believe that the prosperity of their preachers reflects well on the church community and is a sign of godly grace. If a Catholic cleric appeared before the *Hot Bench* tribunal sporting a ruby bishop's ring or a diamond-encrusted cross, would the judges feel entitled to comment and harp in the same derisive way that turned this TV court case into an episode of *Jerry Springer*?

....

With all due disrespect to relics like *Judge Judy* and *Jerry Springer*, the hottest trend in the reality TV industry today is probably an ever-increasing crop of shows with predominantly or completely black casts of mostly female characters, whose popular appeal and high ratings echo what's happening elsewhere on digital, cable, and network technicolored TV, bolstered by the offerings of Tyler Perry as well as Shonda Rhimes. According to an Associated Press report by Nekesa Moody, even Oprah Winfrey winced when Perry began drafting scripts for the first program he created for her network OWN, *The Haves and Have Nots*, which Moody describes as a "prime-time drama fueled by conniving people, sex and blackmail." To Oprah's complaints that the scripts were "too much," "over the top," Perry reportedly replied, "'I know this audience better than you do, I know what the audience wants.'"[22] Four successful shows later, Perry's knowledge of the audience has helped build OWN, just as his ever-expanding rosters of self-produced movies and other TV shows have made him a multimillionaire.

In fact, some call the blackening of the reality TV genre the Tyler Perry effect; I earlier traced the roots of TV's general blacking-up phenomenon to Oprah Winfrey's success. Whatever the cause, black reality shows are attracting large audiences and cornering the market in cable, headlined by a plethora of programs featuring black women frenemies who act out for the cameras, sometimes physically attacking each other and normalizing high-volume verbal smackdowns; Rapunzel-like wigs, weaves, and hair extensions; and conspicuous materialism, backbiting, blackmailing, and betrayal. The cast of characters ranges from the high-maintenance divas of the long-running *Real Housewives of Atlanta* and their catty, cantankerous city cousins the real Atlanta doctors and doctors' wives of *Married to Medicine* (which added a Houston edition in 2016) where female friends frequently come to blows both verbal and physical and undercut each other at every turn; to the cat-fighting, backbiting exes and (in)significant others of the NBA on *Basketball Wives*; and the wild and crazy signifying sistas (and brothas) who populate the sundry city editions and spin-offs of the *Love & Hip Hop* franchise.

Champions of the trend point out that reality TV also shows off plenty of outrageous white people acting out. True enough, and all this voyeuristic, neo-vaudevillian black performativity could well be written off as television

FIGS. 8.5 AND 8.6 The dolled-up doctors, divas, and drama queens of *The Real Housewives of Atlanta* and *Married to Medicine*.

as usual if the medium offered anywhere near as many alternative images of black women and men as it does of white. On the contrary, however, there is an oddly stigmatic homogeneity to the "real" black personas now playing in prime time. In fact, some media watchers have linked the upswing in black girl fighting as public sport and spectacle to the bitch-slapping and female brawling that reality TV has popularized and perhaps even normalized. The sad reality is that a number of girl fights have turned fatal in recent years. A street brawl in a Georgia neighborhood near Augusta that began as fisticuffs between two black teens fighting over a boy led to the death of an eighteen-year-old onlooker and felony murder charges for nine other mostly youthful participant/observers. In another incident in a high school bathroom in Wilmington, Delaware, a sixteen-year-old fighting with another teen, again supposedly over a boy, died of injuries sustained after other girls joined in what became a group beatdown. Videos of such deadly brawls often end up on YouTube or social media sites like Facebook, where in January 2017 four black Chicago teens livestreamed cellphone footage of themselves viciously kicking, beating, and slashing a mentally impaired white teenage boy, as they spewed racial epithets and anti-Trump invectives.

Videos of violence like the Facebook beating are posted on the Internet not as cautionary tales but as entertainment in keeping with—and perhaps inspired by—the outrageous, vulgar, vicious racial spectacles that are all over TV today, masquerading as both the new reality and the new human. Instantly claimed by both the Right and the Left as symbols of a politically raw, racially cleaved nation, the eighteen-year-old perpetrators in the Chicago case, who were charged with hate crimes and a string of other offenses, were called everything from depraved terrorists to sad, sick kids. The arraigning judge asked the teens where was their sense of decency?, a question we might well ask on a broader scale: where is the sense of decency in both our political and popular culture? Jesse Jackson may have gone a long way toward answering that question when he attempted to theorize beyond black and white, calling the Chicago incident "an ethical collapse, not an ethnic affirmation."[23] But in this era of "alternative facts" and post-truth politics; a trash-tweeting, smack-talking, pussy-grabbing presidency; and the celebration of the corrupt, the depraved, and the unprincipled, when we speak of ethical collapse, we have to look way beyond sad, sick teenagers.

Chapter 9

The Autumn of
His Discontent

BILL COSBY, FATHERHOOD,
AND THE POLITICS OF
PALATABILITY

In 1984, when "The Cosby Show" began its fabulously successful run, [Autumn Jackson] was 9. It is hard to imagine how she
could have avoided becoming hurt and confused, at least some of
the time, as this man—in her mind, her father—became known
to all as the greatest father in the land. He was the author of the
hysterically funny best seller "Fatherhood," and the lovably silly
pitchman for Jell-O. As fathers went, there were none better.

—BOB HERBERT, "No Mercy for Autumn," *New York Times*
(July 11, 1997)

A more fitting epigraph for this chapter might be "Oh, how the mighty hero
has fallen," given Bill Cosby's spectacular plunge from grace amid charges
of sexual abuse levied by scores of women claiming to have been drugged
and raped or otherwise sexually assaulted by Cosby over the course of several
decades dating back to the mid-1960s. The first African American actor to
receive a Primetime Emmy Award (1966) and the first to be inducted into the
Television Hall of Fame (1991), Cosby also received the Presidential Medal of
Freedom, the nation's highest civilian honor, awarded to him by George W.
Bush in 2002 for his contributions to the television industry and for using
"the power of laughter to heal wounds and build bridges."[1] As a legendary
comedian, actor, author, and producer, Cosby is a genuine cultural icon, who

in recent years has used his celebrity to criticize the black underclass for what he sees as its social, cultural, and economic failings, ranging from widespread personal and parental irresponsibility to a proclivity for sexual promiscuity, unwed pregnancy, conspicuous consumption, and senseless violence.

In 2004 in a speech delivered at an NAACP event commemorating the fiftieth anniversary of *Brown v. Board of Education*, Cosby effectively endorsed the *Judge Judy* rendition of the African American poor—that is, the same pathological portrait of the black masses that popular culture loves to portray. In the course of what quickly came to be known as his "Pound Cake speech" and in the lecture tour and "call out" crusade that followed, Cosby delineated his diagnosis of what really ails the black community: not structural racism and institutionalized inequality but bad parenting; a "50 percent dropout rate"; parents and children who don't care about education; "women having children by five, six different men"; "people going around stealing" and "getting shot in the back of the head over a piece of pound cake."[2]

Details matter little when such public pronouncements are made from on high, but, like Donald Trump, who retweeted a bogus claim that 81 percent of white homicide victims are killed by blacks, Cosby oversimplified complex socioeconomic dynamics that do unfortunately plague many poor communities and got basic facts wrong in the process. When it comes to calculating the number of black students not finishing high school, any figure is too high, but the sensational statistics that make headlines and further stigmatize disparaged communities are often misleading, according to a number of experts, in part because they do not distinguish between dropout and graduation rates.[3] But whatever the numbers, pontificating about percentages without addressing the larger socioeconomic problems undermining inner-city schools is putting the accent on the wrong syllable, as my Spanish professor used to say. Poverty, unemployment, crime, substandard housing, and abysmal living conditions continue to present untold obstacles to academic achievement in the inner city and elsewhere, but studies show that even in the most disadvantaged communities where, as some analysts have said, the way may block the will, African Americans place a higher value on postsecondary education than any other racial group does.[4] More important than Cosby's skewed facts and figures, however, is his public iteration of the private conviction that the poor debase the race.

Cosby might have taken a different, less preachy, and probably more productive tack, using his own background as a onetime high school dropout who turned his life into something amazing as a way to motivate and encourage rather than shame and belittle the struggling poor. Torn out of the respectability playbook, Cosby's "pull your pants up" critique of ghetto youth is hardly original, but it is odd to hear it from a black celebrity who built an iconic career largely avoiding racial politics while making blackness palatable for white audiences—that is, while being a good, safe, nonthreatening, entertaining Negro who, as Michael Eric Dyson writes, "flatly refused over the years to deal with blackness and color in his comedy," even as he took professional advantage of the achievements of the civil rights movement. "It's ironic that Cosby has finally answered the call to racial leadership forty years after it might have made a constructive difference," Dyson adds. "But it is downright tragic that he should use his perch to lob rhetorical bombs at the poor."[5]

I doubt that Bill Cosby had any idea when he began spouting off in 2004 what trouble was to come from his rhetorical bombs and his new career as the self-appointed moral compass of the black community or how much his own self-righteousness would contribute to his undoing. During a stand-up routine in October 2014, the black comic Hannibal Buress delivered a two-minute sendup of the legendary actor-comedian that called him out as a smug, has-been hypocrite who talks down to black people about their behavior even as he goes around raping women. "Google 'Bill Cosby rape,'" Buress advised as the audience cackled. "It's not funny," he added, pointing to the large number of results such a Google search would yield. It wasn't the first time Buress had alluded to the rape allegations that were better known in some circles than others, but this time his bit was captured on video and posted on the Internet where it spread like wildfire, leading a number of women to come forward with claims that were indeed no laughing matter.

Barbara Bowman, whose earlier rape accusations going back to the mid-1980s when she was a teenager had been dismissed as preposterous by her agent and the attorney whose advice she sought, published a piece in the *Washington Post* under the following headline: "Bill Cosby Raped Me. Why Did It Take 30 Years for People to Believe My Story?"[6] The supermodel Janice Dickinson also came forward, claiming in an interview on *Entertainment Tonight* that Cosby had drugged and raped her thirty-two years earlier.[7] Taking strength from and gaining credibility in their numbers, women began to come forward in droves, including several who had been Jane Doe corroborating witnesses in a 2005 civil suit filed by Andrea Constand. That case was settled out of court, but, as the only charge to fall within the statute of limitations, Constand's claim that she was drugged and sexually assaulted in Cosby's home would become the basis of a criminal prosecution that, after a hung jury in 2017, would see the comedian convicted on three counts of felony indecent aggravated assault in the 2018 retrial.

Many friends, fans, and even a few foes who felt Cosby was being railroaded continued to support the icon in his claims of innocence even as the number of women coming forward with charges of sexual assault climbed into the dozens. Whoopi Goldberg and Cosby's TV wife, Phylicia Rashad, were among those in the entertainment world who spoke out in Cosby's defense, with Rashad suggesting the allegations against him are part of an "orchestrated" attempt to destroy his legacy.[8] But in July 2015, a federal judge, in response to a request from the Associated Press, unsealed court documents from the 2005 civil suit in which Cosby admits to obtaining multiple prescriptions for Quaaludes for the specific purpose of giving the sedatives to women he wanted to have sex with. In deciding to unseal portions of the deposition that Cosby's lawyers fought to keep under wraps, Judge Eduardo Robreno cited the fact that Cosby "has donned the mantle of public moralist and mounted the proverbial electronic or print soap box to volunteer his views on, among other things, childrearing, family, education, and crime." In so doing, the judge asserted, he "voluntarily narrowed the zone of privacy that he is entitled to claim."[9] In other words, Cosby's self-imposed posture as a moral authority unsealed his fate. The upshot of the document release was that Cosby's own words have become the most concrete evidence against him to date, in the degree to which they appear to validate the women's otherwise largely she-said, she-said claims of being drugged in pursuit of what they insist was nonconsensual sex.

A secret life as a sexual predator would be the worst of all possible alter egos for anyone, but for a black man whose performance persona made him not only America's First Father but also a self-proclaimed paragon of virtue and poster boy for racial respectability, the "stark contrast between Bill Cosby, the public moralist" (to use Judge Robreno's phrasing), and Bill Cosby, the accused rapist, is earth-shattering. But the scandal has raised nagging questions about the role of television and mass media in our everyday lives and the larger problem of looking to TV and popular culture for our heroes and our villains.

Malcolm-Jamal Warner, who played Cosby's TV son, Theo Huxtable, on the legendary sitcom that now bears an accused rapist's name, publicly bemoaned the loss of revenue that the misconduct allegations meant for him as a cast member unable to collect residuals for syndicated reruns of *The Cosby Show*, which most TV stations ceased airing for a time.[10] Warner implies that Cosby and perhaps even more so the show that bears his name are victims of a double standard. He points to Woody Allen, Roman Polanski, and Stephen Collins, all of whom have survived allegations of sexual assault without serious injury to their art—without their work products being censored and pulled from public viewing.[11] Is Cosby's case different from theirs, and is that difference skin deep, as Warner's comparison of white men to black implies, though he, like many of those commenting on the scandal early on, stopped short of specifically mentioning race? During and after the 2017 criminal trial, however, Camille Cosby and at least two of the couple's daughters blasted the media and the judicial system for conducting a public lynching. Mrs. Cosby was largely absent from the retrial and was not at her husband's side for the guilty verdict.

Cosby versus Constand and some sixty other accusers is indeed a case about race, but rather than being the thing that brought a black man down, as Warner and others have implied, in this instance, skin color may be the very thing that made a comedian of mediocre talent exceptional and protected an alleged serial rapist from suffering the black man's fate of a high-technicolored lynching. Race so often has been the anchor that has pulled black men down and out of the mainstream; in Cosby's case, however, the particular kind of palatable blackness he performs was the buoy that lifted him up into the arms of the dominant culture, with the blessings of some members of the black middle and upper classes, glad for a representative and a symbol of what blackness looks like on the other side of the stigmatic. As the media theorist Bambi Haggins points out in *Laughing Mad: The Black Comic Persona in Post-Soul America* (2007), Cosby's approach to race relations has long been comfortably optimistic and assimilationist, as announced in his mild-mannered performance manifesto: "I don't think you can bring the races together by joking about the differences between them. I'd rather talk about the similarities, about what's universal in their experience."[12] It's no accident that President Bush chose to quote this particular self-serving pronouncement in awarding Cosby the Medal of Freedom, thus officially entering its conservative message of universalism into the historical record with the White House stamp of approval.

The "palatable blackness" Cosby represents so well is the inverse of what I have defined as stigmatic blackness—the mass-mediated representation of black people as low-Other and a list of additional racial stereotypes ranging from lazy and ineffectual to criminal and dangerous. Palatable blackness, by contrast, is high-Normal, like "us" rather than like "them," blacks whom white people can embrace rather than cross the street to avoid. Palatable blackness is safe rather than sensational, acceptable though not necessarily accommodating or obsequious—a blackness with its own proud, proper but nonthreatening sense of racial self, a kind and quality of racial alterity that offers the dominant culture black bodies without the stereotypical racial embodiment, a face of diversity without the problems of difference, unlike what Judge Judy believes she encounters in her courtroom every day.

The Cosby Show—not the 1980s sitcom but the performance that is Bill Cosby himself—was always on some level a fiction of palatability. Jewel Allison, one of Cosby's accusers, touches upon what I mean in explaining her reticence to out Cosby as a rapist: "Like many of the women who say they were assaulted by Bill Cosby, it took me two decades to gain the courage to reveal it publicly," she writes in the *Washington Post*. Most of Cosby's accusers are white and have had to face retaliation, humiliation, and skepticism in coming forward, but as an African American woman, Allison says she felt the stakes were even higher for her. "Historic images of black men being vilified en masse as sexually violent sent chills through my body," she explains. "Telling *my* story wouldn't only help bring down Cosby; I feared it would undermine the entire African American race." While some of the friends whose advice she sought encouraged her to speak up—torpedoes be damned—others cautioned her to keep quiet, to keep not only Cosby's counsel, as it were, but the black community's, to let "race trump rape," as she puts it.[13]

Allison's description of her dilemma, which linguistically places her outside the race—potentially against rather than of her own black community— evokes Anita Hill's impossible situation in effectively being called to testify against Clarence Thomas during the Senate confirmation hearings for his appointment to the U.S. Supreme Court in 1991. After testifying publicly about having been sexually harassed by Thomas when they worked together in the early 1980s, Hill was essentially derided and dismissed by the all-white, all-male Judiciary Committee and vilified in many quarters of the country, including by some in the black community. While all of her trauma and trouble ultimately did not impede Thomas's ascension to the Supreme Court, it did call unprecedented attention to the problem of sexual harassment in the workplace, although it would be more than twenty-five years before other women would speak out in a way that may effect real change.

I evoke the Hill-Thomas controversy here because a contemporaneous analysis of the incident by the highly respected black sociologist Orlando Patterson reveals exactly the kind of hierarchical thinking about race trumping gender from which Cosby may have benefited. In a *New York Times* op-ed—the venue of all venues—Patterson concedes that Clarence Thomas may well have said the "raunchy things" Anita Hill alleged, but he claims that, as a black woman of the South, Hill surely must have recognized Thomas's advances as his "downhome style of courting" and should have kept her mouth shut instead of giving into what Patterson calls the "legalistic, neo-Puritan and elitist model of gender relations promoted by the dominant school of American feminists."[14] In other words, Hill should have allowed her understanding of race as a black woman from the South to supersede her experience of being sexually harassed by a black man destined to sit on the highest court in the land and potentially adjudicate cases of gender discrimination and sexual misconduct.

Bill Cosby, in an odd and awful way, may have benefited, at least in part, from America's odd and awful history of racism, rape, and lynching—a history that can in certain instances suborn silence for the sake of racial fidelity. We are not so far removed from Emmett Till to have forgotten that, for African American men, just looking at or speaking to a white woman was a hanging offense. Cosby may have gotten away with gross sexual misconduct precisely because few dared call him the thing for which black men historically have been lynched. Who wants to be accused of effectively putting on a hood and facilitating the lynching of yet another black man? Those brave enough or angry enough to point an accusing finger were little ants raging against not only an icon but also the very image of racial respectability, success, and Father Law. Duped and drugged as much by the cult of celebrity as by sedatives, some of Cosby's accusers seem even to have doubted what they now say they experienced as a violation. Others, their own mothers didn't believe. It is a sad commentary on the merit of gender and the gender of merit that it took a black man's crying "rape" in order for women to be heard. It took a male comedian's jest for women's complaints to be taken seriously. It took a boulder from the slingshot of a fellow funnyman to knock a goliath off his high horse.

I feel obliged to acknowledge for the sake of truth in advertising that I have never been a great fan of Bill Cosby's kind of humor or the elements of his performative style. Still, I don't mean to belittle his talent or what some consider his genius when I suggest that good fortune has followed him all the days of his TV life. He first came to prominence as a stand-up comedian in the 1960s with guest appearances on the *Tonight Show* and other TV variety programs. It was his first-of-its-kind costarring role opposite the white actor Robert Culp in the TV series *I Spy* (NBC, 1965–1968), however, which made him an international star and a household name. But it wasn't exactly his acting chops that landed him what turned out to be the role of a lifetime and a watershed moment for the integration of television drama. Sheldon Leonard, the series' executive producer, has said that the seeds for casting a black actor as half of the *I Spy* team were sown in September of 1963 when black actors made cameo appearances in the "That's My Boy??" episode of *The Dick Van Dyke Show* and brought down the house and with it bags of affirmative fan mail.

As detailed in chapter 6, Greg Morris and Mimi Dillard had walk-ons in a flashback episode of *The Dick Van Dyke Show* in which Rob Petrie recounts for friends the story of how he convinced himself the hospital had given him and Laura another couple's baby boy by mistake. Morris and Dillard appear for a hot minute in the flashback as Mr. and Mrs. Peters, new parents whose colored infant, of course, could not have been mistaken for the Petries' white baby. My people know that there is a certain fallacy built into the visual gag on which the episode turns: newborn black babies of brown-skinned parents can in fact be light enough to be taken for white. My own beautiful baby brother entered the world white-skinned with reddish-blonde curls. Two months shy of four years old, I didn't understand much of anything about race at the time of his birth, but I do recall thinking that the adorable infant my parents placed in my doll carriage didn't look like the rest of us. I often overheard my mother telling her friends about snide remarks the white nurses in the maternity ward had made about who the baby's father was, despite seeing my brown-skinned dad at the hospital every day. The punch line of my mother's tale was the pleasure she took in dressing Danny in a baby-yellow outfit she had knitted and taking him back to Harley Hospital in Dorchester "after he had darkened up," my mother would say, to show him off to the nurses who had questioned his paternity.

No matter, the *Van Dyke Show* studio audience went crazy laughing over Rob's faux pas (or perhaps faux pa). Their reaction to the racial gag and the mail the show received in response were both so positive that Sheldon Leonard, who had been nervous about the episode's color-coded climax, was emboldened to cast a black actor in *I Spy*. In the third of a series of five interviews recorded for the TV Legends Archive and in his autobiography, *And the Show Goes On: Broadway and Hollywood Adventures* (1994), Leonard recounts the historic moment in which he came to cast Bill Cosby as Alexander "Scotty" Scott, growing out of his experience with "That's My Boy??"

Part of what turned the tide for him and for television history, Leonard explains, was the difference between the positive response to the appearance of Dillard and Morris and the negative reactions the network had received to previous interactions between white and black characters. Whenever Danny Thomas or any white cast member touched or showed any form of physical affection for Amanda Randolph, the black character actress who played the maid on *The Danny Thomas Show*, hate mail flowed in, Leonard says, with vile comments from what he calls "the land of idiocy," laced with invectives like "When I want to see a white man petting a gorilla, I'll go to the zoo" or "I don't allow niggers in my living room and you got no right to put them there."[15] Sometimes there would be eight or nine or ten postcards all with the same handwriting and postmark but signed with different names, all clearly from the same idiot, trying to make himself look like several idiots, Leonard recalls. But the response to "That's My Boy??" was overwhelmingly favorable, with many writers commenting that it was "very refreshing to see a black man shown with dignity." "We had shown an attractive, cultured black couple going one up on their white counterpart," he adds, and had delighted the audience in the process.[16]

Leonard goes on to say he felt that whoever played opposite the young, attractive Robert Culp, who had been a college athlete, would have to be equally agile and good looking, with a complementary sense of humor, but also physically different enough from Culp so they wouldn't look like "the Gold Dust Twins" (an odd choice for an analogy, since the image of the "Gold Dust Twins" has its own difficult history as racist iconography).[17] He had seen Bill Cosby doing a stand-up routine on a Jack Paar special and thought he fit the bill, but at the time "the networks were very apprehensive about using blacks on the same level as whites," as the costars of *I Spy* would have to be, since they would be working, living, and traveling together as a team. Leonard feared the network would be so afraid of losing southern stations that it wouldn't go for his choice of a black actor. Expecting resistance for that reason and prepared for a fight, Leonard says that when he flew to New York to pitch casting Cosby, he took along a computer printout tabulating the overwhelmingly favorable mail from the *Van Dyke* episode "in which Greg Morris had made a schmuck of Dick" in order to show the executives that the temperature of the country had changed. But when he met with Bob Kintner, the president of NBC at the time, there was no need for the mail or a hard sell. When he mentioned that the actor he wanted for the part was black, Kintner simply said, "What difference does that make?" "Somewhere bells rang, and trumpets blew," Leonard says. "The whole history of television changed in that moment."[18]

Not surprisingly, Cosby's acting was initially so "amateurish" that the NBC brass wanted him replaced, according to Leonard, who says he threatened to quit if his protégé was canned. Cosby grew into the part, and, because of what Leonard calls his "very marked success," soon "everybody wanted a black show." And Cosby, who was not an actor by trade or training like Greg Morris, was nevertheless very successful in the part Morris enabled, earning three successive Best Actor Emmys between 1965 and 1968 for his role as the globetrotting, erudite, multilingual, undercover secret agent, who along with his tennis pro partner got the job done for Uncle Sam without the fantastic paraphernalia and glamorous gadgets James Bond always has at his disposal. The international settings were what made *I Spy* exotic, while also offering a safer, more acceptable foreign backdrop for the black-and-white male bonding the drama depicted at a time when the idea of such interracial togetherness was still controversial.

A trilogy of comic black buddy films with Sidney Poitier followed—*Uptown Saturday Night* (1974), *Let's Do It Again* (1975), and *A Piece of the Action* (1977)—as well as a self-titled sitcom starring Cosby as a gym teacher at an L.A. high school (1969–1971) and the animated series *Fat Albert and the Cosby Kids* (1972–1985), whose title I hated even in my slender days. (I didn't watch *Fat Albert* and therefore am in no position to talk about it, but Beretta E. Smith-Shomade offers a fascinating, extended analysis of the show in her study *Watching while Black: Centering the Television of Black Audiences* [2012].) These outings and regular appearances in TV specials and commercials extended Cosby's popularity.

The documentary *Black History: Lost, Stolen or Strayed*, a CBS News Special that Cosby hosted and narrated in 1968, offers a different side of the actor-comedian, speaking truth to power in both a critique of the omissions, misrepresentations, and "deformed history" taught in American classrooms and a scathing indictment of the demeaning images of blacks depicted in film and television since the dawn of the industries. (This is the same documentary over which Lincoln Perry [Stepin Fetchit] sued CBS for defamation.) I can't imagine that my family wouldn't have watched such a program, but I have no memory of seeing it. Watching it recently on YouTube, I was struck by its crisp, edgy critique—including swipes at what the documentary describes as the "master and pet" relationship between Shirley Temple and her colored costars. The documentary is anything but funny. Its only punch lines are biting witticisms like "If you look history straight in the eye, you get a black eye"—meaning that what you see is what you don't get in the valorized historical record, including the myriad contributions African Americans have made to the wealth and well-being of the nation. None of what comes out of his mouth sounds much like the Bill Cosby most of us think of as avoiding racial politics. The white journalist and writer Andy Rooney, who is probably best known for his closing commentaries on *60 Minutes*, has the sole writing credit—and won an Emmy Award—for the documentary. Oddly enough, the narrative monologue does resemble Rooney's satirical voice rather than Cosby's. Regardless of who may have written the script, however, it was a daring deed for a black actor to be the ventriloquist and visage of such a potent critique.

<hr>

Whatever other roles he played, it was the family-oriented, domestic sitcom *The Cosby Show*, which premiered on NBC in 1984, that made Bill Cosby the nation's most beloved dad, as well as one of the most successful stars in television history. On the show, Cosby, who had earned a doctorate in education from the University of Massachusetts, plays Dr. Heathcliff "Cliff" Huxtable, an obstetrician whose in-home medical practice makes it possible for him to be ever present in the household, overseeing the comings and goings of his five children (four girls and one boy, like Cosby's real-life family), even more so than his superwoman wife, Clair (played by Phylicia Ayers-Allen Rashad), a practicing attorney who makes partner at a prestigious Manhattan law firm early in the series. Focusing on Cliff Huxtable's relationship with the five kids, especially the man-child Theo, *The Cosby Show* not only offered a never-before-seen portrait of an intact, upper-middle-class, male-headed, black household where both parents are successful professionals, it also pictured and promoted responsible black manhood and male domesticity—a common theme in the 1980s that suggested men could not only be good fathers but also be better mothers than many women. In so doing, the show functioned as answer and antidote to decades of negative diagnoses of black family life, such as the infamous *Moynihan Report*, and likewise redressed the myth of the absent black father.

Also unlike most black comedies before it, except, perhaps, *Julia*, *The Cosby Show* played the class card instead of the race card, for which it has been both praised and panned—a welcome departure from the junkyards and ghetto projects for some, a fantasy island of elitism and impossibility for others. On the one hand, the show moved the narrative beyond "a monolithic and one-dimensional view of blackness," in the words of the African American sociologist and media theorist Herman Gray, but on the other, it "seemed unwilling to critique and engage various aspects of black diversity that it visually represented"—as if the junkyards and the projects didn't exist.[19] And in some sense they didn't.

In keeping with its star's universalizing philosophy of touting similarities between the races rather than differences, *The Cosby Show*, as a bourgeois domestic comedy, set out to make black upper-middle-class life with father funny, after the fashion, perhaps, of the smashingly successful Broadway, motion picture, and television vehicle *Life with Father*—Clarence Day Jr.'s hilarious, touching sendup of fatherhood and family life among New York City's white upper crust of the 1890s. Except for the absent servants we don't see scurrying around the various floors of the family's well-appointed Brooklyn Heights brownstone, the Huxtables live every bit as well in the economic recessions of the 1980s as the Clarence Days did in the gay 1890s. And if the teeming colored masses are missing from the Huxtables' upper-middle-class milieu, the point of the show was never to make blackness palpable but rather to make it palatable, accessibly and acceptably comic, safe, silly—the way mainstream America has long loved to see black people, especially black people with money.

Even the black patriarch's name is funny: Heathcliff Huxtable—no African appellation, Negro name, or ghetto-fabulous tag for this brother. Studies show that stereotypically black names like "Jamal" and "DeShawn" are job killers. Voicing his disgust with his own data, Colin Holbrook, the lead investigator of a recent UCLA study exploring racial bias, found that "a character with a black-sounding name was assumed to be physically larger, more prone to aggression, and lower in status than a character with a white-sounding name."[20] Dr. Heathcliff Huxtable (perhaps more the comic-strip cat Heathcliff than the brooding romantic hero) is both safe and funny; Clair, Theodore ("Theo"), Sonia, Denise, Vanessa, and Rudith ("Rudy") are all similarly race neutral. Thus even at the level of naming, *The Cosby Show* effectively disappeared difference as problematic, mostly in favor of funny.

Unfortunately, for the show to have done otherwise in the 1980s—for it to have swaddled itself in racially charged subject matter and politically sensitive social issues—would have been to schedule its own cancellation, perhaps like the award-winning but short-lived black dramedy *Frank's Place* (CBS, 1987–1988), a show that not only featured a black cast but that also immersed itself in African American culture in palpable ways. Instead, *The Cosby Show* used the family's class position effectively to neutralize and normalize them. That is to say, the high-class context of the lowbrow comedy largely exempted the Huxtables from the racist assumptions—not to mention the historical experiences—that typically haunt racially marked bodies. I don't recall that we ever heard Clair Huxtable complain of being surveilled by security guards while shopping at Bloomingdale's, and Dr. Heathcliff Huxtable was spared

FIGS. 9.1 AND 9.2 *The Cosby Show*'s attempts to make life with father funny recall the 1948 film *Life with Father*, based on Clarence Day Jr.'s 1935 memoir of growing up in the 1890s with a stern stockbroker patriarch whose bark was worse than his bite.

the common black male experience of being refused cab service in the city, which even the African American mayor, David Dinkins, experienced, along with celebrities from the actor Danny Glover to the Princeton professor and public intellectual Cornel West. Nor were any of the Huxtables ever picked up by the police in their own upscale neighborhood for walking or driving under the influence of melanin.

But this show, after all, was conceived of and executed within the genre of domestic comedy, not within the contradictory category of reality TV or documentary. We know that off-screen, class doesn't trump color as it did on *The Cosby Show* set. Wealth and education may yield a higher standard of living for the black upper classes, but neither a platinum American Express card nor an Ivy League degree is a shield against the slings and arrows, slights and assaults of racial profiling and retail racism. Indeed, skin color so supersedes not only class but also celebrity that even Oprah Winfrey and Halle Berry, two of the most famous black faces and figures in the world, have been treated rudely and denied service by sales clerks who didn't recognize them and either assumed they were potential shoplifters or presumed they couldn't afford a $38,000 Tom Ford crocodile handbag or an even pricier Birkin at Hermès.

But it's not fair to suggest, as some critics have, that *The Cosby Show* is merely *Father Knows Best* in blackface, with no real colored cultural content. Herman Gray makes the provocative counterpoint that rather than being ignored or disappeared on the *Cosby* set, blackness "was mediated and explicitly figured through home life, family, and middle-classness."[21] The Huxtable brownstone was decorated with African and African American fine art, for example, including museum-quality prints and paintings by Paul Goodnight (one of the talented black Boston-area artists I had the honor of working with during my Arts Council days in the 1970s). The danger, though, is that technicolored outcroppings on *The Cosby Show* often took the form of window dressing and set decoration in much the same way that white Hollywood has long nodded at diversity and exploited difference.

By contrast, the current domestic comedy *Black-ish* makes a point of addressing and confronting everyday issues facing black Americans, from something as mundane as whether the younger generation will continue the old-school tradition of nodding to, smiling at, or otherwise acknowledging other black people when they pass them in the street, to the harmful realities of racism, racial profiling, and police brutality, which affect the lives of even those successful African Americans who have made it out of the ghetto and into the upper echelons of mainstream society like the Johnsons and the

Huxtables. Still operating within the context of comedy, often absurdly so—the *Black-ish* dad mistakes a smoking room for the lavatory and the humidor for the toilet in the home of his son's wealthy white classmate in one episode—the Johnsons can and do talk about Freddie Gray, the young black man whose death in police custody sparked days of protests in Baltimore, Maryland. They can and do protest on behalf of Sandra Bland, the young black woman who also died in police custody. In the second decade of the twenty-first century, *Black-ish* can give a public airing to black America's private hopes vested in the first African American president and its awful fears that he might be gunned down like Medgar Evers, Malcolm X, and Martin Luther King.

In a particularly memorable episode, the Johnsons debate this tension between hope and fear as it played out for many of us watching the inauguration of Barack Obama on January 20, 2009. The mother, Dr. Rainbow "Bow" Johnson (Tracee Ellis Ross), wants her children to be raised on hope; the father, Andre "Dre" Johnson Sr. (Anthony Anderson), wants them to be reared on realism. "Obama ran on hope," he says, before launching into what may be the series' most powerful monologue: "Remember that amazing feeling we had during the inauguration? . . . We were so proud. Then we saw him get out of the limo and walk alongside of it and wave to that crowd. Tell me you weren't terrified when you saw that. Tell me you weren't worried that someone was gonna snatch that hope away from us like they always do. That's the real world, Bow, and our children need to know that that's the world they live in" (S2, E16). I watched every minute of the inauguration that January day, talking on the phone with friends who were likewise glued to their television sets. And what were we saying? "Get back in the limo!" because, yes, we were terrified for the newly sworn-in president, for us, and for a nation those of us who lived through the 1960s and experienced both the rise and fall of hope feared could not survive another slaying.

Thirty years ago, the Huxtables couldn't take up such topics or, at least, they didn't dare do so explicitly. They didn't dare picket Denny's, the restaurant chain notorious for racial discrimination at the time; nor did they risk debating affirmative action or overtly protesting apartheid in South Africa. Instead, a "Free Mandela" poster in Theo's room, black art on the living-room walls, lip-synced jazz lyrics, and, in the latter episodes, twin grandkids named Winnie and Nelson signified both soul and social awareness. It was, I suppose, *The Cosby Show*'s way of being "black-ish," while satisfying white-like-us mythology.

But here, too, it is important to consider what I'm calling the politics of palatability—that is, in this instance, the alchemy *Cosby* performed in turning "black" "white." Patricia Williams, the legal theorist, cultural critic, and *Nation* columnist, makes well the point that *The Cosby Show* did such a convincing job of normalizing certain aspects of black culture that some of those elements were reconstituted as white or raceless—as "ours" rather than "theirs." "As *The Cosby Show*'s warm, even smarmy appeal made it a staple in homes around the country," Williams writes in *The Rooster's Egg: On the Persistence of Prejudice* (1995), "black cultural inflections that were initially quite conspicuous (speech patterns, the undercurrent of jazz music, the role of Hillman College as the fictional black alma mater of the Huxtables, hairstyles ranging from dreadlocks to 'high top fades') became normalized and relatively invisible."[22]

Sheldon Leonard describes a similar appropriative transference effected by Bill Cosby in *I Spy*, as his "natural speech pattern" created an "ad-lib problem" for the show. "A line of dialogue such as 'I can't do a thing like that!' coming from him," Leonard explains, "would naturally and gracefully become 'Hey, that ain't the kind of thing I can do, man!'" Initially, these black interjections weren't a problem. Leonard says, in fact, "Allowing Bill the liberty of adjusting his dialogue eased his transition from being a stand-up comic to being an actor." But as Bill Cosby, the fledgling thespian who started out following his white partner's lead, began attracting attention and winning awards for his performance while Robert Culp, the veteran artist, was relegated to the sidelines, what Leonard describes as "an ironic role reversal" took place. "Bob started interpolating 'Hey, man,' 'real cool,' and 'groovy' into his dialogue." As the producer explains, "The carefully designed characterizations of the two leads, contrasting but complementing each other, became homogenized. What had started as harmless interjections became increasingly intrusive ad-libs, often inconsistent with the story line."[23] Put a bit more bluntly, the white guy's attempt to do the colored thing blackened the show a bit too much.

The normalizing or homogenizing process achieved by Cosby on-screen can create a kind of which-came-first paradox in which cultural origins get lost. "As black cultural contributions are absorbed into mainstream culture," Williams explains, "they actually come to be seen as exclusively white cultural property, with no sense of the rich multiculturalism actually at work." As examples of this phenomenon in play, she cites the judge who not only sides with the employer in ruling cornrows an inappropriate hairstyle for the office but also accuses the black woman wearing them of "'just imitating Bo Derek,'" and the young white student who thinks the moves in her African dance class are borrowed from aerobics.[24] Part of what's interesting about this cultural absorption in relation to *The Cosby Show* is the fact that *Black*

History: Lost, Stolen or Strayed, the 1968 documentary Cosby narrated, makes a point of critiquing and indicting the appropriative gestures that turn African and African American cultural artifacts, music, and dance into European and Anglo-American high art and popular culture without attention or attribution to the roots of, say, Picasso's primitivism or Elvis Presley's rock and roll (although Presley himself often acknowledged his indebtedness to black music and musicians).

Riding the crest of his televisual success, Bill Cosby published a bestselling sendup of family life in 1986 titled, significantly, *Fatherhood*, with an authenticating introduction and afterword by the luminary black Harvard psychiatry professor Alvin Poussaint, MD, who was a consultant to *The Cosby Show*. (I vaguely remember as a girl picking out the handsome, young Dr. Poussaint as my future husband [for that year, anyway] when he appeared in one of *Ebony*'s annual "50 Most Eligible Bachelors" issues.) Cosby also starred in the comedy movie *Ghost Dad* in 1990, which elevated family values and the concept of an omnipotent paternity to even greater heights. Indeed, if on the rival CBS sitcom *Murphy Brown*, the title character's out-of-wedlock pregnancy and single motherhood were an affront to American family values according to then Vice President Dan Quayle, Bill Cosby's upper-middle-class, always-at-home, perpetual parenthood as Dr. Heathcliff Huxtable was a testament to them. Not only did he play the dad of all dads in both TV and film, he also often appeared as a father figure opposite children in Jell-O Pudding commercials, and he hosted a remake of Art Linkletter's old children's vehicle, *Kids Say the Darndest Things*, first as a CBS Special in 1995, then as a weekly series from 1998 to 2000; and he frequently spoke and wrote of his family life with Camille and their five children. As Donald Bogle writes, "Never raunchy or explosive as [Richard] Pryor became, Cosby, even during his early years, was something of a family man who extolled basic American values and a thoroughly American point of view."[25]

I'm not so sure I agree that Cosby's comedy was never raunchy, but I suppose it is a matter of opinion. Ironically, his "Spanish Fly" joke from his 1969 comedy album *It's True! It's True!* effectively makes drugging women with malice of foreplay a laughing matter, as some have been quick to point out. In the joke, Cosby narrates an almost lifelong quest to find an aphrodisiac called Spanish fly, reputed to drive women wild sexually. The joke specifically speaks of putting Spanish fly in a woman's drink to rid her of her sexual inhibitions. In his telling of the tale on the album, Cosby draws Robert Culp into the narrative, joking that as soon as Sheldon Leonard announced that *I Spy* would be shooting in Spain, the first thing he and Culp thought of was finally getting their hands on some Spanish fly. Arriving in what they celebrate as "the land of Spanish fly," they are all set to quiz their local cab driver about where to get the famous Spanish aphrodisiac, when the driver says to them, "You come from America? You can tell me maybe you brought with you some American fly." The live audience, which has been cheering and clapping throughout the narrative, fully bursts into laughter and applause at the American fly punch line.

While the Spanish fly joke may suggest something about changing attitudes toward drugs and sex and the difference between the Quaalude culture of the 1960s and '70s and what today's society would condemn as criminal date-rape behavior, I'm reluctant to jump on the particular bandwagon that reads the joke as inculpatory evidence. I'm mindful of the terrible moment in Zora Neale Hurston's life when she was falsely accused of molesting her landlady's ten-year-old son. She was eventually exonerated—her passport proved she was out of the country at the time of the alleged assault—but not before she was vilified in the black press, which lifted passages from her fiction and quoted them as evidence of her factual depravity and hunger for the knowing and doing love she wrote about in her novels.

What is clear about Cosby is that regardless of what jokes he told, both off- and on-screen he was the clean-cut king of the nuclear household in the eyes of most Americans. On the other side of *I Spy*, his rise to superstardom occurred within the specific context of a *Father Knows Best* narrative and the 1980s Republican platform of Reaganomics and discourse of family values, later winning praise even from the likes of Karl Rove, the Republican strategist and Bush surrogate who dubbed the *Cosby* characters—not the Obamas—the original "African-American first family." "It wasn't a black family," he said of the Cosbys on Fox News the night Barack Obama was elected president. "It was America's family."[26]

The Cosby Show has been much discussed in terms of its appeal to white conservatives as a black success story or, as Rove would have it, an *American* success story, signing off on the universality Cosby claims. What has attracted less attention—and seems to me more relevant now than ever—is the way in which the paternal romance was simultaneously affirmed and upset in January of 1997 by the odd confluence of two startling real-life events: the tragic death of Cosby's "only son," on the one hand, and the potentially scandalous revelation of an "illegitimate" fifth daughter, on the other.

....

In reporting the death of William Ennis Cosby, who was shot and killed during an attempted robbery while he changed a flat tire on the exit ramp of a California freeway, the media constantly referred to the twenty-seven-year-old as Bill Cosby's "only son," as if both the sex and singularity of the deceased as the sole male heir were of particular significance. Cosby jokes in *Father-hood* about asking God for a son to carry on the family name, but would the murder somehow have been less tragic, the loss less acute, if the victim had been one of Cosby's four daughters instead of that sole son?[27] Indeed, Cosby's daughters and even his wife, Camille, were marginal to and in some instances written out of the death notices, as the tragedy was figured as Bill Cosby's alone—a famous sire's loss of son, heir, namesake, and "hero." But the media's coverage of the murder of Ennis Cosby is only part of the sad story that unfolded that January day.

Even as Cosby was receiving the news of his son's murder, his lawyer was on the phone with Autumn Jackson, the young black woman who earlier that day had capped her claim to Cosby daughterhood with a demand for $40 million or else. The "or else" was the threat to go public with the secret Cosby had been paying (remarkably little, some might say) to keep quiet for twenty-two years: a self-described "rendezvous" in the 1970s with the model Shawn Upshaw (née Thompson) that may have spawned permanent consequences in the form of a daughter, Autumn Jackson. Although Upshaw had long maintained and continued to insist that Autumn was Cosby's daughter, another man, Jerald Jackson, whose name is on the birth certificate, had claimed the paternity Cosby himself denied. Denials or not, over the years the actor-comedian had contributed to Autumn's education and set up a trust fund, paying Upshaw well over $100,000 in what even he characterized as hush money, paid out because, in his words, "she could . . . go public with the fact that I had had sex with her."[28]

Donald Bogle once observed that as polite as the comedian always appeared, "audiences sensed that if Cosby were ever crossed, this man would let you have it."[29] Even Bogle couldn't have guessed, however, that the person the paternal, kindhearted, philanthropic "Cos" would let have it would be his own putative daughter, whose attempted blackmail he reported to the FBI, leading to her arrest and eventual conviction for extortion. What I found troubling at the time and what I have continued to stew over is the fact that Cosby wasn't just another vulnerable celebrity who was hit up for cash by a conniving, gold-digging, ne'er-do-well acquaintance; rather, he was at the time, by his own reluctant admission, quite possibly Autumn Jackson's biological father. During her trial, he testified to having been haunted by the question of his paternity ever since Upshaw showed him a baby picture in the 1970s and announced, "This is your daughter." Yet, while an uncharacteristically sympathetic press was willing to advance the image of the actor-comedian as a man both haunted and hounded, the fact was that Cosby himself had long before punted on settling the issue of paternity. Under cross-examination by Jackson's attorney, Cosby conceded that he had backed out of taking a scheduled paternity test several years earlier because he feared news of the test might be leaked to the media, causing him embarrassment.[30] (His attorneys advanced the same personal embarrassment argument in trying to prevent the release of the 2005 sexual assault deposition.)

The fact that Cosby apparently was more concerned with upholding his image as the great American father figure than with determining whether he was indeed Autumn's biological father was of little concern to the courts, the media, and the masses. The fact that, if found guilty of extortion, Autumn faced twelve years in the federal penitentiary was of equally little concern to a populace otherwise preoccupied with fostering good parenting, promoting positive family values, and punishing absentee fathers. In fact, the court ruled the issue of Cosby's alleged paternity irrelevant in Jackson's trial, since extortion is illegal, regardless of the relationship between the blackmailer and the blackmailed.

What seemed relevant to me following the case at the time was the sad absurdity of it all. A kid who thinks she's your daughter—not without good reason—hits you up for $40 million, or else, and you have your lawyers turn her over to the FBI, while pretending to be negotiating a settlement. Five million, ten million—I could see it, but $40 million is such a preposterous king's ransom even for someone as wealthy as Bill Cosby that it sounds more like the pitiful cry for help and attention of a desperate and perhaps even disturbed child than the well-thought-out scheme of a criminal mastermind. Jackson had older and presumably worldlier accomplices, but how did they come up with such a figure? Perhaps they watched *The Cosby Mysteries*. Forty million dollars is pretty close to the $44 million Cosby's character, Guy Hanks, wins in the lottery in the pilot episode of his defunct detective series, and Autumn's extortion plot is just about as far-fetched as most of what happened in that short-lived crime drama.

I felt sorry for the Cosbys at the time, as I would for any parents who have to bury a child, which I watched my own mother and father go through in 1991 when Adrian Jr. died suddenly of a massive coronary a month after his forty-sixth birthday. But there was something that rankled about seeing Cosby mourn the loss of the son he called his hero while throwing away the possibility of a daughter he called a criminal. I, of course, cannot be certain what Autumn Jackson knew and didn't know about her parentage and whether she truly believed Bill Cosby was her father. It must have been heartrending watching him parent the Huxtable kids on TV and the real-life children she would have considered her half-siblings if she did believe "that's my dad." Maybe it was all just a big hoax—a long con with mother and daughter as coconspirators out to bilk a black Daddy Warbucks out of some of his bucks—but even Cosby, who acknowledged that his sexual affair with Jackson's mother coincided with Autumn's conception, had his doubts. Perhaps my sympathies were and remain misplaced, but I'm in accord with the former *New York Times* columnist Bob Herbert, who wrote during Autumn Jackson's trial that looking at her and looking around the courtroom at the judge and jury who could send this barely grown woman to the federal pen for a dozen years, "you cannot escape the queasy feeling that this is something that should not be happening. This is unnecessary."[31]

Most of the media, however—usually overanxious to skewer celebrities who falter—were relatively reticent about the possibility of America's favorite father fathering a forsaken, denied daughter. Like the American public, even muckraking, investigative journalists largely let Cosby off the hook for the philandering that may have spawned a girl child, choosing instead to lay all the blame on a greedy, ungrateful Autumn Jackson and her equally rapacious mother. In fact, his image little tarnished by the scandal, Cosby emerged a sympathetic figure whose approval rating actually went up following Jackson's conviction, as I recall. He got a boost in ratings; Jackson got twenty-six months in federal prison.

And all these years later, when we know or think we know so much more about who Bill Cosby is and is not, I'm left wondering about the moral, if not the legal, relevance of what the court ruled irrelevant: the issue of Cosby's paternity as it relates not only to Autumn Jackson but also to larger questions about the meaning of fatherhood and patriarchy and the politics of palatability that possibly protects a predator from himself. Ironically, Cosby's superstar status as the nation's premier father figure made the assaults on women—on daughters—he now stands accused and convicted of both unthinkable and unspeakable. The deference he received from both the media and the masses in the Autumn Jackson case may have been an act of compassion in the face of the death of his son and a courtesy to Camille Cosby as an innocent party who also lost a child. But this earlier Cosby case may also reveal deeply rooted attitudes about paternal privilege and gender difference, which would play out fifty-fold in the charges of sexual assault that would eventually come to light.

The fact that the nation's premier patriarch—the black man who virtually defined fatherhood as a national narrative, who became synonymous with the concept of father more so even than the white men the country claims as founding fathers—could turn on, turn in, and testify against his black daughter (whether real or a figment of the putative daughter's imagination) ought to be a national disaster, an American tragedy like the collapse of the Washington Monument or the Jefferson Memorial due to footings of clay. Autumn Jackson broke the rule of law, but what of the rules of life that Cosby claims all men, all fathers, must live by? The trial court let the patriarch off the hook by ruling his paternity irrelevant to the daughter's crime, but in the very scheme of things Cosby himself laid out for black men to live by, the father's role can never be immaterial.[32] In my view, then, there is no honest way to reconcile the easy condemnation of Autumn Jackson with Cosby's own much preached-about brand of respectability politics and the national narrative of a responsible paternity in which the daughter is sacred and must be protected at all costs, which, as I argued earlier, has long been used to sanction vigilante justice and the divine rights of men.

In its refusals and its abuses, the case of *Cosby v. Jackson*, like the fictional case of the state against the father who shot his daughter's rapists in *A Time to Kill*, says something disturbingly American about the relative worth not only of black female to white but also of daughter to son. And what of the daughters Cosby does claim—the four young women he has reared with his wife? How does a man with girl children so flagrantly violate the sanctity of "daughter," "woman," "wife," "mother," even "mistress"? Even as he and his diehard supporters continue to maintain his innocence, despite the guilty verdict, we know from the facts in evidence that Bill Cosby is without question a serial philanderer and womanizer, who used his celebrity status and paternal persona to seduce mostly starry-eyed ingénues. And while that is surely first and foremost between and among the principals, I do wonder what such a husband says to his wife, what such a father says to his daughters, what such a self-proclaimed paragon of moral authority says to the rest of us mere mortals.

The issues of fathers and daughters and husbands and wives and the larger questions of filial and familial fidelity necessarily call up final reflections on my father and mother and my own family drama. True to his pronouncement that he was tired of living my mother's kind of life, my father left the still-unfinished house and its occupants behind and drove off into the bright lights of the big city after the divorce, rather quickly remarrying and settling in Boston's South End, where he became a legend in his own time as a community activist and man of the people—one of the "unsung heroes of the South End," the *Boston Globe* once called him.[33] It's somewhat ironic that in the era of women's liberation, it should be the husband and father who escaped the daily drudgeries of domesticity rather than the wife and mother. But Pearl Hogan duCille, at least as she saw it, was born to marriage, parenthood, and family life in ways the man she married was not. That doesn't make one of them good and the other bad, one right and the other wrong. It makes them both, if anything, victims of the limitations and gendered presumptions of a time when men and women met, married, made families, and attempted to live their own *Ozzie and Harriet, Leave It to Beaver* lives. My father might have done better and been happier as a single man of the world seeking, if not great fortune, certainly the fame that came to him in the latter part of his life. My mother, by contrast, was most at home within the home, though she refused the alimony the judge would have awarded her and remained in the workforce, first as a founding staff member of the Greater Brockton Head Start Program in the latter 1960s, then as a caseworker, spending many years patiently and professionally serving clients in the Food Stamp Unit of the Brockton Welfare Office.

My father died in 2006 at the age of eighty-six. I had long before forgiven him the "professional student" slap in the face that had stung so much at the time. I mostly credit my father with having done the best he knew how and make a point of remembering the good things: the artistry and humor of his tall tale telling, the Shakespearean soliloquies he encouraged me to memorize and coached me in reciting with all due drama—"Cry 'Havoc,' and let slip the dogs of war / That this foul deed shall smell above the earth / With carrion men, groaning for burial"—and the gorgeous mint-green dress he made me for my eighth-grade graduation, which lives among my memories as the most beautiful garment I've ever worn.[34]

The same selective way of emplotting the past is how I try to remember my father's namesake son, Adrian Jr., his firstborn and clear favorite, whose misdeeds and increasing psychosocial dysfunction he refused to see. Though there is a lot of troubled water under that bridge, here, again, I cling to the stories my mother used to tell of how much my big brother had wanted a baby sister, how much he had loved and cared for me, how he had protected me as an infant and toddler to the point that I was not to be chastised or punished no matter what I did because I was "just a baby," except for the time I *allegedly* took my two little fists and as soon as Mom's back was turned tore into the birthday cake she had baked for her own big brother, Uncle Francis, instead of eating the cereal in front of me. (Warm homemade pound cake versus cold soggy cereal: who could blame me? I was clearly a child of good taste and discernment.) My mother slapped my hands; I cried; Little Adrian came running poised to defend me as usual—until he saw the cake. My mother said he turned on his heels and left the kitchen without a word. Later, as Mom would tell the tale, he came to her, leading me by the hand and coaxing me to deliver the "I'm sorry, Mummy" speech he had taught me.

Shades of that boyhood goodness remained in the troubled and troublesome adult Adrian grew into. He was the one who was always interested in what I was writing; he was the one who started reading African American authors because I was teaching them. After I got my license at sixteen, he was the one who had let me, his kid sister, drive his car weekdays while he was at work, but he was also the one who would harangue me mercilessly for not putting the seat back exactly where he wanted it and not readjusting the side and rearview mirrors exactly the way he wanted them. There was no reasoning with him about the impossibility of manually adjusting a mirror for someone else's sight lines or a car seat for somebody else's comfort; so, after a while, to avoid his ranting and raving wrath, I began driving the car without changing the positions of the seat and mirrors—quite a perilous proposition, I think now, since Adrian was a good seven inches taller than I am. That there was no reasoning with the adult Adrian is perhaps symptomatic of whatever went wrong with his soul. I still weep sometimes for the loss of the kind, loving little boy who so adored his baby sister and wonder how we might have saved him.

And what of the house the duCilles built and built and built? In 1995, after more than forty years in the same spot, my mother finally sold the old homestead to our neighbor Dick Clayton, a local businessman who as a teen had been one of the first to welcome us to the neighborhood. He purchased the property, I suspect, not because he particularly wanted to add unfinished dwellings (including the house Adrian had built next door, which in the duCille tradition—broken by the third generation of "property brothas"—was also never completed) to his real estate holdings but because he wanted to aid my mother in moving on. I hear he finished the house and made it the thing of beauty my mother always imagined, but I haven't had the heart to go see it for myself.

Just after Christmas 1995, Mom and I moved to San Diego, settling into two new tract houses we had built next door to each other in a subdivision a few miles from the ocean, between La Jolla, where I had an appointment at the University of California, and Del Mar, home to the famous racetrack. For years, I had tried in vain to rescue my mother from a house beginning to crumble around her, but she wouldn't budge. And then the clever folks at UCSD in trying to recruit me invited her along for a look-see visit, during which realtors showed us all manner of manors, most with shock-inducing sticker prices, until we were led into a somewhat more affordable new development, still under construction, where you could pick your own lot and floor plan from among six models the builder offered. All was much as it had been on other house tours until we entered the only single-story model home and there in a corner of the well-staged kitchen sat the built-in breakfast nook and banquette my mother had wanted since first seeing them on TV in the 1950s. The die was cast, but I didn't know how definitively until She-Who-Would-Not-Be-Moved crossed the threshold of the old homestead upon her return east and immediately began going through the rooms saying, "I'm taking this, this, and this, but, no, I'm not taking that or that," her mind clearly made up even if mine was not.

So it was that Mom at last got her breakfast nook, and while I didn't quite get the Blueview Terrace address of my own youthful California dreaming, I did end up on Caminito Exquisito in a subdivision with the grand name of Palacio del Mar. East Coast country bumpkins that we were, dumb to the racial dynamics of Southern California, we didn't understand that all the colored people smiling and waving at us so warmly when we went to pick out our adjoining lots were the help, not the homeowners. Thus it was that forty-three years after we moved to East Bridgewater, we once again found ourselves integrating a white neighborhood. So San Diego became an adventure in ways we hadn't anticipated. We stayed there three and a half years and might be there still but for a turn in my mother's health. The persistent cough that

FIGS. 9.3 AND 9.4 The front and rear views of our adjacent San Diego homes. My house is in the foreground; Mom's is on the left. In fig. 9.3, you can just see Mom standing on the left edge of my driveway, near her home. Fig. 9.4 provides the view of my back patio looking toward Mom's on the left. We took down the fence between the two properties for easy access.

FIG. 9.5 Mom holding her first great-grandchild, Taylor Marie Lovejoy (2000).

FIG. 9.6 Mom with her grandchildren and great-granddaughter Taylor (now a teenager and driving) tickling Great Uncle Danny's neck. Taylor's mother, Beverly Lovejoy, is to the right of Mom, next to her mother, Ingrid. Mom's sister-in-law Aunt Mary Hogan (who lived to be 103) is to the left. Standing left to right are Marie Gordon-Coontz, Dave duCille, and Adrian duCille III.

FIG. 9.7 Mom at home in Taunton, Massachusetts, with Bev and her great-grandchildren, baby Taylor and Bev's stepchildren, Gary, Ashley, and Austin Lovejoy. Michael "Mikey" Paul Lovejoy, not pictured, would come along just after Gramma Pearl passed in June of 2002. Also not pictured are Marie's son, Nicholas Tyler Gordon, likewise born in 2002; Dave and his wife Rachel's daughter, Sienna Pearl duCille, born October 2, 2017; and Elianna Kayin Coontz, born March 7, 2018.

specialists back east had insisted was merely postnasal drip, the San Diego doctors promptly identified as pulmonary fibrosis—a terminal disease of the lungs, unexpected in someone who had never smoked. Mom met the diagnosis with remarkable calm and good cheer, actually seeming to welcome the oxygen tanks and nasal cannula, literally as a breath of fresh air.

Danny, always kind and generous and ever the good son, sold his own much-loved house on the Taunton River and left his job of more than twenty years to join us in San Diego to help with Mom's care. His arrival was a blessing for us, though quite a sacrifice for him, but Danny has always been selfless and quite literally my lifesaver. (As a small boy, he had acted instantly and instinctively when he looked up and saw me tumbling headfirst down the cellar steps, heading for the cement floor. He rushed over and positioned himself to break my fall, almost certainly saving me from serious injury or worse.) As comfortable as the three of us were living next door to each other—and even with the care and kindness of our California friends—I could see as Mom's condition worsened that she longed to end her days among her grandchildren and a rainbow coalition of neighbors, friends, and family in a place where she was Gramma Pearl to multitudes. So in the summer of 1999, we reversed our cross-country journey. I returned to Wesleyan but couldn't persuade Mom to join me in Connecticut. She and Danny settled into a comfortable four-bedroom colonial in southeastern Massachusetts—not new like her San Diego dream house with the breakfast nook, but finished.

On a warm almost summer night in June of 2002, at home in hospice care, with Danny on one side and me on the other, watching TV together one last time, she fell into a peaceful sleep from which she did not wake.

Chapter 10

The "Thug Default"

WHY RACIAL
REPRESENTATION
STILL MATTERS

Some mainstream media outlets seem hell-bent on amplifying the parallel myths of white superiority and black inferiority. African-American men in particular are primarily packaged as "thugs," wrapped in pathology so stifling that even when the opportunity presents itself, mainstream media won't let them breathe. They don't get to be heroes.

—KRISTEN WEST SAVALI, "Why Do All the Superheroes Have to Be White, and All the Thugs Black?," *The Root* (May 27, 2015)

In this final chapter, my reflections on race and representation turn to the figure of the black thug as the repository of contemporary television's criminal intent and popular culture's overdetermined malice aforethought—stigmatic blackness personified and, as the cultural critic Kristen Savali says, African American men pathologized to the point of suffocation.[1] But consider first for a moment a counternarrative of a figure some have dubbed the antithesis of the thug—Wayne Brady, yet another black stand-up comic turned game-show host. Unlike his colleagues Steve Harvey of *Family Feud* and Sherri Shepherd of *The Newlywed Game*, however, Brady runs a squeaky clean ship as head of the revamped version of the old network standard *Let's Make a Deal* on CBS and has managed to keep the show upright and afloat since 2009 without depending on raunchy jokes and sexual innuendo. Clean cut, well spoken, mild mannered, and multitalented, Brady has perhaps the oddest of all possible image problems. He has been dogged throughout his career by claims that he is not black enough.

Some years ago, the African American comedian Paul Mooney in character as the prophet Negrodamus in a *Chappelle Show* skit pegged Brady as a "white folks' Negro" with the now famous line: "White people like Wayne Brady because he makes Bryant Gumbel look like Malcolm X" (S2, E5). In other words, Brady is beloved of white audiences because he is a good, safe, unthuggish, nonthreatening Negro, not unlike Bill Cosby before the fall. The white political satirist Bill Maher has taken a similar tack in joking about his disappointment that the "professorial" Barack Obama turned out to be "President Wayne Brady" instead of the gangsta he thought he was getting when he voted for the first black commander-in-chief. "I thought we were getting Suge Knight," he said in one tasteless quip. In another instance, he criticized Obama for not coming down harder on British Petroleum for the 2010 oil spill in the Gulf of Mexico. "You know, this is where I want a real black president. I want him in a meeting with the BP CEOs, you know, where he lifts up his shirt so you can see the gun in his pants."[2]

Mooney and Maher both mean, of course, to satirize rather than sanction stereotypes, but even out of the mouths of a black comedian and a white liberal who thinks he's so down with the people that he can utter the N-word like a homey, such jokes effectively license a dangerous essentialism. What makes these Obama/Brady jests possible, after all, what resides within them and gives them essence, is the reigning, ruling perception, played out on TV and in popular and political culture, that the quintessential default identity for a black male is "thug," "criminal," "gangster," or, in urban parlance validated by the *Oxford English Dictionary* since 2001, "gangsta." The "real black," the true-blue black brother, is a gun-toting street thug like the rapper and music mogul Suge Knight, who has faced multiple arrests and served jail time on charges ranging from domestic battery to murder.

In a television studio, a joke suggesting the Harvard Law School–educated African American president and the clean-cut African American entertainer are whitewashed Negroes rather than authentic black brothas like Suge Knight may seem harmless enough, but what such dark humor says about the stigmatic presumption that I call "the thug default" has dire, real life-and-death consequences for the black male population perennially typecast and racially profiled as criminal, fearsome, always and forever up to no good. It's such a presumption, for example, that took the life of Trayvon Martin, the unarmed black teenager fatally shot by George Zimmerman, a mixed-race neighborhood watch volunteer patrolling the gated Florida community where Martin was visiting relatives but where his color and clothing seemed out of place to Zimmerman on the evening of February 26, 2012. In his 911 call to the Sanford Police Department before he took matters into his own hands, Zimmerman site/sight-read the black kid in a dark hoodie "just walking around, looking about" as a hood or a thug; he was someone who looked "real suspicious," "like he's up to no good," Zimmerman told the police dispatcher before the altercation that ended Trayvon Martin's life.[3]

Derived from the Sanskrit word "sthagati" (to conceal), a "Thuggee" or "Thug" was originally a member of a secret society of marauding thieves who supposedly roamed throughout India for hundreds of years, murdering travelers and merchants in sacrifices to the goddess Kali, until they were ferreted out and suppressed by the British in the early 1800s.[4] Some contemporary scholars argue, however, that these so-called Thuggee cults were largely an invention of the British colonial imagination as a way to control the Indian population and to justify the brutality with which royal forces suppressed resistance.[5] However real or imagined the subjects, the term "thug" morphed into the English language during the Raj with the more general meaning of robber, rogue, or ruffian. In American urban slang, the term has taken on its own complex meanings, referring, on the one hand, to someone schooled in the ways of the street, living the hard-knocks life—on the fringe, perhaps, but not necessarily outside the law. On the other hand, its association with rap music and hip hop culture has endowed the word with additional, even more complex, culturally resonant connotations often with an aura of lawlessness attached.

For the artist and activist Tupac Shakur, who spoke, wrote, and rapped about "THUG LIFE" and had the words tattooed across his torso, the terminology was of, by, and about the street ethic and survival schemes of urban youth for whom rap music was a form of self-expression and social commentary, a way of telling the hard-luck stories of ghetto existence, which, according to the cultural theorist Tricia Rose, included narratives that "emphasized being trapped by gang life" and addressed how it was that street crime became "a 'line of work' in the context of chronic black joblessness." "Thwarted desires for safe communities and meaningful work were often embedded in street hustling tales," Rose writes in *The Hip Hop Wars: What We Talk about When We Talk about Hip Hop—and Why It Matters* (2008).[6]

Rose, who brought rap into the academy and pioneered the field of hip hop studies, draws a critical distinction between the expressive modalities that emerged out of desperation, featuring complicated representations of ghetto life and street culture, and the commercial commodification of this urban art form. Under the claim of "just keeping it real," Rose explains, commercialized hip hop simplifies, valorizes, promotes, and even caricatures the image of the black street hustler, the gangsta, the pimp, the prostitute, and the thug as nefarious denizens of the hopelessly crime-infested, sex- and drug-crazed inner city, eclipsing other less colorful notions of what it means to be black, while reinforcing the most stigmatizing images of black people.[7]

What I particularly want to address in these final reflections is how widely and deeply entrenched these stigmatic images and narratives of blackness have become, both within and outside of popular culture, finely and I think dangerously reinforced by much of what appears on television today. The "keeping it real" claim of commercialized hip hop is not that different, it seems to me, from the "keeping it human" rationale for the messy, flawed, complicated characters of technicolored TV. Images of the depraved, hustling black thug, con, and criminal, in particular, have floated out into the mainstream, carrying a narrow but universalized understanding of who and what black is beyond the mean streets of the ghetto and even insinuating themselves into the Clinton White House in the 1990s, where during a working dinner on juvenile crime, the president and first lady took note—and, reportedly, literally took notes—as John DiIulio Jr., a distinguished political scientist then at Princeton, promoted his much written- and spoken-about concept of urban youth as "superpredators" with "absolutely no respect for human life and no sense of the future."[8]

Drawing on the conventional wisdom and expert testimony of the time, Hillary Clinton infamously incorporated DiIulio's superpredator rhetoric into a 1996 re-election campaign speech supporting her husband's anticrime agenda, including the federal three-strikes policy and the 1994 Violent Crime Control Act. Talking Republican tough on crime, Mrs. Clinton likened the administration's organized efforts against gangs and urban violence to earlier crusades against the mob, describing inner-city youth as kids no more but, rather, as superpredators without conscience or empathy. "We can talk about why they ended up that way," she said, "but first we have to bring them to heel."[9] This racially charged language, which painted black youths as wild animals that must be tamed, would come back to haunt Secretary of State Clinton during her own presidential run when the Black Lives Matter activist Ashley Williams publicly challenged her and demanded an apology for pathologizing a generation of black Americans as predatory animals.

For Secretary Clinton, the why of ghetto life that supposedly spawned a cohort of young black thugs—schoolchildren who "pack guns instead of lunches," according to DiIulio—seemed to be of secondary importance.[10] I would argue, however, that it is essential to consider the climate and conditions that contributed to the rise of urban gangs—the massive unemployment that made street crime a career and the hopelessness that led young African Americans to feel trapped by gang life, as Tricia Rose describes—all of which fed the superpredator narrative. Deindustrialization and the economic recessions and implosions of the latter decades of the twentieth century were hard on most segments of the population, but nowhere were the consequences of Reaganomics, various financial crises and cutbacks, social policy decisions, and federal legislation—from crime control to welfare reform—more keenly felt than in inner-city black communities across the country.[11] The harsher living conditions became for the disadvantaged, disenfranchised, underemployed, and nonworking poor, the more monstrous the teeming masses appeared in political discourse, news reports, and popular culture, where— in Reagan's race-baiting terminology—"welfare queens" driving Cadillacs gamed the system and young black thugs on the rampage became, in the spirit of the 1993 film, a "Menace II Society."

Born of these brutally hard times, gangsta rap played right into the hands of superpredator mythology, as the marauding black thug replaced the white gangster as public enemy number one. Real-life, highly publicized crimes like the violent rape of a young white woman viciously attacked while jogging in Central Park and left for dead on the night of April 19, 1989, fanned the flames of fear and distrust of out-of-control low-Others, who like the legendary Thugs of old, traveled in packs spreading murder and mayhem far and wide. The five juveniles—four black, one Hispanic—arrested for the Central Park attack and interrogated without counsel were tried and eventually convicted of charges ranging from robbery and assault to rape and attempted murder. Their convictions were based in large part on what the boys claimed were coerced confessions and their supposed ties to gangs of teenagers who attacked and robbed strangers at will as part of a street crime the NYPD and the media would dub "wilding," so-called, some believe, as a consequence of authorities mishearing as "wilding" references to the rap song "Wild Thing" or, more likely, their mishearing and misinterpreting the Afro-urbanism "wilin'" (with no "d" or "g"), meaning to act up or to party hard but without malice or violence.[12]

In the wake of the Central Park tragedy, Donald Trump, channeling Ronald Reagan, placed full-page ads in the *New York Times*, the *Daily News*, the

New York Post, and *New York Newsday* calling for "law and order" and the return of the death penalty. New Yorkers have become "hostages to a world ruled by the laws of the streets," the ad declared, "as roving bands of wild criminals roam our neighborhoods, dispensing their own vicious brand of twisted hatred on whomever they encounter." Vowing to take back the streets, Trump refuted Mayor Koch's caution against "rancor and hate" with his own call for blood, as he insisted that "these muggers and murderers" should be "forced to suffer and, when they kill, they should be executed for their crimes."[13] Others echoed Trump's death knell, arguing for everything from castration to public lynching in Central Park, as the group dubbed "the Central Park Five"—kids of color between the ages of fourteen and sixteen—became the poster boys for lawless youth on the prowl, needing to be not only heeled but executed.[14] Perhaps only the facts that the victim survived, mercifully, and that there was no death penalty in the State of New York at the time spared these teens a fate from which there would have been no return.

The image of predatory black thugs wilding through the streets would influence public policy in terms of both welfare reform and anticrime legislation at the city, state, and federal levels, as mandatory life sentences without parole became the law of the land. But it also would play well in popular culture, giving fodder to a series of films depicting drug and gang violence in the ghetto, including, in addition to *Menace II Society*, *Colors* (1988); *Do the Right Thing* (1989); *Boyz n the Hood* and *New Jack City* (1991); *Deep Cover* and *Juice* (1992); *Above the Rim* (1994); *Clockers*, *Friday*, *New Jersey Drive*, and the Halle Berry vehicle *Losing Isaiah* (1995); *Jackie Brown* (1997); and *Belly* (1998). Later films like *Notorious* (2009) and *Straight Outta Compton* (2015) notwithstanding, the capstone, if not culminating, text of this moment is arguably the urban crime drama *Training Day* (2002), starring Denzel Washington in an Oscar-winning portrayal of a crooked LAPD narcotics detective not on patrol in the ghetto but on the prowl like any other black thug.[15]

Television, too, heard Trump's Reaganesque call for law and order in the wake of the Central Park night of terror in '89, and a year later a crime drama with exactly that title, *Law & Order*, began a long run on NBC that would yield half a dozen similarly themed spin-offs and at least one TV movie, as well as the short-lived 2017 series *Chicago Justice*, whose lead character, State's Attorney Peter Stone (Philip Winchester), is posited as the son of *Law & Order*'s original ADA, Ben Stone (Michael Moriarty). In keeping with the ripped-from-the-headlines format of the series, the flagship show and just about every other drama in the *Law & Order* fleet (especially *Special Victims Unit* [SVU] and *Criminal Intent*) and similar police procedurals—CSI (*Las*

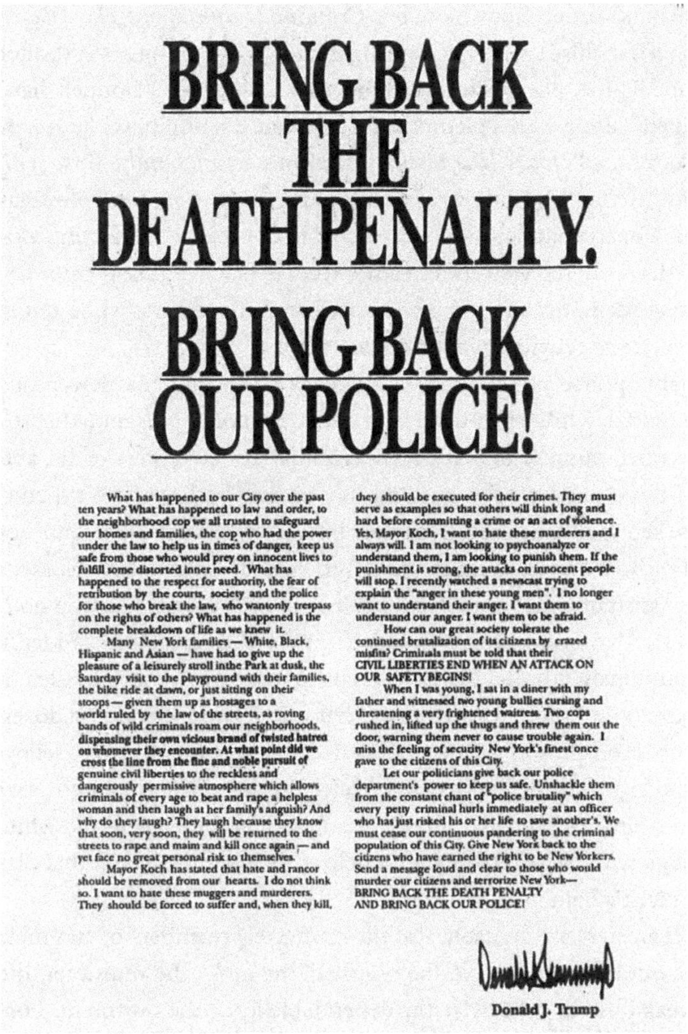

BRING BACK THE DEATH PENALTY.

BRING BACK OUR POLICE!

What has happened to our City over the past ten years? What has happened to law and order, to the neighborhood cop we all trusted to safeguard our homes and families, the cop who had the power under the law to help us in times of danger, keep us safe from those who would prey on innocent lives to fulfill some distorted inner need. What has happened to the respect for authority, the fear of retribution by the courts, society and the police for those who break the law, who wantonly trespass on the rights of others? What has happened is the complete breakdown of life as we knew it.

Many New York families — White, Black, Hispanic and Asian — have had to give up the pleasure of a leisurely stroll in the Park at dusk, the Saturday visit to the playground with their families, the bike ride at dawn, or just sitting on their stoops — given them up as hostages to a world ruled by the law of the streets, as roving bands of wild criminals roam our neighborhoods, dispensing their own vicious brand of twisted hatred on whomever they encounter. At what point did we cross the line from the fine and noble pursuit of genuine civil liberties to the reckless and dangerously permissive atmosphere which allows criminals of every age to beat and rape a helpless woman and then laugh at her family's anguish? And why do they laugh? They laugh because they know that soon, very soon, they will be returned to the streets to rape and maim and kill once again — and yet face no great personal risk to themselves.

Mayor Koch has stated that hate and rancor should be removed from our hearts. I do not think so. I want to hate these muggers and murderers. They should be forced to suffer and, when they kill, they should be executed for their crimes. They must serve as examples so that others will think long and hard before committing a crime or an act of violence. Yes, Mayor Koch, I want to hate these murderers and I always will. I am not looking to psychoanalyze or understand them, I am looking to punish them. If the punishment is strong, the attacks on innocent people will stop. I recently watched a newscast trying to explain the "anger in these young men". I no longer want to understand their anger. I want them to understand our anger. I want them to be afraid.

How can our great society tolerate the continued brutalization of its citizens by crazed misfits? Criminals must be told that their CIVIL LIBERTIES END WHEN AN ATTACK ON OUR SAFETY BEGINS!

When I was young, I sat in a diner with my father and witnessed two young bullies cursing and threatening a very frightened waitress. Two cops rushed in, lifted up the thugs and threw them out the door, warning them never to cause trouble again. I miss the feeling of security New York's finest once gave to the citizens of this City.

Let our politicians give back our police department's power to keep us safe. Unshackle them from the constant chant of "police brutality" which every petty criminal hurls immediately at an officer who has just risked his or her life to save another's. We must cease our continuous pandering to the criminal population of this City. Give New York back to the citizens who have earned the right to be New Yorkers. Send a message loud and clear to those who would murder our citizens and terrorize New York— BRING BACK THE DEATH PENALTY AND BRING BACK OUR POLICE!

Donald J. Trump

FIG. 10.1 Donald Trump's published call for the return of the death penalty in New York in 1989.

Vegas, Miami, New York, and later Cyber), NYPD Blue, Cold Case, Oz, Homicide: Life on the Street, The Wire—would almost all at some point offer a fictional rendition of the Central Park rape and battery case, among a myriad of other heinous crimes often committed by dark perpetrators, who became even darker, more menacing, and more ubiquitous after the O.J. Simpson murder trial and acquittal in the mid-1990s and the attacks on the twin towers of the World Trade Center on September 11, 2001.

Reality law-and-order shows like *Cops*, *Crime and Punishment*, *Hard Copy*, and the *Lockup* franchise (which airs late nights and weekends on MSNBC, after the liberal media-ites like Rachel Maddow and Lawrence O'Donnell have been put to bed), along with a plethora of true-crime docudramas like *America's Most Wanted*, *48 Hours*, *The First 48*, *Dateline*, *20/20*, *On the Case with Paula Zahn*, *City Confidential*, *Forensic Files*, and, since 1996, the Investigation Discovery or ID channel—an entire network devoted to reenacting violent crimes—have offered viewers a steady stream of black pimps, prostitutes, gangstas, thugs, drug dealers, robbers, rapists, and murderers, while doing the public service of providing jobs for black actors.

By and large police procedurals like *Law & Order* and the newer CBS drama *Blue Bloods*, while knee-deep in criminals of color, present a disproportionately small number of black cops, criminal justice professionals, and other would-be good guys. Moreover, racially marked bodies are so expendable on these shows that colored characters in regular, recurring roles are apt to be killed off without warning in any given episode, like Robert Gossett, who played Assistant Chief of Police Russell Taylor for twelve years on both *The Closer* (TNT, 2005–2012) and its sequel *Major Crimes* before suddenly being ignominiously gunned down by a white supremacist serial killer in a bloody courtroom shootout. Taylor goes out with a bang, but after a dozen years, he is not even allowed to die a hero's death, taking a bullet for a fellow officer or blowing away the bad guy as he bites the dust. Instead, a neo-Nazi gunman picks him off like a deer in his headlights, and it's left to the white woman series star (Mary McDonnell) to deliver the heroic kill shot that dispatches the racist villain.

Colored characters are arguably also the most likely members of ensemble casts to turn out to be the crook, the criminal, the mole, the murderer, the patsy, the weak link, or otherwise the expendable fly in the ointment. Lorraine Toussaint as Chief of Police Angela Martin on *Body of Proof* (ABC, 2011–2013)—a clean-cut, straitlaced, by-the-book veteran cop—suddenly turns out to be a multiple murderer with a thirty-year history of crimes and cover-ups in an eleventh-hour plot twist so far out of left field that I laughed myself silly. Corey Reynolds as Sergeant David Gabriel on *The Closer*—Chief Brenda Leigh Johnson's (Kyra Sedgwick) loyal, trusted right-hand driver and go-to gofer—likewise turns out to be the source of a leak that long plagued the squad and undermined the chief in a gross double crossing of the thin blue line. I don't know whether it makes it better or worse that Gabriel was pillow-talked into inadvertently betraying his comrades by his lady love, a planted black Mata Hari he met in church, no less, who sold her body and soul to the chief's arch enemy for $60,000 in paid-off law-school loans. So Chief Johnson's sergeant-at-arms becomes a traitorous, loose-lipped dupe, while the woman he planned to marry turns out to be a Judas and a whore, with the traditional thirty pieces of silver inflated to $60,000, still a paltry sum considering the cost of law school and the dignity and piece of ass the double-crossing girlfriend gives up. At least they could have made her bribe price a tidier sum.

There are exceptions, of course: Andre Braugher's Emmy-winning six-year role as Detective Frank Pembleton on *Homicide*, S. Epatha Merkerson's remarkable seventeen-year run as Lieutenant Anita Van Buren on the original *Law & Order*, and, ironically, the gangsta rapper Ice-T's equally long tour of duty as Detective Odafin "Fin" Tutola on *svu*. But it seems to me, as well, that when African American actors do survive in supporting right-side-of-the-law-and-order roles, they're often flawed in ways that undermine their professionalism or jeopardize the well-being of their colleagues and communities. They screw up or fall short in one way or another and often have to be covered for or saved by white superiority and paternalism. Braugher's character freezes during a shootout, forcing his white partner to step into the line of fire and take a bullet for him. Even the stalwart Lt. Van Buren has to be rescued by two white detectives in her squad who disobey orders and risk their careers to save hers when she faces a grand jury indictment in the fatal shooting (in the back, no less) of an unarmed, mentally disabled teen in an episode from 1994 auspiciously titled "Competence" (s5, E6).

The African American actors Gary Dourdan as Warrick Brown and Laurence Fishburne as Dr. Raymond Langston on the original *CSI* are more classic cases in point. Both characters are given stereotypically colored daddy issues. A Las Vegas native all too fond of the casinos and known to work both sides of the law, Brown is typecast as a misfit hustler whose father abandoned him shortly after birth, while Dr. Langston, a former pathologist and university professor turned initially inept, newbie, entry-level CSI, is endowed with an abusive, alcoholic father and the same genetic predisposition toward violence and antisocial behavior as his paterfamilias. In the series opener, Brown's gambling habit leads to the death of the rookie white female investigator he is supposed to be supervising but leaves behind at a crime scene—to which the killer, of course, returns—while he goes to place a bet for a crooked judge. He survives this fatal faux pas by the grace of the compassionate, accommodating, ultracompetent white bossman, Gil Grissom, PhD (William Petersen), who refuses to fire him and instead mentors and covers for him through eight seasons before Brown is framed for murder and killed off, dying in Grissom's loving arms.

Fishburne's character, Dr. Langston, who succeeds both the dead Warrick Brown and the retired Gil Grissom, also lives up to his paternal pathology, doing away with two suspects, including a serial killer he beats bloody before finishing him off in the eleventh season finale and the Emmy- and Tony-winning, Oscar-nominated actor's own farewell to the series—an episode appropriately titled "In a Dark, Dark House" (s11, E22). Although Langston escapes being charged in either killing, largely through the manipulations of his colleagues, his rogue actions throw the crime lab into such chaos and ill repute during his short tenure that the two white supervisors accused of covering for him, including the long-time series regular (played by Marg Helgenberger)—are demoted and a new director (played by Ted Danson) is brought in from the outside to clean up the mess the black guy left behind.

To be fair, neither of these characters is as flat as my quick sketch paints him, but certain recurrent traits, tropes, faults, and fates so often assigned colored characters do leave me wondering whether the Screen Actors Guild (SAG) has rules governing what kinds of roles black actors are allowed to play. Otherwise, why not give Fishburne's character more of the expertise and command the white authority figure he replaced had in abundance? Why reduce to a thug with an MD a regular but token black character who has already been given one of the most antiheroic backstories of all time? No crime-solving Quincy or Columbo, in his previous position as a hospital pathologist, the criminally myopic Dr. Langston let a mass-murdering Angel of Death colleague kill more than two dozen innocent people right under his nose or "In Front of My Eyes," the title of the book he's scripted as having written about his tunnel vision.

In a generous reading of such flawed specimens, one could make the Rhimesian rationale that television needs messy, complicated black characters who are neither all good nor all bad but human beings in human situations. Fair enough, I suppose, but so many colored characters today beg the question why "human" has to be so dark, deadly, dangerous, and despicable when it happens to be black. Whatever flaws she flaunts and demons she has to conquer, Shonda Rhimes's white feminist physician creation, Dr. Meredith Grey (Ellen Pompeo) on Grey's Anatomy, has managed to survive and even thrive for fourteen seasons without resorting to murder or a host of other heinous crimes that quickly become a way of life, if not a basic instinct, for Shonda-Land's black female leads. Similarly, the pain-pill-popping title character on House (Fox, 2004–2012) is also deeply and humanly flawed, but he, too, gets to be a heroic medical genius with godlike diagnostic powers who miraculously saves rather than takes lives. Even his Sherlockian dependence on Vicodin—the result of life-saving surgery that left him lame and in chronic pain—is couched in sympathetic, even ennobling terms as the essential elixir that keeps a brilliant healer upright and able to leap tall buildings with a single bound.

So what? It's all make-believe, some say. I don't disagree. My concern is the extent to which television's celebrated chorus line of messy, complicated technicolored characters is dancing to the tune of the dominant, default narratives of black pathology, rather than to the progressive beat of a different drummer. Worse, these modalities of black pathology are so deeply ingrained in us by now as a national anthem that we seem willing not only to dance to the music but also to write the lyrics.

That is to say, even innovative new technicolored shows—some well received like *Atlanta* on FX, *Insecure* on HBO, and *Queen Sugar* on the Oprah Winfrey Network—seem to feel the need to insert elements of the stigmatic black familiar into their narratives in order to be authentically black and buyable. *Queen Sugar* the TV series, for example, deviates from Natalie Baszile's bestselling novel in predictably salacious ways, including the addition of a sleazy sex scandal involving a cheating basketball-star husband, a Latina sex worker, and a gang rape, along with a truly troubling opening scene in which the main black male character, newly released from prison (although not an ex-con in the book), leaves his six-year-old son alone in a park while he goes across the street and robs a convenience store at gunpoint—to what end is unclear and underexamined in the narrative, unless it is to excise his thug jones and signal that ex-cons of color have it hard. Add a mystical journalist, activist, and herb-dealing older sister (also not in the novel) who is sleeping with a married white detective on the same police force she is trying to bring down for racial bias and corruption—and who, because the setting is Louisiana (New Orleans adjacent) is also some sort of bisexual voodoo priestess healer—and the narrative becomes cloyingly complicated with excesses that threaten to upstage and undo the well-dones of a promising series.

In both the fictions of television and the facts of real life, Donald Trump has gotten his wish for law and order as a colored containment strategy, including temporary return of the death penalty in New York State as well as minimum sentencing laws, with mandatory life terms without parole for juveniles made to do adult time for adult crime, and color-coded sentencing disparities such as those mandating stiffer penalties for crack cocaine in the black community than for powdered coke in white enclaves, from Wall Street to Beverly Hills. Yet even as the infamous Central Park rape and other crimes of the century (including the murders of Nicole Brown Simpson and Ronald Goldman in 1994) continued to fuel the national narrative of a rising race of superpredators and colored criminals, as well as mass incarceration, DiIulio, now at the University of Pennsylvania, and fellow criminologists such as James Alan Fox of Northeastern University, who likewise had warned of a coming bloodbath of teen, wolf-pack violence, began to see the error of their assertions.

The Thug Armageddon didn't happen; in fact, juvenile crime sharply declined.[16] And as a testament to just how wrong the experts were in their apocalyptic predictions, in 2002, after they had completed prison terms ranging from six to thirteen years, the Central Park Five were exonerated and their convictions vacated due to the confession of a convicted rapist and the DNA evidence and other telling details that confirmed his guilt, although not to the satisfaction of Donald Trump, who remains convinced the colored kids did it. With the foolish consistency that Emerson attributed to little minds, he continues to rail against "the stupidity of the City" in settling a $41 million lawsuit for malicious prosecution brought by the quintet, who, he says, "do not exactly have the pasts of angels."[17] Interestingly enough, at fourteen, fifteen, and sixteen at the time of their alleged crime, none of the boys had prior arrests or criminal records of a piece with Trump's onetime golf partner, Mark Wahlberg, the white, Oscar-nominated actor, who, by his own admission, was dealing drugs, stealing cars, and freebasing cocaine at thirteen and who at sixteen was charged with attempted murder but allowed to plead to a lesser count, serving only forty-five days of a two-year prison sentence for his youthful hate crimes against Asian and African Americans, some left permanently scarred by his nights of wilding laced with racist rants.[18]

Other purveyors of the superpredator panic that turned the criminal justice system from rehabilitating juvenile offenders like Wahlberg to incarcerating them as adults have been more contrite. Both DiIulio and Fox have repudiated their earlier findings and predictions, joining forty-five fellow criminologists in submitting an amicus brief to the Supreme Court in support of the Equal Justice Initiative's pleadings in *Miller v. Alabama* and *Jackson v. Hobbs*, both cases in which fourteen-year-old black boys convicted of capital crimes had received life sentences with no possibility of parole. The two consolidated court cases and the amicus brief attached to them argued that mandatory sentences of life without parole for juveniles violate the Eighth Amendment against cruel and unusual punishment. Pulling no punches in conceding how wrong the experts were in their conclusions and predictions, the amicus brief declares the notion of a juvenile superpredator—much touted in academic and political discourse—"a myth."[19]

By a vote of five to four, the Justices found in favor of the petitioners and the amici, striking down statutes in twenty-nine states that called for mandatory life sentences for juvenile offenders. Bryan Stevenson, the founder and executive director of the Equal Justice Initiative who argued for the plaintiffs, calls the decision "an important win for children."[20] Yet few who have paid close attention to the superpredator panic, and the very real law-and-order backlash it bred, believe the damage wrought can be so easily undone. It's fine to call the superpredator construct a myth twenty-five years after the fact, but that mythology has become both spine and legs of a powerful ideology of fear and loathing of young black males that hasn't been—and perhaps never will be—erased from the public consciousness, despite all the mea culpas. As DiIulio himself has said of his now-defunct theory, "once it was out there, there was no reeling it in."[21]

"Superpredator" and its shorthand simulacrum "thug" have become synonymous not only with "criminal" but also with "black." Through that same racial metonymy by which any black is every black, a colored male is by default a fearsome being, whether he is encountered on a street corner, on the football field, or in the halls of academe. And if you doubt that hail black fellows are not necessarily so well met on the gridiron or the green, I will introduce you to some black male professors I know whose dark presence has on occasion produced shrieks of terror from white women whose paths they crossed on campus. Or you might talk to the Seattle Seahawks cornerback Richard Sherman, salutatorian of his straight-outta-Compton high school class and a Stanford University alum who cannot escape the "thug" label.

Sherman has been referred to repeatedly as a thug on Twitter and elsewhere throughout social and digital media, especially after his rant during a postgame interview with the Fox Sports reporter Erin Andrews following the championship win that sent the Seahawks to the Super Bowl in 2014. In fact, using a keyword search of closed captioning, one source reports that the word "thug" was uttered no fewer than 625 times on TV alone the Monday following the championship game.[22] Asked about the thug label during a press conference later that week, Sherman said it bothers him "because it seems like it's an accepted way of calling somebody the N-word now." He went on to explain that, coming from the inner city, he has fought the thug stereotype all his life. "Just because you hear Compton, you hear Watts, you hear cities like that, you think 'thug,' he's a gangster, he's this, that, and the other," he said. Even a Stanford degree doesn't matter, he suggested. "That's an oxymoron."[23]

The Columbia University linguistics professor John McWhorter agrees that "thug today is a nominally polite way of using the N-word."[24] But seeing Sherman's N-word analogy as simply playing the race card, some posters pointed out in response that Vladimir Putin has been called a thug, as has New Jersey governor Chris Christie. What such rejoinders miss, however, is the critical point that the term doesn't carry the same racial baggage when it's applied to a white man—even a crooked or criminal one, not to mention a dictator or a shady politician. There may be good reason to fear Putin or spurn Christie, but that dread or animus isn't powered by the same Pavlovian response to skin color that has been a death sentence for hordes of black men, women, and children, among whom Amadou Diallo, Eric Garner, Walter Scott, Sandra Bland, Renisha McBride, Tarika Wilson, twelve-year-old Tamir Rice, and twenty-two-year-old Stephon Clark are only a few of the better known names. The default response to the white man walking isn't fear and loathing. Anonymous white guys sitting in Starbucks minding their own business aren't by definition threatening thugs worthy of being handcuffed and arrested for waiting while black.

At the overcrowded intersection of racial profiling and mistaken identity, the thug default means that every black body is suspect, subject to search, seizure, service refusal, and the stalking surveillance of retail racism, in daily assaults, including those in which it is dignity that is damaged rather than a life that is taken. Even a black man as well credentialed and internationally renowned as Dr. Henry Louis Gates Jr., the Harvard professor, TV personality, and distinguished black public intellectual, can be arrested on his front porch like a common criminal, as Gates was in 2009, after a verbal altercation with a white police officer responding to a reported break-in at the professor's address. But even the arrest of the Harvard professor and PBS host doesn't quite reach the same level of absurdity as the takedown at gunpoint of three members of the Harlem Globetrotters basketball team, arrested in downtown Santa Barbara, forced to lie face-down, spread-eagle on the pavement, handcuffed, and detained by police officers who claimed the black ballplayers fit the description of three suspects who had robbed a nearby jewelry store.

"They just looked like somebody we were looking for," a police lieutenant later explained when questioned by reporters about the infamous incident.[25] At 6'10", 6'7", and 6'3", the Globetrotters looked like the actual thieves, described as black males between 5'7" and 5'9" tall, only in terms of their skin color. A half to more than a full foot taller than the actual perpetrators, the Trotters should have been the least likely suspects in town. Instead, their skin color made them look quintessentially like criminals, not only in the eyes of the officers who arrested them but also in the mind of the mayor, Sheila Lodge, who, in attempting to wave away the incident, likened the basketball players' black skin to a blemish or a scar as a distinguishing feature in a white upscale enclave like Santa Barbara, where "some of us look more like others than others do," she said—an inartful way of saying black people not only look alike, they also look unlike Santa Barbarians.[26]

While neither of these infamous incidents turned violent, the thug default is all too often a death sentence, even for those black bodies decidedly on the right side of the law. It may get less press than the skyrocketing numbers of unarmed black men, women, and children dying at the hands of law enforcement officials who see them only as threatening thugs, but it is also a documented, tragic fact that because of who or what they *look like*, a staggering number of black off-duty, undercover, and plainclothes police officers have been shot and wounded or killed by their peers who mistook them for criminals, even in some cases as they were trying to come to the aid of their brothers and sisters in blue.[27]

To cite one recent awful example of many such cases of "mistaken identity," in Prince George's County, Maryland, twenty-eight-year-old Jacai Colson, a black undercover narcotics detective, was fatally shot by a fellow officer who mistook him for a black suspect who opened fire on the police headquarters, pinning down the officers inside and around the perimeter of the precinct. Arriving on the scene in street clothes and an unmarked car, Detective Colson "heroically" (his chief's word) diverted the gunman's fire, allowing other officers to overtake the shooter, but Colson himself was struck by the friendly fire of a fellow officer who confused him with the perpetrators. It was not a stray bullet; Colson didn't accidently get caught in the crossfire. He was "deliberately aimed at" and shot and killed by a comrade at arms, the police chief explained at a press conference.[28] Although the chief did not address the racial dimensions of this tragic case of mistaken identity in which a white policeman fatally shot a black one, it's painfully evident that the fallen officer, close-cropped and clean shaven, resembled the bearded, dreadlocked shooter (and his two similarly outfitted brothers on scene taking pictures to post on the Internet) only in terms of his black skin.

Aiming at and shooting to kill a brother officer has to be a terrible burden to carry, but so is the fear of friendly fire that many, if not most, black police officers drag along with them as an occupational hazard. Part of the Fraternal Order of Police so often accused of racial profiling, African American officers are themselves subject to such profiling and to its most deadly consequence. They take the same oath to protect and serve as their white counterparts, but the presumption of black guilt is such that out of uniform they are as likely to be stopped and frisked while shopping, pulled over while driving, and taken for a thug as any other black male.

The racial logic of black guilt and criminality is so well understood in America and so unrelentingly played out on television that white perpetrators know the best strategy for getting away with murder literally and figuratively is to blame their crimes on generic black male assailants. The false claims of Susan Smith and Charles Stuart live in infamy as two of the most notorious racial hoaxes to attract national and international attention, while doing perhaps irreparable harm to the image of black males. Smith and Stuart both committed heinous homicides, which they attributed to black thugs they invented out of whole cloth steeped in stereotypes as the best of all possible covers for their crimes, and in both cases, print and televisual media played dramatic roles in furthering the reach of their cynical fabrications.

In the fall of 1994, Smith, a young white mother from Union, South Carolina, reported to the police that she had been abducted by a black man who jumped into her car while she was stopped at a traffic light, forced her to drive for several miles, then pushed her out of the car at gunpoint and drove off with her two young sons still in the backseat. It was later revealed that inconsistencies in her statements, gaps in her timeline, and deceptive responses to polygraph questions had led authorities to doubt her story early in the investigation. What the public saw televised, however, was a young white woman handled with kid gloves and put forward as the grieving mother in press conferences and network news reports, while the black-man-did-it ploy was allowed to play out in the local and national media, complete with a police sketch artist's rendering of a dark and forbidding figure with a watch cap and the stereotypically big white lips of a minstrel.

For nine days that were especially hard on the African American citizens of Union, who saw their white neighbors look at them with suspicion or not at all and whose businesses lost white patronage, the image of the black kidnapper thug deepened the black-man-as-monster mythology already gripping a nation preoccupied with the O.J. Simpson double homicides. After a series of crocodile-tear-studded public pleas for the safe return of her beloved babies, Smith was finally forced to admit that there was no black carjacker. She confessed to putting her Mazda in gear, releasing the parking brake, and sending the car careening down a boat ramp into a local lake with her two toddlers still strapped into their car seats.

Given the way race means in America, it doesn't take much imagination to color the usual suspect black, but Smith may have taken inspiration from Charles Stuart's epic racial ruse, which had rocked the City of Boston, the nation, and the world five years before her own fabricated carjacking, almost to the day. On the evening of October 23, 1989, while en route from a birthing class at Brigham and Women's Hospital, Stuart, the upwardly mobile manager of a posh Back Bay fur salon, put a bullet in the head of his pregnant wife and one in his own abdomen (likely wounding himself more seriously than he intended), then, by prior arrangement, handed off the gun and the supposedly stolen goods—his wife's handbag and jewelry—to his younger brother Matthew, before dialing 911 on his car phone and reporting to the state police dispatcher that he and his wife had been shot and robbed by a black gunman. His wife, Carol DiMaiti Stuart, a bright, young tax attorney and expectant mother, died from her head wound later that night; the couple's son, Christopher, delivered two months prematurely by cesarean section, succumbed seventeen days later.[29]

As in the Smith case, television made Charles Stuart all the more a sympathetic character the night he killed his pregnant wife and all the more a hero for what one of the first responders described as the "guts, grizzle, and savvy" the "poor man" showed in summoning help for himself and his dying wife.[30] Mayor Ray Flynn, generally seen as a peacemaker in a racially cleaved city already torn apart by battles over busing and court-ordered school desegregation, promptly appeared on television, vowing to "get the animals responsible" and ordering the police commissioner to enlist every available officer in that dragnet, thereby unleashing a reign of terror on Boston's black communities that turned every African American male of certain age into a usual suspect subject to stop-and-frisk interrogations and strip searches that by some reports required black men to drop their pants in public.[31]

Stuart's story was aided and abetted from the start by the arrival at the crime scene of a TV crew that just happened that night to be shadowing the responding EMS team for an episode of the CBS reality series *Rescue 911*, hosted by William Shatner, *Star Trek*'s kissing Captain Kirk. Endlessly aired video of the blood-soaked crime scene, along with audio of Stuart's emergency call fingering a black gunman as the shooter, helped color-code and sensationalize the tragedy as a gruesome black-on-white crime that would dominate the media and both terrify and mesmerize the masses. *Time* magazine reported, in fact, that on that fate-filled night, the eleven o'clock newscasts of all three major network affiliates attracted 80 percent of the viewership in the Greater Boston market.[32] The *Washington Post* later pointed out how much Stuart benefited from the lucky coincidence of the 911 recording and "the fortuitous arrival of television cameras [that] made his lie more believable by turning it into a multimedia presentation."[33]

Stuart's tall tale played well in Peoria then, as they say, and everywhere else across the country and around the world within the reach of a television signal. There were certainly Doubting Thomas skeptics—my family and I among them—but before Matthew Stuart came forward with the truth (or some semblance thereof) after his big brother upped the ante by falsely identifying a black ex-con named Willie Bennett as the shooter, none of us knew for certain that this latest black crime of the century was actually a macabre puppet show that would turn a dramatis personae of dedicated first responders into bit players acting out roles for a reality TV show. As *Time* put it, Stuart's "fabrication raised the curtain on a drama in which the press and police, prosecutors, politicians and the public played out their parts as though they were following the script for the television movie that CBS will make about the case."[34] The *New York Times* concurred, arguing that rather than just doing their jobs and merely reporting a major news story, as some journalists claimed in response to charges of failed due diligence and bold-face sensationalism, "newspapers and television were pandering to the nightmares of much of their audience." The *Times* went on to spell out the racial dimensions of this shared nightmare: "a loving clean-cut upward-aspiring young white couple attacked by a black predator. It was even scarier than the scene in *The Bonfire of the Vanities* (1990) that it resembled and that called up similar fears."[35]

In the scene from *Bonfire of the Vanities* to which the *Times* referred, Sherman McCoy (Tom Hanks), a wealthy, white Wall Street wheeler-dealer, and his flaky mistress, Maria Ruskin (Melanie Griffith), are driving back to Manhattan from the airport in the dark of night and make a wrong turn that lands them alone within a dead-end alleyway in the bowels of the Bronx, also known as the ghetto. When McCoy gets out of his Mercedes to remove a tire in the road, he is promptly set upon by two "natives"—to use Maria's word for the hulking young black males who approach McCoy—presumably bent on mugging and otherwise doing him and his woman and probably his wheels bodily harm.

There is indeed an eerie similarity between this pivotal scene from the *Bonfire* film and the inner-city setting Stuart—who likewise claimed to have made a fateful wrong turn into harm's way—chose for his own uxorious, lost-in-the-ghetto, mugged-and-thugged theatrical production. Although the *Bonfire* film premiered a full year *after* the Boston tragedy, the Tom Wolfe novel on which it's based was serialized in *Rolling Stone* beginning in 1984. Despite the similarities in plot and setting noted by the *Times*, however, six months after the Central Park assault, Stuart hardly needed yet another fictive or filmic exemplar. The black thug/superpredator narrative was and is so ubiquitous and so well understood that even a dropout who reportedly lacked imagination knew where and to whom to turn for his own deep, dark cover story.[36] As one journalist wrote, reflecting on the tragedy years later, Stuart's ruse worked because it played to whites' worst fears and "tapped into assumptions about race and crime so powerful that they overwhelmed skepticism about his tale."[37] Stuart's deception succeeded, in other words, because the thug default made his lie a universal truth.

So here we return to my central point: the extent to which television constructs, carries on, and carries out into the viewing public the worst of all possible images of the technicolored Other, creating and keeping alive the myth of the superpredator and the image of the black thug. In this sense, TV itself functions as a form of racial profiling with potentially deadly consequences for black males in particular. Far from the instrument of uplift that Ed Sullivan and African Americans of my parents' generation imagined at the dawn of the industry, television today is a weapon of mass distortion that more often than not constitutes colored people not simply as the feeble-minded butlers, buffoons, mammies, maids, and minstrels of yesteryear but as quintessentially conniving, crooked, criminal subjects commanding kingdoms of terrorists and evildoers who steal elections and otherwise defraud the system and murder innocent citizens, or as drug dealers turned hip hop moguls, nightclub owners, and money launderers for whom crime pays very well.

As I said earlier in these reflections, it seems today that many of the best roles for black actors are playing some of the craziest and most sinister characters ever to grace the small screen doing some of the worst, the wildest, and the wackiest deeds ever done in prime time, like bashing in the skull of a wheelchair-bound cripple or blowing out the brains of the love of your life. There is a kind of progress in this, I suppose, compared to the early days when colored people were nowhere as leading men and women but everywhere as window dressing and set decorations. Today, we are everywhere on TV but still nowhere my mother would want us to be. But the critical point most emphatically is not about uplifting the race to show white people how civilized black people are or how well behaved. Police officers and other gun-toting citizens get away with killing unarmed black people because they claim they feared for their lives. At a time when we are more readily taken for thugs, thieves, and threats to life and limb than for human beings, representation is about saving our own lives, about making Black Lives Matter something other than a slogan. How do we flip this script? How do we disable the thug default and other stigmatic definitions of who and what black is?

I wish I had some big, bold, brilliant payoff—what they call in the business a "money shot"—because I know that's what drives decision making in the television industry: money, bang for the buck. What I offer instead is the teaser that there is cultural capital to be had in actively becoming part of the solution rather than the problem. Some years ago a TV commercial for auto insurance seemed to riff that same ghetto scene from *Bonfire of the Vanities* so reminiscent of Charles Stuart's ruse: a city street, screeching tires, the sound of a crash, and the sight of two black teenage boys running. Here we go again, I thought, except the joke was on me. The boys were running toward the scene of an auto accident to render aid and comfort to the white male driver: "You're in good hands with black boys," the commercial seemed to say. It was a small thing, an easy reversal of fortune, yet it suggested to me how effortlessly Hollywood could be part of a radical revolution in the way African Americans are depicted if it dealt its race and casting cards differently.

I am not suggesting systematic censorship that would substitute positive images for negative under some sort of good-role-playing seal of approval, but I am arguing for more variety in narratives. Works like *Hidden Figures* (2016), Margot Lee Shetterly's chronicle of the black women who helped put men in space, and its movie adaptation suggest that there are untold tales to tell through television and film that our children might watch with pride in the past and hope for the future. And there are also models for doing difference differently. By imagining the unimaginable, Lin-Manuel Miranda, the creative genius behind the Broadway blockbuster smash-hit musical *Hamilton*, has blown the lid off casting and programming possibilities for television and other venues beyond the Great White Way. Even a few simple moves much less bold than Miranda's reimagining the founding fathers as technicolored could expand the televisual playing field past the stale and the stigmatic.

Every time I watch an episode of Dan Fogelman's well-acted, well-received series *This Is Us* about a white couple who adopt a black foundling when the third of their triplets is stillborn, I imagine all the less predictable plot twists a chromatic turn in casting could enable. That is to say, what miracles might the show perform if black parents who lost one of their triplets in childbirth adopted an abandoned white baby? The doorstep—or in this case, firehouse—black baby boy abandoned at birth was already a cliché in the '60s when a version of it was used in the "Nebulous Nephew" episode of *Perry Mason*. So are the myths of the absent black drug-addicted mom or dad and the tale of the good white people who take in and rear orphaned, discarded, disadvantaged black children, from sitcoms such as *Diff'rent Strokes* and *Webster*, to films like *Losing Isaiah*, *The Blind Slide*, and other stories of interracial rescue and adoption. In real life, the saviors aren't always white and the rescued aren't always thrown-away colored kids. *Us*, however, like many TV shows, opts for the familiarity of known narratives of blackness as pathos and pathology (even repeating the rescue of an abused, abandoned, neglected black child in the second season—this time through the blackstory and fostering of a damaged teenage girl epithetically named Deja, who is introduced in an episode all-too-self-consciously titled "Déjà Vu").

Rebecca Pearson (Mandy Moore), the white mother of the hybrid triplets in *This Is Us*, is unnerved by and resistant to her black son's persistent attempts to find family, to be with his own people, until a black woman at the community pool tells her that her son wouldn't have all those painful razor bumps on the back of his neck if she took him to a black barber who knows how to cut his kind of hair. On the one hand, the incident raises a critical question about what well-meaning white parents don't know about raising a black child (like whether he needs sunscreen) but are afraid to ask. At the same time, however, nothing could be more banal than white people's not knowing what to do with black hair. But what if the family racial dynamic were inverted? Would a white boy's hair present a challenge to black parents?

How would a white child living in a black family in a black community experience and negotiate his difference? Would his colored siblings resent and belittle him racially as the Pearsons' white son bullies his black brother, calling him "Webster" after the interracially adopted '80s TV character? Would his black mother be mistaken for his nanny? Would his black father be taken for a kidnapper or a child molester, as actual black parents in such unconventional families have experienced? One set of African American parents with a white adopted daughter reports being glared at, followed, and menaced to the point they feared being lynched (their word) by curious Caucasians who couldn't conceive of the black couple's relationship to the white child as benevolent and familial.[38]

And what if the black couple's biological son in my reimagined version of *This Is Us* were a black actor struggling to have a serious career in a profession that sees him only as a body, as Fanon's walking phallus, or as a drug dealer, a thief, a terrorist, or not at all? What if his twin sister in the white plus-size actress Chrissy Metz's much-acclaimed breakout role as Kate Pearson were a morbidly obese black woman struggling not only with the weight of her own flesh but also with the weight of loving herself and letting herself be loved by a rare gem of a black man who sees beyond her size? Hollywood has long been a site of intense struggle for black actors, and while black female fat televisually has been the butt of jokes and the stuffing of stereotypes, it is a particularly critical issue for African American women, whose obesity rate is 51 percent higher than for whites.[39] Black characters negotiating such terrain with a white child would represent real people with real problems, but would theirs be a story worth televisualizing? Would anyone watch?

In Fogelman's real rather than my reimagined *This Is Us*, Randall Pearson (Sterling K. Brown in an Emmy-winning role), the black firehouse foundling originally called Kyle in keeping with the KKK names the writers chose for the Pearson clan (Kevin, Kate, and Kyle), grows into a wealthy, successful perfectionist—the anchor of his adopted white family. On his thirty-sixth birthday, he tracks down and brings into his own happy home his birth father, a recovering heroin addict, poet, horn and piano player, musician composer, chess-playing grandfather griot with dance moves, who is bisexual and dying of cancer, though of course not before he becomes beloved of everyone, even the mailman. Such clichés abound in melodrama, and as race cards played like the ace of spades both high and low, Randall and his newfound, ill-fated father, William (Ron Cephas Jones), carry more than their share of the gut-wrenching, ghetto-pulsing pathology and tear-jerking pathos that help *This Is Us* pull off its masquerade as progressive prestige drama:

the heroin addictions that effectively orphaned a black infant, the emotional breakdown that symbolically infantilizes the adult black sibling in order to elevate his self-centered but suddenly compassionate white brother (Justin Hartley) as his savior, and the Memphis-bound road trip through the South, swinging low in a sweet chariot (a $140,000 Mercedes) that carries a dying man home.

Certain conventional narratives of race and representation, like those masterfully manipulated in the well-intentioned *This Is Us*, persist precisely because they reinforce convention; they endure, at least in part, because they preserve and protect the dominant culture's possessive investment in the stereotypical blackness by which it secures its own supremacy. For that to change, for blackness to be mainstreamed in more variegated ways, television would finally have to surrender its dependence on the very thing that has made it what it is.

Final Spin

"THAT'S NOT MY FOOD"

In one of the last episodes of *Wheel of Fortune* I watched with my mother before she gave up the game in the late 1990s, a black woman played well during the main segment, won the day, and went on to the bonus round where she was asked to solve a one-word, eight-letter puzzle. Between the standard six letters given—R S T L N E—and the optional four letters she selected—C H D I—the puzzle was almost completely filled in: __ __ C C H I N I. "Zucchini," Mom and I urged from our respective armchairs. "Zucchini! Come on! Zucchini!" But however self-evident the solution seemed to us and the rest of the watching world, the woman remained mute until the buzzer sounded, ending the bonus round. When Vanna White lit up the last two letters revealing that the word was indeed ZUCCHINI, the contestant, seemingly unfazed by the groans of disappointment from the studio audience, put her hands on her hips and said emphatically, "That's not *my* food!"

I'm not certain about the hands on her hips after all this time, but the words, "That's not *my* food!," have stayed with me. For years I have used those words to talk about the complex and complicated ways race means even where and when we least expect it to matter. I'm willing to allow for the possibility of overreading, but from body language to intonation, I understood and my mother understood that the contestant was not simply referencing her personal vegetable preferences but, rather, speaking in a larger sense to her cultural experience as a black woman. She was, it seemed to us, declaring that zucchini are not black food, are not soul cuisine. Let me be clear: I neither subscribe to nor mean to promote the idea that black people do not eat zucchini—I know better—but at the same time, in that TV moment, fellow feeling carried me back to the spring of 1974 when I, as a newly minted MFA interviewing for my inaugural full-time teaching position at Hamilton College, had to face down my first ever artichoke while dining with the divisional dean and his family. I looked at this cone-shaped, thorny-edged green thing on my plate and thought but did not say something akin to "That's not my food."

Artichokes were not a part of what we ate at home growing up; neither were zucchini, for that matter, although we regularly consumed their kissing cousin, yellow summer squash. I did think that night more than forty years ago that I had tripped across a cultural and perhaps a class difference, because artichokes are not exactly the everyday fare of the folk. I considered trying to fake my way through the complicated process of eating an artichoke, but as a twenty-five-year-old black woman interviewing at what was at the time a very white men's college in upstate New York, I was already so far out of my element that I decided to own my gastronomic ignorance. I made a joke of never having had that particular vegetable before, and I like to think that the dean and his family laughed with me rather than at me. His ten-year-old daughter took some delight, I think, in teaching the guess-who's-coming-to-dinner guest the fine art of eating an artichoke.

When a twenty-one-year-old Tiger Woods became the youngest and the first nonwhite player to win the prestigious Masters Tournament at the Augusta National Golf Club in 1997, fellow golfer Frank "Fuzzy" Zoeller quipped to reporters that someone should tell Woods not to order fried chicken or collard greens for the following year's championship dinner, for which the defending champion selects the menu.[1] Zoeller's trash talk was widely denounced as racist and ultimately cost him sponsors. It strikes me, however, that Zoeller and the *Wheel* contestant are saying much the same thing. His suggestion that fried chicken and collard greens are black food and the contestant's insinuation that zucchini are not similarly essentialize an entire group and its would-be quintessentially colored cuisine. Or it may be that Zoeller and the contestant are simply telling it as it culturally is? Had the bonus puzzle been FRIED CHICKEN or COLLARD GREENS, would the solution have been "my food" for the black contestant on *Wheel* and the puzzle therefore more solvable? Wouldn't it be racist to assume so?

I stopped watching *Wheel of Fortune* when my mother did. The fun of watching *Wheel* and other game shows was witnessing Mom's wit and word-

FIG. E.1 The *Wheel of Fortune* puzzle for FULL RACK OF BABY BACK RIBS. *Wheel* board re-creation by Arlen Austin.

smithery in action. Without her firing fastball solutions from her recliner, *Wheel of Fortune* was Mudville with no joy in it. But because I began these reflections by drawing on mother wit in writing about game shows as a way of thinking and talking about race and representation, it seemed only right to end them with a return to the scene of the crime, so to speak. So I sat down one Saturday night a while back to watch a repeat episode of Mom's old favorite for the first time in more than fifteen years. Among the three contestants competing that night was a black woman named Latoya. Although she didn't win the game, Latoya did solve one puzzle with a respectable $6,700 in her bank. That one puzzle: FULL RACK OF BABY BACK RIBS.[2]

And now I guess it is my misfortune to contemplate the implications of this final spin of the *Wheel* for the rest of my days. I am, it seems, indeed always and forever my mother's daughter, destined to watch television as she did, through the lens of race, which brings a certain vigilance to TV viewing that disrupts the pleasure principle and carries me back to the haunting question with which I began: was television in general, like my mother's *Wheel of Fortune* particular, easier viewing when it was mostly white? When it was a matter of pleasure rather than politics? I know now that, for me, watching television always was and always will be a political act that never was and never will be neutral or unraced. White is a color, too, that means in its presence, just as blackness means even in its absence.

....

Perry Mason still claims me as a fan. I record old episodes of the original series, along with reruns of *Columbo*, and Danny and I watch them together when he visits, testing our recollections of whodunit. It's just the two of us left of the family that once gathered around the TV set, but I have a recurrent dream that we are five again, riding together in the car. Dad is in his rightful place behind the wheel; Mom is sitting shotgun as always. I'm behind her peering out the window, trying to see into people's houses and mentally re-arrange their furnishings, just as I did in the old days; Danny is in the middle seat and Adrian is to his left. We stop in front of the Prince Hall Grand Masonic Lodge in Dorchester, and Danny and I get out of the car and go into the building. Why Prince Hall, I can't imagine, except that my mother's sole surviving nephews, Cousin Neal and Cousin Sonny—the last of the older generations of Hogans—are masons and the lodge was the site of many happy extended family outings with the crazy cousins back in the day. In dreams, places generally don't look as they are, but, oddly enough, in this dream Prince Hall Masonic Lodge looks very much like itself. It's not clear why Danny and I alone have gone into the building, but when we come out, we can't find the car or its occupants. We search and search and search fitfully and fruitlessly until I finally wake up.

NOTES

Introduction

1. Lynn Spigel, *Welcome to the Dreamhouse: Popular Media and Postwar Suburbs* (Durham, NC: Duke University Press, 2001), 33; Lynn Spigel, *Make Room for TV: Television and the Family Ideal in Postwar America* (Chicago: University of Chicago Press, 1992), 1.

2. Leo Bogart, "TV Viewing in Its Social Gathering," in *The Age of Television: A Study of Viewing Habits and the Impact of Television on American Life*, ed. Leo Bogart (New York: Ungar, 1958), reprinted in *Major Problems in American Popular Culture: Documents and Essays*, ed. Kathleen Franz and Susan Smulyan (Boston: Wadsworth, 2012), 335.

3. Susan Smulyan, *Popular Ideologies: Mass Culture at Mid-century* (Philadelphia: University of Pennsylvania Press, 2007), 1.

4. Paula Groves Price, "'New Normal' in American Television? Race, Gender, Blackness, and the New Racism," in *African Americans on Television: Race-ing for Ratings*, ed. David J. Leonard and Lisa A. Guerrero (Santa Barbara, CA: Praeger, 2013), 434–435. Price rightly references the work of Patricia Hill Collins in her discussion of "the new racism." See Patricia Hill Collins, *Black Sexual Politics* (New York: Routledge, 2004).

5. Price, "'New Normal' in American Television?," 435.

6. Smulyan, *Popular Ideologies*, 1.

7. Toni Morrison, *Playing in the Dark: Whiteness and the Literary Imagination* (Cambridge, MA: Harvard University Press, 1992), 46–47.

8. Veronica Toney, "Jesse Williams Gave One of the Most Memorable Speeches in Award Show History," *Washington Post* (June 27, 2016), https://www.washingtonpost.com/news/arts-and-entertainment/wp/2016/06/27/jesse-williams-gave-one-of-the-most-memorable-speeches-in-award-show-history-full-transcript/.

9. In 1979, Eulia May Love was fatally shot in South Central L.A. by officers responding to her home over a dispute with the gas company about a $22 bill. Margaret LaVerne Mitchell was a mentally ill homeless widow, likewise shot and killed in 1999 by LAPD officers she allegedly threatened with a screwdriver when they questioned whether her shopping cart was stolen. See, for example, Joe Domanick, "A Shooting Reminiscent of the LAPD's Worst Days," *Los Angeles Times* (June 6, 1999), http://articles.latimes.com/1999

/jun/06/opinion/op-44648; and Todd S. Purdum, "A Police Shooting Death, a Study in Contrasts," *New York Times* (June 5, 1999), http://www.nytimes.com/1999/06/05/us/a -police-shooting-death-a-study-in-contrasts.html?pagewanted=all&_r=0.

10. See, for example, Beretta E. Smith-Shomade, *Shaded Lives: African-American Women and Television* (New Brunswick, NJ: Rutgers University Press, 2002); Beretta E. Smith-Shomade, ed., *Watching while Black: Centering the Television of Black Audiences* (New Brunswick, NJ: Rutgers University Press, 2012); Christine Acham, *Revolution Televised: Prime Time and the Struggle for Black Power* (Minneapolis: University of Minnesota Press, 2004); Darnell M. Hunt, ed., *Channeling Blackness: Studies on Television and Race in America* (New York: Oxford University Press, 2005); Gayle Wald, *It's Been Beautiful: Soul! and Black Power Television* (Durham, NC: Duke University Press, 2015); and Leonard and Guerrero, *African Americans on Television*.

11. John Fiske and John Hartley, *Reading Television* (London: Methuen, 1978); rev. ed., with a foreword by Hartley (New York: Routledge, 2003), 2, 3.

12. Jason Mittell, "Narrative Complexity," *Velvet Light Trap* 58 (Fall 2006): 29–40.

13. John Bingham, "TV Drama is the New Literature, Says Salman Rushdie," *Telegraph* (June 12, 2011), http://www.telegraph.co.uk/culture/books/booknews/8571010/TV-drama -is-the-new-literature-says-Salman-Rushdie.html.

14. Thomas Doherty, "Storied TV: Cable Is the New Novel," *Chronicle of Higher Education* (September 17, 2012), http://chronicle.com/article/Cable-Is-the-New-Novel /134420/.

15. Pat Sajak, "Talking about Race," *Ricochet* (August 6, 2010), https://ricochet.com /archives/talking-about-race/.

16. Zora Neale Hurston, "How It Feels to Be Colored Me (1928)," in *Hurston: Folklore, Memoirs, and Other Writings*, ed. Cheryl Wall (New York: Literary Classics, 1995), 826.

17. Quoted by the *Los Angeles Times*, among many other sources. See the obituary for Raymond Burr, *Los Angeles Times* (September 13, 1993), http://articles.latimes.com/1993 -09-13/news/mn-34829_1_perry-mason-revival; the statement is also captured in a YouTube video: https://www.youtube.com/watch?v=6eG3G2sykRQ.

18. George Zimmerman, of course, famously shot and killed the unarmed black teenager Trayvon Martin in Sanford, Florida, in 2012. Less well known perhaps is the name of Michael David Dunn, a Florida software engineer who fired ten rounds into a parked car also in 2012, fatally shooting another black youth, seventeen-year-old Jordan Russell Davis, following a verbal dispute over loud music. Also less well known is the name of Renisha McBride, a nineteen-year-old black woman who, seeking help after a car accident, knocked on the front door of a stranger in Dearborn Heights, Michigan, during the wee hours of November 2, 2013, and was fatally shot by the white homeowner, Theodore Wafer, who claimed both that he thought his house was being broken into and that the gun fired accidentally.

19. Sajak, "Talking about Race."

20. Thomas's remarks are as quoted by the op-ed columnist Charles M. Blow in the *New York Times* (February 12, 2014) and several other sources. No transcript of the talk exists. See "Thomas Speaks . . . Blindly about Race," http://www.nytimes.com/2014/02/13 /opinion/blow-thomas-speaks-blindly-about-race.html?nl=todaysheadlines&emc=edit _th_20140213&_r=0c.

1. What's in a Game?

1. On this point, see Evelyn Brooks Higginbotham, *Righteous Discontent: The Women's Movement in the Black Church, 1880–1920* (Cambridge, MA: Harvard University Press, 1994); and E. Frances White, *Dark Continent of Our Bodies: Black Feminism and the Politics of Respectability* (Philadelphia: Temple University Press, 2001).

2. W. E. B. Du Bois, "The Talented Tenth" (1903), in *W. E. B. Du Bois: A Reader*, ed. David Levering Lewis (New York: Holt, 1995), 347.

3. For a comprehensive and engaging treatment of uplift ideology, see Kevin Gaines, *Uplifting the Race: Black Leadership, Politics, and Culture in the Twentieth Century* (Chapel Hill: University of North Carolina Press, 1996).

4. Higginbotham, *Righteous Discontent*, 14.

5. Higginbotham, *Righteous Discontent*, 15.

6. J. Fred MacDonald, *Blacks and White TV: African Americans in Television since 1948* (Chicago: Nelson Hall, 1992), 4.

7. "Negro Performers Win Better Roles in TV Than in Other Entertainment Medium," *Ebony* 5, no. 8 (June 1950): 23.

8. MacDonald says both that "African Americans regularly appeared on audience participation and quiz programs in the 1950s" and that "blacks occasionally were contestants" during the "quiz-show craze of the mid-1950s." I was a little kid, true enough, but the *occasional* appearance of black contestants is closer to what I remember as far as quiz shows are concerned. As MacDonald points out, however, younger versions of well-known names like Diahann Carroll, Gladys Knight, and Leslie Uggams were big winners on several of the popular talent shows of the era. See *Blacks and White TV*, 17–18.

9. Olaf Hoerschelmann, *Rules of the Game: Quiz Shows and American Culture* (Albany: State University of New York Press, 2006), 1. Hoerschelmann points out that while the terms "game shows" and "quiz shows" are often used interchangeably today, before the cheating scandals that broke in 1958, all such programs were typically called quiz shows. After the revelations that some contestants on *Twenty-One* and other similar programs were fed answers, quiz shows were renamed game shows, as the broadcast industry attempted to remove new and surviving programs from the taint of the cheating scandal.

10. See John Fiske, *Understanding Popular Culture* (London: Routledge, 1989); 2nd ed., with an introduction by Henry Jenkins (New York: Routledge, 2010). Hoerschelmann quotes the 1989 edition on pp. 279–280. See also Fiske's early coauthored work, *Reading Television*, in which he addresses game/quiz shows in a chapter on competition. John Fiske and John Hartley, *Reading Television* (London: Methuen, 1978); rev. ed., with a foreword by Hartley (New York: Routledge, 2003), 113–126.

11. Hoerschelmann, *Rules of the Game*, 2–3, 6.

12. See *Variety*, among several other media sources, Rick Kissell, "Ratings: 'Family Feud' Tops All of Syndication for First Time," *Variety* (June 23, 2015), http://variety.com/2015/tv/news/family-feud-ratings-tops-syndication-1201526217/.

13. On Shonda Rhimes and the women of *Scandal*, see, for example, Kwakiutl L. Dreher, "*Scandal* and Black Women in Television," in *African Americans on Television: Race-ing for Ratings*, ed. David J. Leonard and Lisa A. Guerrero (Santa Barbara, CA: Praeger, 2013), 390–401.

14. Chris Harnick, "Kelly Ripa, Michael Strahan and Gelman Talk 'Live! with Kelly and Michael,'" *Huffington Post* (September 4, 2012), http://www.huffingtonpost.com/2012/09/04/kelly-ripa-michael-strahan-live-with-michael-and-kelly_n_1854576.html.

15. Robert Rorke, "Size Matters," *New York Post* (September 7, 2012), http://nypost.com/2012/09/07/size-matters-3/; Maria Elena Fernandez, "Michael Strahan's Pairing with Kelly Ripa Surprising but Promising," *Daily Beast* (August 29, 2012), http://www.thedailybeast.com/articles/2012/08/29/michael-strahan-s-pairing-with-kelly-ripa-surprising-but-promising.html.

16. Meg James and Greg Braxton, "Black Daytime TV Hosts Are among the Most Bankable Stars," *Los Angeles Times* (November 11, 2013), http://touch.latimes.com/#section/-1/article/p2p-78141247/.

17. According to Temple Black, it was Griffith's idea to introduce a black male presence into her films.

18. Robinson was reportedly anything but an Uncle Tom in real life. See his biography, Jim Haskins and N. R. Mitgang, *Mr. Bojangles: The Biography of Bill Robinson* (New York: William Morrow, 1988).

19. John Fiske, *Media Matters: Everyday Culture and Political Change* (Minneapolis: University of Minnesota Press, 1994), xvii.

20. According to the *Hollywood Reporter*, *Live*'s viewership increased by 15 percent in the first season of Strahan's tenure (2013–2014), with 17 percent more men aged thirty-five to fifty-four tuning in and 0.5 percent more African Americans, with the share of black viewers going from 3.5 to 4 percent. See Alex Ben Block, "Daytime Ratings: Black Viewers Driving Gains for Steve Harvey, 'Live with Kelly and Michael,'" *Hollywood Reporter* (June 6, 2014), http://www.hollywoodreporter.com/news/daytime-ratings-black-viewers-driving-709049.

21. A YouTube video of the scene from the June 28, 2012, episode can be viewed at https://www.youtube.com/watch?v=U90GnDoNraI.

22. Lynne Joyrich, *Re-viewing Reception: Television, Gender, and Postmodern Culture* (Bloomington: Indiana University Press, 1996), 84, 86–88.

23. In a videotaped interview at the Howard Hughes Medical Institute, Dr. Tyson shares an epiphany he had in 1989 watching himself discussing plasma on TV and realizing he had never before seen a black person interviewed on television "for expertise that had nothing to do with being black"—or with sports, or music, or dance. This televisual absence of black scientists, intellectuals, and experts in subjects other than race, he decided then, contributes to the stereotype that African Americans are dumb—a misapprehension he remains committed to changing. See Neil deGrasse Tyson, "A Story about Race," widely available on the Internet, at https://www.youtube.com/watch?v=BtMWvJiFR9E.

24. See Ann duCille, "The Unbearable Darkness of Being: 'Fresh' Thoughts on Race, Sex, and the Simpsons," in *Birth of a Nation'hood*, ed. Toni Morrison and Claudia Brodsky Lacour (New York: Pantheon, 1997), 293–328. The discussion of "Mandingo Syndrome" and "Mapplethorpism" appears on pages 303–308.

25. On othering and racialization, see, for example, Michael Omi and Howard Winant, *Racial Formation in the United States*, 3rd ed. (New York: Routledge, 2014).

26. Joyrich, *Re-viewing Reception*, 87.

27. The "big and brotherly" and other descriptions are from "4 Reasons Michael Strahan Will Shine on *Live! with Kelly*," *The Week* (August 22, 2012), http://theweek.com/articles/472948/4-reasons-michael-strahan-shine-live-kelly.

28. Winfrey withdrew herself and the show from consideration in 1999, after winning seven Emmys for Outstanding Talk Show Host and nine for Outstanding Talk Show, although the program continued to rack up awards in production and technical categories. The program's IMDb listing sets the total number of wins at 67 (out of 104 nominations), but I've also seen other figures. http://www.imdb.com/title/tt0090493/awards.

29. Ann Oldenburg, "For Gayle King, Oprah Casts a Light, Not a Shadow," *USA Today* (January 4, 2011), http://usatoday30.usatoday.com/life/television/news/2011-01-05 -gayleking05_VA_N.htm.

30. Phillip McGraw, PhD, is one of the founders of Courtroom Sciences, Inc. (CSI), a litigation consulting service that advises lawyers and their clients on all aspects of "litigation psychology," from jury selection to witness preparation. McGraw rose to prominence in the latter 1990s when Oprah Winfrey hired his firm CSI to assist her and her legal team in defending a $12 million libel suit brought by agents of the Texas cattle industry after she and a guest made derogatory remarks allegedly linking beef to mad cow disease on an episode of *Oprah* in 1996, supposedly precipitating a dramatic drop in beef prices that cost the plaintiffs millions. McGraw is the self-proclaimed model for, as well as the creator and executive producer of, the TV series *Bull* (CBS, 2016). See http://www .courtroomsciences.com/About-CSI.

31. Bob Minzesheimer, "How the 'Oprah Effect' Changed Publishing," *USA Today* (May 22, 2011), http://usatoday30.usatoday.com/life/books/news/2011-05-22-Oprah -Winfrey-Book-Club_n.htm.

32. Harvey speaks to a group of successful black women on *Oprah* (original air date, March 23, 2009); a YouTube link is https://www.youtube.com/watch?v=_tcghxvhS4U.

33. Steve Harvey, *Act Like a Lady, Think Like a Man: What Men Really Think about Love, Relationships, Intimacy, and Commitment* (New York: HarperCollins, 2011), 183–184.

34. "Steve Harvey: 'Hollywood Is More Racist Than America,'" *Hollywood Reporter* (March 15, 2013), http://www.hollywoodreporter.com/news/is-steve-harvey-next-oprah -427424?page=1; "Steve Harvey—He's the New Oprah Winfrey," *Guardian* (April 14, 2013).

35. Emily Nussbaum, "American Untouchable," *New Yorker* (December 7, 2015), http:// www.newyorker.com/magazine/2015/12/07/american-untouchable.

36. The Nielsen Company, with the National Newspaper Publishers Association, *Resilient, Receptive and Relevant: The African-American Consumer: 2013 Report*, http://nnpa .org/wp-content/uploads/2013/06/African-American-Consumer-Report-2013.pdf.

37. See https://www.reddit.com/r/funny/comments/1069um/have_you_guys_seen _who_wants to_be_a_millionaire/.

38. Greg Braxton and Meg James, "Daytime TV Is Embracing Black Entertainers; Prime Time, Less So," *Los Angeles Times* (November 9, 2013), http://touch.latimes.com /#section/-1/article/p2p-78110838/.

39. Other black game-show hosts as of the summer of 2016 included Sherri Shepherd (*The Newlywed Game*), Alfonso Ribeiro (*Catch-21* and *America's Funniest Home Videos*), DeRay Davis and Tone Bell (*Mind of a Man*), Terry Crews (*Who Wants to Be a Millionaire?*), Jaleel White (*Total Blackout*), Michael Strahan (*$100,000 Pyramid*), Anthony Anderson (*To Tell the Truth*). Also back in the 1990s, Phil Moore hosted two game shows (*Nick Arcade* and *You're On!*) on Nickelodeon, and Spencer Christian hosted *Triple Threat* on BET. Al Roker, the *Today Show*'s longtime weatherman, hosted a summer edition of *Celebrity Family Feud* in 2008 and also briefly subbed for Meredith Vieira as a

guest host of the daytime version of *Who Wants to Be a Millionaire?* Going way back, the rhyming black comedian Nipsey Russell, who was a regular celebrity panelist on several game shows in the 1970s and 1980s, also briefly hosted one.

40. Kyle Smith, "*Family Feud* Is the Raunchiest Show on TV," *New York Post* (October 7, 2015), http://nypost.com/2015/10/07/family-feud-is-an-affront-to-family-values/.

41. For a humorous take on the penis unzipped on-screen, see James Wolcott, "The Hung and the Restless," *Vanity Fair* (February 3, 2012), http://www.vanityfair.com /hollywood/2012/03/wolcott-201203.

42. Tim Kenneally, "MLK's Son Launching 1st African-American-Targeted Broadcast Net," *The Wrap* (April 4, 2011), http://www.thewrap.com/tv/article/martin-luther-king-iii -launching-first-broadcast-network-african-americans-26143/.

43. Adam Buckman, "Sherri Shepherd's Naughty New 'Newlywed Game,'" *Xfinity TV Blog* (November 1, 2010), http://xfinity.comcast.net/blogs/tv/2010/11/01/sherri-shepherds -naughty-new-newlywed-game/.

44. Frantz Fanon, *Black Skin, White Masks* (New York: Grove, 1967), 165.

45. Fanon, *Black Skin, White Masks*, 159.

46. From *Funk and Wagnall's New Practical Standard Dictionary* (1954). I, of course, do not remember the exact definitions from childhood, but luckily the two-volume dictionary, which came with the set of encyclopedias that my parents bought in the mid-1950s, is still in the family. My brother Danny has custody of the volumes and was kind enough to look up the definitions for me.

47. Kristin J. Warner, "If Loving Olitz Is Wrong, I Don't Want to Be Right: ABC's *Scandal* and the Affect of Black Female Desire," *Black Scholar* 45, no. 1 (Spring 2014): 16–20, 17.

48. Warner, "If Loving Olitz Is Wrong," 18.

2. "Those Thrilling Days of Yesteryear"

1. Leo Bogart, "TV Viewing in Its Social Gathering," in *The Age of Television: A Study of Viewing Habits and the Impact of Television on American Life*, ed. Leo Bogart (New York: Ungar, 1958), reprinted in *Major Problems in American Popular Culture: Documents and Essays*, ed. Kathleen Franz and Susan Smulyan (Boston: Wadsworth, 2012), 334–339, quote on p. 335.

2. Lynn Spigel, *Make Room for TV: Television and the Family Ideal in Postwar America* (Chicago: University of Chicago Press, 1992).

3. Spigel, *Make Room for TV*, 65–66.

4. "History: Self Help, Inc.'s 20 Year Campaign . . . in the War on Poverty," http:// selfhelpinc.org.

5. Peter Stallybrass and Allon White, *The Politics and Poetics of Transgression* (Ithaca, NY: Cornell University Press, 1986), 5–6.

6. George Lipsitz, *The Possessive Investment in Whiteness* (Philadelphia: Temple University Press, 1998), vii.

7. *I Love Lucy*, "The Great Train Robbery," CBS, October 31, 1955, written by Jess Oppenheimer, Madelyn (Pugh) Davis, et al., directed by James V. Kern, http://www.imdb .com/title/tt0609361/.

8. The show was originally called *Bandstand* from 1952 to 1957, when it was produced and broadcast locally in Philadelphia. Daniel B. Wood and Gloria Goodale, "Dick Clark: How a Tax-Accountant Look-Alike Changed American Music," *Christian Science Monitor*

(April 19, 2012), http://www.csmonitor.com/USA/Society/2012/0419/Dick-Clark-how-a
-tax-accountant-look-alike-changed-American-music.

9. Andrew Goldman, "Dick Clark, Still the Oldest Living Teenager," *New York Times*
(March 25, 2011), http://www.nytimes.com/2011/03/27/magazine/mag-27Talk-t.html.
See Dick Clark and Richard Robinson, *Rock, Roll and Remember* (New York: Thomas Y.
Cromwell, 1976).

10. Matthew F. Delmont, "Clark Aided Blacks on 'Bandstand'?," *The Root* (April 20,
2012), http://www.theroot.com/clark-aided-blacks-on-bandstand-1790891075. See also
Matthew F. Delmont, *The Nicest Kids in Town: American Bandstand, Rock 'n' Roll, and the
Struggle for Civil Rights in 1950s Philadelphia* (Berkeley: University of California Press,
2012); John A. Jackson, *American Bandstand: Dick Clark and the Making of a Rock 'n' Roll
Empire* (New York: Oxford University Press, 1999).

11. Delmont, *Nicest Kids in Town*, 1–2.

12. Delmont, "Clark Aided Blacks on 'Bandstand'?"

13. Delmont, *Nicest Kids in Town*, 8–9.

14. "Negro Performers Win Better Roles in TV Than in Any Other Entertainment Medium," *Ebony* 5, no. 8 (June 1950): 22–24. Sullivan, who is pictured with Ethel Waters in
the article, is quoted on p. 23.

15. Steve Allen, "Talent Is Color-Blind," *Ebony* 10, no. 11 (September 1955): 41–49, quote
on p. 41.

16. Jan Willis, *Dreaming Me: Black, Baptist, and Buddhist—One Woman's Spiritual
Journey* (Somerville, MA: Wisdom, 2008), 63.

17. Allen, "Talent Is Color-Blind," 41.

18. Ed Sullivan, "Can TV Crack America's Color Line?," *Ebony* 6, no. 7 (May 1951):
58–65, quotes on p. 65.

19. Sullivan, "Can TV Crack America's Color Line?," 65.

20. J. Fred MacDonald, *Blacks and White TV: African Americans in Television since
1948* (Chicago: Nelson Hall, 1992), 12.

21. Allen, "Talent Is Color-Blind," 41.

22. See, for example, Donald Bogle, *Primetime Blues: African Americans on Network
Television* (New York: Farrar, Straus and Giroux, 2001), 51–55.

23. Mandalit Del Barco, "Does Disney's Tonto Reinforce Stereotypes or Overcome
Them?," *Morning Edition*, National Public Radio (July 2, 2013), http://www.npr.org
/sections/codeswitch/2013/07/02/196333864/does-disneys-tonto-reinforce-stereotypes-or
-overcome-them.

24. Robert Lee, "The 'Heathen Chinee' on God's Free Soil," in Franz and Smulyan,
Major Problems in American Popular Culture, 46–49. See also the first chapter of Lee's
book *Orientals: Asian Americans in Popular Culture* (Philadelphia: Temple University
Press, 1999), 15–50.

25. Victor Sen Yung biography, http://www.imdb.com/name/nm0950958/bio.

26. Claudia Luther, "John Forsythe Dies at 92" (obituary), *Los Angeles Times* (April 3,
2010), http://articles.latimes.com/2010/apr/03/local/la-me-john-forsythe3-2010apr03.

27. See Jim Murray, "Dodger Voice Found More Stylish Roles," *Los Angeles Times* (September 10, 2008), http://articles.latimes.com/1990-06-03/sports/sp-1004_1_resonant-voice.

28. Elaine Kim, *Asian American Literature: An Introduction to the Writings and Their
Social Context* (Philadelphia: Temple University Press, 1984), 4.

29. Emily Nussbaum, "Crass Warfare: Raunch and Ridicule on *Whitney* and *2 Broke Girls*," *New Yorker* (November 28, 2011), http://www.newyorker.com/magazine/2011/11/28/crass-warfare.

30. On the "race-face convention," see Richard Slotkin, "Unit Pride: Ethnic Platoons and the Myth of American Nationality," *American Literary History* 13, no. 3 (Autumn 2001): 469–498.

31. Bogle, *Primetime Blues*, 25.

32. In addition to Bogle, *Primetime Blues*, 19–26, see Aniko Bodroghkozy, *Equal Time: Television and the Civil Rights Movement* (Urbana-Champaign: University of Illinois Press, 2013), 20–36; Patricia Turner, *Ceramic Uncles and Celluloid Mammies: Black Images and Their Influences on Culture* (New York: Anchor, 1994), 53, 61–62.

33. Private communication, but see LaBennett's insightful analysis of *Scandal*, "What *Scandal's* Civil Rights–Era Critique Says about Contemporary Black Women and Girls," *Ms.* (October 29, 2015), http://msmagazine.com/blog/2015/10/29/what-scandals-civil-rights-era-critique-says-about-contemporary-black-women-and-girls/.

34. Bogle, *Primetime Blues*, 24–25; Bodroghkozy, *Equal Time*, 34; MacDonald, *Blacks and White TV*, 29–33.

35. Bogle, *Primetime Blues*, 22.

36. Bodroghkozy, *Equal Time*, 32–33.

37. MacDonald, *Blacks and White TV*, 29–30. MacDonald cites his source as the United States Commission on Civil Rights, *Window Dressing on the Set: Women and Minorities in Television* (Washington, DC: Government Printing Office, 1977), 4–5. I am grateful to MacDonald for the tip that led me to this valuable resource.

38. Papers of the NAACP, supplement to part 1, 1951–1955, http://cisupa.proquest.com/ksc_assets/catalog/1415_PapersNAACPPt1Supp195155.pdf.

39. See, for example, Bogle, *Primetime Blues*, 31–40; Bodroghkozy, *Equal Time*, 20–28; and the newspapers themselves, which shed detailed light on the controversies.

40. Bodroghkozy, *Equal Time*, 36.

41. On this point, see Andrew Wiese, *Places of Their Own: African American Suburbanization in the Twentieth Century* (Chicago: University of Chicago Press, 2005).

42. Henry Louis Gates Jr. and Evelyn Brooks Higginbotham, *African American Lives* (New York: Oxford University Press, 2004), 181.

43. See Karen Chilton, *Hazel Scott: The Pioneering Journey of a Jazz Pianist from Café Society to Hollywood to HUAC* (Ann Arbor: University of Michigan Press, 2010).

44. Nat King Cole (as told to Lerone Bennett Jr.), "Why I Quit My TV Show," *Ebony* 13, no. 4 (February 1958): 29.

45. Mary Ann Watson, "*The Nat 'King' Cole Show*," Museum of Broadcast Communications, http://www.museum.tv/eotv/natkingcole.htm.

46. Cole, "Why I Quit My TV Show," 29–30.

3. The Shirley Temple of My Familiar

This chapter revises and extends my essay published in *Transitions* in 1998.

1. From the Stephen Foster minstrel tune "Old Folks at Home" (1851). The songs of Foster's oeuvre were staples of our music education in elementary school during the 1950s.

2. Yunte Huang, *Charlie Chan: The Untold Story of the Honorable Detective and His Rendezvous with American History* (New York: W. W. Norton, 2010). See also Jill Lepore's

review of Huang's book, "Chan, the Man: On the Trail of the Honorable Detective," *New Yorker* (August 9, 2010), http://www.newyorker.com/magazine/2010/08/09/chan-the -man.

3. Jessica Hagedorn, ed., *Charlie Chan Is Dead: An Anthology of Contemporary Asian American Fiction* (New York: Penguin, 1993).

4. Frank Chin and Jeffery Paul Chan, "Racist Love," in *Seeing through Shuck*, ed. Richard Kostelanetz (New York: Ballantine, 1972), 65. Other Asian Americanists who have offered specific critiques of stereotypical figures such as Fu Manchu and Charlie Chan include Elaine Kim, *Asian American Literature: An Introduction to the Writings and Their Social Context* (Philadelphia: Temple University Press, 1984); and Gish Jen, "Changing the Asian Illusion," *New York Times* (August 11, 1991), http://www.nytimes.com/1991/08/11 /arts/challenging-the-asian-illusion.html?pagewanted=all.

5. Matthew Pratt Guterl, *Seeing Race in Modern America* (Chapel Hill: University of North Carolina Press, 2013), 148.

6. Shirley Temple Black, *Child Star* (New York: Warner, 1988), 114–115.

7. Temple Black, *Child Star*, 100–101.

8. Anne Edwards, *Shirley Temple: American Princess* (New York: William Morrow, 1988), 80. Temple's publicized birthday, verified by a fake birth certificate, was April 23, 1929, but Temple was actually born a year earlier. Her stage mother supposedly deducted a year from her daughter's age to make her seem even more precocious.

9. *Biography*, A&E Cable Network, December 8, 1996.

10. George Lipsitz, *The Possessive Investment in Whiteness* (Philadelphia: Temple University Press, 1998), 1.

11. Graham Greene, "Review of *Captain January*," *Spectator* (August 1936), in *The Graham Greene Film Reader: Reviews, Essays, Interviews and Film Stories*, ed. David Parkinson (New York: Applause, 1995), 128.

12. Christopher Hawtree, ed., *Night and Day: Selections* (London: Chatto and Windus, 1986), 204. See also Cecil Smith, "The 'Lolita' Libel Case: Shirley Temple's 'Dimpled Depravity'?," *Los Angeles Times* (June 22, 1986), http://articles.latimes.com/1986-06-22 /entertainment/ca-20446_1_libeling.

13. Jeanine Basinger, *A Woman's View: How Hollywood Spoke to Women, 1930–1960* (Hanover, NH: Wesleyan University Press, 1993), 282–284.

14. Basinger, *Woman's View*, 284.

15. Basinger, *Woman's View*, 284.

16. Temple Black, *Child Star*, 98.

17. Temple Black, *Child Star*, 90.

18. Temple Black, *Child Star*, 98.

19. James Snead, *White Screens/Black Images: Hollywood from the Dark Side*, ed. Colin MacCabe and Cornel West (New York: Routledge, 1994), 56.

20. Patricia Turner, *Ceramic Uncles and Celluloid Mammies: Black Images and Their Influences on Culture* (New York: Anchor, 1994), 83.

21. Quoted by Temple Black in *Child Star*, 154.

22. Edwards, *Shirley Temple*, 85.

23. Betty Bao Lord, *In the Year of the Boar and Jackie Robinson* (New York: HarperCollins, 1984). My then ten-year-old friend Rachel Woodhull, who is grown up now and married, introduced this book to me in the mid-1990s.

24. Snead, *White Screens/Black Images*, 60. For provocative readings of race in Shirley Temple movies and other media, see Donald Bogle, *Toms, Coons, Mulattoes, Mammies, and Bucks* (New York: Continuum, 1973); Herman Gray, *Watching Race: Television and the Struggle for "Blackness"* (Minneapolis: University of Minnesota Press, 1995); and Susan Gubar, *Racechanges: White Skin, Black Face in American Culture* (New York: Oxford University Press, 1997).

25. Zora Neale Hurston, "Characteristics of Negro Expression," in *Hurston: Folklore, Memoirs, and Other Writings*, ed. Cheryl Wall (New York: Literary Classics, 1995), 839.

26. African American Policy Forum and Center for Intersectionality and Social Policy Studies, "Black Girls Matter: Pushed Out, Overpoliced and Underprotected" (December 30, 2014), http://www.atlanticphilanthropies.org/app/uploads/2015/09 /BlackGirlsMatter_Report.pdf.

27. For an insightful, detailed discussion of the novel and the film and the difference between the two, see Rebecca Wanzo, *The Suffering Will Not Be Televised: African American Women and Sentimental Political Storytelling* (Albany: State University of New York Press, 2009), 127–136.

4. *Interracial* Loving

1. Quotations are from the Virginia Code cited as [Footnote 4] in *Loving v. Virginia*. 338 U.S. 1. Sup. Ct. 1967, http://caselaw.findlaw.com/us-supreme-court/388/1.html. In homage to the descendants of John Rolfe and Pocahontas, the Virginia Code also classified as white "persons who have one-sixteenth or less of the blood of the American Indian and have no other non-Caucasic blood."

2. *Loving v. Virginia*.

3. On civil rights and *Loving*, see Dorothy E. Roberts, *"Loving v. Virginia* as a Civil Rights Decision," *New York Law School Law Review* 59, no. 1 (2014–2015): 177, http://www .nylslawreview.com/wp-content/uploads/sites/16/2015/02/Volume-59-1.Roberts.pdf.

4. Renee C. Romano, *Race Mixing: Black-White Marriage in Postwar America* (Cambridge, MA: Harvard University Press, 2003), 191.

5. Romano, *Race Mixing*, 83.

6. The "mask" quotation is from a poem by Paul Laurence Dunbar, "We Wear the Mask."

7. See the British Film Institute website at http://www.screenonline.org.uk/tv/id/537722/. See also Sheena McKenzie, "Uncovered Footage Reveals TV's 'First' Interracial Kiss, Long before Star Trek," CNN (November 20, 2015), http://www.cnn.com/2015/11/20/world/first -interracial-kiss-on-tv/.

8. David Cole Stein, "The First Interracial Black/White Kiss in U.S. TV History," https:// www.youtube.com/watch?v=L14hByoODIw.

9. See the stars' respective biographies: William Shatner, *Star Trek Memories* (New York: HarperCollins, 1993), 282–285; and Nichelle Nichols, *Beyond Uhura: Star Trek and Other Memories* (New York: G. P. Putnam's Sons, 1994), 194–197.

10. Shatner, *Star Trek Memories*, 282.

11. Donald Bogle, *Primetime Blues: African Americans on Network Television* (New York: Farrar, Straus and Giroux, 2001), 138.

12. In his biography, Norman Lear quotes this familiar lyric as "moving on up to a *duplex* apartment in the sky," rather than the emphasized "deee-lux."

13. Mel Watkins, "Sherman Hemsley, 'Jeffersons' Star, Is Dead at 74," *New York Times* (July 24, 2012), http://www.nytimes.com/2012/07/25/arts/television/sherman-hemsley -star-of-the-jeffersons-dies-at-74.html.

14. Lisa Woolfork, "Looking for Lionel: Making Whiteness and Blackness in *All in the Family* and *The Jeffersons*," in *African Americans on Television: Race-ing for Ratings*, ed. David J. Leonard and Lisa A. Guerrero (Santa Barbara, CA: Praeger, 2013), 48.

15. Woolfork, "Looking for Lionel," 48.

16. Henry Louis Gates Jr., "TV's Black World Turns—but Stays Unreal," *New York Times* (November 12, 1989), http://www.nytimes.com/1989/11/12/arts/tv-s-black-world-turns-but -stays-unreal.html?pagewanted=all&src=pm.

17. In this sentence, I had meant to write "backstory," but with my infamously bad typing, it accidentally came out "blackstory," a typo I decided to keep and make use of.

18. James Joyce, *Dubliners* (New York: Penguin Classics, 1993), 108.

19. Roger Ebert, "Review of *I Spy*," *Chicago Sun-Times* (November 1, 2002), http://www.rogerebert.com/reviews/i-spy-2002; "Twenty-Third Annual Razzie—Movies from 2002—Nominees—Worst Screen Couple/Worst Screen Ensemble," https://www .filmaffinity.com/en/awards.php?award_id=razzie&year=2003&cat_id=worst_screen _couple_ensemble.

20. Lois Armstrong, "Interracial Love in the Afternoon? TV Soaps Aren't Ready for It, Tina Andrews Finds," *People* 7, no. 24 (June 20, 1977), http://www.people.com/people /archive/article/0,,20068128,00.html.

21. William K. Knoedelseder, "It's Kaput for TV Soapdom's Only Interracial Couple," *Washington Post* (May 31, 1977), https://www.washingtonpost.com/archive/lifestyle /1977/05/31/its-kaput-for-tv-soapdoms-only-interracial-couple/fa351e52-e368-4d9d-bf3c -83a3156a6db6/.

22. Armstrong, "Interracial Love in the Afternoon?"

23. Romano, *Race Mixing*, 250, 253.

24. Braden Goyette, "Cheerios Commercial Featuring Mixed Race Family Gets Racist Backlash," *Huffington Post* (May 31, 2013), http://www.huffingtonpost.com/2013/05/31 /cheerios-commercial-racist-backlash_n_3363507.html.

5. "A Credit to My Race"

1. Kayla Webley, "How the Nixon-Kennedy Debate Changed the World," *Time* (September 23, 2010), http://content.time.com/time/nation/article/0,8599,2021078,00.html; "1960: First Televised Presidential Debate," *60 Minutes Overtime* (October 3, 2012), http://www .cbsnews.com/news/1960-first-televised-presidential-debate/.

2. Donald Bogle, *Primetime Blues: African Americans on Network Television* (New York: Farrar, Straus and Giroux, 2001), 97.

3. United States Commission on Civil Rights, *Window Dressing on the Set: Women and Minorities in Television* (Washington, DC: Government Printing Office, 1977), 5. The original source: Richard Lemon, "Black Is the Color of TV's Newest Stars," *Saturday Evening Post* (November 30, 1968): 82.

4. See Mel Watkins, *Stepin Fetchit: The Life and Times of Lincoln Perry* (New York: Vintage Books, 2005), 268–274, quote on p. 273.

5. Hattie McDaniel accepting the Best Supporting Actress plaque at the 12th Academy Award ceremony, February 29, 1940: https://www.youtube.com/watch?v=e7t4pTNZshA.

6. Seth Abramovitch, "Oscar's First Black Winner Accepted Her Honor in a Segregated 'No Blacks' Hotel in L.A.," *Hollywood Reporter* (February 19, 2015), http://www.hollywoodreporter.com/features/oscars-first-black-winner-accepted-774335. The black comedian Flip Wilson often included a skit in his namesake show (NBC, 1970–1974) that revolved around his alter ego Geraldine (Wilson in drag) meeting her boyfriend Killer "at a booth in the back in the corner in the dark." They were looking for seclusion, of course, while the seating of Hattie McDaniel in such a location was about her exclusion.

7. See, for example, Jill Watts, *Hattie McDaniel: Black Ambition, White Hollywood* (New York: Amistad, 2007).

8. As quoted on the blurb on the box housing the fiftieth-anniversary *Julia* Barbie doll.

9. Ruth Feldstein, *How It Feels to Be Free: Black Women Entertainers and the Civil Rights Movement* (New York: Oxford University Press, 2013), 116–117.

10. Christine Acham, *Revolution Televised: Prime Time and the Struggle for Black Power* (Minneapolis: University of Minnesota Press, 2004), 117.

11. Daphne Brooks's provocative observation about "imaginative activism" and "progressive representations of black womanhood" is quoted on the back cover of Feldstein's study *How It Feels to Be Free* and, according to Brooks, does not currently exist elsewhere.

12. Feldstein, *How It Feels to Be Free*, 117.

13. Acham, *Revolution Televised*, 2–3.

14. See, for example, Bogle, *Primetime Blues*, 108–113, and especially Aniko Bodroghkozy, *Equal Time: Television and the Civil Rights Movement* (Urbana-Champaign: University of Illinois Press, 2013), chapter 6, 155–179. Bodroghkozy offers a detailed, well-researched analysis of the series and its reception and its two most discussed episodes, "Who Do You Kill?" and "No Hiding Place." My own discussion is based primarily on admittedly sketchy memories of seeing the show in the 1960s, refreshed by contemporary screenings. Before I watched these episodes on YouTube recently, I didn't remember that it was James Earl Jones who played the father in "Who Do You Kill?," but the character's hopeless despair and the mother's stultifying anguish have stayed with me for more than half a century.

15. Stephen W. Bowie, "*East Side/West Side*," http://classictvhistory.com/EpisodeGuides/east_side_west_side.html.

16. Bogle, *Primetime Blues*, 112.

17. Bowie, "*East Side/West Side*."

18. Nichelle Nichols, *Beyond Uhura: Star Trek and Other Memories* (New York: G. P. Putnam's Sons, 1994), 161–165. Nichols writes that fed up and feeling she could no longer allow herself to be treated "as less of a person than [her] coworkers," she informed Roddenberry she was leaving the series. The very next evening at an NAACP fundraiser, she was introduced to "her biggest fan," who turned out to be Dr. King.

19. Nichols, *Beyond Uhura*, 165.

20. Norman Lear, *Even This I Get to Experience* (New York: Penguin, 2014), 267.

21. Shonda Rhimes, http://www.whosay.com/status/shondaland/460562.

22. Lear, *Even This I Get to Experience*, 267.

23. Lear, *Even This I Get to Experience*, 268.

24. Lear, *Even This I Get to Experience*, 270.

25. Lear, *Even This I Get to Experience*, 271.

26. The disagreements among cast members are legendary and were much discussed in the media even during the show's heyday. See, for example, Louie Robinson, "Bad

Times on the 'Good Times' Set," *Ebony* 30, no. 11 (September 1975): 33–36, 38, 40, 42. For a contemporary commentary, see Tammy L. Brown, "An Interview with John Amos," in *African Americans on Television: Race-ing for Ratings*, ed. David J. Leonard and Lisa A. Guerrero (Santa Barbara, CA: Praeger, 2013), 34–44.

27. Robinson, "Bad Times on the 'Good Times' Set," 34–35; Brown, "Interview with John Amos."

28. Lear, *Even This I Get to Experience*, 276.

29. Lear, *Even This I Get to Experience*, 268.

30. Lear, *Even This I Get to Experience*, 269.

31. Lear, *Even This I Get to Experience*, 269.

32. "For Classic TV Producer, Good Times No Longer," narrated by Katia Dunn, *Weekend Edition*, National Public Radio (July 29, 2006).

33. Lear, *Even This I Get to Experience*, 274–275.

34. See Matthew F. Delmont, *Making "Roots": A Nation Captivated* (Berkeley: University of California Press, 2016).

35. Lena Dunham, "It's No SCANDALOUS Secret, I Worship Kerry Washington," *Marie Claire* (April 2015): 200, 244.

36. Matt Webb Mitovich, "*Scandal's* Kerry Washington: Olivia Pope Should Be 'Nobody's Role Model,'" *TVLine* (August 4, 2015), http://tvline.com/2015/08/04/scandal-season-5-olivia-fitz-still-together/.

37. Frantz Fanon, *Black Skin, White Masks* (New York: Grove, 1967), 165.

38. Mitovich, "*Scandal's* Kerry Washington."

39. Mike Ayers, "The Soul of 'Scandal': How Shonda Rhimes Soundtracks TV's Most Dramatic Show," *Billboard* (April 17, 2014), http://www.billboard.com/articles/columns/pop-shop/6062363/the-soul-of-scandal-how-shonda-rhimes-soundtracks-tvs-most.

40. Oneka LaBennett, "What *Scandal's* Civil Rights–Era Critique Says about Contemporary Black Women and Girls," *Ms.* (October 29, 2015), http://msmagazine.com/blog/2015/10/29/what-scandals-civil-rights-era-critique-says-about-contemporary-black-women-and-girls/.

41. The African American actor Julius Carry was sometimes listed as a regular on *Murphy Brown*, but he only appeared in five episodes of a show that ran for ten years. Other black actors who crossed paths with the show primarily appeared in bit parts or as guest artists, usually in a single episode. Aretha Franklin appeared as herself in one episode, as did the black TV journalist and *60 Minutes* veteran Ed Bradley.

42. The listing for the soundtrack album appears here: https://www.amazon.com/Sounds-Murphy-Brown-Television-Soundtrack/dp/B000002OE8.

43. United States Commission on Civil Rights, *Window Dressing on the Set*, 4.

6. A Clear and Present Absence

Note on the epigraph: Raymond Burr's remarks regarding the impact of *Perry Mason* were widely quoted at the time of his death in 1993. See obituary for Raymond Burr, *Baltimore Sun* (September 21, 1993), http://articles.baltimoresun.com/1993-09-21/news/1993264194_1_raymond-burr-perry-mason-burr-died.

1. A villain in "Weary Watchdog," Keye Luke turns up again in "The Case of the Feather Cloak" (1965), set in Hawaii with Arthur Wong as the presiding judge. Benson Fong, whose character Mason defends in "The Case of the Caretaker's Cat," likewise turns

up again in a number of episodes, including "The Case of the Blushing Pearls," where he plays a Japanese gem merchant and the murder victim, supposedly killed by his niece, Mitsou Kamuri (Nobu McCarthy), whom Mason successfully defends. Mitsou's good Japanese friend and eventual love interest (once she dumps the white guy who she figures out was only courting her to annoy his racist father) is played by none other than George Takei, who would go on to star as Lt. Hikaru Sulu in the original *Star Trek* series.

2. J. Fred MacDonald, *Blacks and White TV: African Americans in Television since 1948* (Chicago: Nelson Hall, 1992), 88.

3. Garfield Hinton, "The 'Man with a Thousand Faces' Comes to Baltimore," *Baltimore Afro-American* (April 2, 1956), https://news.google.com /newspapers?id=ReclAAAAIBAJ&sjid=bPUFAAAAIBAJ&pg=3807,1918500&dq =frank+silvera+actors+studio&hl=en.

4. "'Civil Rights' Theater Has New Show on Broadway," *St. Joseph News-Press* (May 9, 1965), https://news.google.com/newspapers?id=idBTAAAAIBAJ&sjid =xDgNAAAAIBAJ&pg=740,1497104&dq=frank+silvera+the+theatre+of+being&hl=en. See also Donald Bogle, *Primetime Blues: African Americans on Network Television* (New York: Farrar, Straus and Giroux, 2001), 136–137; Henry Louis Gates Jr., "Which Black Actor Was Paid to Be White?," *The Root* (October 27, 2014), http://www.theroot.com /articles/history/2014/10/which_black_actor_who_passed_for_white/; and Silvera's *New York Times* obituary on June 12, 1970, http://www.nytimes.com/1970/06/12/archives/frank -silvera-actordirector-electrocuted-in-coast-mishap.html.

5. "When We Speak TV," https://www.youtube.com/watch?v=RTL10Fc3vS0.

6. Golden Age Radio Research, "Introduction to the Perry Mason Connection," http:// www.digitaldeliftp.com/DigitalDeliToo/dd2-Research-Perry-Mason-Main.html.

7. In the series premiere, a young white couple (Mandy Moore and Milo Ventimiglia), who lose their third triplet in childbirth, adopt a black foundling and raise him along with the surviving boy and girl siblings. To flesh out the stereotype even further, on his thirty-sixth birthday, the foundling (Sterling K. Brown), who has learned from a private detective that his mother was a crack addict who died in childbirth, seeks out the father who abandoned him, who, of course, was also an addict and claims not even to remember what he did with his infant son.

8. Neil Genzlinger, "Adorable Baby, Doubting Dad, Teachable Moment: Revisiting 'That's My Boy??' on *The Dick Van Dyke Show*," *New York Times* (September 24, 2013), http://www.nytimes.com/2013/09/25/arts/television/revisiting-thats-my-boy-on-the-dick -van-dyke-show.html.

9. Genzlinger, "Adorable Baby."

10. Peter Dreier, "Sanford and Its Sons: From Jackie Robinson to Trayvon Martin," *Huffington Post* (September 13, 2013), http://www.huffingtonpost.com/peter-dreier /sanford-and-its-sons-from_b_3595577.html. See also Jules Tygiel, *Baseball's Great Experiment: Jackie Robinson and His Legacy* (New York: Oxford University Press, 1983).

11. Nsenga K. Burton, "How Did Blacks Travel during Segregation?," *The Root* (July 9, 2012), http://www.theroot.com/articles/culture/2012/07/black_history_road_trip_negro _motorist_green_book_destinations/.

12. Eugene L. Meyer, "A Welcoming Enclave with Roots in a Snub," *New York Times* (September 9, 2009), http://www.nytimes.com/2009/09/04/greathomesanddestinations

/04Highland.html?_r=0; Nurith C. Aizenman, "Chesapeake Summer: A Haven for Blacks and History," *Washington Post* (August 20, 2002), B1, B7.

13. See, for example, Chris Lamb, "Jackie Robinson—Crossing the Line," *Los Angeles Times* (February 27, 2012), http://articles.latimes.com/2012/feb/27/opinion/la-oe-lamb -jackie-robinson-20120227.

14. Michel duCille, "Documenting with Dignity in the Ebola Zone," *Washington Post* (October 19, 2014), https://www.washingtonpost.com/lifestyle/style/documenting-with -dignity-in-the-ebola-zone/2014/10/19/07c41fd2-5638-11e4-ba4b-f6333e2c0453_story.html ?utm_term=.086bd8f5bb43.

15. Emilie Raymond, *Stars for Freedom: Hollywood, Black Celebrities, and the Civil Rights Movement* (Seattle: University of Washington Press, 2015), 162.

16. Carl M. Cannon, "Hollywood Who's Who Marched with King in '63," *Real Clear Politics* (August 29, 2013), http://www.realclearpolitics.com/articles/2013/08/29 /hollywood_whos_who_marched_with_king_in_63__119762.html.

17. Tim Gray, "Hollywood Turned Out for Historic 'I Have a Dream' Speech," *Variety* (August 28, 2015), http://variety.com/2015/biz/columns/1963-march-on-washington -hollywood-bob-dylan-sidney-poitier-1201580118/; and Ted Johnson, "When Brando Marched with Heston: How *Variety* Covered the March on Washington," *Variety* (August 27, 2013), http://variety.com/2013/voices/columns/when-marlon-brando-marched -with-charlton-heston-how-variety-covered-the-march-on-washington-1200589376/.

18. Haeyoun Park, Josh Keller, and Josh Williams, "The Faces of American Power, Nearly as White as the Oscar Nominees," *New York Times* (February 26, 2016), http:// www.nytimes.com/interactive/2016/02/26/us/race-of-american-power.html?_r=1; see also Brooks Barnes and John Koblin, "Channing Dungey to Succeed Paul Lee as Chief of ABC Entertainment," *New York Times* (February 17, 2016), http://www.nytimes.com/2016/02/18 /business/media/paul-lee-resign-abc-entertainment.html.

19. Obituary for Raymond Burr, *Baltimore Sun* (September 21, 1993), http://articles .baltimoresun.com/1993-09-21/news/1993264194_1_raymond-burr-perry-mason-burr-died.

7. "Soaploitation"

1. John Nichols, "Edward Brooke and the Republican Party That Might Have Been," *Nation* (January 7, 2015), https://www.thenation.com/article/edward-brooke-and -republican-party-might-have-been/.

2. Leah Wright Rigueur, *The Loneliness of the Black Republican* (Princeton, NJ: Princeton University Press, 2015), 120. Rigueur offers a detailed, balanced critique of Brooke in her pivotal, comprehensive study of black Republicanism.

3. This figure is as cited by Rigueur, who also points out that Brooke received 86 percent of the black vote: *Loneliness of the Black Republican*, 118.

4. Some critics and fans maintain that Olivia Pope is suffering from posttraumatic stress disorder and self-medicating with fine wine. On the subject of Olivia's untreated mental health issues, see Stacia L. Brown, "*Scandal* Keeps Missing Opportunities to Address Olivia's Mental Health," *Washington Post* (April 8, 2016), https:// www.washingtonpost.com/news/act-four/wp/2016/04/08/scandal-keeps-missing -opportunities-to-address-olivia-popes-mental-health/?utm_term=.e328eb5cdb91.

5. The phrase was coined by David Brock, author of *The Real Anita Hill* (New York: Free Press, 1993), as part of a smear campaign in which he has since admitted using lies

and every other trick in the book to discredit her, a story he tells in the apologia *Blinded by the Right: The Conscience of an Ex-conservative* (New York: Crown, 2002).

6. Jasmine Lester, "How to Get Away with Rape Culture," *Black Girl Dangerous* (December 2, 2014), https://www.bgdblog.org/2014/12/get-away-rape-culture/. I'm grateful to Lester for her insightful commentary, which helped me understand my own discomfort with this aspect of the show.

7. This may have been a fairly common sentiment, because Renee Romano quotes a black female source saying something similar, although that woman posits the end of the marriage rather than the end of the husband. See Renee C. Romano, *Race Mixing: Black-White Marriage in Postwar America* (Cambridge, MA: Harvard University Press, 2003), 85.

8. Roxane Gay, "Not Here to Make Friends," in *Bad Feminist* (New York: Harper Perennial, 2014), 83–95.

9. Emily Nussbaum, "Difficult Women: How 'Sex and the City' Lost Its Good Name," *New Yorker* (July 29, 2013), http://www.newyorker.com/magazine/2013/07/29/difficult-women.

10. Willa Paskin, "Shonda Rhimes: 'Calling a Show a "Guilty Pleasure"—It's Like Saying It's a Piece of Crap,'" *Salon.com* (February 10, 2013), http://www.salon.com/2013/02/10/shonda_rhimes_calling_a_show_a_guilty_pleasure_—_it's_like_saying_its_a_piece_of_crap/.

11. Paskin, "Shonda Rhimes."

12. Robin Nelson, *TV Drama in Transition: Forms, Values and Cultural Change* (London: Palgrave, 1997), 23–25.

13. Daisy Hernandéz, "4 Reasons Why *Scandal* Is a Telenovela—and a Good One," *Code Switch*, National Public Radio (November 20, 2014), http://www.npr.org/sections/codeswitch/2014/11/20/365457210/4-reasons-why-scandal-is-a-telenovela-and-a-good-one.

14. See, for example, Raymond Williams, *Television: Technology and Cultural Form* (London: Fontana, 1974; rev. ed., New York: Routledge, 2003); and John Ellis, *Visible Fictions* (London: Routledge, 1982).

15. Christopher Wilson, "The Scandalous Truth about *Downton Abbey*'s Royal Gigolo 'Jack Ross,'" *Telegraph* (October 14, 2013), http://www.telegraph.co.uk/culture/tvandradio/downton-abbey/10377794/The-scandalous-truth-about-Downton-Abbeys-royal-gigolo-Jack-Ross.html.

8. The Punch and Judge Judy Shows

1. Molly Ladd-Taylor, "Eugenics, Sterilisation and Modern Marriage in the USA: The Strange Career of Paul Popenoe," *Gender and History* 13, no. 2 (August 2001): 298–327.

2. On Popenoe, see Jill Lepore, "Fixed: The Rise of Marriage Therapy, and Other Dreams of Human Betterment," *New Yorker* (March 29, 2010), http://www.newyorker.com/magazine/2010/03/29/fixed; Sara Boboltz, "Awful '50s Marriage Advice Shows What Our Mothers and Grandmothers Were Up Against," *Huffington Post* (September 26, 2014), http://www.huffingtonpost.com/2014/09/26/can-this-marriage-be-saved-advice_n_5829870.html.

3. "Meet Judge Lynn," https://www.divorcecourt.com/meet-judge-lynn/.

4. Amelia Robinson, "Dayton Man: 'I've Got 12 Sons and 15 Daughters. I Have 27 All Together,'" *Dayton Daily News* (September 6, 2013), http://www.daytondailynews.com/news/news/crime-law/dayton-man-ive-got-12-sons-and-15-daughters-i-have/nZpKr/.

5. Rene Lynch, "Man Who Had 30 Kids with 11 Women Wants Child-Support Break," *Los Angeles Times* (May 18, 2012), http://articles.latimes.com/2012/may/18/nation/la-na-nn-tennessee-man-has-30-kids-20120518; Robinson, "Dayton Man"; "Orlando Shaw,

Nashville Father with 22 Children by 14 Women, Sued for Unpaid Child Support," *Huffington Post* (June 7, 2013), http://www.huffingtonpost.com/2013/06/06/orlando-shaw -father-22-children-14-women_n_3397397.html.

6. Andrew Goldman, "Order! Order in Judge Judy's Court!," *New York Times Magazine* (June 24, 2011), http://www.nytimes.com/2011/06/26/magazine/judge-judy-has-her-day -in-court.html?_r=0.

7. My mother used to watch *Judge Judy*, but I had no idea how long I had been follow-ing the show with the intention of writing about it, until I came across a copy of the AARP magazine *Modern Maturity* from July–August 2001 with a cover story about the judge and marginal notes I hadn't remembered making.

8. Goldman, "Order!"

9. See Camille Dodero, "*Judge Judy*'s Cat-Killing-Hipster Plaintiff Speaks: An Interview with Teeth Mountain's Kate Levitt and Andrew Burt," *Village Voice* (March 30, 2010), http://www.villagevoice.com/music/judge-judys-cat-killing-hipster-plaintiff-speaks-an -interview-with-teeth-mountains-kate-levitt-and-andrew-burt-6646226.

10. David Firestone, "While Barbie Talks Tough, G.I. Joe Goes Shopping," *New York Times* (December 31, 1993), http://www.nytimes.com/1993/12/31/us/while-barbie-talks -tough-g-i-joe-goes-shopping.html?sec=&spon=&pagewanted=all.

11. Soraya Nadia McDonald, "The Lasting Appeal of TV's Top Woman: Judge Judy," *Washington Post* (March 3, 2015), https://www.washingtonpost.com/news/morning-mix /wp/2015/03/03/the-lasting-appeal-of-tvs-top-woman-judge-judy/.

12. Taunya Lovell Banks, "Here Comes the Judge! Gender Distortion on TV Reality Court Shows," *Law Forum* 39, no. 1 (Fall 2008): 37–56, quote on p. 39.

13. See, for example, in addition to Banks, Kimberlianne Podlas, "As Seen on TV: The Normative Influence of Syndi-Court on Contemporary Litigousness," *Jeffrey S. Moo-rad Sports Law Journal* 11, no. 1 (2004), https://digitalcommons.law.villanova.edu/cgi /viewcontent.cgi?referer=https://www.google.com/&httpsredir=1&article=1123&context =mslj; Lawrence M. Friedman, "Judge Judy's Justice," *Berkeley Journal of Entertainment and Sports Law* 1, no. 2 (April 2012): 123–133; and Philip Z. Kimball, "Syndi-Court Justice: Judge Judy and Exploitation of Arbitration," http://www.americanbar.org/content/dam /aba/migrated/dispute/essay/syndicourtjustice.authcheckdam.pdf.

14. Debra K. Japp, "*Judge Judy* and *Dr. Phil*: Advice with an Attitude," in *Communica-tion Ethics, Media, and Popular Culture*, ed. Phyllis M. Japp, Mark Meister, and Debra K. Japp (New York: Peter Lang, 2005), 291–292.

15. ConsumerAffairs.com reveals a different kind of complaint about *Judge Judy*, with numerous respondents claiming to have been bullied into bringing their small-claims lawsuits to the show or tricked into participating by assurances from the producers that they would win their cases "hands down," only to be sent packing without having been given a chance to present their evidence. See http://www.consumeraffairs.com/misc /judge_judy.html.

16. "Judge Judy DESTROYS Obama-Supporting Welfare Cheat," *Political Insider* (December 28, 2015), http://www.thepoliticalinsider.com/judge-judy-destroys-obama -supporting-welfare-cheat/.

17. "Judge Judy Unloads on Obama Welfare Moocher Mom," https://www.youtube.com /watch?v=wcksRQjMAGs; "Judge Judy and the Production of the Welfare State," https:// www.youtube.com/watch?v=etYoz5GCXOk.

18. As per the full transcript of the unedited video of Romney's remarks provided by *Mother Jones*. See *Mother Jones* (September 19, 2012), http://www.motherjones.com /politics/2012/09/full-transcript-mitt-romney-secret-video#47percent.

19. Roberton C. Williams, "Why Do People Pay No Federal Income Tax?," *Tax Policy Center* (July 27, 2011), http://www.taxpolicycenter.org/taxvox/why-do-people-pay-no -federal-income-tax; Lucy Madison, "Fact-Checking Romney's '47 Percent' Comment," CBS News (September 25, 2012), http://www.cbsnews.com/news/fact-checking-romneys -47-percent-comment/.

20. *Kabia v. Koch*, 186 Misc.2d 363 (N.Y. Misc. 2000), https://casetext.com/case/kabia-v -koch.

21. The Pringles' bios can be found at the following blog: https://atlantapowercouple .wordpress.com.

22. Nekesa Mumbi Moody, "Critics Aside, Perry Reaches New Heights with OWN, More Hits," Associated Press (April 5, 2016), http://bigstory.ap.org/article/eoeb828b634d4 cdca096dadc81ea3cf0/critics-aside-perry-reaches-new-heights-own-more-hits.

23. Mitch Smith and Monica Davey, "4 Black Suspects Charged in Videotaped Beating of White Teenager in Chicago," *New York Times* (January 5, 2017), http://www.nytimes .com/2017/01/05/us/chicago-racially-charged-attack-video.html.

9. The Autumn of His Discontent

1. George H. W. Bush, "Remarks by the President at Presentation of Medal of Free- dom," White House press release (July 9, 2002), http://georgewbush-whitehouse.archives .gov/news/releases/2002/07/20020709-8.html.

2. William H. Cosby Jr., "Dr. Bill Cosby Speaks," transcript provided by Cosby's PR representatives, http://www.rci.rutgers.edu/~schochet/101/Cosby_Speech.htm.

3. For an insightful analysis of the difference, see Ivory A. Toldson, "Think You Know the Dropout Rates for Black Males? You're Probably Wrong," *The Root* (June 4, 2014), http://www.theroot.com/think-you-know-the-dropout-rates-for-black-males-you-r -1790875915.

4. Rice University News and Media, "African-Americans Are the Most Likely to Value Postsecondary Education, According to First-Ever Houston Education Survey" (Novem- ber 12, 2013), http://news.rice.edu/2013/11/12/african-americans-are-the-most-likely-to -value-postsecondary-education/.

5. Michael Eric Dyson, *Is Bill Cosby Right? Or Has the Black Middle Class Lost Its Mind?* (New York: Basic Civitas, 2006), 3.

6. Barbara Bowman, "Bill Cosby Raped Me: Why Did It Take 30 Years for People to Believe My Story?," *Washington Post* (November 13, 2014), https://www.washingtonpost .com/posteverything/wp/2014/11/13/bill-cosby-raped-me-why-did-it-take-30-years-for -people-to-believe-my-story/.

7. Antoinette Bueno, "Janice Dickinson Details Bill Cosby Sexual Assault Accusations: He Raped Me," *Entertainment Tonight Online* (November 18, 2014), http://www.etonline .com/news/154076_janice_dickinson_details_alleged_bill_cosby_sexual_assault/.

8. Roger Friedman, "Exclusive: Bill Cosby Co-star Tony Winner Phylicia Rashad Speaks Out for the First Time, Defends Her Friend," *ShowBiz 411* (January 6, 2015), http:// www.showbiz411.com/2015/01/06/exclusive-bill-cosby-co-star-tony-winner-phylicia -rashad-speaks-out-for-first-time-defends-her-friend.

9. Andrew Blankstein, Tom Winter, and Daniel Arkin, "Judge Explains Why He Unsealed Bill Cosby Court Documents," NBC News (July 7, 2015), http://www.nbcnews.com/news/us-news/judge-explains-why-he-unsealed-bill-cosby-court-documents-n387861.

10. Bounce TV, which along with other networks had ceased broadcasting *The Cosby Show* in 2014, resumed airing reruns as of December 19, 2016, drawing a mixed response from viewers. TV One resumed airing the series in May 2017.

11. Peter Sblendorio, "'Cosby Show' Star Malcolm-Jamal Warner Says Bill Cosby Scandal Is Costing Him Money," *Daily News* (March 6, 2016), http://www.nydailynews.com/entertainment/tv/cosby-show-star-show-cancelation-costing-article-1.2552090.

12. Bambi Haggins, *Laughing Mad: The Black Comic Persona in Post-Soul America* (New Brunswick, NJ: Rutgers University Press, 2007), 24. Michael Dyson and several others also quote this particular pronouncement.

13. Jewel Allison, "Bill Cosby Sexually Assaulted Me," *Washington Post* (March 6, 2015), https://www.washingtonpost.com/posteverything/wp/2015/03/06/bill-cosby-sexually-assaulted-me-i-didnt-tell-because-i-didnt-want-to-let-black-america-down/.

14. Orlando Patterson, "Race, Gender and Liberal Fallacies," *New York Times* (October 20, 1991), http://www.nytimes.com/1991/10/20/opinion/op-ed-race-gender-and-liberal-fallacies.html?pagewanted=all.

15. Sheldon Leonard, *And the Show Goes On: Broadway and Hollywood Adventures* (New York: Proscenium, 1994), 131. Where page numbers are given, quotations are from the autobiography.

16. Leonard, *And the Show Goes On*, 131.

17. Leonard, *And the Show Goes On*, 145.

18. Sheldon Leonard, archive interview, part 3 of 5, https://www.youtube.com/watch?v=asxkvWyhyRE. Quotations are from my transcription unless otherwise indicated. Leonard, *And the Show Goes On*, 131, 145–147.

19. Herman Gray, *Watching Race: Television and the Struggle for "Blackness"* (Minneapolis: University of Minnesota Press, 1995), 91.

20. Alison Hewitt, "'Black'-Sounding Name Conjures a Larger, More Dangerous Person," UCLA News (October 7, 2015), https://www.universityofcalifornia.edu/news/5494/black-sounding-name-conjures-larger-more-dangerous-person.

21. Gray, *Watching Race*, 80.

22. Patricia J. Williams, *The Rooster's Egg: On the Persistence of Prejudice* (Cambridge, MA: Harvard University Press, 1995), 83.

23. Leonard, *And the Show Goes On*, 171–172.

24. Williams, *Rooster's Egg*, 84.

25. Donald Bogle, *Primetime Blues: African Americans on Network Television* (New York: Farrar, Straus and Giroux, 2001), 372–373.

26. Tim Arango, "Before Obama, There Was Bill Cosby," *New York Times* (November 7, 2008), http://www.nytimes.com/2008/11/08/arts/television/08cosb.html?_r=0.

27. William H. Cosby Jr., *Fatherhood* (New York: Berkley, 1986), 15; Bob Herbert, "No Mercy for Autumn," *New York Times* (July 11, 1997), http://www.nytimes.com/1997/07/11/opinion/no-mercy-for-autumn.html?rref=collection%2Ftimestopic%2FJackson%2C%20Autumn&action=click&contentCollection=timestopics&region=stream&module=stream_unit&version=latest&contentPlacement=4&pgtype=collection.

28. John J. Goldman, "Cosby Testifies about Secret Payments," *Los Angeles Times* (July 16, 1997), http://articles.latimes.com/1997/jul/16/news/mn-13121.

29. Bogle, *Primetime Blues*, 372–373.

30. Goldman, "Cosby."

31. Herbert, "No Mercy for Autumn."

32. In 1999, the U.S. Court of Appeals overturned Jackson's conviction on the grounds that the judge erred in instructing the jury that the issue of paternity was irrelevant, ruling, according to the *New York Times*, that "the jury should have been allowed to consider whether Ms. Jackson believed she had a rightful claim to the money in light of her contention that Mr. Cosby was her father." Jackson was briefly released from prison, but the Appeals Court promptly reversed itself and reinstated her conviction in light of a U.S. Supreme Court ruling on jury instruction that came down just one day after the Appeals Court's decision in Jackson's favor. The Supreme Court ruled that errors in jury instruction are deemed "harmless when they could not have affected the jury's verdict." The prosecuting U.S. attorney argued that no rational juror would have agreed with Jackson's sense of entitlement. The Appeals Court three-judge panel agreed, and Jackson's conviction was reinstated. I'm not a lawyer; I just see them played on TV. But if jurors are allowed to consider "intent" in felony murder cases—that is, the accused's state of mind, what he or she believed—why not here? See Benjamin Weiser, "Judges Reinstate Conviction in Extortion of Bill Cosby," *New York Times* (November 10, 1999), http://www.nytimes.com/1999/11/16 /nyregion/judges-reinstate-conviction-in-extortion-of-bill-cosby.html.

33. My father is mentioned several times in J. Anthony Lukas's Pulitzer Prize–winning study of race relations in Boston before and during the turbulent years surrounding the desegregation and busing orders in the 1970s. See J. Anthony Lukas, *Common Ground: A Turbulent Decade in the Lives of Three American Families*, rev. ed. (New York: Vintage Books, 1986), 407–411, 633, 637. See also Gloria Negri, "Adrian duCille, Affordable Housing Activist," *Boston Globe* (August 1, 2006): E8.

34. *Julius Caesar*, 3.1.254–275.

10. The "Thug Default"

1. Kristen West Savali, "Why Do All the Superheroes Have to Be White, and All the Thugs Black?," *The Root* (May 27, 2015), http://www.theroot.com/why-do-all-the -superheroes-have-to-be-white-and-all-th-1790859955.

2. "Bill Maher Calls Obama 'Wimpy,' 'Wussy,' on 'Fareed Zakaria GPS,'" *Huffington Post* (December 12, 2010), http://www.huffingtonpost.com/2010/12/05/bill-maher-obama-cnn _n_792223.html; Natalie Finn, "Wayne Brady Slams Bill Maher over Obama Comparison, Says *Real Time* Host No Expert on Being Black," *E! News* (May 15, 2013), http://www .eonline.com/news/419411/wayne-brady-slams-bill-maher-over-obama-comparison-says -real-time-host-no-expert-on-being-black.

3. Transcript of George Zimmerman's 911 call to the Stanford Police Department, February 26, 2012, https://www.documentcloud.org/documents/326700-full-transcript -zimmerman.html.

4. From the *Oxford English Dictionary*, http://www.oxforddictionaries.com/us/definition /american_english/thug.

5. See, for example, Martine van Woerkens, *The Strangled Traveler: Colonial Imaginings and the Thugs of India* (Chicago: University of Chicago Press, 2002); and Lakshmi

Gandhi, "What a Thug's Life Looked Like in 19th Century India," *Code Switch*, National Public Radio (November 18, 2013), http://www.npr.org/sections/codeswitch/2013/11/18 /245953619/what-a-thugs-life-looked-like-in-nineteenth-century-india.

6. Tricia Rose, *The Hip Hop Wars: What We Talk about When We Talk about Hip Hop—and Why It Matters* (New York: Basic Books, 2008), 2–3.

7. Rose, *Hip Hop Wars*, 138–139.

8. Kevin Drum, "A Very Brief History of Super-Predators," *Mother Jones* (March 3, 2016), http://www.motherjones.com/kevin-drum/2016/03/very-brief-history-super-predators.

9. Clips of Hillary Clinton's remarks, delivered during a campaign speech at Keene State College on January 28, 1996, are widely available for viewing on YouTube.

10. John J. DiIulio Jr., "The Coming of the Super-Predators," *Weekly Standard* (November 27, 1995), http://www.weeklystandard.com/the-coming-of-the-super-predators/article /8160.

11. Clyde Haberman, "When Youth Violence Spurred 'Superpredator' Fear," *New York Times* (April 7, 2014), http://www.nytimes.com/2014/04/07/us/politics/killing-on-bus -recalls-superpredator-threat-of-90s.html.

12. Cara Shousterman, "Anything You Say Can and Will Be Used against You: The Case of 'Wilding,'" *Word* (July 3, 2014), https://africanamericanenglish.com/2014/07/03 /anything-you-say-can-and-will-be-used-against-you-the-case-of-wilding/.

13. Oliver Laughland, "Donald Trump and the Central Park Five: The Racially Charged Rise of a Demagogue," *Guardian* (February 17, 2016), http://www.theguardian.com/us -news/2016/feb/17/central-park-five-donald-trump-jogger-rape-case-new-york.

14. The designation became official with the release of the 2012 PBS documentary *The Central Park Five*, directed by the legendary filmmaker Ken Burns and his daughter Sarah Burns.

15. Washington's Best Actor Oscar for *Training Day* was his second Academy Award. His first was for a supporting role in *Glory* in 1989. Halle Berry, who played a crack addict in *Losing Isaiah*, won Best Actress honors for *Monster's Ball* in 2002.

16. Haberman, "When Youth Violence Spurred 'Superpredator' Fear."

17. Donald Trump, "Central Park Five Settlement Is a 'Disgrace,'" *Daily News* (June 21, 2014), http://www.nydailynews.com/new-york/nyc-crime/donald-trump-central-park -settlement-disgrace-article-1.1838467.

18. Leslie Bennetts, "Rogue Star," *Vanity Fair* (February 7, 2011), http://www.vanityfair .com/news/2001/08/mark-wahlberg-200108.

19. Brief for Jeffrey Fagan, Deborah Baskin, Frank R. Baumgartner, et al. as Amicus Curiae, p. 8, *Jackson v. Hobbs* and *Miller v. Alabama*, Supreme Court of the United States 10-9647, 10-9646 (2012), https://eji.org/sites/default/files/miller-amicus-jeffrey-fagan.pdf.

20. "U.S. Supreme Court Bans Mandatory Life-without-Parole Sentences for Children Convicted of Homicide," Equal Justice Initiative (June 25, 2012), https://eji.org/news/supreme -court-bans-mandatory-life-without-parole-sentences-for-children-miller-v-alabama.

21. Haberman, "When Youth Violence Spurred 'Superpredator' Fear."

22. Kyle Wagner, "The Word 'Thug' Was Uttered 625 Times on TV on Monday. That's a Lot," *Deadspin.com* (January 21, 2014), http://regressing.deadspin.com/the-word-thug -was-uttered-625-times-on-tv-yesterday-1506098319.

23. Ryan Wilson, "Richard Sherman: 'Thug' Is Accepted Way of Calling Someone N-Word," CBS Interactive (January 22, 2014), http://www.cbssports.com/nfl/eye-on-football /24417234.

24. Melissa Block, interview with John McWhorter, *All Things Considered*, National Public Radio (April 30, 2015), http://www.npr.org/2015/04/30/403362626/the-racially -charged-meaning-behind-the-word-thug.

25. "Globetrotters Cleared," *Spokane Chronicle* (December 14, 1983), A6.

26. Mary A. Fischer, "Three Harlem Globetrotters Come Up Short in a Case of Jewel-Heist Mistaken Identity," *People* 21, no. 6 (February 13, 1984), http://people.com/archive /three-harlem-globetrotters-come-up-short-in-a-case-of-jewel-heist-mistaken-identity -vol-21-no-6/.

27. See Roger L. Abel, *The Black Shields* (Bloomington, IN: AuthorHouse, 2006).

28. Dana Ford, "Chief: Shot That Killed Detective 'Deliberately Aimed' by Another Officer," CNN (March 16, 2016), http://www.cnn.com/2016/03/16/us/maryland-police-officer -killed/index.html.

29. Accounts of the Stuart case are legend and legion. See among the many detailed summaries, Fox Butterfield with Constance Hays, "A Boston Tragedy: The Stuart Case—a Special Case; Motive Remains a Mystery in Deaths That Haunt a City," *New York Times* (January 14, 1990), http://www.nytimes.com/1990/01/15/us/boston-tragedy-stuart-case -special-case-motive-remains-mystery-deaths-that-haunt.html?pagewanted=all.

30. Montgomery Brower, Dirk Mathison, and S. Avery Brown, "A Dark Night of the Soul in Boston," *People* 32, no. 20 (November 13, 1989), http://www.people.com/people /archive/article/0,,20115915,00.html.

31. Delores Handy, "The Murder That Forced a Divided Boston to Reflect," WBUR News, Boston Public Radio (October 23, 2009), http://legacy.wbur.org/2009/10/23/charles -stuart-anniversary.

32. Margaret Carlson, "Presumed Innocent," *Time* (June 24, 2001), http://www.time .com/time/magazine/article/0,9171,153650,00.html.

33. Jim Naughton, "The Murder That Ravaged Boston," *Washington Post* (January 8, 1990), https://www.washingtonpost.com/archive/lifestyle/1990/01/08/the-murder-that -ravaged-boston/d87d8b55-cff5-44a0-9668-f6aee4214ca6/?utm_term=.dce7c6ad44ca.

34. Carlson, "Presumed Innocent."

35. Walter Goodman, "Review/Television; the Role of Journalists in the Stuart Case *New York Times* (January 25, 1990), http://www.nytimes.com/1990/01/25/arts/review -television-the-role-of-journalists-in-the-stuart-case.html.

36. Butterfield, "Boston Tragedy."

37. Carlson, "Presumed Innocent."

38. Tony Dokoupil, "What Adopting a White Girl Taught One Black Family," *Newsweek* (May 4, 2009), http://www.newsweek.com/what-adopting-white-girl-taught-one-black -family-77335.

39. Alice Randall, "Black Women and Fat," *New York Times* (May 5, 2012), http://www .nytimes.com/2012/05/06/opinion/sunday/why-black-women-are-fat.html.

Epilogue

1. Richard Sandomir, "Zoeller Learns Race Remarks Carry a Price," *New York Times* (April 24, 1997), http://www.nytimes.com/1997/04/24/sports/zoeller-learns-race-remarks -carry-a-price.html.

2. This particular episode aired on January 16, 2013.

BIBLIOGRAPHY

Abel, Roger L. *The Black Shields*. Bloomington, IN: AuthorHouse, 2006.

Abramovitch, Seth. "Oscar's First Black Winner Accepted Her Honor in a Segregated 'No Blacks' Hotel in L.A." *Hollywood Reporter*, February 19, 2015. http://www.hollywoodreporter.com/features/oscars-first-black-winner-accepted-774335.

Acham, Christine. *Revolution Televised: Prime Time and the Struggle for Black Power*. Minneapolis: University of Minnesota Press, 2004.

African American Policy Forum and Center for Intersectionality and Social Policy Studies. "Black Girls Matter: Pushed Out, Overpoliced and Underprotected." December 30, 2014. http://www.atlanticphilanthropies.org/app/uploads/2015/09/BlackGirlsMatterReport.pdf.

Aizenman, Nurith C. "Chesapeake Summer: A Haven for Blacks and History." *Washington Post*, August 20, 2002, B1, B7.

Alexander, Michelle. "Why Hillary Clinton Doesn't Deserve the Black Vote." *The Nation*, February 10, 2016. http://www.thenation.com/article/hillary-clinton-does-not-deserve-black-peoples-votes/.

Alexander, Michelle. *The New Jim Crow: Mass Incarceration in the Age of Colorblindness*. New York: New Press, 2011.

Allen, Steve. "Talent Is Color-Blind." *Ebony* 10, no. 11 (September 1955): 41–49.

Allison, Jewel. "Bill Cosby Sexually Assaulted Me." *Washington Post*, March 6, 2015. https://www.washingtonpost.com/posteverything/wp/2015/03/06/bill-cosby-sexually-assaulted-me-i-didnt-tell-because-i-didnt-want-to-let-black-america-down/.

Arango, Tim. "Before Obama, There Was Bill Cosby." *New York Times*, November 7, 2008. http://www.nytimes.com/2008/11/08/arts/television/08cosb.html?_r=0.

Armstrong, Lois. "Interracial Love in the Afternoon? TV Soaps Aren't Ready for It, Tina Andrews Finds." *People* 7, no. 24 (June 20, 1977). http://www.people.com/people/archive/article/0,,20068128,00.html.

Ayers, Mike. "The Soul of 'Scandal': How Shonda Rhimes Soundtracks TV's Most Dramatic Show." *Billboard*, April 17, 2014. http://www.billboard.com/articles/columns/pop-shop/6062363/the-soul-of-scandal-how-shonda-rhimes-soundtracks-tvs-most.

Banks, Taunya Lovell. "Here Comes the Judge! Gender Distortion on TV Reality Court Shows." *Law Forum* 39, no. 1 (Fall 2008): 37–56.

Barnes, Brooks, and John Koblin. "Channing Dungey to Succeed Paul Lee as Chief of ABC Entertainment." *New York Times*, February 17, 2016. http://www.nytimes.com/2016/02/18/business/media/paul-lee-resign-abc-entertainment.html.

Basinger, Jeanine. *A Woman's View: How Hollywood Spoke to Women, 1930–1960.* Hanover, NH: Wesleyan University Press, 1993.

Bennetts, Leslie. "Rogue Star." *Vanity Fair*, February 7, 2011. http://www.vanityfair.com/news/2001/08/mark-wahlberg-200108.

"Bill Maher Calls Obama 'Wimpy,' 'Wussy' on 'Fareed Zakaria GPS.'" *Huffington Post*, December 12, 2010. http://www.huffingtonpost.com/2010/12/05/bill-maher-obama-cnn_n_792223.html.

Bingham, John. "TV Drama Is the New Literature, Says Salman Rushdie." *Telegraph*, June 12, 2011. http://www.telegraph.co.uk/culture/books/booknews/8571010/TV-drama-is-the-new-literature-says-Salman-Rushdie.html.

Blankstein, Andrew, Tom Winter, and Daniel Arkin. "Judge Explains Why He Unsealed Bill Cosby Court Documents." NBC News, July 7, 2015. http://www.nbcnews.com/news/us-news/judge-explains-why-he-unsealed-bill-cosby-court-documents-n387861.

Block, Alex Ben. "Daytime Ratings: Black Viewers Driving Gains for Steve Harvey, 'Live with Kelly and Michael.'" *Hollywood Reporter*, June 6, 2014. http://www.hollywoodreporter.com/news/daytime-ratings-black-viewers-driving-709049.

Block, Melissa. Interview with John McWhorter. *All Things Considered*, National Public Radio, April 30, 2015. http://www.npr.org/2015/04/30/403362626/the-racially-charged-meaning-behind-the-word-thug.

Blow, Charles M. "Thomas Speaks . . . Blindly about Race." *New York Times*, February 12, 2014. http://www.nytimes.com/2014/02/13/opinion/blow-thomas-speaks-blindly-about-race.html?nl=todaysheadlines&emc=edit_th_20140213&_r=0c.

Boboltz, Sara. "Awful '50s Marriage Advice Shows What Our Mothers and Grandmothers Were Up Against." *Huffington Post*, September 26, 2014. http://www.huffingtonpost.com/2014/09/26/can-this-marriage-be-saved-advice_n_5829870.html.

Bodroghkozy, Aniko. *Equal Time: Television and the Civil Rights Movement.* Urbana-Champaign: University of Illinois Press, 2013.

Bogart, Leo. "TV Viewing in Its Social Gathering." In *The Age of Television: A Study of Viewing Habits and the Impact of Television on American Life*, edited by Leo Bogart. New York: Ungar, 1958.

Bogle, Donald. *Primetime Blues: African Americans on Network Television.* New York: Farrar, Straus and Giroux, 2001.

Bogle, Donald. *Toms, Coons, Mulattoes, Mammies, and Bucks.* New York: Continuum, 1973.

Bowie, Stephen W. "*East Side/West Side.*" http://classictvhistory.com/EpisodeGuides/east_side_west_side.html.

Bowman, Barbara. "Bill Cosby Raped Me: Why Did It Take 30 Years for People to Believe My Story?" *Washington Post*, November 13, 2014. https://www.washingtonpost.com/posteverything/wp/2014/11/13/bill-cosby-raped-me-why-did-it-take-30-years-for-people-to-believe-my-story/.

Braxton, Greg, and Meg James. "Daytime TV Is Embracing Black Entertainers; Prime Time, Less So." *Los Angeles Times*, November 9, 2013. http://touch.latimes.com /#section/-1/article/p2p-78110838/.

Brief for Jeffrey Fagan, Deborah Baskin, Frank R. Baumgartner, et al. as Amicus Curiae, p. 8, *Jackson v. Hobbs* and *Miller v. Alabama*, Supreme Court of the United States 10-9647, 10-9646 (2012). https://eji.org/sites/default/files/miller-amicus-jeffrey-fagan .pdf.

Brock, David. *Blinded by the Right: The Conscience of an Ex-conservative*. New York: Crown, 2002.

Brock, David. *The Real Anita Hill*. New York: Free Press, 1993.

Brower, Montgomery, Dirk Mathison, and S. Avery Brown. "A Dark Night of the Soul in Boston." *People* 32, no. 20 (November 13, 1989). http://www.people.com/people/archive /article/0,,20115915,00.html.

Brown, Stacia L. "*Scandal* Keeps Missing Opportunities to Address Olivia's Mental Health." *Washington Post*, April 8, 2016. https://www.washingtonpost.com/news/act -four/wp/2016/04/08/scandal-keeps-missing-opportunities-to-address-olivia-popes -mental-health/?utm_term=.e328eb5cdb91.

Brown, Tammy L. "An Interview with John Amos." In *African Americans on Television: Race-ing for Ratings*, edited by David J. Leonard and Lisa A. Guerrero, 34–44. Santa Barbara, CA: Praeger, 2013.

Buckman, Adam. "Sherri Shepherd's Naughty New 'Newlywed Game.'" *Xfinity TV Blog*, November 1, 2010. http://xfinity.comcast.net/blogs/tv/2010/11/01/sherri-shepherds -naughty-new-newlywed-game/.

Bueno, Antoinette. "Janice Dickinson Details Bill Cosby Sexual Assault Accusations: He Raped Me." *Entertainment Tonight Online*, November 18, 2014. http://www.etonline .com/news/154076_janice_dickinson_details_alleged_bill_cosby_sexual_assault/.

Burton, Nsenga K. "How Did Blacks Travel during Segregation?" *The Root*, July 9, 2012. http://www.theroot.com/articles/culture/2012/07/black_history_road_trip_negro _motorist_green_book_destinations/.

Bush, George H. W. "Remarks by the President at Presentation of Medal of Freedom." White House press release, July 9, 2002. http://georgewbush-whitehouse.archives.gov /news/releases/2002/07/20020709-8.html.

Butterfield, Fox, with Constance Hays. "A Boston Tragedy: The Stuart Case—a Special Case; Motive Remains a Mystery in Deaths That Haunt a City." *New York Times*, January 14, 1990. http://www.nytimes.com/1990/01/15/us/boston-tragedy-stuart-case -special-case-motive-remains-mystery-deaths-that-haunt.html?pagewanted=all.

Cannon, Carl M. "Hollywood Who's Who Marched with King in '63." *Real Clear Politics*, August 29, 2013. http://www.realclearpolitics.com/articles/2013/08/29/hollywood _whos_who_marched_with_king_in_63__119762.html.

Carlson, Margaret. "Presumed Innocent." *Time*, June 24, 2001. http://content.time.com /time/magazine/article/0,9171,153650,00.html.

The Central Park Five. Directed by Ken Burns, Sarah Burns, and David McMahon. Walpole, NH: Florentine Films, 2012.

Chilton, Karen. *Hazel Scott: The Pioneering Journey of a Jazz Pianist from Café Society to Hollywood to HUAC*. Ann Arbor: University of Michigan Press, 2010.

Chin, Frank, and Jeffery Paul Chan. "Racist Love." In *Seeing through Shuck*, edited by Richard Kostelanetz, 65–79. New York: Ballantine, 1972.

"'Civil Rights' Theater Has New Show on Broadway." *St. Joseph News-Press*, May 9, 1965, 21. https://news.google.com/newspapers?id=idBTAAAAIBAJ&sjid=xDgNAAAAIBAJ&pg =740,1497104&dq=frank+silvera+the+theatre+of+being&hl=en.

Clark, Dick, and Richard Robinson, *Rock, Roll and Remember*. New York: Thomas Y. Cromwell, 1976.

Cole, Nat King. "Why I Quit My TV Show." *Ebony* 13, no. 4 (February 1958): 29.

Cosby, William H., Jr. "Dr. Bill Cosby Speaks." http://www.rci.rutgers.edu/~schochet/101 /Cosby_Speech.htm.

Cosby, William H., Jr. *Fatherhood*. New York: Berkley, 1986.

Del Barco, Mandalit. "Does Disney's Tonto Reinforce Stereotypes or Overcome Them?" *Morning Edition*, National Public Radio, July 2, 2013. http://www.npr.org/sections /codeswitch/2013/07/02/196333864/does-disneys-tonto-reinforce-stereotypes-or -overcome-them.

Delmont, Matthew F. "Clark Aided Blacks on 'Bandstand'?" *The Root*, April 20, 2012. http://www.theroot.com/clark-aided-blacks-on-bandstand-1790891075.

Delmont, Matthew F. *Making "Roots": A Nation Captivated*. Berkeley: University of California Press, 2016.

Delmont, Matthew F. *The Nicest Kids in Town: American Bandstand, Rock 'n' Roll, and the Struggle for Civil Rights in 1950s Philadelphia*. Berkeley: University of California Press, 2012.

DiIulio, John J., Jr. "The Coming of the Super-Predators." *Weekly Standard*, November 27, 1995. http://www.weeklystandard.com/the-coming-of-the-super-predators/article/8160.

Dodero, Camille. "*Judge Judy*'s Cat-Killing-Hipster Plaintiff Speaks: An Interview with Teeth Mountain's Kate Levitt and Andrew Burt." *Village Voice*, March 30, 2010. http:// www.villagevoice.com/music/judge-judys-cat-killing-hipster-plaintiff-speaks-an -interview-with-teeth-mountains-kate-levitt-and-andrew-burt-6646226.

Doherty, Thomas. "Storied TV: Cable Is the New Novel." *Chronicle of Higher Education*, September 17, 2012. http://chronicle.com/article/Cable-Is-the-New-Novel/134420/.

Dokoupil, Tony. "What Adopting a White Girl Taught One Black Family." *Newsweek*, May 4, 2009. http://www.newsweek.com/what-adopting-white-girl-taught-one-black-family-77335.

Domanick, Joe. "A Shooting Reminiscent of the LAPD's Worst Days." *Los Angeles Times*, June 6, 1999. http://articles.latimes.com/1999/jun/06/opinion/op-44648.

Dreher, Kwakiutl L. "*Scandal* and Black Women in Television." In *African Americans on Television: Race-ing for Ratings*, edited by David J. Leonard and Lisa A. Guerrero, 390–401. Santa Barbara, CA: Praeger, 2013.

Dreier, Peter. "Sanford and Its Sons: From Jackie Robinson to Trayvon Martin." *Huffington Post*, September 13, 2013. http://www.huffingtonpost.com/peter-dreier/sanford-and -its-sons-from_b_3595577.html.

Drum, Kevin. "A Very Brief History of Super-Predators." *Mother Jones*, March 3, 2016. http://www.motherjones.com/kevin-drum/2016/03/very-brief-history-super-predators.

Du Bois, W. E. B. "The Talented Tenth." In *W. E. B. Du Bois: A Reader*, edited by David Levering Lewis, 347. New York: Holt, 1995.

duCille, Ann. "The Unbearable Darkness of Being: 'Fresh' Thoughts on Race, Sex, and the Simpsons." In *Birth of a Nation'hood*, edited by Toni Morrison and Claudia Brodsky Lacour, 293–328. New York: Pantheon, 1997.

duCille, Michel. "Documenting with Dignity in the Ebola Zone." *Washington Post*, October 19, 2014. https://www.washingtonpost.com/lifestyle/style/documenting-with -dignity-in-the-ebola-zone/2014/10/19/07c41fd2-5638-11e4-ba4b-f6333e2c0453_story .html?utm_term=.086bd8f5bb43.

Dunham, Lena. "It's No *SCANDALOUS* Secret, I Worship Kerry Washington." *Marie Claire*, April 2015.

Dunn, Katia, narr. "For Classic TV Producer, Good Times No Longer." *Weekend Edition*, National Public Radio, July 29, 2006.

Dyson, Michael Eric. *Is Bill Cosby Right? Or Has the Black Middle Class Lost Its Mind?* New York: Basic Civitas, 2006.

Ebert, Roger. "Review of I Spy." *Chicago Sun-Times*, November 1, 2002. http://www .rogerebert.com/reviews/i-spy-2002.

Edwards, Anne. *Shirley Temple: American Princess*. New York: William Morrow, 1988.

Ellis, John. *Visible Fictions*. London: Routledge, 1982.

Fanon, Frantz. *Black Skin, White Masks*. New York: Grove, 1967.

Feldstein, Ruth. *How It Feels to Be Free: Black Women Entertainers and the Civil Rights Movement*. New York: Oxford University Press, 2013.

Fernandez, Maria Elena. "Michael Strahan's Pairing with Kelly Ripa Surprising but Promising." *Daily Beast*, August 29, 2012. http://www.thedailybeast.com/articles/2012/08/29 /michael-strahan-s-pairing-with-kelly-ripa-surprising-but-promising.html.

Finn, Natalie. "Wayne Brady Slams Bill Maher over Obama Comparison, Says *Real Time* Host No Expert on Being Black." *E! News*, May 15, 2013. http://www.eonline.com/news /419411/wayne-brady-slams-bill-maher-over-obama-comparison-says-real-time-host -no-expert-on-being-black.

Firestone, David. "While Barbie Talks Tough, G.I. Joe Goes Shopping." *New York Times*, December 31, 1993. http://www.nytimes.com/1993/12/31/us/while-barbie-talks-tough-g -i-joe-goes-shopping.html?sec=&spon=&pagewanted=all.

Fischer, Mary A. "Three Harlem Globetrotters Come Up Short in a Case of Jewel-Heist Mistaken Identity." *People* 21, no. 6 (February 13, 1984). http://people.com/archive /three-harlem-globetrotters-come-up-short-in-a-case-of-jewel-heist-mistaken-identity -vol-21-no-6/.

Fiske, John. *Media Matters: Everyday Culture and Political Change*. Minneapolis: University of Minnesota Press, 1994.

Fiske, John. *Understanding Popular Culture*. London: Routledge, 1989.

Fiske, John. *Understanding Popular Culture*. 2nd ed., with an introduction by Henry Jenkins. New York: Routledge, 2010.

Fiske, John, and John Hartley. *Reading Television*. London: Methuen, 1978.

Fiske, John, and John Hartley. *Reading Television*. Revised ed., with a foreword by John Hartley. New York: Routledge, 2003.

Ford, Dana. "Chief: Shot That Killed Detective 'Deliberately Aimed' by Another Officer." CNN, March 16, 2016. http://www.cnn.com/2016/03/16/us/maryland-police-officer -killed/index.html.

"4 Reasons Michael Strahan Will Shine on *Live! with Kelly*." *The Week*, August 22, 2012. http://theweek.com/articles/472948/4-reasons-michael-strahan-shine-live-kelly.

Franz, Kathleen, and Susan Smulyan, eds. *Major Problems in American Popular Culture: Documents and Essays*. Boston: Wadsworth, 2012.

Friedman, Lawrence M. "Judge Judy's Justice." *Berkeley Journal of Entertainment and Sports Law* 1, no. 2 (April 2012): 123–133.

Friedman, Roger. "Exclusive: Bill Cosby Co-star Tony Winner Phylicia Rashad Speaks Out for the First Time, Defends Her Friend." *ShowBiz 411*, January 6, 2015. http://www .showbiz411.com/2015/01/06/exclusive-bill-cosby-co-star-tony-winner-phylicia-rashad -speaks-out-for-first-time-defends-her-friend.

Gaines, Kevin. *Uplifting the Race: Black Leadership, Politics, and Culture in the Twentieth Century.* Chapel Hill: University of North Carolina Press, 1996.

Gandhi, Lakshmi. "What a Thug's Life Looked Like in 19th Century India." *Code Switch*, National Public Radio, November 18, 2013. http://www.npr.org/sections /codeswitch/2013/11/18/245953619/what-a-thugs-life-looked-like-in-nineteenth -century-india.

Gates, Henry Louis, Jr. "TV's Black World Turns—but Stays Unreal." *New York Times*, November 12, 1989. http://www.nytimes.com/1989/11/12/arts/tv-s-black-world-turns -but-stays-unreal.html?pagewanted=all&src=pm.

Gates, Henry Louis, Jr. "Which Black Actor Was Paid to Be White?" *The Root*, October 27, 2014. http://www.theroot.com/articles/history/2014/10/which_black_actor_who _passed_for_white/.

Gates, Henry Louis, Jr., and Evelyn Brooks Higginbotham. *African American Lives.* New York: Oxford University Press, 2004.

Gay, Roxane. *Bad Feminist.* New York: Harper Perennial, 2014.

Genzlinger, Neil. "Adorable Baby, Doubting Dad, Teachable Moment: Revisiting 'That's My Boy??' on *The Dick Van Dyke Show.*" *New York Times*, September 24, 2013. http:// www.nytimes.com/2013/09/25/arts/television/revisiting-thats-my-boy-on-the-dick-van -dyke-show.html.

"Globetrotters Cleared." *Spokane Chronicle*, December 14, 1983, A6.

Golden Age Radio Research. "Introduction to the Perry Mason Connection." http://www .digitaldeliftp.com/DigitalDeliToo/dd2-Research-Perry-Mason-Main.html.

Goldman, Andrew. "Dick Clark, Still the Oldest Living Teenager." *New York Times*, March 25, 2011. http://www.nytimes.com/2011/03/27/magazine/mag-27Talk-t.html.

Goldman, Andrew. "Order! Order in Judge Judy's Court!" *New York Times Magazine*, June 24, 2011. http://www.nytimes.com/2011/06/26/magazine/judge-judy-has-her-day -in-court.html?_r=0.

Goldman, John J. "Cosby Testifies about Secret Payments." *Los Angeles Times*, July 16, 1997. http://articles.latimes.com/1997/jul/16/news/mn-13121.

Goodman, Walter. "Review/Television; the Role of Journalists in the Stuart Case." *New York Times*, January 25, 1990. http://www.nytimes.com/1990/01/25/arts/review -television-the-role-of-journalists-in-the-stuart-case.html.

Goyette, Braden. "Cheerios Commercial Featuring Mixed Race Family Gets Racist Backlash." *Huffington Post*, May 31, 2013. http://www.huffingtonpost.com/2013/05/31 /cheerios-commercial-racist-backlash_n_3363507.html.

Gray, Herman. *Watching Race: Television and the Struggle for "Blackness."* Minneapolis: University of Minnesota Press, 1995.

Gray, Tim. "Hollywood Turned Out for Historic 'I Have a Dream' Speech." *Variety*, August 28, 2015. http://variety.com/2015/biz/columns/1963-march-on-washington -hollywood-bob-dylan-sidney-poitier-1201580118/.

Greene, Graham. "Review of Captain January." *Spectator*, August 1936. In *The Graham Greene Film Reader: Reviews, Essays, Interviews and Film Stories*, edited by David Parkinson, 128. New York: Applause, 1995.

Gubar, Susan. *Racechanges: White Skin, Black Face in American Culture*. New York: Oxford University Press, 1997.

Guterl, Matthew Pratt. *Seeing Race in Modern America*. Chapel Hill: University of North Carolina Press, 2013.

Haberman, Clyde. "When Youth Violence Spurred 'Superpredator' Fear." *New York Times*, April 7, 2014. www.nytimes.com/2014/04/07/us/politics/killing-on-bus-recalls -superpredator-threat-of-90s.html.

Hagedorn, Jessica, ed. *Charlie Chan Is Dead: An Anthology of Contemporary Asian American Fiction*. New York: Penguin, 1993.

Haggins, Bambi. *Laughing Mad: The Black Comic Persona in Post-Soul America*. New Brunswick, NJ: Rutgers University Press, 2007.

Handy, Delores. "The Murder That Forced a Divided Boston to Reflect." WBUR News, Boston Public Radio, October 23, 2009. http://legacy.wbur.org/2009/10/23/charles -stuart-anniversary.

Harnick, Chris. "Kelly Ripa, Michael Strahan, and Gelman Talk 'Live! with Kelly and Michael.'" *Huffington Post*, September 4, 2012. http://www.huffingtonpost.com/2012/09 /04/kelly-ripa-michael-strahan-live-with-michael-and-kelly_n_1854576.html.

Harvey, Steve. *Act Like a Lady, Think Like a Man: What Men Really Think about Love, Relationships, Intimacy, and Commitment*. New York: Amistad, 2009.

Haskins, Jim, and N. R. Mitgang. *Mr. Bojangles: The Biography of Bill Robinson*. New York: William Morrow, 1988.

Hawtree, Christopher, ed. *Night and Day: Selections*. London: Chatto and Windus, 1986.

Herbert, Bob. "No Mercy for Autumn." *New York Times*, July 11, 1997. http://www.nytimes .com/1997/07/11/opinion/no-mercy-for-autumn.html?rref=collection%2Ftimestopic% 2FJackson%2C%20Autumn&action=click&contentCollection=timestopics&region =stream&module=stream_unit&version=latest&contentPlacement=4&pgtype =collection.

Hernandéz, Daisy. "4 Reasons Why *Scandal* Is a Telenovela—and a Good One." *Code Switch*, National Public Radio, November 20, 2014. http://www.npr.org/sections/codeswitch /2014/11/20/365457210/4-reasons-why-scandal-is-a-telenovela-and-a-good-one.

Hewitt, Alison. "'Black'-Sounding Name Conjures a Larger, More Dangerous Person." UCLA News, October 7, 2015. https://www.universityofcalifornia.edu/news/5494/black -sounding-name-conjures-larger-more-dangerous-person.

Higginbotham, Evelyn Brooks. *Righteous Discontent: The Women's Movement in the Black Church, 1880–1920*. Cambridge, MA: Harvard University Press, 1994.

Hill Collins, Patricia. *Black Sexual Politics*. New York: Routledge, 2004.

Hinton, Garfield. "The 'Man with a Thousand Faces' Comes to Baltimore." *Baltimore Afro-American*, April 2, 1956. https://news.google.com/newspapers?id=ReclAAAAIBAJ&sjid =bPUFAAAAIBAJ&pg=3807,1918500&dq=frank+silvera+actors+studio&hl=en.

Hoerschelmann, Olaf. *Rules of the Game: Quiz Shows and American Culture*. Albany: State University of New York Press, 2006.

Huang, Yunte. *Charlie Chan: The Untold Story of the Honorable Detective and His Rendezvous with American History*. New York: W. W. Norton, 2010.

Hunt, Darnell M., ed. *Channeling Blackness: Studies on Television and Race in America.* New York: Oxford University Press, 2005.

Hurston, Zora Neale. "Characteristics of Negro Expression." In *Hurston: Folklore, Memoirs, and Other Writings*, edited by Cheryl Wall, 839. New York: Literary Classics, 1995.

Hurston, Zora Neale. "How It Feels to Be Colored Me (1928)." In *Hurston: Folklore, Memoirs, and Other Writings*, edited by Cheryl Wall, 826. New York: Literary Classics, 1995.

Jackson, John A. *American Bandstand: Dick Clark and the Making of a Rock 'n' Roll Empire.* New York: Oxford University Press, 1999.

James, Meg, and Greg Braxton. "Black Daytime TV Hosts Are among the Most Bankable Stars." *Los Angeles Times*, November 11, 2013. http://touch.latimes.com/#section/-1/article/p2p-78141247/.

Japp, Debra K. "*Judge Judy* and *Dr. Phil*: Advice with an Attitude." In *Communication Ethics, Media, and Popular Culture*, edited by Phyllis M. Japp, Mark Meister, and Debra K. Japp, 291–292. New York: Peter Lang, 2005.

Jen, Gish. "Challenging the Asian Illusion." *New York Times*, August 11, 1991. http://www.nytimes.com/1991/08/11/arts/challenging-the-asian-illusion.html?pagewanted=all.

Johnson, Ted. "When Brando Marched with Heston: How *Variety* Covered the March on Washington." *Variety*, August 27, 2013. http://variety.com/2013/voices/columns/when-marlon-brando-marched-with-charlton-heston-how-variety-covered-the-march-on-washington-1200589376/.

Joyce, James. *Dubliners.* New York: Penguin Classics, 1993.

Joyrich, Lynne. *Re-viewing Reception: Television, Gender, and Postmodern Culture.* Bloomington: Indiana University Press, 1996.

"Judge Judy DESTROYS Obama-Supporting Welfare Cheat." *Political Insider*, December 28, 2015. http://www.thepoliticalinsider.com/judge-judy-destroys-obama-supporting-welfare-cheat/.

Kabia v. Koch, 186 Misc.2d 363 (N.Y. Misc. 2000). https://casetext.com/case/kabia-v-koch.

Kenneally, Tim. "MLK's Son Launching 1st African-American-Targeted Broadcast Net." *The Wrap*, April 4, 2011. http://www.thewrap.com/tv/article/martin-luther-king-iii-launching-first-broadcast-network-african-americans-26143/.

Kim, Elaine. *Asian American Literature: An Introduction to the Writings and Their Social Context.* Philadelphia: Temple University Press, 1984.

Kimball, Philip Z. "Syndi-Court Justice: Judge Judy and Exploitation of Arbitration." http://www.americanbar.org/content/dam/aba/migrated/dispute/essay/syndicourtjustice.authcheckdam.pdf.

Kissell, Rick. "Ratings: 'Family Feud' Tops All of Syndication for First Time." *Variety*, June 23, 2015. http://variety.com/2015/tv/news/family-feud-ratings-tops-syndication-1201526217/.

Knoedelseder, William K. "It's Kaput for TV Soapdom's Only Interracial Couple." *Washington Post*, May 31, 1977. https://www.washingtonpost.com/archive/lifestyle/1977/05/31/its-kaput-for-tv-soapdoms-only-interracial-couple/fa351e52-e368-4d9d-bf3c-83a3156a6db6/.

LaBennett, Oneka. "What *Scandal*'s Civil Rights–Era Critique Says about Contemporary Black Women and Girls." *Ms.*, October 29, 2015. http://msmagazine.com/blog/2015/10/29/what-scandals-civil-rights-era-critique-says-about-contemporary-black-women-and-girls/.

Ladd-Taylor, Molly. "Eugenics, Sterilisation and Modern Marriage in the USA: The Strange Career of Paul Popenoe." *Gender and History* 13, no. 2 (August 2001): 298–327.

Lamb, Chris. "Jackie Robinson: Crossing the Line." *Los Angeles Times*, February 27, 2012. http://articles.latimes.com/2012/feb/27/opinion/la-oe-lamb-jackie-robinson-20120227.

Laughland, Oliver. "Donald Trump and the Central Park Five: The Racially Charged Rise of a Demagogue." *Guardian*, February 17, 2016. http://www.theguardian.com/us-news/2016/feb/17/central-park-five-donald-trump-jogger-rape-case-new-york.

Lear, Norman. *Even This I Get to Experience*. New York: Penguin, 2014.

Lee, Robert. "The 'Heathen Chinee' on God's Free Soil." In *Major Problems in American Popular Culture*, edited by Kathleen Franz and Susan Smulyan, 46–49. Belmont, CA: Wadsworth, 2012.

Lee, Robert. *Orientals: Asian Americans in Popular Culture*. Philadelphia: Temple University Press, 1999.

Lemon, Richard. "Black Is the Color of TV's Newest Stars." *Saturday Evening Post*, November 30, 1968, 82.

Leonard, David J., and Lisa A. Guerrero, eds. *African Americans on Television: Race-ing for Ratings*. Santa Barbara, CA: Praeger, 2013.

Leonard, Sheldon. *And the Show Goes On: Broadway and Hollywood Adventures*. New York: Proscenium, 1994.

Lepore, Jill. "Chan, the Man: On the Trail of the Honorable Detective." *New Yorker*, August 9, 2010. http://www.newyorker.com/magazine/2010/08/09/chan-the-man.

Lepore, Jill. "Fixed: The Rise of Marriage Therapy, and Other Dreams of Human Betterment." *New Yorker*, March 29, 2010. http://www.newyorker.com/magazine/2010/03/29/fixed.

Lester, Jasmine. "How to Get Away with Rape Culture." *Black Girl Dangerous*, December 2, 2014. https://www.bgdblog.org/2014/12/get-away-rape-culture/.

Lipsitz, George. *The Possessive Investment in Whiteness*. Philadelphia: Temple University Press, 1998.

Lord, Betty Bao. *In the Year of the Boar and Jackie Robinson*. New York: HarperCollins, 1984.

Loving v. Virginia. 338 U.S. 1. Sup. Ct. 1967. http://caselaw.findlaw.com/us-supreme-court/388/1.html.

Lukas, J. Anthony. *Common Ground: A Turbulent Decade in the Lives of Three American Families*. New York: Knopf, 1985.

Lukas, J. Anthony. *Common Ground: A Turbulent Decade in the Lives of Three American Families*. Revised ed. New York: Vintage, 1986.

Luther, Claudia. "John Forsythe Dies at 92." *Los Angeles Times*, April 3, 2010. http://articles.latimes.com/2010/apr/03/local/la-me-john-forsythe3-2010apr03.

Lynch, Rene. "Man Who Had 30 Kids with 11 Women Wants Child-Support Break." *Los Angeles Times*, May 18, 2012. http://articles.latimes.com/2012/may/18/nation/la-na-nn-tennessee-man-has-30-kids-20120518.

MacDonald, Fred J. *Blacks and White TV: African Americans in Television since 1948*. Chicago: Nelson Hall, 1992.

Madison, Lucy. "Fact-Checking Romney's '47 Percent' Comment." CBS News, September 25, 2012. http://www.cbsnews.com/news/fact-checking-romneys-47-percent-comment/.

McDonald, Soraya Nadia. "The Lasting Appeal of TV's Top Woman: Judge Judy." *Washington Post*, March 3, 2015. https://www.washingtonpost.com/news/morning-mix/wp/2015/03/03/the-lasting-appeal-of-tvs-top-woman-judge-judy/.

McKenzie, Sheena. "Uncovered Footage Reveals TV's 'First' Interracial Kiss, Long before *Star Trek*." CNN, November 20, 2015. http://www.cnn.com/2015/11/20/world/first-interracial-kiss-on-tv/.

Meyer, Eugene L. "A Welcoming Enclave with Roots in a Snub." *New York Times*, September 9, 2009. http://www.nytimes.com/2009/09/04/greathomesanddestinations/04Highland.html?_r=0.

Minzesheimer, Bob. "How the 'Oprah Effect' Changed Publishing." *USA Today*, May 22, 2011. http://usatoday30.usatoday.com/life/books/news/2011-05-22-Oprah-Winfrey-Book-Club_n.htm.

Mitovich, Matt Webb. "*Scandal*'s Kerry Washington: Olivia Pope Should Be 'Nobody's Role Model.'" *TVLine*, August 4, 2015. http://tvline.com/2015/08/04/scandal-season-5-olivia-fitz-still-together/.

Mittell, Jason. "Narrative Complexity." *Velvet Light Trap* 58 (Fall 2006): 29–40.

Moody, Nekesa Mumbi. "Critics Aside, Perry Reaches New Heights with OWN, More Hits." Associated Press, April 5, 2016. http://bigstory.ap.org/article/e0eb828b634d4cdca096dadc81ea3cf0/critics-aside-perry-reaches-new-heights-own-more-hits.

Morrison, Toni. *Beloved*. New York: Alfred A. Knopf, 1987.

Morrison, Toni. *The Bluest Eye*. New York: Holt, Rinehart and Winston, 1970.

Morrison, Toni. *Playing in the Dark: Whiteness and the Literary Imagination*. Cambridge, MA: Harvard University Press, 1992.

Mother Jones. "Full Transcript of the Mitt Romney Secret Video." September 19, 2012. http://www.motherjones.com/politics/2012/09/full-transcript-mitt-romney-secret-video#47percent.

Murray, Jim. "Dodger Voice Found More Stylish Roles." *Los Angeles Times*, September 10, 2008. http://articles.latimes.com/1990-06-03/sports/sp-1004_1_resonant-voice.

Naughton, Jim. "The Murder That Ravaged Boston." *Washington Post*, January 8, 1990. https://www.washingtonpost.com/archive/lifestyle/1990/01/08/the-murder-that-ravaged-boston/d87d8b55-cff5-44a0-9668-f6aee4214ca6/?utm_term=.dce7c6ad44ca.

Negri, Gloria. "Adrian duCille, Affordable Housing Activist." *Boston Globe*, August 1, 2006, E8.

"Negro Performers Win Better Roles in TV Than in Any Other Entertainment Medium." *Ebony* 5, no. 8 (June 1950): 22–24.

Nelson, Robin. *TV Drama in Transition: Form, Values and Cultural Change*. London: Palgrave, 1997.

Nichols, John. "Edward Brooke and the Republican Party That Might Have Been." *Nation*, January 7, 2015. https://www.thenation.com/article/edward-brooke-and-republican-party-might-have-been/.

Nichols, Nichelle. *Beyond Uhura: Star Trek and Other Memories*. New York: G. P. Putnam's Sons, 1994.

The Nielsen Company, with the National Newspaper Publishers Association. *Resilient, Receptive and Relevant: The African-American Consumer: 2013 Report*. http://nnpa.org/wp-content/uploads/2013/06/African-American-Consumer-Report-2013.pdf.

"1960: First Televised Presidential Debate." *60 Minutes Overtime*, October 3, 2012. http://www.cbsnews.com/news/1960-first-televised-presidential-debate/.

Nussbaum, Emily. "American Untouchable." *New Yorker*, December 7, 2015. http://www.newyorker.com/magazine/2015/12/07/american-untouchable.

Nussbaum, Emily. "Crass Warfare: Raunch and Ridicule on *Whitney* and *2 Broke Girls*." *New Yorker*, November 28, 2011. http://www.newyorker.com/magazine/2011/11/28/crass -warfare.

Nussbaum, Emily. "Difficult Women: How 'Sex and the City' Lost Its Good Name." *New Yorker*, July 29, 2013. http://www.newyorker.com/magazine/2013/07/29/difficult -women.

Obituary for Raymond Burr. *Baltimore Sun*, September 21, 1993. http://articles .baltimoresun.com/1993-09-21/news/19932641941raymond-burr-perry-mason-burr -died.

Obituary for Raymond Burr. *Los Angeles Times*, September 13, 1993. http://articles.latimes .com/1993-09-13/news/mn-34829 1perry-mason-revival.

Oldenburg, Ann. "For Gayle King, Oprah Casts a Light, Not a Shadow." *USA Today*, January 4, 2011. http://usatoday30.usatoday.com/life/television/news/2011-01-05 -gaylekingo5_VA_N.htm.

Omi, Michael, and Howard Winant. *Racial Formation in the United States*. 3rd ed. New York: Routledge, 2014.

"Orlando Shaw, Nashville Father with 22 Children by 14 Women, Sued for Unpaid Child Support." *Huffington Post*, June 7, 2013. http://www.huffingtonpost.com/2013/06/06 /orlando-shaw-father-22-children-14-women_n_3397397.html.

Papers of the NAACP, supplement to part 1, 1951–1955. http://cisupa.proquest.com/ksc _assets/catalog/1415_PapersNAACPPt1Supp195155.pdf.

Park, Haeyoun, Josh Keller, and Josh Williams. "The Faces of American Power, Nearly as White as the Oscar Nominees." *New York Times*, February 26, 2016. http://www .nytimes.com/interactive/2016/02/26/us/race-of-american-power.html?_r=1.

Paskin, Willa. "Shonda Rhimes: 'Calling a Show a "Guilty Pleasure"—It's Like Saying It's a Piece of Crap.'" *Salon.com*, February 10, 2013. http://www.salon.com/2013/02/10 /shonda_rhimes_calling_a_show_a_guilty_pleasure_—_it's_like_saying_its_a_piece _of_crap/.

Patterson, Orlando. "Race, Gender and Liberal Fallacies." *New York Times*, October 20, 1991. http://www.nytimes.com/1991/10/20/opinion/op-ed-race-gender-and-liberal -fallacies.html?pagewanted=all.

Podlas, Kimberlianne. "As Seen on TV: The Normative Influence of Syndi-Court on Con- temporary Litigiousness." *Jeffrey S. Moorad Sports Law Journal* 11, no. 1 (2004): 1–48.

Price, Paula Groves. "'New Normal' in American Television? Race, Gender, Black- ness, and the New Racism." In *African Americans on Television: Race-ing for Ratings*, edited by David J. Leonard and Lisa A. Guerrero, 434–442. Santa Barbara, CA: Praeger, 2013.

Purdum, Todd S. "A Police Shooting Death, a Study in Contrasts." *New York Times*, June 5, 1999. http://www.nytimes.com/1999/06/05/us/a-police-shooting-death-a-study -in-contrasts.html?pagewanted=all&_r=0.

Randall, Alice. "Black Women and Fat." *New York Times*, May 5, 2012. http://www.nytimes .com/2012/05/06/opinion/sunday/why-black-women-are-fat.html.

Raymond, Emilie. *Stars for Freedom: Hollywood, Black Celebrities, and the Civil Rights Movement*. Seattle: University of Washington Press, 2015.

Rice University News and Media. "African Americans Are the Most Likely to Value Post- secondary Education, According to First-Ever Houston Education Survey." November 12,

2013. http://news.rice.edu/2013/11/12/african-americans-are-the-most-likely-to-value
-postsecondary-education/.

Rigueur, Leah Wright. *The Loneliness of the Black Republican*. Princeton, NJ: Princeton
University Press, 2015.

Roberts, Dorothy E. "*Loving v. Virginia* as a Civil Rights Decision." *New York Law School
Law Review* 59, no. 1 (2014–2015): 175–209. http://www.nylslawreview.com/wp-content
/uploads/sites/16/2015/02/Volume-59-1.Roberts.pdf.

Robinson, Amelia. "Dayton Man: 'I've Got 12 Sons and 15 Daughters. I Have 27 All
Together.'" *Dayton Daily News*, September 6, 2013. http://www.daytondailynews.com
/news/news/crime-law/dayton-man-ive-got-12-sons-and-15-daughters-i-have/nZpKr/.

Robinson, Louie. "Bad Times on the 'Good Times' Set." *Ebony* 30, no. 11 (September 1975): 33–36, 38, 40, 42.

Romano, Renee C. *Race Mixing: Black-White Marriage in Postwar America*. Cambridge,
MA: Harvard University Press, 2003.

Rorke, Robert. "Size Matters." *New York Post*, September 7, 2012. http://nypost.com/2012
/09/07/size-matters-3/.

Rose, Tricia. *The Hip Hop Wars: What We Talk about When We Talk about Hip Hop—and
Why It Matters*. New York: Basic Books, 2008.

Sajak, Pat. "Talking about Race." *Ricochet*, August 6, 2010. https://ricochet.com/archives
/talking-about-race/.

Sandomir, Richard. "Zoeller Learns Race Remarks Carry a Price." *New York Times*,
April 24, 1997. http://www.nytimes.com/1997/04/24/sports/zoeller-learns-race-remarks
-carry-a-price.html.

Savali, Kristen West. "Why Do All the Superheroes Have to Be White, and All the Thugs
Black?" *The Root*, May 27, 2015. http://www.theroot.com/why-do-all-the-superheroes
-have-to-be-white-and-all-th-1790859955.

Sblendorio, Peter. "'Cosby Show' Star Malcolm-Jamal Warner Says Bill Cosby Scandal
Is Costing Him Money." *Daily News*, March 6, 2016. http://www.nydailynews.com
/entertainment/tv/cosby-show-star-show-cancelation-costing-article-1.2552090.

Shatner, William. *Star Trek Memories*. New York: HarperCollins, 1993.

Shousterman, Cara. "Anything You Say Can and Will Be Used against You: The Case
of 'Wilding.'" *Word*, July 3, 2014. https://africanamericanenglish.com/2014/07/03
/anything-you-say-can-and-will-be-used-against-you-the-case-of-wilding/.

Slotkin, Richard. "Unit Pride: Ethnic Platoons and the Myth of American Nationality."
American Literary History 13, no. 3 (Autumn 2001): 469–498.

Smith, Cecil. "The 'Lolita' Libel Case: Shirley Temple's 'Dimpled Depravity'?" *Los Angeles
Times*, June 22, 1986. http://articles.latimes.com/1986-06-22/entertainment/ca-20446_1
_libeling.

Smith, Kyle. "*Family Feud* Is the Raunchiest Show on TV." *New York Post*, October 7, 2015.
http://nypost.com/2015/10/07/family-feud-is-an-affront-to-family-values/.

Smith, Mitch, and Monica Davey. "4 Black Suspects Charged in Videotaped Beating of
White Teenager in Chicago." *New York Times*, January 5, 2017. http://www.nytimes.com
/2017/01/05/us/chicago-racially-charged-attack-video.html.

Smith-Shomade, Beretta E. *Shaded Lives: African-American Women and Television*. New
Brunswick, NJ: Rutgers University Press, 2002.

Smith-Shomade, Beretta E., ed. *Watching while Black: Centering the Television of Black Audiences*. New Brunswick, NJ: Rutgers University Press, 2012.

Smulyan, Susan. *Popular Ideologies: Mass Culture at Mid-century*. Philadelphia: University of Pennsylvania Press, 2007.

Snead, James. *White Screens/Black Images: Hollywood from the Dark Side*. Edited by Colin MacCabe and Cornel West. New York: Routledge, 1994.

Spigel, Lynn. *Make Room for TV: Television and the Family Ideal in Postwar America*. Chicago: University of Chicago Press, 1992.

Spigel, Lynn. *Welcome to the Dreamhouse: Popular Media and Postwar Suburbs*. Durham, NC: Duke University Press, 2001.

Stallybrass, Peter, and Allon White. *The Politics and Poetics of Transgression*. Ithaca, NY: Cornell University Press, 1986.

"Steve Harvey—He's the New Oprah Winfrey." *Guardian*, April 14, 2013.

"Steve Harvey: 'Hollywood Is More Racist Than America.'" *Hollywood Reporter*, March 15, 2013. http://www.hollywoodreporter.com/news/is-steve-harvey-next-oprah-427424?page=1.

Sullivan, Ed. "Can TV Crack America's Color Line?" *Ebony* 6, no. 7 (May 1951): 58–65.

Temple Black, Shirley. *Child Star*. New York: Warner, 1988.

Toldson, Ivory A. "Think You Know the Dropout Rates for Black Males? You're Probably Wrong." *The Root*, June 4, 2014. http://www.theroot.com/think-you-know-the-dropout-rates-for-black-males-you-r-1790875915.

Toney, Veronica. "Jesse Williams Gave One of the Most Memorable Speeches in Award Show History." *Washington Post*, June 27, 2016. https://www.washingtonpost.com/news/arts-and-entertainment/wp/2016/06/27/jesse-williams-gave-one-of-the-most-memorable-speeches-in-award-show-history-full-transcript/.

Trump, Donald. "Central Park Five Settlement Is a 'Disgrace.'" *Daily News*, June 21, 2014. http://www.nydailynews.com/new-york/nyc-crime/donald-trump-central-park-settlement-disgrace-article-1.1838467.

Turner, Patricia. *Ceramic Uncles and Celluloid Mammies: Black Images and Their Influences on Culture*. New York: Anchor, 1994.

Tygiel, Jules. *Baseball's Great Experiment: Jackie Robinson and His Legacy*. New York: Oxford University Press, 1983.

United States Commission on Civil Rights. *Window Dressing on the Set: Women and Minorities in Television*. Washington, DC: Government Printing Office, 1977.

"U.S. Supreme Court Bans Mandatory Life-without-Parole Sentences for Children Convicted of Homicide." Equal Justice Initiative, June 25, 2012. https://eji.org/news/supreme-court-bans-mandatory-life-without-parole-sentences-for-children-miller-v-alabama.

van Woerkens, Martine. *The Strangled Traveler: Colonial Imaginings and the Thugs of India*. Chicago: University of Chicago Press, 2002.

Wagner, Kyle. "The Word 'Thug' Was Uttered 625 Times on TV on Monday. That's a Lot." *Deadspin.com*, January 21, 2014. http://regressing.deadspin.com/the-word-thug-was-uttered-625-times-on-tv-yesterday-1506098319.

Wald, Gayle. *It's Been Beautiful:* Soul! *and Black Power Television*. Durham, NC: Duke University Press, 2015.

Wanzo, Rebecca. *The Suffering Will Not Be Televised: African American Women and Sentimental Political Storytelling*. Albany: State University of New York Press, 2009.

Warner, Kristin J. "If Loving Olitz Is Wrong, I Don't Want to Be Right: ABC's *Scandal* and the Affect of Black Female Desire." *Black Scholar* 45, no. 1 (Spring 2014): 16–20.

Watkins, Mel. "Sherman Hemsley, 'Jeffersons' Star, Is Dead at 74." *New York Times*, July 24, 2012. http://www.nytimes.com/2012/07/25/arts/television/sherman-hemsley -star-of-the-jeffersons-dies-at-74.html.

Watkins, Mel. *Stepin Fetchit: The Life and Times of Lincoln Perry*. New York: Vintage Books, 2005.

Watson, Mary Ann. "The Nat 'King' Cole Show." Museum of Broadcast Communications. http://www.museum.tv/eotv/natkingcole.htm.

Watts, Jill. *Hattie McDaniel: Black Ambition, White Hollywood*. New York: Amistad, 2007.

Webley, Kayla. "How the Nixon-Kennedy Debate Changed the World." *Time*, September 23, 2010. http://content.time.com/time/nation/article/0,8599,2021078,00.html.

Weiser, Benjamin. "Judges Reinstate Conviction in Extortion of Bill Cosby." *New York Times*, November 10, 1999. http://www.nytimes.com/1999/11/16/nyregion/judges -reinstate-conviction-in-extortion-of-bill-cosby.html.

White, E. Frances. *Dark Continent of Our Bodies: Black Feminism and the Politics of Respectability*. Philadelphia: Temple University Press, 2001.

Wiese, Andrew. *Places of Their Own: African American Suburbanization in the Twentieth Century*. Chicago: University of Chicago Press, 2005.

Williams, Patricia J. *The Rooster's Egg: On the Persistence of Prejudice*. Cambridge, MA: Harvard University Press, 1995.

Williams, Raymond. *Television: Technology and Cultural Form*. London: Fontana, 1974.

Williams, Raymond. *Television: Technology and Cultural Form*. Revised ed. New York: Routledge, 2003.

Williams, Roberton C. "Why Do People Pay No Federal Income Tax?" *Tax Policy Center*, July 27, 2011. http://www.taxpolicycenter.org/taxvox/why-do-people-pay-no-federal -income-tax.

Willis, Jan. *Dreaming Me: Black, Baptist, and Buddhist—One Woman's Spiritual Journey*. Somerville, MA: Wisdom, 2008.

Wilson, Christopher. "The Scandalous Truth about *Downton Abbey*'s Royal Gigolo 'Jack Ross.'" *Telegraph*, October 14, 2013. http://www.telegraph.co.uk/culture/tvandradio /downton-abbey/10377794/The-scandalous-truth-about-Downton-Abbeys-royal -gigolo-Jack-Ross.html.

Wilson, Ryan. "Richard Sherman: 'Thug' Is Accepted Way of Calling Someone N-Word." CBS Interactive, January 22, 2014. http://www.cbssports.com/nfl/eye-on-football/24417234.

Wolcott, James. "The Hung and the Restless." *Vanity Fair*, February 3, 2012. http://www .vanityfair.com/hollywood/2012/03/wolcott-201203.

Wood, Daniel B., and Gloria Goodale. "Dick Clark: How a Tax-Accountant Look-Alike Changed American Music." *Christian Science Monitor*, April 19, 2012. http://www .csmonitor.com/USA/Society/2012/0419/Dick-Clark-how-a-tax-accountant-look-alike -changed-American-music.

Woolfork, Lisa. "Looking for Lionel: Making Whiteness and Blackness in *All in the Family* and *The Jeffersons*." In *African Americans on Television: Race-ing for Ratings*, edited by David J. Leonard and Lisa A. Guerrero, 45–68. Santa Barbara, CA: Praeger, 2013.

INDEX

A&E Biography, 90

abandoned at birth cliché, 163–167, *165*, 169, 281, 302n7

ABC Entertainment, 181

absence, presence of, 159–160, 166, 169–170, 181–182

Acham, Christine, 139, 140

Acker, Tanya, 227–228

Act Like a Lady, Think Like a Man (Harvey), 37–38

actors, African American: burden of representation, 16, 17, 136–137, 144–145, 152–153, 157, 159, 282; civil rights movement and, 139–140, 162, 178–180, *180*; guest roles, 135–136; payment, 64–65; stigmatic blackness portrayed by, 183–208, 280; Uncle Tom characters, 34, 95, 105, 137, 292n18. *See also specific actors, characters, shows, and concepts*

Adventures of Ozzie and Harriet, The, 60, 80

advertising, 81–82, 218, 241, 280

African American Dream, 24–29, 50

age-appropriate programming, 45–48

Agnew, Spiro, 184

Aidman, Charles, 127–128

All about Eve, 21

Allen, Byron, 217

Allen, Steve, 30, 31, 61, 63–64, 140

All in the Family, 126–128

Allison, Jewel, 237

Ally McBeal, 73

Alonso, Daniella, 107, 108

American Bandstand, 15, 61–63

American Bar Association, 220

American Dream, 24–29, 50, 80, 106, 129

American Negro Theatre of Harlem, 162

America's Next Top Model, 46

Amos, John, 16, 144–145, 147, 150

Amos 'n' Andy, 71, 84, 88, 104, 127, 157; driven off air, 15, 80; radio show, 6, 75, 79

analepses and prolepses, 206

Anderson, Anthony, 246

Anderson, Eddy, 65

Andrews, Erin, 273

Angelou, Maya, 162

Another World, 16

antimiscegenation laws, 16, 95, 112–113, 132

"any black is every black," 3, 24, 103–104, 213, 221–222, 274

Apana, Chang, 87

appropriation of black culture, 247–248

Arc TV, 13, 17

Arkin, Alan, 203

Arnaz, Desi, 60, 188, *189*

Ashe, Arthur, 131

Asians, 86, 170; Chinese immigrants, 67–68; stereotypes about, 67–73, 87, 159–160, 297n4. *See also* Charlie Chan films

Astaire, Fred, 94–95

As the World Turns, 131

Autobiography of Miss Jane Pittman, The (Gaines), 147, 148, 150, *151*

Ayers, Mike, 155

Baby Burlesks, 91, 92, 93, 103

Bachelor Father, 2, 15, 57, 67–73, *72*, 87, 88

Bakman, Larry, 228

Baldwin, James, 70

Ball, Lucille, 60, 188, *189*

Baltimore Sun, 182

Banks, Taunya Lovell, 218

Banks, Tyra, 37

Barbie Liberation Organization, 216

Barker, Bob, 40

Basinger, Jeanine, 91–92

Basketball Wives, 229

Bass, Lance, 46

Baszile, Natalie, 173, 271

Beat Shazam, 32

Beavers, Louise, 75, 77

Belafonte, Harry, 179, *180*

Beloved (Morrison), 112

Ben Casey, 138

Benevides, Robert, 181

Bennett, Tony, 81

Bennett, Willie, 278

Benson, 65

Berkus, Nate, 37

Berry, Halle, 200, 245, 266

Best, Willie, 84, 101, 103, 104

Bethune, Mary McLeod, 79

Beulah Show, The, 4, 6, 15–16, 75–79, *78*, 138

Bewitched, 130

Big Beat, The, 63

Billy Daniels Show, The, 81

Birth of a Nation, The, 33, 90

Black, Shirley Temple, 88, 90, 111. *See also* Temple, Shirley

Black Entertainment Television (BET), 5, 11

blackface/minstrelsy, 46, 67–68, 88, *102*; as concept, 108, 122, 126, 245

#BlackGirlsMatter, 109

"black gold," 14–15

Black History: Lost, Stolen, or Strayed (documentary), 137, 241–242, 247–248

Black-ish, 245–246

Black Lives Matter, 5, 108–109, 264

Black Panthers, 146

Blacks and White TV: African Americans in Television since 1948 (MacDonald), 11, 30

Black Skin, White Masks (Fanon), 15, 45, 153, 282

blackstory, 129, 167, 199, 281, 299n17

Black Twitter, 195, 201

Bland, Sandra, 5, 246, 274

blaxploitation films, 17, 201

Blind Slide, The, 281

Bloody Sunday (March 7, 1965), 171

Blue Angel, The, 92

Blues for Mister Charlie (Baldwin), 70

Bluest Eye, The (Morrison), 83–84, 97–98, 199

Bodroghkozy, Aniko, 75, 77, 78–79, 300n14

Body of Proof, 268

Bogart, Leo, 1, 52–53

Bogle, Donald, 11, 75, 77, 78, 125, 136, 248, 250

Bolden, Kamal Angelo, 106

Boles, John, 101

Bonanza, 15, 69, 88

Bonfire of the Vanities, The, 278–279

Booth, Shirley, 75

bootstrap stories, 129

Boston, school desegregation, 171

Boston Globe, 254

Boston Red Sox, 56

Bowman, Barbara, 234

Brady, Wayne, 40, 261–262

Brando, Marlon, 179, *180*

Braugher, Andre, 269

Bridges, Ruby, 114, *116*

Bright Eyes, 89, 92

British television, 123

Brock, David, 303–304n5

Brooke, Edward William, III, 183–186, *185*, 303n2

Brooke Girls, 184, *185*

Brooks, Daphne, 140, 300n11

Brooks, Duane, Jr., 221–222, 224

Brown, Billy, 192, 202

Brown, Michael, 5

Brown, Sterling K., 282, 302n7

Brown v. Board of Education, 29, 62, 105, 113, 233

Bullock, Sandra, 109

Bunche, Ralph, 79

Buress, Hannibal, 234, 238

Burns, Sarah, 192

Burr, Raymond, 17, 136, 159, 162, 179, 186; obituaries, 159, 181–182, 301n

Bush, George H. W., 33

Bush, George W., 232, 236

butler characters, 65, 84, 94, 104

Buying Naked, 45–46

Cabrini-Green housing project (Chicago), 145–146

capitalism, black, 129

Capra, Frank, 19

Captain January, 91, 92

Carey, Drew, 40

Carmichael, Stokely, 183–184

Carr, Gary, 206

Carroll, Diahann, 16, 138–140, 157, 179

Carry, Julius, 301n41

Carter, Nell, 75

Carter, Ralph, 145

Cash, Rosalind, 130

Cedric the Entertainer, 40, 41, 43

Celebrity Family Feud, 46

Central Park rape and battery case, 265–267, *267*, 272

Chan, Charlie. *See* Charlie Chan films

Chan, Jeffery Paul, 87–88

Chappelle Show, 262

Charlie Chan films, 4, 83, 87, 97, 104

Charlie Chan Is Dead, 87

Cheerios TV commercial, 132–133

Chew, The, 33

Chicago Justice, 266

Childress, Alvin, 75

Child Star (Temple), 88–89, 94

Chin, Frank, 87–88

Chinese immigrants, 67–68

churchwomen, 24–25

cinema, 4, 65–66, 92, 95. *See also* Temple, Shirley

Cisco Kid, The, 74, 75

civil rights movement, 17, 61–62, 137, 170–172; actors and, 139–140, 162, 178–180, *180*; desegregation, 143; "Leading Six," 179; March on Washington, 166–169, 179–180, *180*; televised, 135, 179, *180*

Clark, Dick, 36, 61–63

Clark, Kenneth, 105

Clark, Mamie, 105

class narratives, 97, 140, 156, 242–243; "ethnic" and working-class comedies, 80; television courtrooms increase tensions, 214, 221–222

Claws, 46, 157

Clinton, Bill, 264

Clinton, Hillary, 183, 264–265

Closer, The, 106, 268–269

Colbert, Claudette, 19, 89, 91, 96

Cole, Maria, 82

Cole, Nat King, 81–82

Coles, Julius, *98*

colonialism, 263

"colored," as term, 12

Color Purple, The (Walker), 199

Colson, Jacai, 275–276

comedy, 40, 85; civil rights and, 140; real-world experiences in, 143–147; romantic genre, 71, 94, 96. *See also* situation comedies (sitcoms)

Comedy Central, 140

Communication Ethics, Media and Popular Culture (Japp), 221

Compton, 107

Concentration, 22

Connor, Eugene "Bull," 135, 170

Connors, Mike, 122

Constand, Andrea, 234

consumers, black, 135, 169

Cooley High, 147

Cooper, Anderson, 39

Cooper, Chris, 109

Cooper, Gary, 92

Copeland, Misty, 106

Corcoran, Noreen, 67, *72*

Correll, Charles, 75

Cosby, Bill, 18, 37, 131, 168; allegations of sexual abuse against, 232, 234–235, 253; awards received, 232, 236; *Black History: Lost, Stolen, or Strayed*, 137, 241–242, 247–248; career, 238–239; *The Cosby Mysteries*, 251; as cultural icon, 232–233; *Fat Albert and the Cosby Kids*, 143, 241; *Fatherhood* (book), 248, 250; *Ghost Dad*, 248; *It's True! It's True!*, 248–249; Jell-O Pudding commercials, 232, 248; *Kids Say the Darndest Things*, 248; as moral

Cosby, Bill (continued)
    authority, 232–234, 235; "Pound Cake
    speech," 233; racialization of allegations,
    235–236; "Spanish Fly" joke, 248–249
Cosby, Camille, 236, 248, 250, 253
Cosby, William Ennis, 250, 252
Cosby Show, The, 4, 11, 18, 39, 141, 143,
    156, 232, 242–248, 244; appeal to white
    conservatives, 249–250; normalization of
    blackness, 246–247; taken off air, 235–236,
    307n10
Coupling Convention, The (duCille), 120, 121
Couric, Katie, 39
courtrooms, television, 12, 14, 18, 209–231;
    arbitration agreements, 220, 225–226;
    attraction of, 220–221; black judges, 218;
    class and color warfare increased by,
    214, 221–222; courtroom demeanor, 228;
    Divorce Court, 210–214, 220; doctors and
    lawyers as litigants, 225; misrepresen-
    tation about law, 220; Other and, 218;
    The People's Court, 32, 209, 214, 215–216,
    225–226; phony cases, 217–218; produc-
    tion staff, 217; slander in, 225–226; "syndi-
    courts," 220; "welfare fraud" focus, 18, 213,
    215–226. See also Judge Judy
Cover, Franklin, 126, 128
Crenshaw, Kimberlé, 109
Cristal, Linda, 123
CSI, 266–267, 269
Culp, Robert, 131, 238, 240, 249
cultural differences, 285–286

Dacascos, Mark, 73
Daktari, 136
Dallas, 202, 208
Daly, Tim, 50
Dandridge, Ruby, 76
Danes, Claire, 200
Daniels, Billy, 81, 82
Danny Thomas Show, The, 75, 239–240
Danson, Ted, 270
Dating Naked, 45
Davis, Bette, 21, 89
Davis, Ossie, 179
Davis, Sammy, Jr., 64, 123, 179
Davis, Viola, 17, 51, 186, 197
Dawson, Richard, 48

Day, Clarence, Jr., 243
Days of Our Lives, 131–132
deadbeat dads, 213–215
death penalty, 265–266, 267, 271–272
"debase relief," 60, 103
Dee, Ruby, 131, 141, 179
DeGeneres, Ellen, 37
de jure segregation, 112–113
Delmont, Matthew F., 61–62
Democratic National Convention (2016), 183
Depp, Johnny, 66–67
Depression era, 89–90, 92, 97
Diallo, Amadou, 5, 274
Diana Ross and the Supremes, 63
Diary of Anne Frank, 86
Dickinson, Janice, 234
Dick Van Dyke Show, The, 167–169, 239
Dietrich, Marlene, 91, 92
Diff'rent Strokes, 143, 281
DiIulio, John, Jr., 264–265, 272, 273
Dillard, Mimi, 168, 239
DiMango, Judge, 226–227
Dinkins, David, 245
Disney, Walt, 90
Divorce Court, 210–214, 220
Divorce Hearing, 210
Dixon, Ivan, 136, 141, 164, 165, 166
dog-whistle politics, 194–195
Doherty, Thomas, 13
double consciousness, 114
Douglass, Charles, 174
Douglass, Frederick, 174
Douglass, Laura, 174
Dourdan, Gary, 269–270
Downton Abbey, 17, 201, 203–204, 206–207
Dreaming Me: Black, Baptist, and Buddhist—
    One Woman's Spiritual Journey (Willis), 64
drive-in theater, 55–56
Driving Miss Daisy, 66
Dr. Kildare, 131, 138
Dr. Oz, 37, 39
Dr. Phil, 37, 39
Du Bois, W. E. B., 24
duCille, Adrian, Jr., 6–8, 9, 26, 27, 47, 55, 84,
    113–115, 114, 116, 134, 148, 148, 251, 255
duCille, Adrian Everard, 6, 10, 24, 58, 118,
    119, 120, 308n33
duCille, Ann, 7, 26, 27, 98, 117, 119, 149, 212

duCille, Danny, 10, *26*, *27*, *54*, 55, 84, 114, 115, *117*, 118, 148, *148*, 259–260, 287–288

duCille, Michel (Michelangelo Everard), 176–178, *177*

duCille, Pearl Louise (Hogan), 6, 22–30, 69–70, 118, *119*, 120, 212, 254–260, *258*, *259*

duCille family, *54*, *148*, *152*, 254; polio epidemics and move, 6, 8–10; trip to South and Jamaica, 172–178, *177*

Duffy, Patrick, 208

Duncan, Sandy, 150

Dungey, Channing, 181

Dunham, Lena, 153

Dunn, Michael David, 290n18

DuVernay, Ava, 173, 208

Dynasty, 70

Dyson, Michael Eric, 234

East Bridgewater, Massachusetts, 10, 113, 171

East Side/West Side, 136, 141–143, 300n14

Ebert, Roger, 131

Ebony, 63, 64–65, 82, 145, 248

Ed Sullivan Show, The, 15, 30–31, 61, 63–65

education and school, 15; as African American value, 233; *Brown v. Board of Education* ruling, 29, 62, 105, 113, 233; college campuses, 190–191, 273; informal "escort service" for black students, 115, 118; northern schools, 114–122, 142; "slave auctions" as high school fundraisers, 84–85, 142

Edwards, Anne, 89, 90

Eighth Amendment, 272–273

Ellison, Nan, 98, *98*

Ellison, Ralph, 56, 199

Emmy Awards, 36–37, 131, 142, 148; Outstanding Game Show Host, 48; Outstanding Lead Actress in a Drama Series, 76; Outstanding Talk Show, 39, 48

Empire, 32–33, 40, 157, 201

Enoch, Alfred, 187

Equal Justice Initiative, 272–273

Equal Time: Television and the Civil Rights Movement (Bodroghkozy), 75, 77, 78–79, 300n14

Erickson, Leif, 123

essentialism, 106, 262, 286

ethical collapse, 231

"ethnic" and working-class comedies, 80

Eubanks, Bob, 44

eugenics, 210

Evans, Michael "Mike," 146–147

Even This I Get to Experience (Lear), 143–145

Extant, 200

"Faces of American Power, Nearly as White as the Oscar Nominees, The" (*New York Times*), 180–181

Fair, Peggy (character, *Mannix*), 122, 125–126, 136, 138

Falahee, Jack, 187

family dynamic and television, 52–57; negative effects, 53, 57–59

Family Feud, 14, 32, 37–39, 41–44, 261; *Celebrity Family Feud*, 46; Fast Cash bonus round, 42; penis fetish, 43–44

Fanon, Frantz, 15, 45, 46, 153

Farrer, John, 74

Fat Albert and the Cosby Kids, 143, 241

Fatherhood (Cosby), 248, 250

fatherhood as national narrative, 251–253. See also *Bachelor Father*; *Cosby Show, The*; *Father Knows Best*

Father Knows Best, 74, 80, 245, 249

FBI in Peace and War, The, 6

Feldstein, Ruth, 139

Fellowes, Julian, 206

female-headed households, 138–139

feminism, 188

feminization of black masculinity, 35–36, 71, 73, 79, 95

Fenway Park, 56

Feuerstein, Mark, 74

5th Dimension, 78

#FindKaylaWeber (*Major Crimes*), 106–109

Fishburne, Laurence, 269–270

Fisher, Gail, 122, 136

Fiske, John, 12–13, 31, 34

Flack, Roberta, 155

flexi-narratives, 201

Flying Down to Rio, 95

Flynn, Ray, 277

Fogelman, Dan, 167, 281

Foley, Scott, 153

Fong, Benson, 160

Ford, Gerald, 90

Forsythe, John, 67, 71, *72*, 79

42 (film), 174
Foster, Stephen, 86, 296n2
Fourteenth Amendment, 113
Fox, James Alan, 272
Foxx, Jamie, 32
Frank's Place, 243
Freed, Alan, 63
Freeman, Al, Jr., 181
Freeman, Morgan, 65–66
Fu Manchu (character, *Charlie Chan* movies), 73, 87

Gable, Clark, 19, 96, 137
Gaines, Ernest, 147–148
Gaines, Kevin, 291n3
Game Show Network (GSN), 32, 48
game shows, 4–5, 12, 22–51; changes in color and content, 31–32, 291n8; hosts, 294–295n39; inappropriate material, 45–48; lowbrow, 41–44; of 1950s, 60; upscale, 41. *See also specific shows*
Gandolfini, James, 197
Gardner, Erle Stanley, 170
Garner, Eric, 5, 274
Garner, James, *180*
Garrity, Arthur, 82
Gates, Henry Louis, Jr., 129, 274
Gay, Roxane, 196
Gelman, Michael, *33*
Get Christie Love!, 76
Ghost Dad, 248
Gibbins, Wes (character, *How to Get Away with Murder*), 187, 190, 196, 201, 204, 207
Gibbs, Marla, 127
Gimme a Break!, 75
girl fights, 231
girls, black, 15–16, 109; effect of Shirley Temple on, 83–84, 97–99
girls, sexualization of, 90–92
Glover, Danny, 245
Goldberg, Whoopi, 235
Goldbergs, The, 80
Golden Globes, 76
Golden Razzie for Worst Screen Couple, 131
Goldman, Ronald, 272
Goldwater, Barry, 184
Goldwyn, Tony, 49
Gone with the Wind, 16, 76, 137–138

Good Morning America (GMA), 36
Goodnight, Paul, 245
"Goodnight Sweet Blues" (*Route 66*), 135–136
Good Times, 11, 16, 65, 143, 144–147, 300–301n26
Gosden, Freeman, 75
Go Set a Watchman, 46–47
Gossett, Robert, 268
Grant, Cary, 25, 71
Graves, Teresa, 76
Gray, Freddie, 5, 246
Gray, Herman, 11, 242
Green, Nathaniel, 214–217, 218
Green, Shambala (character, *Law & Order*), 203
Greene, Graham, 91–92
Gregory, Dick, 62, 179
Grey's Anatomy, 33, 194, 270
Griffith, D. W., 33, 90, 94
Griffith, Melanie, 278–279
Grisham, John, 109
Guess Who's Coming to Dinner, 130
Guiding Light, 131
Guillaume, Robert, 65
Gunsmoke, 13, 60–61, 74, 75
Guterl, Matthew, 88
Guthrie, Richard, 132

Haggins, Bambi, 236
Haley, Alex, 147–148, 150–151
Hallelujah Voices, *98*
Hamilton, 281
Hamilton, Kim, 127
Hanks, Tom, 278–279
Harlem Globetrotters, 274–275
Harris, Bud, 76
Hart, John, 66
Hartley, Justin, 283
Harvey, Steve, 14, 32–33, 42, 51, 261; *Celebrity Family Feud*, 46; *Family Feud*, 41–44; relationship advice books, 37–38; *Steve Harvey*, 37, 39
Hatchett, Desmond, 213
hate mail, 132, 142, 143, 239–240
Haves and Have Nots, The, 229
Hawaii Five-0, 73
Hawkins, Coleman, 136
Hawkins-Byrd, Petri, 219

Hazel, 75
Hazel Scott Show, The, 81
Hearst, Patty, 203
"'Heathen Chinee' on God's Free Soil, The"
   (Lee), 68
Helgenberger, Marg, 270
Hemings, Sally, 158
Hemsley, Sherman, 127
Herbert, Bob, 232, 252
Hernández, Daisy, 201
heroes, television personalities as, 235
hero worship, 170–171
Heston, Charlton, 130, 179, *180*
Hidden Figures (Shetterly), 280–281
Higginbotham, Evelyn Brooks, 23
High Chaparral, The, 123, 162
Highland Beach, Maryland, 174
Hill, Anita, 191, 237–238, 303–304n5
hip hop studies, 263–264
*Hip Hop Wars: What We Talk about When
   We Talk about Hip Hop—and Why It
   Matters, The* (Rose), 263–264
Hoerschelmann, Olaf, 31, 291n9
Hogan's Heroes, 136, 141, 164
Holbrook, Colin, 243
Hollywood High School, 170
Hollywood Reporter, 38
Homeland, 200
Homicide, 269
Honeymooners, The, 80
Hooks, Robert, 136, 141
Hopalong Cassidy, 75
Hopper, William, 164
Horne, Lena, 139
Hoskins, Allen, 84
Hot Bench, 218, 226–229, *227*
House, 270–271
"houseboy," as term, 71
"How It Feels to Be Colored Me" (Hurston), 16
*How It Feels to Be Free: Black Women Enter-
   tainers and the Civil Rights Movement*
   (Feldstein), 139
How to Get Away with Murder, 5, 12, 14,
   17, 18, 51, 154, 157, 183–208, *195, 198*, 213;
   flashbacks, 190, 197–199, 204–205; online
   response to, 190–191; plot, 186–189;
   racially coded commentary, 194–196; as
   sign of the times, 207

Hurston, Zora Neale, 16, 105, 199, 249
Hutchinson, Leslie "Hutch," 206
Hyman, Earle, 141

Ice-T, 269
identity, racial, 15, 25, 105–106, 128
identity politics, 40, 128
ideological formations, 19, 31
I'll Fly Away, 75, 76
I Love Lucy, 60, 73
imaginative activism, 140, 300n11
India, colonialism, 263
Indian stereotypes, 66–67
intentional fallacy, 196
interracial adoption stories, 281–283
interracial relationships: antimiscegenation
   laws, 16, 112–113, 132; naturalized, 193;
   northern schools and, 114–122; white fear
   of miscegenation, 62–63
interracial relationships on television, 16, 21,
   49, 60, 130–132; bedroom scenes, 94, 96,
   187–189, *189*; early forays into, 122–126;
   The Jeffersons, 16, 126–129; male costars,
   130–131; *Star Trek* kiss, 16, 115, 123–126,
   128, 136
In the Year of the Boar and Jackie Robinson
   (Lord), 97, 297n23
"inverse racism," 146–147
Invisible Man (Ellison), 56, 199
Ironside, 136, 162, 181
I Spy, 18, 131, 168, 238–241, 247, 249
It Happened One Night, 19, 89, 96
It's True! It's True! (Cosby), 248–249

Jack Benny Program, The, 65, 75
Jackson, Autumn, 18, 232, 250–253, 308n32
Jackson, Jerald, 250
Jackson, Jesse, 231
Jackson, Michael, 88
Jackson, Samuel L., 109
Jackson v. Hobbs, 272–273
Janssen, Famke, 191
Japp, Debra, 221
Jefferson, Thomas, 158
Jeffersons, The, 16, 126–129, 143, 146, 172
Jeopardy, 22, 41
Jet, 63
Jim Crow South, 17, 113, 122, 173–174

Johnson, Lyndon, 56–57
Joker's Wild, The, 32
Jones, James Earl, 131, 141–142, 300n14
Jones, Ron Cephas, 282
Joyce, James, 130
Joyrich, Lynne, 15, 34–35
Judge Faith, 14
Judge Judy, 12, 14, 18, 214–224, 223, 233, 305n15; cat-astrophe incident, 216; production staff, 217
Judge Mathis, 14
Julia, 4, 11, 16, 80, 138–140, 162, 242
Jungle Fever, 63
Just around the Corner, 103

Kanter, Hal, 140
Keating, Annalise (character, *How to Get Away with Murder*), 17, 183, 186–202; complexity of, 197–199
Keating, Sam (character, *How to Get Away with Murder*), 186–187, 190–194, 196, 205–206
Kelly, RaeVen, 109
Kennedy, John, Jr., 49
Kennedy, John F., 135
Key, Keegan-Michael, 140
Key and Peele, 140
Kid 'n' Africa, 103
Kid 'n' Hollywood, 92, 93
Kids Say the Darndest Things, 248
Killing Affair, A, 129–130
Kim, Elaine, 72
King, Gayle, 37
King, Martin Luther, Jr., 139, 143, 153, 170, 300n18; March on Washington, 166, 179
King, Martin Luther, III, 44
King, Rodney, 170
King's English, 104, 105
Kintner, Bob, 240
Kite, Jonathan, 73
Knight, Gladys, 61
Knight, Suge, 262
Koch, Ed, 225, 266
Kotto, Yaphet, 162
Kung Fu, 88

LaBennett, Oneka, 75, 155–156
Ladies' Home Journal, 210

Lake, Lauren, 214
Lake, Ricki, 39
L.A. Law, 170
Lassie, 60
Laughing Mad: The Black Comic Persona in Post-Soul America (Haggins), 236
Lauren Lake's Paternity Court, 214
Law & Order, 203, 266, 268, 269
"Leading Six," 179
Lear, Norman, 39, 65, 143–147
Leave It to Beaver, 57, 60
Lee, Johnny, 84
Lee, Peggy, 81
Lee, Robert, 68
Lee, Spike, 63
Lemon, Richard, 136
Lenox, Adriane, 74
Leonard, Sheldon, 168, 238–241, 247, 249
Leoni, Téa, 50
Lester, Jasmine, 304n6
Let's Make a Deal, 32, 40, 261–262
Lewis, Joe, 63
Lewis, John, 171
Life of Riley, The, 57, 80
Life with Father, 242, 244
Life with Luigi, 80
Linkletter, Art, 37
Lipsitz, George, 59, 90
Little Big Shots, 37
Little Black Sambo, 85
Little Colonel, The, 94–96, 95, 100
Little Miss Broadway, 92
Little Miss Marker, 89, 92, 96
Little Rascals, The (*Our Gang*), 75, 84, 104
Littlest Rebel, The, 92, 94, 99–103, 102, 110
Liu, Lucy, 73
Live!, 33–36, 35, 94
Live! with Regis and Kelly, 33
Living Color: Race and Television in the United States (Torres), 11
living conditions, 249, 265; Jim Crow South, 17, 113, 122, 173–174
Lodge, Sheila, 275
Loew's Grand Theater, 137
Loneliness of the Black Republican, The (Rigueur), 186, 303n2
Lone Ranger, The, 66–67, 74, 75

"Looking for Lionel: Making Whiteness and Blackness in *All in the Family* and *The Jeffersons*" (Woolfork), 128

Lord, Bette Bao, 97

Los Angeles Unified School District, 170

Los Angeles uprising of 1992, 170

Losing Isaiah, 281

Love, Eulia May, 5, 289n9

Love & Hip Hop franchise, 229

Loving, Mildred Jeter, 112, 122

Loving, Richard, 112, 122

Loving v. Virginia, 16, 21, 112–113, 126, 129, 132

low-Other, 59, 127, 236

Loy, Myrna, 89

Luke, Keye, 88, 89, 160, 301–302n1

Lymon, Frankie, 63

lynching, 36, 111, 236, 238, 266

MacDonald, J. Fred, 11, 30, 65, 79, 291n8

Mack, Ted, 61

Madame Secretary, 50

magazines, 209–210

Magic Mike, 34

Maharis, George, 135

Maher, Bill, 262

maid roles, 75–76

Major Crimes, 16, 106–109, 268

Make Room for Daddy, 2, 74, 75

Make Room for TV: Television and the Family Ideal in Postwar America (Spigel), 53

mammy characters, 75, 78, 99, 126; male roles, 65–66; Mammy (character, *Gone with the Wind*), 16, 137–138

Mandingo (Onstott), 35

"Mandingoism," 35

Manifest Destiny, 86

Mannix, 122, 125–126, 136, 138

"Man, the," 70

Mapplethorpe, Robert, 35

"Mapplethorpism," 35

March on Washington, 166–169, 179–180, 180

marketing, 39–40, 168–169; advertising, 81–82, 218, 241, 280; collective buying power of African Americans, 39–40

Marlowe, Hugh, 163, 169

Married to Medicine, 40, 229–231, 230

Marshall, Thurgood, 79, 171

Martha & Snoop's Pot Luck Dinner, 32

Martin, Ross, 87

Martin, Trayvon, 5, 18–19, 174, 262–263

masculinity, black: feminization of, 35–36, 71, 73, 79, 95; hypermasculinity projected onto, 34–36, 48; white female actresses and, 33–34

Massachusetts Council on the Arts and Humanities, 82

mass consumption, 59–60

Master of None, 208

Match Game, 44

Mathis, Greg, 219

Maude, 65, 75, 144

Maury, 214

Mays, Benjamin, 79–80

McBride, Renisha, 274, 290n18

McCarthy, Nobu, 302n1

McConaughey, Matthew, 109

McDaniel, Hattie, 16, 60, 75, 77, 78, 84, 96, 134, 137–138; fair housing campaigns and, 179

McDaniel, Sam, 60

McDonnell, Mary, 268

McEachin, James, 181

McGraw, Phillip (Dr. Phil), 37, 293n30

McQueen, Butterfly, 76

McWhorter, John, 274

Menace II Society, 265

Menjou, Adolphe, 96

Merkerson, S. Epatha, 269

Metz, Chrissy, 282

Mexicans, 74, 86

microaggression, 227

middle-class blacks, 6, 24, 105, 236; fictional, 140, 142, 168, 242–243; racial profiling of, 243, 245

middle-class whites, 24–25, 140

Milian, Marilyn, 214, 215, 216–217, 219–220, 225

Miller v. Alabama, 272–273

Million Dollar Baby, 66

Mills, Alison (Newman), 162

Milner, Martin, 135

Miranda, Lin-Manuel, 281

Mission Impossible, 136, 141

Miss Universe Pageant, 39

"Mister Charlie" and "Miss Ann," 70

Mitchell, Don, 162, 181

Mitchell, Margaret LaVerne, 5, 289n9
Mittell, Jason, 13
Modern Family, 73–74
Mod Squad, The, 136, 141
Monte, Eric, 146–147
Montgomery, Elizabeth, 129–130
Moody, Nekesa, 229
Mooney, Paul, 262
Moonlighting, 50
Moore, Clayton, 66
Moore, Mandy, 281, 302n7
Moore, Mary Tyler, 167, 188, *189*
Moore, Tim, 84
Moreland, Mantan, 87, *89*, 104
Moriarty, Michael, 203, 266
Morris, Garrett, 73
Morris, Greg, 125, 141, 168, 239–241
Morrison, Toni, 4, 83–84, 97–98, 112, 199
Morton, Joe, 152
Motown music, 155–156
Movin' with Nancy, 123
Moy, Matthew, 73
Moynihan, Daniel Patrick, 138–139
Moynihan Report, 138–139, 242
Murphy, Eddie, 48, 131
Murphy Brown, 156, 248, 301n41
Murrow, Edward R., 6
music, 155–156, 201; rap, 263–264
music shows, 61–63
Mutiny on the Bounty, 142
"My Brother's Keeper" self-help initiative, 224

NAACP. See National Association for the Advancement of Colored People
Naish, J. Carrol, 87
Naked and Afraid, 45
Naked Castaway, 45
Naked City, The, 47
Naked Vegas, 45
Name That Tune, 32
narrative, 13–14, 17
National Association for the Advancement of Colored People (NAACP), 137–138, 157, 233; NAACP Image Award, 39, 76, 137; protests of black television stereotypes, 16, 78, 79–81
Native Americans, 86, 112, 123

Nat "King" Cole Show, The, 81–82
Negro Family: A Case for National Action, The, 138–139
Negro Motorist Green Book, The, 174
Nelson, Robin, 201
Newlywed Game, The, 32, 44–45, 261
news coverage, 5, 249–253, 265–268, *267*, 276–278
New York Times, 168, 180–181, 237, 278
Nicest Kids in Town: American Bandstand, Rock 'n' Roll, and the Struggle for Civil Rights in 1950s Philadelphia (Delmont), 61–62
Nichols, John, 184
Nichols, Nichelle, 123–125, *124*, 136, 143, 153, 300n18
Nielsen market ratings, 39–40
Night and Day, 91
Nixon, Richard, 90, 129, 135, 184
noble savage mythology, 15, 66–67
"No Mercy for Autumn" (Herbert), 232
Norman, Jessye, 106
Not for Black Only, 148
Nowalk, Peter, 187
Now and Forever, 92
*NSYNC, 46
Nussbaum, Emily, 39, 73, 197
N.Y.P.D., 136, 141
Nyro, Laura, 78

Obama, Barack, 15, 140, 184, 221, 222, 224, 249, 262; black fears for, 246
Obama, Michelle, 156
Obama effect, 36
O.J.: Made in America, 130
Oland, Warner, 87
Omega Man, The, 130
"one-drop rule," 112
$100,000 Pyramid, The, 32, 36
Onstott, Kyle, 35
Oprah effect, 36
Oprah's Book Club, 37
Oprah Winfrey Network (OWN), 32, 229
Oprah Winfrey Show, The, 36–38
orientalism, 15
Original Amateur Hour, 61
Orman, Suze, 37
Oscars, 16, 32, 66, 89, 96, 180

Other, 5, 87–88; black masculinity and, 35–36, 224; courtroom television and, 218, 220–223, *223*; high-Normal, 236; low-Other, 127, 236; whiteness as unmarked category, 90
Oz, Mehmet (Dr. Oz), 37
Ozzie and Harriet, 60, 80

"Painful Case, A" (Joyce), 130
palatable blackness, 236–237, 243–247
Parker, Sarah Jessica, 197
Parks, Rosa, 113
Password, 22
paternal gaze, 92
Patterson, Orlando, 237–238
Peele, Jordan, 140
People's Court, The, 32, 209, 214, 215–216, 225–226
Perry, Lincoln (Stepin Fetchit), 84, 87, 104, 106, 136–137, 241
Perry, Tyler, 229
Perry Mason, 2, 17, 115, 125, 126, 159, 181–182, 186, 287–288; "The Case of the Blushing Pearls," 160, 302n1; "The Case of the Borrowed Baby," 169; "The Case of the Caretaker's Cat," 159–160, 301n1; "The Case of the Fancy Figures," 160, 162; "The Case of the Nebulous Nephew," 163–167, *165*, 169, 281; "The Case of the Runaway Racer," 160; "The Case of the Skeleton's Closet," 160, *161*; "The Case of the Weary Watchdog," 160
Petersen, William, 269–270
Peyton Place, 131
Philadelphia, 61–62
Picatinney Arsenal, 29, *30*
Pickler, Kellie, 46
"Plato's Stepchildren" (*Star Trek*), 16, 115, 123–126, 128, 136
Playing in the Dark: Whiteness and the Literary Imagination (Morrison), 4
Poitier, Sidney, 179, 241
police officers, black, 275–276
police procedurals, 14, 16, 106, 266–270; true-crime docudramas, 268
political thrillers, 50
Pompeo, Ellen, 194
Pope, Olivia (character, *Scandal*), 16, 40, 49, 133, 152–158, 303n4; as female fixer, 33, 75–76, 154; undoing of black female

heroics, 188–189; verbal assaults on as black woman, 194, 196
Popeil, Ron, 48
"Popeil Galactic Prophylactic" (Murphy), 48
Popenoe, Paul, 210
Popular Ideologies: Mass Culture at Midcentury (Smulyan), 2
Possessive Investment in Whiteness, The (Lipsitz), 59
postracial television, 3, 153, 156, 158, 202; racist subtext in, 193–197
Poussaint, Alvin, 248
Povich, Maury, 214
pregnancy plots, 97, 151, 187–188, 191–192, 195–196, 200
Price, Paula Groves, 3
Price Is Right, The, 40
Primetime Blues: African Americans on Network Television (Bogle), 11, 75, 77, 78
prime-time dramas, 4, 40, 201, 229. See also *How to Get Away with Murder*; *Scandal*
Prince Hall Grand Masonic Lodge, Dorchester, 288
Pringle, Bishop Otis Craig, 226–228, *227*
Pringle, Tiffany Anisette, 226
prism of race, 14, 22, 51
Private Practice, 33
Probst, Jeff, 39
progressive programs, 61–62, 65, 73
Project Runway All Stars, 46
Pryor, Richard, 248

Quayle, Dan, 248
Queen Latifah, 33
Queen Sugar, 173, 196, 208, 271
quiz shows, 291n9. *See also* game shows

race-face convention, 74
Race Mixing: Black-White Marriage in Postwar America (Romano), 115, 304n7
"Racial Integrity Act" (Virginia), 16, 112–113, 298n1
racialization. *See* stigmatic blackness
racial metonymy, 3, 104, 221, 273
racial performativity, 84
racial profiling, 19, 30, 245; of black police officers, 275–276; television as form of, 5, 279; uplifting, 50

racial representation, 16, 19; burden of, 16, 17, 136–137, 144–145, 152–153, 157; disappeared, 17, 71, 243, 245

racial self-making, 128–129

racism: "any black is every black," 3, 24, 103–104, 213, 221–222, 274; in Hollywood, 137–139; internalized, myth of, 105–106; "inverse," 146–147; under new guises, 2–3; sexualization of race, 34–36, 45–46, 59, 153, 199; slapstick approach fails, 127–128; traumatic encounters with in school, 84–86, 113–114

radio, 65, 162; *Amos 'n' Andy*, 6, 75, 79; talk radio, 18, 222

Ramsey, JonBenét, 91

Randolph, Amanda, 75, 239–240

rap music, 263–264

Rashad, Phylicia Ayers-Allen, 235, 242

ratings, 39, 50

Ray, Rachael, 37

Raymond, Emilie, 179

Reading Television (Fiske), 12–13

Reagan, Nancy, 50

Real Housewives of Atlanta, 40, 229–231, 230

reality TV, 18, 31, 40; blackening of, 229–230. *See also* courtrooms, television

real-world experiences on television, 143–144

Reckford, Barry, 123

Reiner, Carl, 168

Republican Party, 184, 249

Rescue 911, 278

resistance, 3–4

resorts, black, 174

respectability, black, 18, 186

respectability, politics of, 23–25, 29–30, 144–145, 186, 224

retail racism, 245

Revolution Televised: Prime Time and the Struggle for Black Power (Acham), 139, 140

Reynolds, Burt, 60–61

Reynolds, Corey, 268

Reynolds, James, 132

Rhimes, Shonda, 16, 33, 49, 51, 144, 153, 155, 181, 187, 208, 229, 270

Rhodes, Hari, 136

Rice, Tamir, 5, 274

Richards, Beah, 162

Riddle, Nelson, 81

Rigueur, Leah Wright, 186, 303n2

Ripa, Kelly, 33–36, *35*, 94

Robeson, Paul, 106

Robinson, Bill "Bojangles," 34, *35*, 84, 94–96, 100, 103, 104

Robinson, Jackie, 5–6, 63, 174, 175

Robinson, Rachel, 175

Robreno, Eduardo, 235

Rock, Roll and Remember (Clark), 61

Roddenberry, Gene, 143

Rogers, Ginger, 94–95

Roker, Roxie, 126, 128

Rolle, Esther, 16, 65, 144–145, 147

Romano, Renee, 115, 304n7

romantic comedy genre, 71, 94, 96

Romney, Mitt, 222–224

Rooney, Andy, 241–242

Roosevelt, Franklin Delano, 89–90

Rooster's Egg: On the Persistence of Prejudice, The (Williams), 247

Roots: The Next Generation (Haley), 147

Roots: The Saga of an American Family (Haley), 39, 147–148, 150–151

Rose, Tricia, 3, 263–265

Ross, Tracee Ellis, 246

Route 66, 135–136

Rove, Karl, 249

Royal Pains, 74

Rules of the Game: Quiz Shows and American Culture (Hoerschelmann), 31

Rushdie, Salman, 13

Ryan, Meg, 44

Sajak, Pat, 14, 20, 22

S&H Green Stamps, 55

Sands, Diana, 141–142

Sanford, Isabel, 162

Sanford and Son, 143

Sanger, Mark, 181

Saturday Evening Post, 136

Saturday Night Live, 48

Savali, Kristen West, 261

Scandal, 5, 14, 16, 33, 40, 75–76, 133, 152–158, 200, 207, 303n4; black women fall from power, 188–189; plot, 49–50; soundtrack, 155–156

Scott, George C., 136, 141, 143

Scott, Hazel, 81, 82
Scott, Kelsey, 203
Scott, Walter, 5, 274
Sedgwick, Kyra, 268
Seeing Race in Modern America (Guterl), 88
Self Help, Inc., 56–57, 171–172
self-help ethos, 25
self-making, 128–129
Selznick, David O., 137
Senate Judiciary Committee, 237
Sen Yung, Victor, 67, 69, 88, *89*
September 11, 2001, attacks, 267
Serial Mom, 202–203
serials: Arc TV, 13, 17; long-form, 13–14
Sex and the City, 197
sexual harassment, 237
sexuality, 187–188; children's understanding,
   46–48; college campuses, 190–191; girls,
   sexualization of, 90–92; racialized, 34–36,
   45–46, 59, 153, 199; same sex, 12, 144,
   187–188, 192–193
Shakur, Tupac, 263
shame, 23–24
Shatner, William, 123–125, *124*, 136, 278
Shaw, Orlando, 213
Sheindlin, Judith Blum (Judge Judy),
   215–216, 218, 219–220
Shepherd, Cybill, 50
Shepherd, Sherri, 44, 261
Sherman, Richard, 273–274
Shetterly, Margot Lee, 280–281
ShondaLand Productions, 49, 153–156, 187,
   188, 194, 201, 270
shootings of unarmed black people, 5,
   18–19
Showtime at the Apollo, 37
Shyamalan, M. Knight, 167
sight gags: "The Case of the Nebulous
   Nephew," 163–167, *165*, 169; *The Dick Van
   Dyke Show*, 167–169, 239
Silvera, Frank, 123, 160, 162–163, *180*
Silverheels, Jay (Harold Smith), 66
Simone, Nina, 139
Simpson, Nicole Brown, 272
Simpson, O.J., 129–130, 267, 272, 277
Sinatra, Nancy, 123
Sinclair, Madge, 150
Singer, Stuffie, *78*

situation comedies, 4, 11–12, 15, 39, 140;
   real-world experiences and, 143–147;
   technicolored, 16, 126–128. *See also
   specific sitcoms*
16th Street Baptist Church bombing, 135,
   167, 169
Sixth Sense, The, 167
$64,000 Question, The, 22
Skin Wars, 46
slavery, 86, 99–101, 158, 173
Slotkin, Richard, 74
Smith, Edward, 217
Smith, Judy, 33
Smith, Nathaniel, 213
Smith, Susan, 276–277
Smith-Shomade, Beretta E., 241
Smulyan, Susan, 2
Snead, James, 94, 99–100
Snoop Dogg, 32
Soap, 65
"soaploitation," 17, 18, 19, 201
soap operas, 17, 49, 71, 200–201; interracial
   romance, 131–132. *See also How to Get
   Away with Murder*
social media, 19–20, 56; Black Twitter, 195,
   201; racist comments on, 132–133
Sommerfield, Diane, 132
Song of the South, 90
Sopranos, The, 197, 202
Soul Train, 61
Sounder, 160
Sounds of Murphy Brown, The, 156
South Shore Citizens Club, 184
South Shore Conservatory of Music, *98*
Spigel, Lynn, 1, 53
Stallybrass, Peter, 59
Stanis, Bern Nadette, 145
Stanwyck, Barbara, 55
Starr, Ron, 163
*Stars for Freedom: Hollywood, Black Celebri-
   ties, and the Civil Rights Movement*
   (Raymond), 179
Star Trek: The Original Series, 16, 115,
   123–126, 128, 136, 143
Stepin Fetchit. *See* Perry, Lincoln
Steve, 37
Steve Harvey, 37, 39
Stevenson, Bryan, 273

Stewart, Martha, 32

stigmatic blackness, 15, 52, 157; acceptable and unacceptable counterweights, 87–88; black children, effect on, 83–88, 97–99, 103–106; black stupidity, myth of, 66, 76, 88, 100–101, 103–104, 292n23; buffoon character, 3, 38, 48, 87, 105, 127, 145; butler characters, 65, 84, 94, 104; in Charlie Chan films, 87; classed-up side, 127; current examples, 106–109; family as flawed, 138–139, 199; judiciary, black, representation of, 160; maid roles, 75–76; mammy characters, 16, 65, 75, 78, 99, 126, 137–138; mass consumption and, 59–60; news coverage, 5, 249–253, 265–268, 267, 276–278; palatable blackness compared with, 236–237; in police procedurals, 267–270; progressive programs, 73; race-face convention, 74; servant characters, 65–68, 72, 84; slavery, myths of, 86, 99–101; stock figures, 65–66; variety show performers, 61–65; white family as more important than own family, 76, 79. See also Asians; Indian stereotypes; Native Americans; "thug" figure

Stowaway, 92

Strahan, Michael, 33–36, 35, 48, 94, 292n20

Straight Talk, No Chaser: How to Find, Keep, and Understand a Man (Harvey), 37–38

Stuart, Carol DiMaiti, 277

Stuart, Charles, 276–278, 277–279

Stuart, Matthew, 278

Student Nonviolent Coordinating Committee (SNCC), 139, 171

Sula (Morrison), 199

Sullivan, Ed, 30–31, 61, 63–65, 82, 135, 140, 279

superpredator rhetoric, 264–265, 272–273

Susanna of the Mounties, 92

tabloid talk shows, 14, 18, 164, 213–214, 217–218

Takei, George, 115, 302n1

talent competitions, 61

"Talented Tenth" (Du Bois), 24

Talk, The, 33

talk radio, 18, 222

talk shows, 14, 18, 33–39; The Oprah Winfrey Show, 36–38

Talman, William, 164

Tatum, Channing, 34

Taylor, Regina, 75, 76

"technicolored," as term, 12

telenovelas, 201

television studies, 12–13, 31, 206

Temple, Shirley, 4, 15–16, 33–34, 35, 241; Baby Burlesks, 91, 92, 93, 103; body language, 91–92; Child Star (autobiography), 88–89, 94; effect on black girls, 83–84, 97–99; international fame, 97; The Little Colonel, 94–96, 95; Little Miss Marker, 89, 92, 96–97; as perfect-10 white girl, 90, 111; sexualizing of girls, 90–92, 94; on television, 83, 85, 86, 88

Temptations, 63

Tenney, Jon, 154

That Hagen Girl, 90

"That's My Boy??" (Dick Van Dyke Show), 168, 239–240

That's My Mama, 143

theaters, segregated, 55

Theatre of Being, 162

Their Eyes Were Watching God (Hurston), 199

This Is Us, 167, 281–283, 302n7

Thomas, Clarence, 20–21, 191, 237–238, 290n20, 303–304n5

Thomas, Danny, 239–240

Thomas, Willie, 84

"thug default," 262, 274

"thug" figure, 19, 261; adult sentencing of juveniles, 271–273; black police officers in danger, 275–276; Central Park rape and battery case, 265–267, 267, 272; death penalty called for, 265–266, 267, 271–272; hip hop music and, 263–264; hoaxes, 276–279; "superpredator" rhetoric, 264–265, 272–273; "thug" as new N-word, 273–274

Thuggee cults, 263, 265

Till, Emmett, 111, 238

Time to Kill, A, 109–111, 253

Toast of the Town, 63. See also Ed Sullivan Show, The

To Kill a Mockingbird, 46–47

Tolbert, Berlinda, 126
Toler, Lynn, 212–213
Toler, Sidney, 87
Tong, Sammee, 67, 69, 71, 72
Tonto (character, *The Lone Ranger*), 66–67
Tormé, Mel, 81
Torres, Sasha, 11
To Tell the Truth, 32
Toussaint, Lorraine, 203, 268
traveling while black, 172–178
Trebek, Alex, 41
trickster figure, 127, 129, 137, 158, 190
Trump, Donald, 20, 38, 129, 219, 223, 233;
    death penalty, call for, 265–266, *267*, 271
Turner, Kathleen, 202–203
Turner, Patricia, 95
TV trays, 55
Twenty-One, 22, 291n9
2 Broke Girls, 73
typecasting, 5, 15, 41, 69, 108, 262, 269. *See
    also* stigmatic blackness
Tyson, Cicely, 131, 136, 141–142, 149, *151*, 198
Tyson, Neil deGrasse, 35, 292n23

Uggams, Leslie, 150–151
Uhura, Lt. (character, *Star Trek: The Original
    Series*), 16, 115, 123–126, 128, 136, 143
Uncle Tom characters, 34, 95, 105, 137,
    292n18
Unforgiven, 66
uplift, racial, 15, 23–24, 29–30, 104, 152; as
    profiling, 50
Upshaw, Shawn (Thompson), 250–252

Van Dyke, Dick, 167, 188, *189*
Vanzant, Iyanla, 37
variety shows, 15, 30–31, 61–65; *American
    Bandstand*, 15, 61–63; *The Ed Sullivan
    Show*, 15, 30–31, 61, 63–65; *The Nat "King"
    Cole Show*, 81–82
Ventimiglia, Milo, 302n7
Vergara, Sofia, 73
Verica, Tom, 187
View, The, 33
violence, videos of, 231
Violent Crime Control Act (1994), 264
Virginia, "Racial Integrity Act," 16, 112–113,
    298n1

Wade, Ernestine, 84
Wahlberg, Mark, 272
Walker, Alice, 199
Walker, Jimmie, 145
Walker, William "Bill," 160
Wallace, George, 170, 171
Wapner, Joseph, 214
Warner, Kristin J., 49–50
Warner, Malcolm-Jamal, 235–236
War on Poverty, 56–57, 172
Warren, Earl, 113
Washington, Booker T., 24
Washington, Denzel, 266
Washington, Hannah, 99–100, *100*
Washington, Kerry, 16, 49, 51, 75–76, 153, 158.
    See also Pope, Olivia
*Watching Race: Television and the Struggle
    for "Blackness"* (Gray), 11
*Watching while Black: Centering the Television
    of Black Audiences* (Smith-Shomade), 241
Waters, Ethel, 75, 77, 135–136
Waters, John, 202
Waterston, Sam, 76, 203
Watkins, Mel, 137
Watts riots, 139, 170
We, the Women, 148
Weber, Charlie, 191
Webster, 281, 282
"Wedding Bell Blues" (5th Dimension), 78
Wee Willie Winkie, 91, 92
"welfare fraud," courtroom television and,
    18, 213, 215–226
West, Cornel, 245
westerns, 60–61, 74, 123
What's Happening!, 143
Wheel of Fortune, 14, 22–23, 41, 51, 285–287,
    287
When Harry Met Sally, 44
White, Allon, 59
White, Vanna, 22–23, 285
whiteness: blackness as bleaching agent
    for, 109; projection of sexuality, 45; as
    unmarked category, 90; white woman
    represents social order, 34
*White Screens/Black Images: Hollywood from
    the Dark Side* (Snead), 94
"white" shows, 51, 57–58, 80
Whitman, Ernest, 76, 77, *78*

Who Wants to Be a Millionaire?, 32, 40, 41, 43
"Why I Quit My TV Show" (Cole), 82
"wilding" incident, 265–266
Wilkins, Roy, 79
Williams, Anissa, 214–217, 218
Williams, Clarence, III, 136, 141
Williams, Jesse, 5
Williams, Michael Kenneth, 201
Williams, Patricia, 247
Williams, Spencer, 75
Williams, Vanessa, 132
Williams, Wendy, 33, 37
Williamson, Mykelti, 104
Willis, Bruce, 50
Willis, Jan, 64
Wilson, Dooley, 76, 77
Wilson, Flip, 137, 300n6
Wilson, Owen, 131
Wilson, Tarika, 274
Winchell, Walter, 97
Winchester, Philip, 266
Winfield, Paul, 160

Winfrey, Oprah, 15, 35–37, 173, 245, 293n28;
    Oprah Winfrey Network (OWN), 32, 229;
    The Oprah Winfrey Show, 36–38
Winters, Roland, 87, 89
Wire, The, 201
womanhood, black, 49–50
Woman's View, A (Basinger), 91–92
Woods, Tiger, 286
Woolfork, Lisa, 128

yellowface, 87, 88
You in Your Small Corner, 123
Young, Andrew, 44
Young, Bellamy, 194
Young, Robert, 92
Young Thug, 106
YouTube, 42

Zimmerman, George, 18–19, 262–263,
    290n18
Zoeller, Frank "Fuzzy," 286
Zorro, 75